<u>British Locomotive Catalogue 1825-1923</u>

<u>4: Scottish and remaining English Companies in the LMS Group</u>

D1437692

BRITISH LOCOMOTIVE CATALOGUE

1825-1923

compiled by the late Bertram Baxter
edited by David Baxter

Volume 4
Scottish and remaining English Companies
in the LMS Group

MOORLAND PUBLISHING COMPANY

Printed in Great Britain by:
Dotesios (Printers) Ltd,
Bradford-on-Avon, Wilts.
For the Publishers:
Moorland Publishing Company Ltd,
9-11 Station Street,
Ashbourne, Derbyshire, DE6 1DE.

Contents

EDITORIAL NOTE AND ACKNOWLEDGEMENTS

This volume completes the catalogue of locomotives owned by all the remaining companies in the LMS group as set up by the Railways Act 1921.

The LMS company came into being on 1 January 1923, absorbing the locomotives of all the constituent companies except the Caledonian on that date. The Caledonian continued to be independent for a further six months as financial arrangements were not complete and it became part of the LMS on 1 July 1923.

The three Scottish companies became the Northern Division of the LMS and the English companies were added to the LNW system to become the Western Division. The Somerset and Dorset Joint Railway was not affected by the grouping as it continued to be a joint railway controlled by the Southern and LMS companies and the locomotive stock continued to be independently managed by the Joint Committee, responsibility for which passed from the Midland to the LMS.

In 1930, however, for reasons of economy, the Joint Committee relinquished control of the locomotives which were absorbed into LMS stock from 1 January of that year and for locomotive purposes the joint line became part of the Midland Division of the LMS. Details of S&DJ locomotives are therefore included until 1930.

All the locomotive stock of the North Staffordshire Railway and most of the minor companies had been withdrawn by the LMS before Nationalisation took effect on 1 January 1948 and although a single locomotive of the former Glasgow and South Western Railway was still in service on that date it was withdrawn shortly afterwards without carrying its allotted BR number.

Locomotives of the former Caledonian, Highland, Furness, Somerset and Dorset Joint Railways and the single ex L&Y 2-4-2T on the Wirral Railway did however survive long enough to be given BR numbers and the dates of their renumberings are given, where known, in a separate list at the end. The vast majority of these were Caledonian which had dominated the Northern Division of the LMS and enjoyed a certain amount of autonomy in locomotive matters.

Throughout the volume numbers known not to have been carried are either stated as 'allotted' or given in brackets.

Grateful thanks are due to correspondents who have assisted with information about the more obscure Companies and their locomotives. In particular I should like to thank Mr V. Williams Goudie for assistance with information regarding the Scottish North Eastern Railway and its constituents, the Scottish Central and Dundee, Perth and Aberdeen Junction Railways. Mr Williams Goudie is preparing a book on the history of the railways of North East Scotland which will be entitled *Two-and-tenpence Return to Dundee*. This it is hoped will help to fill an existing void in recorded railway history due to the lack of surviving records. The only other work is George Maclennan Steel's book *Dundee's Iron Horses* which gives some information derived from surviving records of the locomotive builders in Dundee.

It should be stressed that the information given by J.F. McEwan in the *Locomotive Magazine* in the 1940s concerning these pre-amalgamation Caledonian constituent companies is very speculative and should not be taken too literally as to numbers and wheel arrangements. With Mr Williams Goudie's help it has been possible to indicate areas where other recorded facts and the contemporary railway press indicate an alternative version to that given by McEwan with varying degrees of certainty.

In the case of the Scottish Midland Junction Railway (which McEwan largely ignored) only the number of locomotives is certain fact and it is only possible to be conjectural as to their identity. A similar difficulty has been encountered with the later SNE, SC and Aberdeen locomotives.

I should also like to thank Dr H.L. Holland of Ontario, Canada for information concerning the Garstang and Knott End Railway locomotives and Gordon Lowther concerning the Maryport and Carlisle locomotives.

In addition Peter Mitchell gave assistance with bibliographical references and BR numbering dates and I should also like to record my thanks to the librarians

and the staff of the public libraries in Manchester, Edinburgh and Liverpool and
the Rylands Library in Manchester, and in particular to Christine Heap, the
archivist of the Greater Manchester Museum of Science and Industry.

Abbreviations

BHS	Boiler heating surface
Blr	Boiler. Length of barrel x outside diameter
Cyls	Cylinders. Diameter x stroke in inches
diam	diameter
DW	Driving wheels
LW	Leading wheels
no(s)	number(s)
O/S	Outside
S'heat	Superheated
THS	Total heating surface
TW	Trailing wheels
WB	Wheelbase
WP	Working pressure
Wt	Weight in working order excluding tender

CALEDONIAN RAILWAY

INTRODUCTION

Unlike the London and North Western Raulway, Midland Railway and Lancashire and Yorkshire Railway the Caledonian was not formed by an amalgamation. It was incorporated on 31 July 1845 and promoted with strong English backing as a railway linking England with Scotland as a natural extension of the already authorised Lancaster and Carlisle Railway, engineered by Joseph Locke, which was opened in 1847, providing a through line from London and Carlisle. Joseph Locke had already made a preliminary survey in 1836 at the instigation of the Lancaster and Carlisle promoters, directors of the Grand Junction Railway. Two routes were possible: the Nithsdale route to the west through Dumfries and the more direct mountainous route up Annandale, through the Vale of Elvan and down Clydesdale, the route followed by Telford's coach road. Locke favoured the former since he feared that the ten-mile Beattock bank would be too steep for locomotive operation.

John James Hope Johnstone MP, the proprietor of the Annandale estates, however disagreed with Locke's decision. Fearing that Annandale would be by-passed and seeking a more direct access to Edinburgh (there was a general opinion at the time that only one Anglo-Scottish railway would be viable) he persuaded Locke to resurvey the route. Locke eventually agreed in a new survey of 1837 that a railway through Lockerbie and Beattock was a possibility.

Meanwhile largely Glasgow interests had succeeded in obtaining an Act for the Glasgow, Paisley, Kilmarnock and Ayr Railway, so that railway construction was already going on along part of the Nithsdale route.

So contraversial was the choice of route that a Royal Commission was appointed and this reported in 1841 in favour of Annandale with a branch to Edinburgh from Symington through Biggar.

Glasgow interests were still trying to promote the Nithsdale route by a proposed Glasgow, Dumfries and Carlisle Railway (eventually incorporated 16/7/1846), when active promotion of the Caledonian Railway started in 1844 with the issue of a prospectus.

To win over Scottish support to what had been until then a largely English scheme an aggressive nationalistic policy was followed influencing the choice of name and using the Scottish coat of arms and motto *Nemo me impune lacessit* (No one provokes me with impunity) and calling itself the 'National Line'.

It continued to promote this image throughout its existence. As the northern operating partner of the L&NW 'the Premier Line' in the west coast Anglo-Scottish route the CR considered itself the principal Scottish Railway - 'The True Line'.

The line from Carlisle to Beattock was opened on 10/9/1847 and throughout to Glasgow and Edinburgh on 15/2/1848, though the Edinburgh line took an amended route via Midcalder from Carstairs rather than through Biggar.

The Glasgow, Dumfries and Carlisle Railway joined the CR line at Gretna on 23/8/1848 and on completion in 1850 amalgamated with the Glasgow, Paisley, Kilmarnock and Ayr Railway to form the Glasgow and South Western Railway. This line was ultimately destined to carry the Glasgow traffic from the Midland line.

The Scottish Central Railway was joined at Castlecary on 7/8/1848 and with it access to the north. Access to Glasgow was originally via the already well established Glasgow, Garnkirk and Coatbridge line until the Clydesdale Junction was opened in 1849 connecting the CR with the Pollock and Govan Railway, the south side of Glasgow and the Glasgow, Paisley and Greenock Railway. Buchanan Street station was opened on 12/8/1849.

To the north a complicated chain of companies, some promoted earlier to serve purely local needs and originally built to the 4ft 6in and 5ft 6in gauges, eventually provided a through route from England to Aberdeen which was completed on 1/4/1850, nearly all of it engineered by Joseph Locke. This utilised the lines of the Wishaw and Cottness, Monkland and Kirkintilloch, Scottish Central, Scottish Midland Junction, Newtyle and Coupar Angus, Newtyle and Glammis, Arbroath and Forfar and Aberdeen railways.

The CR was the first railway able to convey through traffic from any Scottish railway to any English railway, which gave it a tremendous advantage.

Having already absorbed the Garnkirk, Wishaw and Pollock lines and amalgamated with the Glasgow, Paisley and Greenock Railway it stood in a strong position. The north-eastern companies were absorbed by the Aberdeen and the SMJ who in turn amalgamated in 1856 to form the Scottish North Eastern Railway.

The Dundee and Perth and Aberdeen Junction Railway joined with the Scottish Central Railway in 1863, having already leased the Dundee and Newtyle Railway in 1846.

The SC was amalgamated with the CR in 1865 and the SNE in 1866.

Of the Aberdeen main line only the Monkland and Kirkintilloch Railway did not pass into Caledonian hands, becoming eventually part of the North British and throughout its existence, and indeed until Nationalisation, the short 50-chain section was a foreign line over which the CR only had running powers.

A scheme to quarter the Lowlands with a line from Ayr to Berwick through Peebles and Galashiels failed in 1846 through lack of capital. It was ultimately replaced by a branch line to Peebles where it connected with the North British Peebles loop, the line to Galashiels, and to Berwick, Carlisle, Hexham and Morpeth having been built by that company.

In the west the Oban line through Crianlarich was completed on 1/7/1880 and the Bullachulish branch on 24/8/1903. This line, the Callander and Oban was an independent company worked by the Caledonian until absorbed by the LMS in 1923 as were the Killin, Brechin and Edzell District, Cathcart District, Lanarkshire and Ayrshire, and the Solway Junction railways. The Arbroath and Forfar Railway, and the Dundee and Newtyle Railway continued as independent leased companies until 1923 and the CR was a member of the Portpatrick and Wigtownshire Joint Committee along with the L&NW, Midland and Glasgow and South Western Railways.

The Caledonian was one of the British companies to adopt the Westinghouse automatic air brake after George Westinghouse had brought out his British patent in 1874 following an ideal specification suggested by The Engineer, but when the LMS took over they converted Caledonian stock to the vacuum brake. The driver's position on the footplate was on the left.

Locomotive policy originated in Crewe designs under the influence of Sinclair and Alexander Allan on the Scottish Central but did not develop along the same lines, the Caledonian adopting a large engine policy from quite early on. Conner, Drummond and McIntosh had the most influence on locomotive design. In the Drummond and McIntosh periods the railway achieved a status of considerable repute, with its elaborate livery, as a line of distinction and elegance somewhat comparable with that of the Midland. It gained much credit from its part in the famous 'Races' between London and Edinburgh in 1888, and London and Aberdeen in 1895 between the west coast and east coast routes.

It was, however, a railway of contrast. While its permanent way was not considered to be up to the standard of the L&NW or the Midland some of its stations were very fine indeed, well up to the Midland standard. On its Aberdeen and Oban services it provided carriages with a high standard of comfort and ran Pullman services on some lines; much of its carriage stock on lesser services was of a far more spartan kind however.

On the Aglo-Scottish services it operated with the L&NW the West Coast Joint Stock which was mostly of LNWR design.

A decline in standards set in, however, during World War I and continued well into LMS days. Under the LMS the Caledonian became the largest of the three Scottish companies absorbed and created into a new Northern Division along with the G&SW and the Highland. Its biggest rival, the North British Railway, went into the LNE grouping.

Locomotive Superintendents

Robert Sinclair 1847-56 Resigned
Benjamin Conner 1857-76 Died
George Brittain 1876-82 Resigned
Dugald Drummond 1882-90 Resigned
Hugh Smellie 1890-1 Died
John Lambie 1891-5 Died
John Farquharson McIntosh 1895-1914 Retired
William Pickersgill 1914-23 Formation of LNS

Robert Sinclair had been the locomotive superintendent of the Glasgow, Paisley and Greenock since 1844 having served his apprenticeship with Scott, Sinclair & Co at Greenock of which firm his uncle, Robert, was a partner. From there he worked under Buddicom in the Grand Junction Railway works at Edge Hill. When Buddicom left the GJ in 1841 to set up, at Joseph Locke's suggestion, the locomotive building firm of Allcard, Buddicom & Co at Les Chartreux, Rouen, Sinclair was appointed works manager moving from there to Greenock on Joseph Locke's recommendation. From 1851 he became resident engineer of the CR in addition to Locomotive Superintendent.

During this period the Greenock works became the main locomotive works for the CR, the Glebe Street works of the Glasgow, Garnkirk and Coatbridge and the Holytown works of the Wishaw and Coltness being retained for repairs only. His designs were largely, if not wholly, based on the GJ/LNW 'Crewe' types in some cases, on drawings supplied from Crewe works. He introduced a livery of light blue for passenger locos and light green for goods locos.

He left the CR in 1856 to become locomotive superintendent of the Eastern Counties and was also its chief engineer from 1857 until 1866, the EC having become the Great Eastern in 1862. A founder member of the Institution of Mechanical Engineers, he became a member of the Institution of Civil Engineers in 1858, and was in the forefront of the steam locomotive technology of his day along with Alexander Allan on the Scottish Central from 1853. Early locomotive types, particularly the 4-class passenger singles, on the CR, SC and SMJ were all basically to the same pattern.

Somewhat in advance of the standards of the times, he advocated large bearing surfaces and structural rigidity. He was a pioneer in the use of steel in locomotives and probably the first to use steel regularly for axles and tyres. He was a good leader of men, always straight-forward and firm, but also considerate and was much liked and respected.

He laid a firm foundation for his successor Benjamin Conner who had been introduced to locomotive engineering at Murdoch, Aitken & Co, Glasgow. He later became works manager of Neilson and Mitchell (later Neilson & Co) whose works were adjacent to the CR works at St Rollox and who built many locos for the CR.

Situated north of Inchbelly level crossing on the old G, G & C line on Springburn Road, plans for the CR works were prepared under Sincair in 1853 and the works opened in 1856 as Conner took over, the Greenock works being closed. St Rollox works were extended in 1870-1.

Conner was also conversant with marine engineering. On the CR he retained the 'Crewe' type framing and outside cylinders, but developed the design into much larger and more powerful machines than was the current practice at Crewe. His 8ft 2in singles had, marginally, the largest driving wheels ever used on the standard gauge. For goods traffic he favoured the 0-4-2 type and the classic 0-6-0 design of goods engine was late in coming to the CR, not being introduced by Conner in any number until his 631 class in 1874. Coal burning was standardised.

This period also saw the amalgamation of the SC and SNE in 1865/6. The rather rudimentary works of the SNE at Arbroath were closed, but the SC works at Perth were retained as a repair shop, later becoming a wagon building shop. The blue livery of the passenger locos became ultramarine under Conner and black lining was added to the green on the goods locos.

The last five years of Conner's period of office were beset by continued ill health and much responsibility fell on George Brittain, the all-line outside superintendent since 1870 who eventually succeeded Conner when he died in 1876.

Brittain had been locomotive superintendent of the Dundee and Perth and Aberdeen Junction Railway during 1859-63 and was appointed assistant to Alexander Allan on the SC when the two companies merged.

When the CR took over the SC in 1865 he was appointed outside superintendent on the Stirling-Aberdeen section. His 2-4-2Ts, designed for the Oban line which was completed in 1880, were not a success but their replacements, the 'Oban bogies', were highly successful. All but two lasted into LMS days, the last three being withdrawn in 1930 having worked on the Oban line for many years.

By 1882 Brittain's health was failing and he resigned, dying shortly afterwards. The board felt that the locomotive stock as a whole was falling short of requirements and in fact Brittain's resignation followed 5 months after the appointment of Dugald Drummond at twice Brittain's salary, the board having decided that Brittain should be retained as a consultant only.

Drummond had made a name for himself as a designer of locomotives on the North British where he had introduced highly successful 4-4-0, and 0-6-0 designs and brought about considerable improvements in their locomotive affairs. Despite his rather aggressive and obstinate character the CR board set out to attract him with a lucrative offer and they were not disappointed.

In eight years he produced standard classes of the above types and set patterns on which future locomotive engineers would build. He modernised the works at St Rollox and brought about a transformation in CR locomotive affairs. Under him royal blue was introduced as the livery for all locomotives.

He resigned in 1890 to establish his own business in Australia later returning, of course, to join the LSWR. His replacement, Hugh Smellie, had been locomotive superintendent of the G&SW and prior to that on the Maryport and Carlisle Railway. His designs for the G&SW had been highly successful but, tragically, he was not to design any locomotives for the CR having, literally, given his life for the company.

In the 1890-1 railway strike in Scotland a goods train driven by a volunteer driver got out of control and crashed at Buchanan Street. Smellie, himself, turned out with a makeshift breakdown crew in pouring rain. This, coupled with overwork due to the strike, led to a chill which developed into pleurisy and he died just over a year after taking office.

John Lambie was essentially a 'running' man with a wide knowledge of CR engines and men, having been in the position of all line outdoor superintendent since September 1876, succeeding George Brittain on his promotion. His designs showed consideration for the needs of engine men by the provision of cab doors, longer handrails and additional footsteps. He designed the condensing locomotives for the Glasgow low level line and brought out a further variation of the Drummond 4.4.0 with a boiler that had already been designed by Smellie.

He was popular with both board and men but became ill in 1894 and died in office on 1/2/1895. His father had been traffic manager of the Wishaw and Coltness Railway.

McIntosh had similar experience on the running side having worked his way up from fireman and driver on the SNE, completing his apprenticeship at Arbroath in 1867. In 1876 he lost his right hand in an accident while at Montrose works and on recovery was appointed a district locomotive inspector. In 1886 he became locomotive foreman at Polmadie, Glasgow and succeeded Lambie as running superintendent in 1891.

Under McIntosh the CR locomotive department reached its zenith. His original appointment was provisional, subject to review after six months, but his period of office equalled that of Conner, lasting nineteen years. He continued the work of developing and modernising the basic Drummond designs and also introduced the 0.4.4Ts and 0.6.0Ts which were later to become so much associated with Caledonian practice.

His four versions of the *Dunalastair* 4-4-0s and the subsequent 140 class and superheated 139 class, together with the 4-6-0 classes, particularly 903 *Cardean* class, won the CR much favoured publicity in the contemporary press and placed the company in the forefront of locomotive practice. He was also in charge of the carriage and wagon department. A popular and much liked practical engineer he was made a Member of the Royal Victorian Order in 1911. He introduced variations in the shade of the livery on the passenger engines, but from about 1898 goods engines were painted black.

After McIntosh's retirement in 1914 William Pickersgill, the former locomotive superintendent of the Great North of Scotland was appointed. He had formerly been on the Great Eastern as a locomotive inspector being DLS at Norwich before going to the GN of S in 1894. As a pupil at Stratford in 1876 he had the honour of being a Whitworth Exhibitioner.

He started with the CR on 4/5/1914. When the war started three months later the CR was soon presented with many difficulties. Heavier loads caused more maintainence and repair work, but the loss of skilled men meant that locos had to be overhauled by outside contractors and a locomotive shortage developed. When the twenty-five 0-6-0 'Jumbos' were acquired by the War Department in 1917 the Railway Executive Committee had to draft four Fletcher 0-6-0s from the North Eastern and seven Great Central 0-6-0s to the CR to help make good the loss.

The 113 class 4-4-0s were authorised in October 1914, but were not completed until 1916. In fact only twenty-nine locomotives were built at St Rollox in the years 1915-17, although others were supplied by outside manufacturers. All these difficulties are often overlooked when Pickersgill is sometimes compared unfavourably with McIntosh, although it has to be said that his most original design, the three-cylinder 956 class, was a disappointment. At the end of hostilities he was awarded a CBE for his services during the war to the Railway Executive Committee. Due to delay in finalising the financial arrangements the Caledonian was not taken over by the LMS until 1 July 1923 and Pickersgill was appointed mechanical engineer to the newly created Northern Division comprising the CR, G&SW and Highland railways whose headquarters continued to be at St Rollox. He retired in 1925.

CALEDONIAN RAILWAY Constituent Companies

Garnkirk and Glasgow (4ft 6in gauge)

Incorporated 1826, opened 5/1831 (minerals), 1/6/1831 (passengers), ceremonial opening 27/9/1831. Double line from Gartsherrie where it formed a junction with the Monkland and Kirkintilloch railway (see North British Vol 6) to Townhead (St Rollox) Glasgow adjoining Monkland canal basin. A Stephenson railway with locomotives of similar design to Liverpool and Manchester railway using 'fish belly' wrought iron rails on stone blocks (except for a one mile section over marshy ground laid on longitudinal or transverse wooden sleepers) and in direct competition for coal traffic with the Monkland canal. For ten years Townhead station was the only station in Glasgow.
On amalgamation with the Caledonian Railway it formed the original approach into Glasgow until the line was diverted and regraded to cross under the Monkland canal into Buchanan Street in 1849, and the Clydesdale Junction line was opened from Motherwell to South Side station 1/6/1849. Extended from Gartsherrie to make connection with Wishaw and Coltness at Whifflet 1845. Name changed to **Glasgow, Garnkirk and Coatbridge** 1844. Purchased by Caledonian 30/6/1846 by annuity and converted to standard gauge 1847/8.
13 locomotives as under.
Locomotives not numbered until 1839

2-2-0 Built by Robert Stephenson & Co
DW 5ft 0in, LW 3ft 3in, Cyls 11 x 20, Blr 6ft 0in x 3ft 0in, THS 298.5 sq ft, Wt 6 tons approx.
Updated version of *Planet* class Liverpool and Manchester railway.

Name	Date	
St Rollox	1831	Sold to Paisley & Renfrew railway contractors 1836 for £350 later being spare engine. Not renumbered in GPK&A list in 1847 when P&R amalgamated. Sold for scrap at Paisley 22/12/1848

0-4-0 Built by Robert Stephenson & Co   (RS)
              Johnston & McNab   (JM)
              Murdoch & Aitken & Co   (MA)
DW 4ft 0in, Cyls 11 x 16, Blr 6.91ft x 3ft, Wt as below (empty)
1839

No	Name	Date	
1	*George Stephenson* (RS)	1831	Wt 8 tons. McEwan gives blr 7ft 0in x 3ft 3in, THS 319.17 sq ft. Pressure 50lbs/sq in (above dimensions as Whishaw) Withdrawn 1846
2	*Glasgow* (JM)	2/1832	Wt 8½ tons. Scrapped 1847
3	*Garnkirk* (MA)	3/1834	Wt 9 tons* Works no 3. McEwan states probably had horizontal O/S cyls. Scrapped 1847

*Some sources give weight 8½ tons.

0-6-0 Built by Murdoch & Aitken & Co
DW 4ft 0in, Cyls 12½ x 21, Wt 13 tons (empty). Unusual placing of inclined O/S cyls level with top of boiler at footplate end with a connecting rod rocking a crank at chimney end of boiler with second connecting rod connecting to centre pair of wheels. (McEwan states DW 3ft 9in). WB 5ft + 5ft 0in. Lowe gives DW 4ft 4in
1839

No	Name	Date	
4	*Gartgill*	6/1833	Withdrawn 1847

0-4-0 Built by St Rollox Foundry Co
  DW 4ft 0in, Cyls 13 x 18 O/S, Wt 11 tons 8½ cwts. Horizontal cylinders.
  Pressure 50 lbs/sq in, WB 5ft 6in
  1839

No	Name	Date	
5	*Frew*	1835	Withdrawn 1848

2-2-0 Built by Murdoch & Aitken & Co
  DW 4ft 0in, LW 3ft 0in, Cyls 11 x 16*, Wt 10 tons (empty)
  Copy of *Planet* type
  * Some sources give cyls 11 x 24
  1839

No	Name	Date	
6	*Jenny*	1836	McEwan stated BHS reputed to have been 294 sq ft, grate area 8.25 sq ft. Scrapped c1847

0-6-0 Built by St Rollox Foundry Co
  DW 3ft 10in, Cyls 13 x 18, Blr (inside) 13ft 6in x 3ft 9in (approx). Vertical
  cyls connecting a crank between leading and centre DW which were more widely
  spaced than centre and rear DW. Later altered, effectively, to 0-4-2 simply
  by removing connecting rod to rear wheels due to excessive wear on track.
  Blr was an adaptation of the Cornish boiler with large diameter flue which
  divided into four smaller flues which passed into the smokebox.

No	Name	Date	
7	*Victoria*	1840	Sold to contractors 1847
8	*St Rollox*	1840	Sold to contractors 1847
9	*Carfin*	1840	Sold to contractors 1847

0-4-0 Built by Neilson & Mitchell Works nos 1-3
  DW 4ft 0in, Cyls 14 x 20. Altered to standard gauge 1847/8

No	Name	Date	
10	*Alchymist*	1843	To Caledonian no **80** 1848
			Rebuilt 0-4-2 TW 2ft 9in 1850
			Withdrawn 1854
11	*Astrologer*	1843	To Caledonian no **81** 1848
			Withdrawn 1850
12	*Magician*	1843	To Caledonian no **82** 1848
			Withdrawn 1850

NB Whishaw states that nos 1-6 had tenders built at the Company's St Rollox
works but not known whether this applies to the later locos. He also states
that the engines burnt coal rather than coke and that 50lbs/sq in was the
usual pressure.

Glasgow, Paisley and Greenock

Incorporated 1837, opened 29/3/41 (joint line 14/7/40). Joint line with
Glasgow, Paisley, Kilmarnock & Ayr (see G&SW page no   ) from Paisley into
Bridge St station (on south bank near present Central station). Worked by CR
from 1848 under amalgamation Act of 1847 but not fully implemented until 1851.
Company's works at Greenock formed first Caledonian works until St Rollex
opened in 1856.
19 locomotives as under
Not numbered until 1842.

2-2-0 Built by Rothwell & Co (works nos 48-50)
  DW 5ft 0in, LW 3ft 6in, Cyls 12 x 18, Blr 8ft 0in x 3ft 4in, Wt 12½ tons
  (empty), WB 5ft 3in + 5ft 3in, THS 530.7 sq ft, WP 55lbs/sq in.
  All rebuilt as 2-2-2, TW 3ft 6in in 1841

1842

No	Name	Date*	
1	*Lucifer*	1839	To Caledonian no **77** 1848
	renamed *Fireking*		Replaced 1851
2	*Zamiel*	1840	Boiler exploded 9/1844
			Replaced with boiler from *Hawk* (no 8 below).
			To Caledonian no **67** 1848. Replaced 1854
3	*Hecate*	1840	To Caledonian no **78** 1848
	May have been		Replaced 1851
	named *Glasgow*		

*Lowe gives dates of building as 1838, 1/1839, 2/1838 respectively.

2-2-2 Built by Sharp Roberts & Co, works nos 89, 90, 93, 109
DW 5ft 0in, LW & TW 3ft 6in, Cyls 13 x 18, Blr 7ft 8in x 3ft 3in, WB 5ft 8in
+ 5ft 2in
Standard Sharp singles with Sharp's gab motion.
1842

No	Name	Date	
4	*Eagle*	1840	To Caledonian no **70** 1848
			Withdrawn 1854
5	*Falcon*	1840	To Caledonian no **71** 1848
			Withdrawn 1854
7	*Curlew*	1840	To Caledonian no **73** 1848
			Withdrawn 1853
6	*Petrel*	1841	To Caledonian no **72** 1848
			Withdrawn 1855

2-2-2 Built by Barr & MacNab Paisley (BM)
          Caird & Co Greenock works nos E1 & E2 (C)
DW 5ft 0in, LW & TW 3ft 6in, Cyls 13 x 18, Blr 7ft 8in x 3ft 5in, Gab motion.
1842

No	Name		Date	
8	*Hawk*	BM	1840	Withdrawn after accident 1844. Motion used
				to drive machinery in works. Boiler used to
				repair *Zamiel* (no 2 above)
11	*Greenock*	C	1840	To Caledonian **68** 1848
				Withdrawn 1855
12	*Glasgow*	C	1840	To Caledonian **69** 1848
				Withdrawn 1854

2-2-2 Built by Tayleur & Co, works nos 103/4, 106/7*
DW 5ft 0in, LW & TW 3ft 6in, Cyls 13 x 18, Blr 8ft 0in x 3ft 4in, THS 469.71
sq ft, WP 60lbs/sq in. Estimated weight (empty) 14 tons.
*Whishaw gives second pair of Tayleur nos as 105/6
1842

No	Name	Date	
9	*Witch*	1840	To Caledonian no **65** 1848
			Withdrawn 1852
10	*Phantom*	1840	To Caledonian no **66** 1848
			Withdrawn 1855
13	*Paisley*	1841	To Caledonian no **74** 1848
			Withdrawn 1855
14	*Clyde*	1841	To Caledonian no **75** 1848
			Withdrawn 1855

0-4-2 Built by Hawthorn & Co, works no 352.
DW 4ft 6in, TW 2ft 3½in, Cyls 14 x 18, Blr 8ft 5in x 3ft 6in, WP 50lbs/sq in,
WB 5ft 0in + 5ft 0in. Improved Hawthorn gab motion.
1842

No	Name	Date	
15	*Hercules*	1841	To Caledonian no **76** 1848. Sold to contractor 1855

2-2-2 Built by Sharp Roberts, works no 205.
DW 5ft 6in, LW & TW 3ft 6in, Cyls 14 x 18, Blr 8ft 0in x 3ft 4in, THS
385.65 sq ft, WP 60lbs/sq in. Improved Sharp gab motion.

No	Name	Date	
16	*Willington*	1842	To Caledonian no **79** 1848. On duplicate list from 1851. May have carried no 82 during this period. Withdrawn 1860.

2-2-2 Built by GP & G Rly at Greenock
DW 5ft 6in, LW & TW 3ft 6in, Cyls 14 x 20 O/S. Sinclair design, the
progenitor of the first standard CR class 4 with similar boilers (see below)
hence numbered 1-3 in CR list. Not named. Worked CR main line.

No	Date	
17	1846	To Caledonian no 1 1847
		Hauled first train from Carlisle to Beattock when first portion of line opened on 26/8/47. Later rebuilt 2-4-0 15 x 20 cyls.
	1869	Renumbered **57**. Withdrawn 1869
18	1846	To Caledonian no **2** 1847
	1859	Sold to Dundee and Arbroath no 3
	1862	To Scottish North Eastern no 12. Scrapped 1866
19	1846	To Caledonian no **3** 1847
		Later rebuilt 2-4-0 15 x 20 cyls
	1869	Renumbered **58**. Withdrawn 1874

Pollok and Govan (4ft 6in gauge)

Incorporated 1830. Act of Parliament has older spelling Polloc in name.
Opened 22/8/1840. Originally a tramway with horse haulage. Extension of this
line from Rutherglen formed the Clydesdale Junction line (originally a seperate
company) which is the present main line into central station from the south.
(Central station opened 1879). Both companies purchased by CR. (P & G
29/1/1845, CJR 3/2/1845 confirmed by Act of August 1846). Gauge widened and
through line from Motherwell to South Side station opened 1st June 1849.
3 locomotives as under: (steam haulage introduced April 1842)

0-4-0 Build by Jas M. Rowan & Co, Glasgow
Tenders built by Wm Dixon & Son, Govan ironworks who were owners of the
line.
DW 4ft 6in, Cyls 12 x 18, Blr 8ft 3in x 3ft 0in (inside), WP 40lbs/sq in,
WB 6ft 3in.
Cast iron parallel chimneys, gab type motion and hand operated water pump on
fireman's side of the footplate. These locomotives were not regauged but
transferred to Cleland and Omoa branches of Wishaw and Coltness railway where
4ft 6in gauge continued in use after 1846-8. Eventually regauged by
Wm Dixon when rebuilt as saddle tanks. Not numbered on P & G.

Name	Date	
Pollok	4/1842	To Caledonian 83 1848
	1852	Sold to Wm Dixon
	c1854	Rebuilt 0-4-OST standard gauge
		Withdrawn about 1865
Govan	1842	To Caledonian 84 1848
	1852	Sold to Wm Dixon and rebuilt about same time as 0-4-OST standard gauge.
		Withdrawn about 1865
Tradeston	1842	To Caledonian 85 1848
	1854	Sold to Wm Dixon and rebuilt about same time as 0-4-OST standard gauge.
		Withdrawn about 1865

Wishaw and Coltness (4ft 6in gauge)

Incorporated 1829 (originally Garturk & Garion). Opened Whifflet - Holytown
23/1/1834
            to Newarthill 31/3/1834
            throughout to Coltness Iron works 9/3/1844
Extension of Monkland & Kirkintilloch. Agreement to widen gauge and double
track 1844. Caledonian joined the line at Gariongill. Horse haulage only used
until 1838 then Garnkirk and M & K locos allowed to work over line. Purchased
by Caledonian 6/1/1846 confirmed by Act of 1848 (by annuity).
15 locomotives as under:
Not numbered on W & C. Painted green.

0-4-0 Built by James Rowan & Co, Glasgow
   DW 4ft 0in, Cyls 10½ x 24, Blr 9ft 3in x 4ft 6½in, WP 50lbs/sq in, Wt 10 tons
   12 cwt.
   Designed George Dodds, Locomotives Superintendent of the M & K based on
   Stockton and Darlington *Locomotion* but with orthodox fire tube boiler. All
   are thought to have been put to stationary work by 1848 and were not taken
   into CR stock.

Name	Date
Wishaw	11/1840
Coltness	11/1840
Cleland	12/1840

0-4-0 Built by Murdoch & Aitken & Co, Glasgow in 9/1831, works no 2. Purchased
       from M & K 1841 ex M & K no 2 *Kirkintilloch*. Believed to have been
       overhauled on M & K in 1840.
   DW 3ft 9in, Cyls 10½ x 24, Blr 9ft 0in x 4ft 6in, WP 40lbs/sq in, Wt 9 tons
   18 cwt.
   Similar to Rowan locos but slightly smaller.

Name		
Jenny	1841	Not taken into CR stock

2-2-2 Built by James M Rowan & Co, Glasgow in 1839.
       Purchased from M & K in 1842.
       Ex Slamannon Rly (see North British Vol 6)
   DW 5ft 0in, Cyls 15 x 18
   Purchased to work passenger trains then being introduced

Name	Date	
Boanerges	1842	Stationery work c1847. Broken up 1858
Borealis	1842	Rebuilt 0-4-2 1847 using DW from Boanerges, larger
Renamed		boiler and cyls 16 x 20. Altered to standard gauge.
Mercury	1847	To Caledonian **94** 1848
		Withdrawn 1864

0-4-0 Built by James Rowan & Co, Glasgow
   DW 4ft 6in, Cyls 14 x 20, WB 6ft 9in, Wt 12 tons 2 cwts. Copy of Bury
   design with firebox crown in half sphere.

Name	Date	
Meteor	1843	Rebuilt 1847 as 0-4-2, TW 2ft 4in, and altered to
		standard gauge.
	1848	To Caledonian no **93** and name removed.
		Rebuilt 1861 (believed). Withdrawn 1864.

0-4-0 Built be Neilson & Mitchell, works nos 6 & 7
   DW 5ft 0in, Cyls 14 x 18, WB 7ft 8in
   Similar to G & G 10-12 (above) but with modified dimensions. Both rebuilt
   as 0-4-2, TW 2ft 9in in 1847 and altered to standard gauge. Fitted with
   Sinclair boilers by CR.

Name	Date	
Sirocco	1844	To Caledonian no **90** 1848. Withdrawn 1861

Talisman   1844 To Caledonian no **92** 1848. Withdrawn 1861.

Names probably removed by CR

O-4-2 Built by R & W Hawthorn, works nos 388/9, 421/2, 454/5.
DW 4ft 6in, TW 2ft 11in, Cyls 14 x 20, WP 60lbs/sq in later increased to
70lbs/sq in. Probably built to standard gauge.

Name	Date	
Jupiter	1844	To Caledonian no **89** 1848
		Withdrawn 1861
Hercules	1844	To Caledonian no **95** 1848
	1856	Sold to Wm Dixon
Vulcan	1845	To Caledonian no **91** 1848
		Withdrawn 1861
Venus	1845	To Caledonian no **87** 1848
	1854	Renumbered **84**. Withdrawn 1863
Vesta	1845	To Caledonian no **88** 1848
	1854	Renumbered **85**. Withdrawn 1859
Lucifer	1845	Derailed, colliding with *Hercules* (above) prior to
		amalgamation.
		To Caledonian no **86** 1848
		Withdrawn 1860

General Terminus and Glasgow Harbour

Incorporated 1846. Opened 30/3/1849
Branches from *Pollok and Govan, Glasgow, Paisley, Kilmarnock and Ayr,
Glasgow, Barrhead and Neilson*. Direct railways to general terminus at
Glasgow Harbour. Amalgamated with Caledonian 1864
4 locomotives as under:

O-4-O Built by J.M.Rowan & Co
DW Not known, Cyls 15in diameter, stroke not known

No	Date	CR no 1864	
1	2/1851	**116**	Scrapped 1867
2	2/1851	**117**	Scrapped 1867

O-4-OST Built by Neilson & Co, works nos 338-9.
DW 3ft 6in, Cyls 12 x 18 O/S

No	Date	CR no 1864	1865 no	1872 no	1877 no	
3	2/1855	**93**	**240**	**145**	**519**	Scrapped 1880
4	2/1855	**94**	**241**	**146**	**520**	Scrapped 1882

Portpatrick

Incorporated 1857. Opened to Stranraer 12/3/1861, to Portpatrick 28/8/1862.
Connection with G & SW at Castle Douglas. Worked by CR from 1864. In 1885 the
company was amalgamated with Wigtownshire to form *Portpatrick and Wigtownshire
Joint Committee* (managed by Joint Committee representing LNW, CR, Midland and
G & SW).
9 locomotives as under:

O-4-2 Built by Sharp Stewart & Co, works nos 1219-21, 1322.
DW 5ft 1in, TW 3ft 6in, Cyls 16 x 24, Blr 10ft 9in x 4ft 1¼, WB 7ft + 7ft 9in,
THS 1051.03 sq ft, Wt 25 tons 18½ cwts. Designed by McConnell of LNW
Southern Division.

No	Date	CR no 1864	1885 no	
1	1861	**262**	262A	Withdrawn 1888

```
2      1861      263      263A    Withdrawn 1890. Stationery work at Perth.
3      1861      264              Scrapped 1874 after accident Dalbeattie.
4      1862      265      265A    Withdrawn 1888
```

0-6-0 Built by LNW at Crewe, Crewe no 475
DW 5ft 2in, Cyls 16 x 24, WB 7ft 3in + 8ft 3in, Blr 10ft 6in x 4ft 2in, THS
1099 sq ft, Wt 29 tons. Ramsbottom design DX goods, open splashers, no cab.
Purchased new from LNW (ex LNW no 550, see Vol 2A p127).

```
No     Date
4      3/1861    Returned to LNW in exchange for no 5 below
```

0-6-0 Built by LNW at Crewe, Crewe no 575.
DW 5ft 2in, Cyls 17 x 24, WB 7ft 3in + 8ft 3in, Blr 10ft 6in x 4ft 2in, THS
1099 sq ft, Wt 29 tons. As DX goods above but with larger cylinders. The
standard DX size adopted from 5/1861, (see Vol 2A p131) (ex LNW 638).

```
                 CR no
No     Date      1864
5      10/1862   266       Sold 1885 to cement maker, Dumfries and later to Shap
                           Granite Quarry in both cases as portable boiler.
```

2-2-2 Built by Sharp Stewart & Co, works nos 1282-3.
DW 6ft 0in, LW & TW 3ft 9in, Cyls 15 x 22, WB 7ft + 7ft 9in, Blr 10ft 9in x
3ft 10⅝in, THS 907.7 sq ft, WP 140lbs/sq in, Wt 27 tons 2cwts.

```
                 CR no    1885
No     Date      1864     no     Withdrawn
6      1861      267      267A    1888
7      1861      268      268A    1888
```

2-4-0 Built by Sharp Stewart & Co, works no 1397.
DW 6ft 0in, LW 3ft 9in, Cyls 16 x 22, WB 7ft 0in + 7ft 6in, Blr 10ft 6in x
3ft 10¼in, WP 140lbs/sq in (reduced by CR to 130lbs/sq in), THS 865.5 sq ft,
Wt 26 tons 18¼ cwts.

```
                 CR no    1885
No     Date      1864     no     Withdrawn
8      1863      269      269A    1888
```

Dundee and Newtyle (4ft 6in gauge)

Incorporated 1826. Part horse, stationary engine operation from 16/12/1831.
(Also reputed to have used wind power) Loco haulage from 1833. Altered to
standard gauge 1849. Leased by **Dundee and Perth** 27/7/1846. Continued as leased
company until absorbed by LM & SR under Railways Act 1921 from 1/ /1923.
4 locomotives as under: (nos retained on D & P and D & P & AJct)

0-2-4 Built by J & C Carmichael, Dundee
DW 4ft 5in, Cyls 11 x 18* vertical, WP 50lbs/sq in, Wt 9 tons 10 cwts*
Drive through return cranks and connecting rods. Crosshead was above the
cylinder.
*Cyls of no 2 were 11¼ x 18, Wt of no 3 8 tons 3cwts. Altered to standard
gauge 9/1849 (except no 3)

			DP no	DPAJ	
No	Name	Date	1846	no 1847	
1	*Earl of Airlie*	9/1833	1	1*	Stationary work 1854
2	*Lord Wharncliffe*	9/1833	2	2*	Stationary work 1854
3	*Trotter*	3/1834	3	3	Withdrawn 9/1849

*McEwan records 1850 nos 10 & 11

0-4-0 Built by Robert Stephenson & Co, works no 137
DW 4ft 4in, Cyls 11 x 16, WB 4ft 10in, Blr 7ft 0in x 3ft 0in, THS 330.82
sq ft, WP 50lbs/sq in, Wt 9.3 tons approx. Altered to standard gauge 9/1849.

No	Name	Date	DP no 1846	DPAJ no 1847	Scrapped
4	*John Bull*	4/1836	4	4*	1854

*McEwan records 1850 no 12

Dundee and Perth

Incorporated 1845. Opened 25/5/1847. Leased **Dundee and Arbroath** 1847 and
name changed **Dundee and Perth and Aberdeen Junction**. Lease discontinued
9/3/1850. Amalgamated with **Scottish Central** 28/7/1863.

16 locomotives as under (nos 1-4 ex Dundee & Newtyle above). Some confusion
exists on pre-1850 numbering. Numbers recorded by McEwan are not verified by
subsequent research (see note below and under **Dundee and Arbroath** p 33). In
1863 Allan of **Scottish Central** advised that only five D&P&AJ locomotives were
suitable for taking into SC stock. These were not specified, but McEwan
records all but five being scrapped 1863/4. SC and CR numbers are as recorded
by him but cannot be confirmed.

0-4-2* Built by Kinmond, Hutton & Steel
DW 5ft 0in, TW 3ft 6in, Cyls 15 x 20. Double frames. Boilers similar to
D&A 5ft 6in singles of 1840-1
*Details recorded by McEwan cannot be confirmed.

Date	1850 no	SC no 1863	CR no 1865	Scrapped
1847	2	68		1864
1847	3	69	**379**	1869
1847	4	70	**378**	1869

2-2-2* Built by Kinmond, Hutton & Steel
DW 5ft 0in, LW & TW 3ft 6in, Cyls 15 x 20
Double frames, boilers similar to above
*Details recorded by McEwan cannot be confirmed

Date	Name	1850 no	SC no 1863	Scrapped
1847	*Vulcan*	5	74	1864
1847	*Lucifer*	6	75	1864
1847	*Dundee*	7	76	1864

2-2-2-0 Crampton. Built by Tulk & Ley, works no 14
DW 7ft 0in, LW 3ft 9in, Cyls 16 x 20 O/S, Blr length 11ft 0in, THS 989 sq ft,
Total WB 13ft 0in, WP 50lbs/sq in, Wt 24 tons. O/S Gooch valve gear. McEwan
states not taken into stock until 1850, but in use on D&P 10/1847. Built
1846, delivered date below.

Date	Name	1850 no	SC no 1863	Scrapped
8/1847	*Kinnaird*	1	66	1864

McEwan records four locomotives built by Stirling & Co, Dundee in 1847-9
which he states went to the **Dundee and Arbroath,** in 1850 at the expiration
of the lease, but there is no record of any purchase of locos by the company
between the Crampton (above) and the George England tank loco (below). The
Dundee and Arbroath recorded however at their meeting in October 1847 that
four new engines had been ordered. These are thought to have been built by
Kinmond & Co and are listed under **Dundee and Arbroath** (page no   ) (Amends
information in Vol 1: Summary).

2-2-2WT Built by George England & Co
   DW 4ft 6in, LW & TW 3ft 0in, Cyls 9 x 12, Blr length 11ft 0in, THS 577.2 sq
   ft, WB 8ft 0in + 7ft 0in

Date	Name	1850 no	SC no 1863	Scrapped
6/1849*	*Eclipse*	9**	67	1864

   *Taken into stock 1850, having been sent on approval.
   McEwan records No 8 was ex **Dundee and Arbroath retained by DPAJ at
   expiration of lease 1850.

0-4-0 Built by Bury, Curtis & Kennedy
   Purchased second hand 1854 and rebuilt at Perth.
   DW 5ft 0in, Cyls 14 x 20, WB 7ft 0in, Wt 18 tons 5 cwts.
   McEwan recorded possibly ex-LNW Southern Division, but not identified as such.
   Known on DPAJ as 'Tods' (Scottish word for foxes), but reason for this not
   known. Replaced **Dundee and Newtyle** Locos. Possibly named *Balbeuchley, Hatton*
   and *Law* but not confirmed and order not known.

No	Date	SC no 1863	Scrapped
10	1854	63	1863
11	1854	64	1863
12	1854	65	1863

2-4-0 Built by George England & Co
   DW 4ft 9in, Cyls 16 x 22. Purchased from stock. Sold to Scottish Central
   4/1860 and names removed.

No	Name	Date	SC no 1860	CR no 1865	Withdrawn
13	*Scorpion*	1855	6	**353**	1881
14	*Spitfire*	1855	23	**352**	1882

2-4-0 Built by George England & Co
   DW 5ft 0in, Cyls 15 x 22, Similar to 13/14 but 'close coupled' (McEwan's
   description).

No	Name	Date	SC no 1863	Rebuilt Perth	CR no 1865	Withdrawn
15	*Sprite*	1855	71	1864	**351**	1879

   Possibly worked on Carmyllie railway after 1866

0-4-0 Built by Robert Stephenson & Co, works nos 1311/2
   DW 4ft 8in, Cyls 15 x 22, WB 7ft 0in

No	Date*	SC no 1863	CR no 1865	1883 no	Withdrawn
13	1863	72	**350**	350A	5/1892
14	1863	73	**349**	349A	12/1883

   *McEwan gives dates as 1860 in each case.

Scottish Central

   Incorporated 1845. Opened Stirling to Greenhill 1/3/1848, throughout 23/5/1848,
   connection with Caledonian at Castlecary (by running powers over Monkland and
   Kirkintilloch, Garnqueen to Gartsherrie, 50 chains) 7/8/1848. Connection with
   Edinburgh and Glasgow (later North British) at Greenhill giving access to
   Glasgow Queen Street and at Larbert via Stirlingshire Midland Junction
   (incorporated 1846, promoted by E & G) giving access to Edinburgh. Connection
   with Scottish Midland Junction at Perth giving access to Aberdeen Railway at
   Forfar (from 1/4/1850 to Aberdeen itself). Worked Scottish Midland Junction
   from opening on 2/8/1848. From 3/1/1849 until October 1849 the Scottish
   Central (and presumably the SMJ also) was itself worked jointly by the

Caledonian, Lancaster and Carlisle and LNW following an abortive attempt by these companies to lease the SC. The agreement, which was for 25 years, ended abruptly when the southern companies discovered that they had made a bad bargain and the Caledonian in particular refused to pay its share of the guaranteed interest of 6% on capital to the SC (the traffic receipts only just covered the guarantee leaving the operating companies with nothing). The SC then started a legal action against the three companies, which failed in law because the working agreement had never been ratified by Parliament and was finally settled out of Court and, of course, resumed working as before, including the SMJ. From 12/2/1851 until 31/7/1854 the SC also operated the Aberdeen Rly and for a further twelve months until 31/7/1855 the locos of the three companies continued to be operated as a common pool (see **Scottish Midland Junction** page no 28 and **Aberdeen** page no 30) and were repaired and rebuilt in the SC works at Perth. Absorbed **Dundee and Perth and Aberdeen Junction** 28/7/1863. Locomotives were superintended by Sinclair of the Caledonian until 1/10/1853, when Alexander Allan came from the LNW at Crewe to take charge. When the company amalgamated with the Caledonian in July 1865 he left shortly afterwards in 1866 to become manager of the Worcester Engine Co.

91 locomotives as under (amends information in Vol 1: Summary). Numbering is as given by McEwan but cannot be confirmed SMJ and Aberdeen locos numbered into SC series during periods of joint working as above.

2-2-2 Built by Jones & Potts, works nos as below.
          Vulcan Foundry Co, works nos as below.
          Scott, Sinclair & Co, works nos as below.
DW 6ft 0in, LW & TW 3ft 6in, Cyls 15 x 20 O/S.
As Caledonian 4 class (qv). Stephenson link motion. Dome on raised firebox casing. No cabs. Double frames.

Built by Jones & Potts, works nos believed to be 142-7 with two pillar type safety valves on first and third ring of boiler casing. Rebuilt without cabs.

No	Date	Rebuilt etc	Withdrawn
1	1847	4/1854, 1/1857 patent leading springs	
		6/1859 New cylinders	1863
2	1847	1/1854	1863
3	1847	8/1855 Used to repair Aberdeen 2-2-2 ex 48	
		(Pool no 48). Renewed 2/1856	1860
4	1847	7/1856	1864
5	1847	9/1855	1864
6	1847	Renumbered 3 1860	
		Rebuilt 6/1854, Boiler ex no 3 1860	1863

Built by Vulcan Foundry Co, works no 269-76.
Pillar safety valve on centre ring of boiler casing. Salter safety valve on dome. Rebuilt with cabs. Two more were ordered but taken up by CR (see page 40).

No	Date	Rebuilt	CR No	Withdrawn
7	1847	1/1860	330	1872
8	1847	8/1857 18in diam cyls		
		1/1858 cyls lined to 15in	326	1872
9	1847	8/1859	325	1872
10	1847	2/1858	338	1869
11	1847	9/1861	318	1877
12	1847	3/1861, 1867 Reboilered with	316	
		blr from **333** and **renumbered**	333	1872
13	1847	7/1858	337	1869
14	1847	7/1862	317	1875

Built by Jones and Potts, works nos 169-76, 225-8, 230, 235.
Safety valves as 1847 locos but rebuilt with cabs.
Two more were ordered but taken up by CR (page no 41)

No	Date	Rebuilt	CR no 1865	1877	1878	1881	1885	Withdrawn
				no	no	no	no	
36	1848	9/1860	320					1875
37	1848	4/1860	319	675	712	(723)		1881
38	1848	6/1860	315	674	711			1880
39	1848	7/1862	314	703				1881
40	1848	1857*						
		11/1862	313					1877
41	1848	7/1863	312					1877
42	1848	4/1863	311	673	710			1879
43	1848	3/1863	310					1877
15	1848	9/1857	324					1872
16	1848	8/1855**						1864
17	1848	10/1859***	321					
		1874						
							321A	1888
18	1848	8/1855						1864
19	1848	4/1864	322	676	713	(721)		1881
20	1848	3/1864	323	677	714	722		1881

   * No 40 was in an accident on Forth & Clyde Rly 10/7/1857 and had new frames, buffer plate and buffers fitted.

  ** No 16 had balance weights added to the driving wheels in 1855 and had cast iron patent slide valves in 1857.

*** No 17 had patent (yellow metal) tubes fitted in 1859 and 16in diameter cylinders in 1874.

Built by Scott Sinclair & Co, works nos 4-12.
Safety valves as Vulcan locos, rebuilt with cabs. Three more ordered taken up by CR (see page no 40)

No	Date	Rebuilt		CR nos 1865	Withdrawn
27	1848	10/1859		336	1869
28	1848	8/1859		335	1870
29	1848	4/1859	Had new tender after accident at Greenhill 31/3/1857	334	1869
30	1849	12/1859	Brick arch fitted in firebox	333	1867
31	1849	6/1859	(Accident Aberdeen Rly 1/1854)	332	1871
32	1849	2/1859	Copper facings on boiler	331	1872
33	1849	6/1855	Cast iron slide valves		
		4/1857	cab and special steam drying system	329	1872
34	1849	9/1859	Huntsman patent springs fitted to tender	328	1871
35	1849	10/1859	Volute spring buffers	327	1872

0-4-2 Built by Vulcan Foundry Co, works nos 311-5 (VF)
        Scott, Sinclair & Co, works nos 13-17 (SS)
DW 4ft 7in, TW 3ft 6in, Cyls 16 x 18 O/S, WB 7ft 2in + 5ft 10in, Blr 10ft 2in x 3ft 10in. Fourteen locos ordered, but Vulcan Foundry agreed to retain four for resale. It is possible that the three supplied by them to the Liverpool, Crosby & Southport 7/1848, works nos 318-20 were from these four (see Vol 3B, p17).

No	Date	Rebuilt etc		CR no 1865	Withdrawn
21	1848 VF	10/1855		374	1870
22	1848 VF	4/1854		373	1869
23	1848 VF	5/1855, 1860 after accident and sold to Banff, Portsoy & Strathisla (later Banffshire) No 3 *Strathisla* see Great North of Scotland Vol 6			

24	1848	VF	2/1855		**375**	1869
25	1848	VF	4/1857		**372**	1870
44	1848	SS	7/1857, New tender 1869 after			
			accident		**377**	1870
45	1849	SS	1/1855		**376**	1870
46	1849	SS	12/1854 after accident Stirling.			
			Accident Denry 10/1871			
			16 x 20 cyls fitted 1872		**371**	1877
47	1849	SS	3/1855, 4/1868		**370**	1876
26	1849	SS	12/1854, 11/1857, cast iron piston			
			rings fitted 4/1858		**369**	1868

2-2-2 Built by Jones & Potts
DW 6ft 0in, LW & TW 3ft 6in, Cyls 15 x 20 O/S
Other dimensions as CR 4 class (qv)
Two pillar safety valves on first and third rings of boiler casing.
Stephenson link motion. Double frames. McEwan records these locos as
diverted to Aberdeen railway before delivery, but SC accounts published in
contemporary railway press show that they were sold for £8750 to Aberdeen
Railway in the six monthly period ended 31/1/1854 retaining the same numbers.
See also **Aberdeen** page no 30.   Special note.

		SNE	CR no			
No	Date	no 1855	1866	Rebuilt	Withdrawn	
48	1848	14	**445**	8/1855*	1874	
49	1848	15	**444**	1/1855	1874	
50	1848	16	**443**		1871	
51	1848	17	**442**		1873	
52	1848	18	**441**		1873	

* No 48 rebuilt after accident at Cove Bay using parts of no 3.

0-6-0 Built by Hawthorn's of Leith
DW 5ft 6in, Cyls 18 x 20, WB 5ft 6in + 8ft 3in, Blr 11ft 9in x 4ft 0in,
Wt 32 tons 15 cwts. Experimental mid feather in firebox.

		7/1855	CR no	
No	Date	no	1865	Withdrawn
75	1853	48	**368**	1875
76	1853	49	**367**	1875

0-4-2 Built by Vulcan Foundry Co, works nos 403-6.
DW 4ft 7¼in, TW 3ft 7¼in, Cyls 16 x 20 O/S, WB 6ft 0in + 7ft 0in, Blr
10ft 3¼in x 3ft 11in, THS 1165 sq ft, WP 120lbs/sq in. Four-wheel tender.
No cab.

		7/1855	CR no	1887		With-
No	Date	no	1865	no	Rebuilt	drawn
81	3/1855	51	**365**		8/1858 cast iron	
					piston rings, 1875	1885
82	3/1855	50	**366**	366A	1877	1888
(83)	4/1855	52	**364**	364A	1857 Allan's patent	
					springs on loco, 1880	1888
(84)	4/1855	53	**363**	363A	5/1857 patent cylinder	
					cocks, 1859 after	
					accident on turntable	
					at Perth	1888

0-4-2 Built by SC at Perth
DW 4ft 7¼in, TW 3ft 7¼in, Cyls 16 x 22 O/S, THS 1049 sq ft. Other
dimensions as Vulcan locos above. Rebuilt with flush boiler, THS 1165 sq ft.

		CR no		1885	
No	Date	1865	Rebuilt	no	Withdrawn
54	12/1856	**362**	1879	362A	1888
55	5/1857	**361**	1877		1885

No 54 had Ramsbottom patent piston valve rings and ran with an old tender
until 7/1857.
No 55 had Beattie type coal burning firebox.

0-4-2 Built by Neilson & Co, works no 396.
DW 5ft 0in, TW 3ft 6in, Cyls 16 x 22, WP 130lbs/sq in, WB 6ft 3in + 7ft 3in.
Probably similar in appearance to 0-4-2s above. Coal burning.

No	Date	Rebuilt etc	CR no 1865	With-drawn
56	6/1857	10/1857 fitted with Fenton patent blast pipe also warming cock, firebrick arch in firebox cyls made 16½in diam.	360	11/1879

2-4-0 Built by Fairbairn & Sons
DW 5ft 2in, LW 3ft 6in, Cyls 16 x 22 O/S, WB 6ft 6in + 7ft 10in, Blr 10ft
4in x 3ft 11in. 'Crewe' type, Allan link motion, mid-feather in firebox.
Steel fireboxes replaced on rebuilding when canopy supported on poles also
provided. Six-wheel tenders.

No	Date	CR no 1865	1884* no	Duplicate no	year	Rebuilt	With-drawn
57	1857	359		359A	1886	3/1871, 1880	1888
58	1857	358		358A	1886	3/1871, 1881	1888
59	1857	357		357A	1886	9/1868, 1881	1888
60	1857	356		356A	1886	12/1870, 1880	1888
61	1857	355		355A	1886	2/1871, 1880	1888
62	1857	354	360	354A	1883	4/1870, 1880	
				360A	1886		1888

*Restored to Capital List

2-4-0 Built by Neilson & Co, works nos 954-9.
DW 5ft 2in, LW 3ft 7½in, Cyls 17 x 24 O/S, WB 6ft 8½in + 8ft 4in, THS 920.3
sq ft, WP 120lbs/sq in, Wt 33 tons 18 cwts. 'Crewe' type but single framed.
Raised steel fireboxes. Four-wheel tenders. Canopy supported on
weatherboard and rear poles when built, replaced by Connor type cab about
1870. Raised firebox casing possibly removed, but not otherwise rebuilt.

No	Date	2nd no 1863	CR no 1865	1887 no	Withdrawn
63	1863		348	348A	1888
64	1863		347	347A	1888
65	1863		346	346A	1888
66	1863	1	345	345A	1888
67	1863	2	344	344A	1888
68	1863	3	343	343A	1888

2-4-0 Built by Sharp Stewart & Co, works no 1521-4
DW 5ft 2in, LW 3ft 7½in, Cyls 17 x 24 O/S, WB 6ft 9in + 8ft 9in,
Blr 10ft 3in x 3ft 11in, THS 1329 sq ft, WP 130lbs/sq in, Wt 35 tons 4¼ cwts.
Six-wheel tenders, 'Crewe' type mid-feather firebox.

No	Date	CR no 1865	1887 no	Withdrawn
66	1864	342	342A	1888
67	1864	341	341A	1888
68	1864	340	340A	1888
74	1864	339	339A	1888

2-2-2 Built by Sharp Stewart & Co, works nos 1533-6, 1554-5.
DW 6ft 1½in, LW & TW 3ft 7½in, Cyls 17 x 22 O/S, WB 6ft 9in + 7ft 9in,
Blr 9ft 11in x 3ft 9in, THS 1079.2 sq ft.
'Crewe' type, canopy as 57 class, mid-feather firebox. First locos fitted
with reverse hook on front buffer beam for dropping winding rope after
ascending Cowlairs bank when working out of Glasgow Queen Street (E & G).

No	Date	CR no 1865	1882 no	Duplicate no	year	Rebuilt	Withdrawn
75	1864	303	248	248A	1887	1882 16½in diam	
				1229	1899	cyls and flush	
						Brittain boiler	11/1900
76	1864	302		302A	1883		3/1884
77	1864	301		301A	1883		5/1888
78	1864	300		300A	1883		6/1888
79	1864	305					7/1882
80	1864	304		304A	1883		8/1885

2-2-2 Built by SC at Perth

DW 6ft 1in, LW & TW 3ft 7¾in, Cyls 16 x 20 O/S, WB 6ft 9in + 7ft 3in, Blr 9ft 6¾in x 3ft 9in, WP 125lbs/sq in, THS 1014.7 sq ft.

Allan design of 'Crewe' type with trough in crown plate (as hitherto) but with transverse mid-feather in firebox dividing it into four parts with fore and aft ash pans. Boiler centre 5ft 10⅞in. Cabs with half depth side plates and two rear poles. Intended for light passenger work and all types of branch traffic. Boilers intended for rebuilds but found unsuitable were used. Four-wheel tenders. Mid-feathers removed by Connor. Nos 83 & 84 used spare parts from original locos 1-14. Last four completed after amalgamation.

No	Date	CR no 1865	Duplicate no	year		Withdrawn
4	3/1864	306				1882
5	9/1864	307	307A	1883	6 wheel tender 8/1868	1884
16	11/1864	308	308A	1883	6 wheel tender 1868	1884
81	3/1865	299	299A	1883		1888
18	3/1865	309	309A	1886		1888
82	6/1865	298	298A	1883		1888
(84)	10/1865	296				1883
(83)	11/1865	297	297A	1883		1892
	1866	295				1883
	1866	294				1882

Two more locomotives were built at Perth, CR nos 472 & 473 (2-4-0). These are listed on page no 58 under the date given by McEwan, 1868, but some sources give the date as 1864-6.

Newtyle and Glamiss* (4ft 6in gauge)

Incorporated 1835. Opened 4/6/1838. Purchased by Scottish Midland Junction 1845 and converted to standard gauge.
*Act has older spelling Glammis

McEwan records an 0-4-0 locomotive built by James Stirling and Co, Dundee in 1837 named *Victoria* and gives DW 4ft 3in, Cyls 12 x 16, which he states was sold to contractors by the SMJ, but there is no evidence that this company ever owned a locomotive. At times of heavy traffic, eg, on market days, **Dundee and Newtyle** locos 1, 2 & 3 were hired on a day-by-day basis. At other times horses were used.

Newtyle and Coupar Angus (4ft 6in gauge)

Incorporated 1835. Opened 2/1837. Purchased by Scottish Midland Junction 1845 and converted to standard gauge.

No record of any locomotives.

Scottish Midland Junction

Incorporated 1845. Opened 2/8/1848. Connections with Aberdeen Railway at
Forfar and Scottish Central at Perth. Kirriemuir branch opened 2/1855,
Blairgowrie 8/1855. Worked by Scottish Central from opening until 31/7/1855
then formed Joint Board of Management with Aberdeen Railway until **Scottish
North Eastern** formed by amalgamation of the two companies 29/7/1856.

Special Note

McEwan did not identify any locomotives as belonging to the SMJ and recorded
only Scottish Central and Aberdeen locos, assuming that as the SMJ was worked
by the SC until 1855 that there were none but this was not so. The accounts
of the three companies published in *Herapath's Railway and Commercial Journal*,
particularly those of the SC which were published in greater detail and
included a schedule of the number of locos and rolling stock employed by type
and which company owned them, record the following

Locomotives employed	SC	SMJ	Aberdeen
Period 12/2/1851 to 31/7/53			
Passenger	42	7 }	20
Goods	10	- }	
Period 1/8/1853 to 31/7/54			
Passenger	37	7 }	20
Goods	12	2 }	
Period 1/8/1854 to 31/1/55			
Passenger	37	7 }	23
Goods	12	4 }	

In addition the Aberdeen accounts for 8/4/1856 record a total (Aberdeen and
SMJ) of 44 locomotives employed and the SMJ accounts for 31/3/1856 record
7 passenger and 7 goods locos.

These figures correlate for the pre-1855 SC details already given, but
difficulty is encountered in identifying the SMJ and Aberdeen locos (see
page no 30)

Taking into consideration all the available information, none of which is
conclusive and, in particular, the accounts and reports of the six-monthly
meetings of the SMJ, it would seem likely that the seven passenger locos
would be 2-2-2s and built by Jones & Potts as given below. The four goods
locos as at 31/1/1855 would most likely be those given below. The
remaining three locos cannot be positively identified as they were probably
delivered after the Joint Board of Management had been set up with the
Aberdeen in 1/8/1855. They are amongst those listed for the SNE on page
no 35. All of these are recorded by McEwan, but as of SC or SNE origin as
recorded below. The information is only conjectural.

11 locomotives as under (plus three others not identified listed under SNE)

2-2-2 Built by Jones & Potts

Probable dimensions DW 6ft 0in, LW & TW 3ft 6in, Cyls 15 x 20 O/S. These
locos are recorded by McEwan as being built from 11/1855 to 1857, the first
6 by John Jones and Sons (successors to Jones & Potts in 1852) and the last
at the SNE works at Arbroath. It is here conjectured, but cannot be
positively stated, that the above dates are rebuild dates as below.
Rebuilt 16 x 20 cyls

Nos	Date	SNE no 1855*	CR no 1866	Rebuilt	Withdrawn
not	1850	4	**451**	11/1855	1870**
known	1850	5	**450**	11/1855	1868
	1851	6	**449**	12/1855	1876
	1851	7	**448**	1/1856	1876
	1851	8	**447**	2/1856	1873

```
           1851          9        446      2/1856          1873
           1851         10        453       1857           1870
        *SNE numbers uncertain
       **Used to rebuild no 452 (page no 35)
```

O-6-O Built by Hawthorn's of Leith
   DW 5ft 0in, Cyls 17 x 20, Rebuilt O-4-2, DW 4ft 6in

			1864	CR no		2nd CR		
				1866				
No*	Date	Rebuilt	no	1866	no	year	Withdrawn	
77	11/1853	4/1856	1	488	660	1873	1876	
78	11/1853	4/1856		497	664	1875	1877	

   *Number recorded by McEwan retained on SNE.

O-6-O Built by John Jones & Son, Liverpool
   DW 4ft 6in, Cyls 17 x 20

		Rebuilt	CR no	1876		
No*	Date	O-4-2	1866	no	Withdrawn	
79	3/1854**	1857	498	670	1877	
80	3/1854**	1857	499	671	1877	

   *Number recorded by McEwan, retained on SNE
  **Date given by McEwan but not recorded in accounts until 1/8/1854. See
     also note Aberdeen Railway page no 30).

Arbroath and Forfar (5ft 6in gauge)

   Incorporated 1836. Opened Arbroath-Leysmill 24/11/1838 (horse operation).
   Throughout 4/12/1838. Locomotive operation from 31/1/1839. Junction with
   Dundee and Arbroath at Arbroath harbour. Leased to **Aberdeen** 1846 and converted
   to standard gauge.
   7 locomotives as under

   2-2-2 Built by James Stirling, Dundee Foundry Co.
      DW 5ft 0in, LW & TW 3ft 6in, Cyls 14½ x 18 O/S, Blr 8ft 6in x 4ft 0in,
      Wt 13 tons.
      Report by Robert Marshall, D & A Manager, gives cyls 12 x 16.

Name	Date	
Victoria	12/1838	Altered to standard gauge 1846. To stationary work 1849.

   2-2-2 Built by James Stirling, Dundee Foundry Co.
      DW 5ft 0in, LW & TW 3ft 6in, Cyls 13 x 18 O/S, Blr 8ft 5in x 3ft 9in,
      Wt 13 tons.

Name	Date	
Britannia	5/1839	Sold 12/1848. Shipped to Canada
Caledonia	3/1839	Altered to standard gauge 1846. Stationary work 1849

   O-4-2 Built by James Stirling, Dundee Foundry Co.
      DW 4ft 6in, TW 3ft 0in, Cyls 12 x 18, Blr 8ft 6in x 4ft 0in, Wt almost 14 tons.
      Report by Robert Marshall, D & A Manager, gives cyls 14 x 18

Name	Date	
Albert	1840	Sold 12/1848

   O-4-2 Built by James Stirling, Dundee Foundry Co.
      Specifications uncertain

Name	Date	
Princess	5/1841	Sold 12/1848. Shipped to Canada

   O-4-2 Built by Simpson & Co, Aberdeen
      DW 5ft 0in, TW 3ft 0in, Cyls 13 x 18 (15 x 18), Blr 8ft 6in x 3ft 7in,
      WB 6ft 9in + 6ft 0in. Above specifications as given by McEwan, but not

confirmed. Also stated by McEwan to have double frames, cast iron wheels
and O/S cranks. Rebuilt with Salter safety valves and dome over and
cylinders enlarged to 15 x 18. Screw reversing gear. Names removed by
Aberdeen Railway.

Name	Date	Aberdeen loco stock 1848	SNE no* 1856	Rebuilt	CR no 1866	Withdrawn
Lucifer	1845	1848	53	2/1855	**475**	1867
Mercury	1846	1848	54	7/1855	**474**	1867

*SNE numbers as given by McEwan

McEwan records two other locos, named *Sirocco* and *Hercules*, built by
Kinmond, Hutton and Steel. These 0-4-2s, similar to the above, were ordered
by the Aberdeen Railway, the first being dated 29/12/1846 for £2,100. A
badly written minute book of the Aberdeen Railway held in the Scottish Record
Office records on 8/4/1847 that an offer was made of payment of £1,000 on
account to KHS in response to a letter from them requesting payment. Two
further entries suggest that the Aberdeen Railway resold these locos. An
undated note refers to a *"Letter from Mr. Cubitt re locomotives; write
Edinburgh and Northern as to two engines and write to makers"*. The other,
dated 15/4/1847, records a letter from Hawthorn's presumably referring to
the 1848 0-4-2s below concluding with the note: *"To take engines and give a
few wagons in exchange as part of the price"*. It is known that Kinmond & Co
(who had succeeded KHS on 23/7/1847) delivered at least one loco to the
Aberdeen Railway because in October of that year it was in collision with the
Dundee and Arbroath loco preparing to work the 12 o'clock up train while in
transit to Aberdeen. On 2/11/1847 the Aberdeen company offered a bill at
three months to cover the balance price of the engines. There is thus no
conclusive proof of resale, but the fact that the Aberdeen accounts (see
pages 23 and 28) only recorded 20 locos until 8/1854 would seem to make
this likely. Had they come into Aberdeen stock as stated by McEwan the
figure would have been 22.

Aberdeen

Incorporated 1845. Formal opening 27/1/1848. Opened Montrose to Brechin and
Forfar 1/2/1848. Throughout Guthrie to Aberdeen 1/4/1850. Formed northern
section of main line to Aberdeen. From 12/2/1851 until 31/7/1854 the line
was worked by the Scottish Central and for a further twelve months until
31/7/1855 the locomotives were pooled with those of the SC and the Scottish
Midland Junction. The Aberdeen and the SMJ then formed a Joint Board of
Management to operate the two railways independently of the SC and
amalgamated 29/7/1856 to form the **Scottish North Eastern**.

Special note (see page no 28)

From the published accounts it will be seen that the total locomotive stock
remained constant at 20 until 31/7/1854, despite the fact that 5 locos were
sold to the Aberdeen by the SC in the period ended 31/1/1854. These are
seen to come off the SC total as at 31/7/1854, but curiously do not go onto
the Aberdeen total which only increases to 23 as from 1/8/1854. The half-
yearly meeting of the company was informed in March 1854 that "two new
locomotives have recently been delivered and a third is due in a few days" and
these are obviously those added to capital stock in the period ended 31/1/1855.
However according to the received dates given by McEwan and others only six
locos were acquired by the three companies in 1853/4, two 5ft 6in 0-6-0s
from Hawthorn's of Leith in 1853 which from their CR numbers would appear to
have gone to the Scottish Central (page no 29), two 5ft 0in 0-6-0s from
Hawthorn's of Leith and two 4ft 6in 0-6-0s from John Jones & Son which have
already been given conjecturally as SMJ property. It is possible that the
three Aberdeen locos acquired in 1854 relate to three of these, but if so
then the SC and SMJ totals would no longer correlate as the SC record two

additional goods locos from 1/8/1853 and the SMJ two more from the same
date and a further two from 1/8/1854.

A second possibility is that the three 'new' locos were in fact three of the
five ex SC 2-2-2s (page no 25) which the SC had taken into their works at
Perth for overhaul or rebuild (it will be noted that two are recorded as
being rebuilt in 1855, but the other three have no rebuild dates recorded)
to be handed over to order from the Aberdeen Railway as and when they had
the funds available. (The company had serious financial problems throughout
its independent existence and never paid any dividend until merged into the
SNE). This would seem quite possible. A third possibility, of course, is
simply that some of the received dates are wrong.

In the later period the Aberdeen total would seem (by deduction of the 14
SMJ locos from the combined total of 44 given for 8/4/1856) to have risen to
30. Again there is difficulty reconciling this total, but this may be due
to locomotives being out of traffic (the figure is only a note of 'locomotives
employed' and not part of the accounts themselves). The Aberdeen Board in
1856 complained that locomotives had been returned from the SC in a bad state
of **repair** and there is a reference at one of the meetings to locos having
had to be hired at first when independent operation was resumed.

22 locomotives as under (plus 2 from Arbroath & Forfar, 5 from SC and one
other, unidentified listed under SNE) (Amends Vol 1: Summary). Numbering
given by McEwan is not considered to be reliable and is omitted.

0-4-2 Built by R & W Hawthorn, works nos 534-42.
DW 5ft 0in, TW 3ft 0in, Cyls 15 x 21, THS 597.8 sq ft (or 592.5 sq ft),
WP 85lbs/sq in. Hawthorn standard design built in 1847, but not delivered
until 1848. 12 were originally ordered but this was revised and the other
three were taken up by the Caledonian becoming CR 111/2, 118. These three
locos are recorded, however, as having 4ft 6in DW, Cyls 14 x 21 by McEwan.

Date	1851 no	SNE no 1856	CR no 1866	Rebuilt	With- drawn
1848	57	57	**487**		1877
1848	58	58		1854 at Perth after accident 5/1854, cyls lined to 14½in, Salter safety valves. Sold 1865	1865
1848	59	59	**486**		1878
1848	60	60	**485**		1868
1848	61	61	**484**		1868
1848	62	62	**483**	1854 at Perth	1868
1848	63	63	**482**		1868
1848	64	64	**481**		1868
1848	65	65		1/1855 at Perth	1864

0-4-2 Built by Gourlay Mudie & Co   (G)
            Simpson & Co, Aberdeen   (S)
            Blackie & Co   (B)
DW 5ft 0in, TW 3ft 0in, Cyls 13 x 18 (15 x 18), Blr 8ft 6in x 3ft 7in,
WB 6ft 9in + 6ft 0in. Similar to Arbroath & Forfar Simpson locos of
1854/6, but with cast iron wheel bosses only. Similarly rebuilt with cyls
15 x 18.

Date	1851 no	SNE no 1856	CR no 1866	Rebuilt	With- drawn
1848* (G)	66	66	**479**		1867
1848 (S)	67	67	**476**		1867
1848** (G)	68	68	**480**	12/1854	1868
1848 (B)	69	69	**478**	8/1855	1867
1848 (B)	70	70	**477**	6/1854	1867
1848 (S)	71	71			
		40	(renumbered 1858)		1861

*Not listed by Lowe. McEwan records built 1847.
**Lowe states possibly 0-4-0

0-4-0 Built by Kinmond, Hutton & Steel 1845.
    Purchased second hand from contractors of line 1849/50 and name removed.
DW 4ft 0in, Cyls 13 x 18, Blr 7ft 3in x 4ft 0in. Double frames O/S cranks,
raised firebox casing.

		1851	SNE no	1859	CR no	
Name	Date	no	1856	no	1866	Rebuilt
Dandie	1849/50	72	72	34	**472**	1855/6 0-4-0PT with
(May have						Neilson indirect
been named						valve motion
Caledonia						
earlier)	Sold to contractors of Dingwall and Skye railway 1865. Scrapped
	1869.					

4-2-0 Crampton. Built by E B Wilson & Co c1849
    DW 7ft 0in, LW 4ft 6in & 3ft 6in, Cyls 16 x 20, THS 920 sq ft, WP 50lbs/sq in,
Wt 25tons 18 cwts. Purchased from stock. Rebuilt as 2-2-2.

	1851	SNE no	1859	CR no	1868	Rebuilt	With-
Date	no	1856	no	1866	no	2-2-2	drawn
1850	73	73	2	**455**	**563**	1861	1871
1850	74	74	3	**454**	**562**	1861	1871

0-6-0 Built by Hawthorn's of Leith
    DW 5ft 0in, Cyls 16 x 24, WB 7ft 8½in + 7ft 8½in, Boiler diameter 4ft 1in,
THS 1136 sq ft, WP 90lbs/sq in, Wt 32 tons 8 cwts. Six-wheel tenders, wheels
3ft 6in, later replaced with four-wheel tenders. Rebuilt 1861-6, 0-4-2
TW 3ft 7¼in.

		CR no	1875	1877		
SNE no	Date	1866	no	no	Withdrawn	
81	2/1855	**493**	**666**	**462**	1880	
82	2/1855	**494**	**667**	**463**	1880	
83	3/1855	**495**	**668**	**464**	1881	
84	3/1855	**496**	**669**		1877	Dismantled
						for spares

Dundee and Arbroath (5ft 6in gauge)

Incorporated 1836. Opened 6/10/1838 (three temporary stations in Dundee
before completion of permanent station, later Dundee (East) in 1851). Leased
to **Dundee and Perth and Aberdeen Junction** 30/4/1847 and converted to standard
gauge. Lease discontinued 9/3/1850 and D & A returned to independent
operation and locomotives returned except one.
Leased by **Scottish North Eastern** 1/2/1862. The line became joint with the
North British 1/1/1880 together with part of the Arbroath and Forfar and the
Carmyllie prior to the NB line from St Vigeon's Junction to Kinnaber Junction
opening in 1881-3.

13 locomotives as under: (plus 2 from Caledonian. Amends Vol 1: Summary)

2-2-2 Built by Kinmond, Hutton & Steel
    DW 5ft 0in, LW & TW 3ft 6in, Cyls 13 x 18 O/S, Wt 12 tons, WP 50lbs/sq in.
Inside framing, centre dome with brass cover with smaller dome between it
and chimney, later removed. Safety valve on raised firebox casing.
O/S crank.

Name	Date	Withdrawn
Wallace	1838	1847
Fury	1838	1847
Griffen	1839	1847

2-2-2 Built by Kinmond, Hutton & Steel
DW 5ft 6in, Cyls 13 x 18 O/S, Wt 13 tons 13 cwts. Other dimensions and
details as 5ft 0in locos above. Converted to standard gauge 1845/6 *Rapid* is
believed to have been retained by the DPAJ the others being returned.

Name	Date	
Rapid	1840	Retained DPAJ, 1850
		To SC 77 1863, Withdrawn 1864
Dart	1840	Withdrawn 1859
Queen	1841	Withdrawn 1859

O-4-O Built by Kinmond & Co (see page no 21)
DW 4ft 6in, Cyls 14 x 18 (in 1865).
McEwan records these locos as of DPAJ origin but not so.

Name	Date	SNE no 1862	CR no 1866	Withdrawn
Caledonia	1847	38	**471**	1867
Gowrie	1848	39	**470**	1868

O-4-2 Built by Kinmond & Co (see page no 17)
DW 4ft 6in, Cyls 14 x 20

Name	Date	SNE no 1862	Withdrawn
Craigie	1849	36	1866
Carlogie	1849	37	1866

2-2-2 Built by Kinmond & Co*
DW 5ft 6in, LW & TW 3ft 6in, Cyls 15 x 18. Similar to 1840/1 KHS locos with
larger cylinders and patent injector. Not named, numbers not known.

Date*	SNE no 1862	CR no 1866	Withdrawn
c1852	19	**439**	1873
c1852	20	**438**	1873
c1852	21	**437**	1873

*McEwan records these locos as being replacements for the three original
locos of 1838/9 and gives the date as 1855. As these original locos were not
regauged and in any case Kinmond & Co moved their business to Canada in 1852
this information must be regarded with suspicion. It is possible that the
locos were acquired second hand as two locos were offered for sale in 1852
(one partly completed) when Kinmond & Co sold the Wallace Foundry in Dundee,
or they could have been by Gourlay Mudie & Co. Evidence for their exact
identification is lacking.

2-2-2 ex Glasgow, Paisley and Greenock
DW 5ft 6in, LW & TW 3ft 6in, Cyls 14 x 20 O/S. Purchased from Caledonian
1859.

ex GP & G no 18/CR no 2.
To SNE 12 1862, see page no

2-2-2 ex Caledonian
DW 6ft 0in, LW & TW 3ft 6in, Cyls 15 x 20 O/S. Purchased from Caledonian
1859.

e x CR no 16. To SNE 13 1862. See page no 39.

Perth, Almond Valley and Methven

Incorporated 1856, opened 1857. From junction with Scottish Midland Junction
near Dunkeld to Methven. Worked by Scottish Central for a few months in 1857,
then by Scottish North Eastern until 1861, when company purchased rolling
stock and locomotive and took over operation themselves. Amalgamated with
SNE 1/1/1864.

One locomotive as under:

0-4-OT Built by Hawthorn of Leith
DW 4ft 0in, Cyls 13 x 18. Standard Hawthorn design. Not named or
numbered.

Date	
1861	To Scottish North Eastern no 35 1864
1866	To Caledonian no **468** and exchanged with Alyth engine
1868	Renumbered **450**
1877	Renumbered **679**
1878	Renumbered **716**
1881	Renumbered **719**. Withdrawn 1883

Alyth

Incorporated 1858. Opened 2/9/1861.
Junction with Scottish North Eastern at Meigle to Alyth. Leased by Scottish
North Eastern 1863 confirmed by Act of 23/6/64.

One locomotive as under:

0-4-OWT Built by E.B. Wilson & Co.
DW 4ft 0in, Cyls 12 x 15 O/S, THS 319 sq ft, WP 100lbs/sq in. Tank capacity
310 gallons.

Name	Date	
	1858	To SNE 33 1863
	1866	To Caledonian 466
	1868	Renumbered 454
	1877	Renumbered 264
	1883	Sold to Thos Wheatley, Wigtown.
		Worked Methven branch from about 1866 and transferred to
		Stranraer in 1874 replacing former Portpatrick no 264.

Carmyllie

Private railway to Carmyllie Quarry from Elliott Junction on Dundee and
Arbroath Railway near Arbroath, built 1853-5. Statements by McEwan concerning
the dates of building of the line, purchase of a locomotive from the Arbroath
and Forfar and, particularly, his statement that the line was 5ft 6in gauge
must be treated with caution. It seems highly unlikely that a line constructed
six years after the line with which it connected had been converted to standard
gauge would be of a different gauge. Line purchased by Scottish North
Eastern 6/1865.

One locomotive as under:
Stated by McEwan to be property of Quarry Company, but not definately
established as such and might have come from any of the independent branches on
the SNE.

0-4-OST Built by Neilson & Co
DW 3ft 6in, Cyls 10 x 18, WB 5ft 8in.
Tank capacity 450 gallons. Standard Neilson industrial loco with indirect
valve gear and regular valve in smokebox. Building date 1858.

Date	
1865	To SNE 32
1866	To Caledonian no **467**
1868	Renumbered **455**
1877	Renumbered **678**
1878	Renumbered **715** Cut up 1/1881

Scottish North Eastern (including Joint Board of Management Aberdeen and Scottish Midland Junction 1855-6)

Amalgamation of Aberdeen (including leased Arbroath and Forfar) and Scottish Midland Junction incorporated 29/7/1856, but effective under Joint Board from 1/8/1855. Amalgamated with CR 10/8/1866, effective from 1/8/1866.

44 locomotives as under: (amends Vol 1: Summary)
Three of the 1855/6 locos below were SMJ stock not identified and one was Aberdeen stock (see pages 28 & 31). Locomotive Superintendent Thomas Yarrow.

O-6-O Built by E B Wilson & Co, works nos 504-7
DW 5ft 0in, Cyls 16 x 24. Details and rebuilding to O-4-2 TW 3ft 7½in as Aberdeen 81 class 1861-6.

No	Date	CR no 1866	1875 no	1877 no	Withdrawn	
49	12/1855	489			1872	Dismantled for spares
50	12/1855	490	661	459	1880	
51	12/1855	491	662	460	1880	
52	1/1856	492	663	461	1881	

O-6-O Built by John Jones & Sons (formerly Jones, Turner & Evans)
DW 5ft 0in, Cyls 17 x 20. Tender brake gear. Rebuilt O-4-2 1857 by Scottish Central at Perth.

No	Date	CR no 1866	1875 no	Withdrawn
45	11/1855	500	665	1877

2-4-O Built by Brassie, Jackson, Betts & Co, works nos 37/8, 42.
DW 5ft 2in, LW 3ft 7½in, Cyls 17 x 20 O/S, THS 842 sq ft, WP 120lbs/sq in, WB 7ft 0in + 8ft 0in, Wt 30 tons 15 cwts. 'Crewe' type, raised firebox casing, Salter type safety valve over firebox and pillar type on boiler barrel.

No	Date	CR no 1866	1876 no	1878 no	Rebuilt	Withdrawn
46	1855	501	672	706	4/1868	1879
47	1855	502	673		9/1868	1877
48	1857	503				1872 after exploding at Bridge of Dun 23/3/1872

2-2-2 Built by SNE at Arbroath
DW 6ft 0in, Cyls 16 x 20 O/S. Similar to rebuilds of locos listed conjecturally under SMJ, (page no 28)

No	Date	CR no 1866	1870 no	1872 no	Withdrawn
11	1859	452	451*	486	1878

*Rebuilt with spare parts of 451 and renumbered 451

O-4-2 Built by Neilson & Co, works nos as below
          Brassey, Jackson, Betts & Co, works nos as below
          Vulcan Foundry Co, works nos as below
DW 5ft 1½in, TW 3ft 8½in, Cyls 17 x 20 O/S, WB 6ft 10in + 7ft 6in, THS 1073 sq ft, WP 120lbs/sq in, Wt 26 tons 6¼ cwts. Yarrow patent transverse water division (mid-feather), raised firebox casing, with dome and safety valve on top. Pillar type safety valve in centre of boiler. No cabs.

Built by Neilson & Co, works nos 478-82

No	Date	CR no 1866	1876 no	1877 no	1884 no	Withdrawn
71	1859	515		684	684A	1888

72	1859	**514**	(S685)*				1876	*Scrap np.
73	1859	**513**		**683**			1883	
74	1859	**512**		**682**			1881	
75	1859	**511**		**681**	681A		1888	

Built by Brassie, Jackson, Betts & Co, works nos 48-50

		CR no	1876	1877	1878	1881	1885	
No	Date	1866	no	no	no	no	no	Withdrawn
40	1861	**504**	**674**	**670**	**704**	**721**		1885
41	1861	**505**	**675**	**671**	**705**	**720**		1887
42	1862	**506**	**697**				691A	1888

Built by Vulcan Foundry, works nos 490-493

		CR no	1877	1881	1882	
No	Date	1866	no	no	no	Withdrawn
43	1862	**510**	**702**	**538**		1886
44	1862	**509**	**701**	**725**	**539**	1884
54	1862	**508**	**700**	**724**		1882
76	1862	**507**	**699**			1881

Built by Neilson & Co, works nos 1161-6, 1202-7 with larger diameter boiler
and no mid-feathers in firebox. THS 969.3 sq ft, Wt 27 tons 6¼ cwts.

		CR no	1877	1884	1885	
No	Date	1866	no	no	no	Withdrawn
58	1865	**516**	**686**			1883
77	1865	**517**	**687**	687A		1888
85	1865	**518**	**688**	688A		1889
86	1865	**519**	**689**	689A		1888
87	1865	**520**	**690**			1883
88	1865	**521**	**691**		691A	1885
89	1866	**527**	**696**		696A	1887
(90)	1866	**522**	**685**	685A		1888
(91)	1866	**523**	**692**			1883
(92)	1866	**524**	**693**		693A	1888
(93)	1866	**525**	**694**		694A	1888
(94)	1866	**526**	**695**		695A	1888

O-4-2WT Built by Robert Stephenson & Co, works no 1490
DW 5ft 2in, TW 3ft 9in, Cyls 16 x 24, WB 6ft 10in + 7ft 6in, THS 877.8 sq ft,
WP 120lbs/sq in.
Partly Stephenson standard design modified to Yarrow's instructions.

No	Date	
65	1864	To Caledonian **469** 1866
		Renumbered **369** 1868. Withdrawn 1876

2-2-2 Built by Vulcan Foundry Co, works nos 550-3
DW 7ft 1¼in, LW & TW 3ft 10½in, Cyls 16 x22, WB 7ft 3in + 7ft 9in, THS 1301.75
sq ft, WP 120lbs/sq in. 'Crewe' type to Yarrow's design. Double frames.
Intended for main line passenger work. Raised firebox casing, pillar safety
valve on boiler and dome with Salter safety valve on firebox casing. Yarrow
patent firebox division. Rebuilt with Connor flush boilers.

		CR no	1877	1886		
No	Date	1866	no	no	Rebuilt	Withdrawn
22	12/1865	**456**	**312**	312A	1875	1888
23	12/1865	**457**	**313**	313A	1878	1891
24	12/1865	**458**	**314**	314A	1876	1889
25	12/1865	**459**	**315**	315A	1878	1889

2-2-2 Built by Vulcan Foundry Co
   DW 7ft 0½in, LW & TW 3ft 10¼in, Cyls 16½ x 22.
   As 22 class above but with some difference in firebox division. Bent weather
   board. Stated by McEwan to be built at Arbroath, but photograph shows it in
   Vulcan's yard.

No	Date	CR no 1866	1877 no	Rebuilt	Withdrawn
(26)	4/1866	**461**	**311**	1870	1885

2-2-2 Built by SNE at Arbroath
   DW 6ft 0in, Cyls 15½ x 20. Renewal of SNE 12 (ex G p & G)

No	Date	CR no 1866	
(12)	1866	**460**	Withdrawn 1871

2-2-2 Built by Vulcan Foundry Co, works nos 570-3
   DW 7ft 1¼in, LW & TW 3ft 10¼in, Cyls 16 x 22.
   As 22 class Connor flush boilers on rebuilding.

No	Date	CR no 1866	1877 no	1886 no	1899 no	Rebuilt	Withdrawn
(27)	9/1866	**462**	**316**	316A	(1231)	1879	1899*
(28)	9/1866	**463**	**317**	317A		1880	1898
(29)	9/1866	**464**	**318**	318A		1878**	1888
(30)	9/1866	**465**	**319**	319A		1875**	1888

   *Stationary work, Dundee shed until 1906.
   **Fitted with simple air brake 1888 for branch working. Yarrow fireboxes
   removed from all locos by CR.

Forth and Clyde Navigation

Incorporated 1768. Canal completed 1790.
Railway from Grabamston to Grangemouth, built as a private line, opened 1860
(goods), 1861 (passenger). Company purchased by CR 1867.

2 locomotives as under:

0-4-0ST Built by Andrew Barclay & Co, Kilmarnock (or Sharp Stewart)
   Dimensions uncertain, but cylinders probably 12in diameter.

Name	Date	CR no 1867		
Carron	1862	**116**	Sold 1876	May have been renumbered
Grange	1862	**117**	Sold 1877	676/7 in 1875

Monkland Navigation

Incorporated 1770. Canal completed 1790. Act of 1843 authorised the
construction of a short railway, sometimes called the Drumpellier railway, near
Cuilhill Colliery. Included inclined planes from Rosehall to the Luggie Burn,
from the Luggie Burn to the Edinburgh road and short locomotive-hauled section
to the canal. Powers for the Monkland Navigation company to purchase. Opened
1849-50 after company had been amalgamated with the Forth and Clyde Navigation
in July 1846 and railway purchased by them. F & C N purchased by CR 1867.

1 locomotive as under:

0-4-0ST Built by A Barclay & Son, works no 12.
   DW 3ft 0in, Cyls 8 x 16.
   Always known as 'Canal no 1". Not taken into CR stock. McEwan states 'was
   never wholly owned by Caledonian railway'. Possibly purchased jointly by the
   colliery and the F & C Navigation who continued to be part owners when the

CR took over the canal.
Date
1862   Scrapped 1889

Solway Junction

Incorporated 1864. Opened 13/9/1869 (goods), 8/8/1870 (passenger). Line from
Kirtlebridge (CR) to Brayton (Maryport & Carlisle) including running powers over
North Bristol Silloth branch between Kirkbride and Abbeyholme. Annan to
Kirtlebridge section purchased by CR (confirmed by Act of 21/7/1873).
Company absorbed by CR 1895 but line worked by CR from opening.

7 locomotives as under: (Solway Jct nos never carried)

0-4-2WT Built by Neilson & Co, works nos 1217-8
    DW 5ft 6in, TW 4ft 0in, Cyls 16 x 20, WB 7ft 6in + 9ft 6in, THS 1009.2 sq ft,
    WP 130lbs/sq in, Wt 36 tons 2½ cwts. Originally ordered by Northampton and
    Banbury Junction (see page no 262) but not taken up. Weather board only when
    built. Canopy provided shortly after.

No	Date	CR no 1869	Duplicate no	year	Withdrawn
(1)	1866	**540**	540A	1892	
			1354	1899	1900
(2)	1866	**541**	541A	1892	
			1355	1899	
			1541	1901	1901

0-4-2 Built by Neilson & Co, works nos 1219-20
    DW 5ft 6in, TW 4ft 0in, Cyls 16 x 20, WB 7ft 6in + 7ft 0in, THS 1009.2 sq ft,
    Wt 28 tons 13 cwts. Cylinders, motion, wheels and boilers interchangeable
    with 0-4-2WTs above. Four-wheel tenders. Ordered by Northampton & Banbury Jct
    as above.

No	Date	CR no 1869	1877 no	Duplicate no	year	Withdrawn
(3)	1866	**452**	**322**	322A	1887	
				1279	1899	1899
(4)	1866	**453**	**323**	323A	1887	
				1280	1899	
				1323	1900	1906

0-6-0 Built by Neilson & Co, works nos 1388-9.
    DW 5ft 1¼in, Cyls 17 x 24, WB 7ft 3in + 7ft 9in, Blr 4ft 1in diam, THS 1044 sq
    ft. Six-wheel tenders. Rebuilt standard 0-6-0T boiler.

No	Date	CR no 1868	1892 no	1897 no	Rebuilt	LMS no	Withdrawn
(5)	8/1868	**542**	542A	**381***	3/1902	17101	1927
(6)	1868	**543**	543A	**382***	2/1903	17102	1928

    *Restored to Capital list

0-6-0T Built by Manning Wardle & Co, works no 196.
    DW 3ft 0in, Cyls 11 x 16
    Supplied new to Eckersley & Bayliss (Chesterfield) in 1866. Sold 1867 to
    Brassey & Co who were contractors of the SJ.

No	Date	
(7)	1868/9	To Caledonian no **539** 1869
	1/1872	Sold to T. Wheatley To Wigtownshire No 6 *Bradby* 1882
	1894	Withdrawn

CALEDONIAN RAILWAY

Sinclair Locomotives 1847-1858

2-2-2 Built by: CR at Greenock
Vulcan Foundry Co, works nos as below
Jones & Potts, believed works nos as below
Scott Sinclair & Co, works nos as below
DW 6ft 0in, LW & TW 3ft 6in, Cyls 15 x 20 O/S, WB 5ft 6½in + 6ft 6½in,
Blr 9ft 9in x 3ft 6¾in, THS 779.88 sq ft, WP 90lbs/sq in, Wt 19 tons (empty).
Based on LNW SFB Pass design from drawings supplied by Crewe. Double frames,
Stephenson link motion. Two pillar type safety valves, one centre and one
on dome on raised firebox. Four-wheel tenders, 800 gallons, 3 tons coal,
WB 7ft 11¼in.
2-4-0 rebuilds had open splashers filled in.
2-2-2WT rebuilds had hand brake fitted acting on DW & TW, weatherboard added
and splashers filled in.
One loco preserved until the late seventies when scrapped, but not known
which.

Built by CR Greenock

No	Date	Renumbered no	year	Rebuilt	Withdrawn
4	1847			2-4-0	1869
5	1847				1869
6	1847	42	1869		1871
7	1847	48	1869		
		50	1870		1874
8	1847	26	1869		
		41	1871		1873
9	1847	44	1870		1872
42	1847				1869
43	1847				1873
44	1847			2-4-0	1869

Built by Vulcan Foundry Co, works nos 299-308

No	Date	Renumbered no	year	Rebuilt	
10	1847				Withdrawn 1869
11	1847	27	1869		
		49	1871	1865 2-2-2WT	Withdrawn 1872
12	1847	38	1869		
		42	1872		
		118	1874		Withdrawn 1874
13	1847	39	1869		
		45	1872		Withdrawn 1873
14	1847	41	1869		Withdrawn 1871
15	1847				Withdrawn 1868
16	1847				Sold to **Dundee and Arbroath**
					No 4 1859
					To SNE 13 1862
					To CR **440** 1866
					Withdrawn 1873
17	1847				Withdrawn 1870
18	1847				Withdrawn 1869
19	1847	48	1870		Withdrawn 1871

Built by Jones & Potts. No domes, safety valves on centre of boiler and over firebox. Works nos believed to be as below.

No	Date	Works no	Renumbered no	year	Rebuilt	Withdrawn
25	1847	236				1869
26	1847	220	23	1868	1865 2-2-2WT	1870
27	1847	221				1869
20	1847	229	57	1870	1866 2-2-2WT	
			320	1875		1878
21	1847	231	29	1869		1871
22	1847	232	40	1870	2-4-0	1872
23	1847	233				1868
24	1847	234	49	1870	2-4-0	1871

Built by CR, Greenock. Locos marked * had larger boilers, THS 831 sq ft.

No	Date	Renumbered no	year	Rebuilt	Withdrawn
31*	1848	32	1869		1872
32*	1848				1869
45	1848				1872
46	1848			1856 2-4-0	1872
47	1848				1874
48	1848			1856 2-4-0	1870
49	1848			2-4-0	1870
50	1848			2-4-0	1870
51	1848				1874
52	1848				1873
53	1848				1869
54	1848	615	1873		1874
55	1848				1869
56	1848	53	1869		1873
57	1848				1869
58	1848				1869

Built by Vulcan Foundry Co, works nos 277/8.
Ordered by Scottish Central (see page no 23)

No	Date	Renumbered no	year	Withdrawn
29	1848			1869
30	1848	(50)	1871	1871

Built by Scott Sinclair & Co, works nos 1-3
Ordered by Scottish Central (see page no 24)

No	Date	Renumbered no	year	Rebuilt	Withdrawn
28	1848			2-4-0	1870
40	1849				1869
41	1849	57	1869		1870

Built by CR, Greenock. Large boilers as above

No	Date	Renumbered no	year	Rebuilt	Withdrawn
33	1849	48	1872		1874
34	1849			2-4-0	1871
35	1849	46	1872	1856 2-4-0	1873
36	1849	44	1872	2-4-0*	1873
37	1849	46	1873	2-4-0*	1874

*Cylinders experimentally 16 x 20, later lined back to 15 x 20.

Built by Jones & Potts, works nos 177-8.
Ordered by Scottish Central (see page no 24)

		Renumbered		
No	Date	no	year	Withdrawn
38	1849	31	1869	
		49	1872	1874
39	1849			1868

2-2-2 Built by Jones & Potts, works nos 239-44.
DW 6ft 0in, LW & TW 3ft 6in, Cyls 15¼ x 20 O/S, WB 6ft 4in + 7ft 6in, larger
boiler as 31-7 above. Other details as 4 class. Later fitted with Blr
8ft 7in length of barrell, THS 850 sq ft, WP 100lbs/sq in. Rebuilt 2-4-0
as below.

No	Date	Rebuilt	Withdrawn
59	1848	c1857 2-4-0 15½in cyls	
		1870	1884
60	1848	1864 2-4-0 16½in cyls	
		1871	1885
61	1852	1864 2-4-0 15½in cyls	1880
62	1852	c1857 2-4-0 15½in cyls	
		1864	1882
63	1852	c1857 2-4-0 15½in cyls	
		1870	1882
64	1852	1865 2-4-0 15½in cyls	1883

2-2-2 Built by CR at Greenock
DW 7ft 2in, LW & TW 3ft 6in, Cyls 15½ x 20*O/S, THS 891 sq ft, WP 110lbs/sq
in, Wt 30 tons approx.
*Stroke assumed.
More powerful main line passenger locomotive to eliminate double heading.
Dome and Salter safety valve on raised firebox casing. Gooch box link valve
gear. Four-wheel tender 900 gallons, 3½tons of coal. Rebuilt with
identical boilers and 16in cylinders.

No	Date	Rebuilt	Withdrawn
65	7/1854	1864	1881
66	7/1854	1869	1883
67	9/1854	1863, 1872 after accident Kirtlebridge	1884
68	10/1854	1871	1882
69	11/1854	1871	1882
70	1/1855	1863	1881
71	5/1855	1867	1879
72	5/1855	1864	1882
73	7/1855	1863	1879
74	9/1855	1869	1880
75	9/1855	1869	1880
76	10/1855	(Exploded Rockcliffe 18/4/1856)	
		Scrapped	1859

2-4-0 Built by George England 1852-3
DW 5ft 0¾in, LW 3ft 0⅜in, Cyls 15 x 22 O/S*
WB 5ft 11½in + 5ft 6in, THS 850 sq ft, Wt 10¾ tons.
Part of cancelled order for Russia which were purchased from stock in 1854.
Intended for goods traffic. All wheels in front of firebox.
*Lowe records cylinders as 16 x 22.

No	Date	1872 no	Withdrawn
144	1854	182	1874
145	1854		1872
146	1854		1872
147	1854		1872
148	1854	183	1873
149	1854		1872

150	1854	**184**	1872
151	1854	**185**	1872

2-4-0 Built by CR, at Greenock

DW 5ft 2in, LW 3ft 2in, Cyls 16 x 20, WB 6ft 1in + 7ft 5in, Blr 9ft 4⅜ x 3ft 6in, BHS 696.4 sq ft, WP 120lbs/sq in, Wt 22½ tons.
Based on LNW LFB goods (see vol 2A p110). Four-wheel tenders, 900 galls, 2½ tons coal. Rebuilt with flush boilers and Ramsbottom safety valves instead of Salter's in some cases.

		1880	Renumbered			
No	Date	no	no	year	Rebuilt	Withdrawn
152	9/1854				1864	1880
153	9/1854				1867	1880
154	10/1854				1866	1879
155	10/1854	**167**	**680**	1881	1875	1883
156	11/1854	**181**			1869	1881
157	11/1854	**184**			1868	1882
158	11/1854	**255**			1875	1885
159	12/1854	**320**			1875	1886
160	12/1854				1865	1880
161	1/1855				1865	1880
162	1/1855	**351**			1867	1881
163	2/1855	**360**	**360A**	1884	1869	1885
164	2/1855	**369**			1869	1884

2-4-0 Built by CR at Greenock

DW 5ft 2in, LW 3ft 2in, Cyls 17 x 20 O/S.
As 152 class with larger cylinders.

		1880	1881	1887		
No	Date	no	no	no	Rebuilt	Withdrawn
165	2/1855	**370**		**370A**	1870	1888
166	3/1855	**680**			1868	1881
167	3/1855				1867	1879
168	3/1855		**682**		1865 at Perth	1883
169	4/1855		**698**		1865 at Perth	1882
170	4/1855		**172**		1867	1884

0-4-2 Built by R & W Hawthorn & Co, works nos 543-5.

DW 4ft 6in, TW 3ft 0in, Cyls 14 x 21, THS 597.8 sq ft.
Last three of order for Aberdeen Railway (see page no 31).
Dimensions differed as recorded

No	Date	
111	1847	Withdrawn 1863
112	1847	Withdrawn 1867
118	1849	Withdrawn 1864

0-4-2 Built by Neilson & Mitchell, works nos 28-30, 35-7.

DW 5ft 0in, TW 3ft 4in, Cyls 16 x 20, WB 6ft 5in + 6ft 7in, THS 788 sq ft, WP 90lbs/sq in. Double sandwich frames, raised firebox, one safety valve on manhole cover centre boiler and one on dome over firebox. Three locos ordered by Scottish Midland Junction taken over by CR and increased to six. SMJ had specified bar frames, but these were supplied as plate sandwich frames.

No	Date	Withdrawn	Scrapped
113	1847	1862	
114	1847	1864	
115	1847	1863	
119	1847	1865	1867
120	1847	1867	
121	1847	1871	

0-4-2 Built by CR at Greenock
    DW 4ft 6in, TW 3ft 6in, Cyls 16 x 18, WB 7ft 2in + 5ft 10in, Blr 10ft 11in
    x 3ft 5in, THS 974 sq ft, WP 90lbs/sq in, Wt 24 tons 13 cwts, DW springs
    were under-slung. Gooch link motion. Safety valves and domes as on 4 class
    singles. Raised firebox. Rebuilt 17 x 18 cyls shortly after building.

No	Date	Renumbered no	year	Rebuilt	Withdrawn
101	1848	**528**	1867		
		707	1878		1880
102	1848	**529**	1867	1870	
		708	1878		
		722	1881		Sold 1886
103	1848	**530**	1867		
104	1848	**531**	1867		
		709	1878		
		723	1881		1882
105	1848	**532**	1867		1871

0-4-2 Built by CR at Greenock
    DW 4ft 6in, TW 3ft 6in, Cyls 17 x 18, Wt 26 tons 2 qrs.
    As 101 class above, but built with 17 x 18 cyls.

No	Date	Renumbered no	year	Rebuilt	Withdrawn
106	1849	**533**	1867		1881
107	1849	**534**	1867		1870
108	1849	**535**	1867		
		532	1872	1870	1881
109	1849	**536**	1867		
		534	1871		1880
110	1849	**537**	1867		1871

0-4-2 Built by Neilson & Co, works nos 53-6
    DW 5ft 0in, TW 3ft 6in, Cyls 17 x 20 O/S, WB 6ft 9in + 6ft 3in, THS 838 sq ft,
    WP 100 lbs/sq in. Underslung springs on DW. Boiler feed driven off
    crosshead. Round 'haystack' firebox as built, but conventional raised
    firebox fitted 1856-60.

No	Date	Renumbered no	year	Withdrawn
132	1853			1869
133	1853	**185**	1872	
		118	1874	
		370	1876	1878
134	1853	**115**	1870	1875
135	1853	**132**	1870	
		255	1874	1877

0-4-2 Built by CR at Greenock
    DW 5ft 2in, TW 3ft 2in, Cyls 15 x 22 O/S, WB 6ft 1in + 8ft 3in, THS 840 sq ft,
    Wt 23¼ tons. Last locos built completely at Greenock. Flush topped boilers
    as new and as rebuilt 16 x 20 cyls as rebuilt with Ramsbottom safety valves
    instead of Salter.

No	Date	1884 no	Rebuilt	Withdrawn
171	1855		1871	1884
172	1855		1867	1881
173	1855	**173A**	1867	1885

0-4-2 Built by CR at St Rollox
    DW 5ft 2in, TW 3ft 2in, Cyls 15 x 22 O/S.
    As 171 class above, but built with 16 x 22 cyls. May have been only
    assembled at St Rollox.

No	Date	Renumbered no	year	Rebuilt	Withdrawn
174	1856			1866	1882
175	1856	175A	1884	1873	1885
176	1857			1867	1881
177	1857			1875	1885
178	1857			1868	1885
179	1858	724	1882	1868	1884
180	1858	698	1882	1866	1889
181	1858			1868	1880

2-4-OT Built by Hawthorn's of Leith, works nos 5/6 1850.
  DW 5ft 0in, Cyls 14 x 21
  Purchased 1854.

No	Date	
80	1854	from Coltness Iron Co. Withdrawn 1860
81	1854	from Russell & Co. Withdrawn 1861

O-4-OST Built by CR at Greenock
  DW 4ft 7in, Cyls 12 x 18. Dummy crankshaft. WB 12ft 0in, Blr 9ft 4in x
  2ft 9in, WP 110lbs/sq in. Built for shunting work. Rebuilt by 1855
  probably to O-4-O tender. 137-41 and 143 ultimately to O-4-2ST

No	Date	1870 no	1871 no	Rebuilt O-4-2ST	Withdrawn
136	1853				1869
137	1853	182		*	1872
138	1853			*	1870
139	1853	562	590	*	1871
140	1853	563	591	1865	1872
141	1853		592	*	1872
142	1853				1871
143	1853			*	1871

  *Dates of rebuilding to O-4-2ST not recorded

O-4-OST Built by Hawthorn's of Leith, works no 50 1851
  DW 4ft 6in, Cyls 15 x 18
  Purchased 1854 from Summerlee Iron Co.

No	Name	Date	1862 no	1864 no	Withdrawn
83	*Neilson*	1854	240	118	1873

O-4-2ST Built by Hawthorn's of Leith 1850
  DW 5ft 0in, Cyls 16 x 20 O/S.
  Purchased 1854 from Kidson & Russell.

No	Name	Date	1862 no	1864 no	Withdrawn
87	*Newton*	1854	241	255	1874
88	*Arch Russell*	1854		242	1872

2-2-2WT Built by CR at Greenock
  DW 5ft 1in, LW & TW 3ft 1in, Cyls 9 x 15, Blr 8ft 7½in x 2ft 8in, THS
  386.1 sq ft, WP 100lbs/sq in, WB 6ft 7in + 6ft 5in, Wt 26 tons 13½ cwts.
  Gooch box link valve gear. Coal capacity 30 cwts. 450 gallon tanks between
  frames (2 x 225 galls) and underslung wooden brake blocks on TW only.

No	Date	Renumbered no	year	Withdrawn
77	1851	2	1859	
		55	1869	
		444	1874	
		487	1877	1879

78	1851	**16**	1859	
		56	1869	
		445	1874	
		530	1877	
		486	1878	1880
79	1851			Replaced 1861*

*Not recorded by McEwan. Possibly renewed as no 79 of 2-2-2 76 class
(page no 46)

0-4-0 Built by Fairbairn & Co.
DW 4ft 9in, Cyls 15 x 22, WB 7ft 6in, Blr 4ft 9in diam, THS 580 sq ft,
Wt 21 tons. Believed to have been ordered by SMJ. Gab motion. Raised
firebox. Single safety valve on dome over firebox.

No	Date	Rebuilt
116	1848	1858 0-4-2T, TW 3ft 9in. Bunker and side tanks. THS 725 sq ft, Wt 18½tons. Link motion.
	1863	Sold to buyer in Cardiff area*
117	1848	Not rebuilt
	1863	Sold to buyer in Cardiff area*

*It has been suggested that these were the two purchased by the Bristol
Port Railway and Pier in c1865 (see Vol 3A p36) but this is unlikely as
they were supplied by J. Cross & Co of St. Helens.

0-6-0 Built by Jones & Potts, works nos 154-8 (96-100).
CR at Greenock (remainder)
DW 4ft 7in, Cyls 16 x 20 O/S, WB 6ft 6in + 6ft 6in, THS 1050 sq ft,
WP 90lbs/sq in.
Crewe type 0-6-0, but very soon rebuilt to 0-4-2.   TW 3ft 0in, Cyls 17 x 20
O/S, Wt 28 tons 3 qrs. Single frames. Rebuilt dates below refer to later
rebuild.

No	Date	Renumbered no	year	Rebuilt	Withdrawn
96	1849	**113**	1866		
		503	1875	1863	1876
97	1849	**115**	1866	1862	1870
98	1849	**111**	1867	1873	
		119	1868		
		316	1876		
		371	1877		
		371A	1886		1890
99	1849	**112**	1867	1864	
		538	1868		
		121	1877		1872
100	1849	**114**	1867	1865	
		264	1875		
		255	1877		
		487	1880		1881
122	1849	**449**	1876	1866	
		698	1877		1879
123	1849				1864
124	1849			1864	1875
125	1849			1863	1876
126	1850	**182**	1876	1867	1882
127	1850	**183**	1876	1863	
		699	1882	1873	1886
128	1850			1862	1876
129	1850	**184**	1876	1868	1880
130	1850	**185**	1876	1867	1882
131	1850			1865	1872

Connor Locomotives 1857-81

2-2-2 Built by CR at St Rollox

DW 8ft 2in, LW & TW 3ft 8in, Cyls 17 x 24 O/S, WB 7ft 2in + 8ft 6in, Blr
11ft 7½in x 3ft 10⅜in, THS 1169 sq ft, WP 120lbs/sq in, Wt 30 tons 13 cwts.
A famous design based on Crewe type, but with running plate curved over
wheel bosses, a feature of all Connor's 2-4-0 and 2-2-2 designs. Double
frames, raised firebox with dome on top. Horizontal cylinders rather than
inclined facilitated by large DW diameter. Salter safety valves. Six-wheel
tender, 2016 gallons, 3½ tons capacity. Open splashers, O/S bearings on
LW & TW. 'Half cabs' fitted later. Rebuilt by Drummond with flush boilers,
Ramsbottom safety valves, dome on second ring of boiler casing, Drummond
chimney replacing Connor's 'stove pipe' type and full cab. Cyls 17¼ x 24
O/S (or 17½ x 24), DW 8ft 4in, THS 1190 sq ft, Wt 35 tons 6 cwts.

No	Date	Duplicate no	year	Rebuilt	Withdrawn
76	1859	76A	1889	1872	
				1887	5/1893
77	1859	77A	1889	1869	6/1893
78	1861	78A	1889	1868	7/1891
79	1861	79A	1889	1869	
				1882	6/1895
80	1861			1870	7/1886
81	1861	81A	1887	1870	1/1891
82	1861	82A	1887	1872*	6/1895
83	1863	83A	1891	1870	1/1895
84	1864	84A	1889	1871	11/1894
85	1864			1871	7/1886
86	1864	86A	1888	1871	2/1891
87	1865	87A	1889	1872	6/1894

*after accident Kirtlebridge

2-2-2 Built by CR at St Rollox

DW 8ft 2in, LW & TW 3ft 8in, Cyls 17½ x 24 O/S, THS 947.5 sq ft, WP 140lbs/
sq in, Wt 32 tons 16 cwts, WB as 76 class.
Built with flush top boilers, cabs, Ramsbottom safety valves on firebox
cover and dome to the rear of DW centre on boiler. Other details as 76 class.

No	Date	Duplicate no	year	Withdrawn
113	1875			7/1891
114	1875	114A	1891	7/1896
115	1875	115A	1891	
		1228	1899	12/1900
116	1875	116A	1887	1/1891

2-2-2 Built by CR at St Rollox

DW 7ft 2in, LW & TW 3ft 8in, Cyls 17 x 22 O/S, WB 6ft 10in + 8ft 2in, Blr
10ft 5in x 3ft 11½in, THS 1127 sq ft, WP 120lbs/sq in, Wt 30¼ tons approx.
Raised fireboxes with dome over and Salter safety valves. 'Half cabs' as
76 class. Rebuilt with flush boilers 10ft 5in x 4ft 4in. THS 882 sq ft,
Wt 32 tons 5¾ cwts, larger cabs, dome on middle ring of boiler casing,
Ramsbottom safety valves on firebox, except no 90 which had dome and Salter
safety valves on middle ring. On rebuilding the original six-wheel tenders
were replaced with four-wheel ones giving 1750 gallons and 2¼ tons capacity.

No	Date	Duplicate no	year	Rebuilt	Withdrawn
88	1864	88A	1891	1872	1895
89	1864	89A	1891	1873	
		1231	1899		1899
90	1864	90A	1891	1875	1887
91	1864	91A	1891	1872	1895

2-2-2 Built by A. Barclay & Co, works no 119
DW 7ft 2in, LW & TW 3ft 8in, Cyls 16½ x 22 (16¾). Other dimensions as 88
class.
Built to demonstrate invention of John Miller Ure to lift DW from rails when
coasting saving retarding friction and wear. CR agreed to take the engine
if there was no purchaser when experiments discontinued. Rebuilt 1880, Cyls
16¾in diameter.

No	Date	1877 no	Duplicate no	year	Withdrawn
460	9/1871	310	310A	1886	
			1230	1899	
			1310	1900	1901

O-4-2 Built by Hawthorn's of Leith, works nos 83/4, 1852.
DW 4ft 6in, Cyls 14 x 21.
Purchased from Coltness Iron Co 1857

No	Possible name	Date	Withdrawn
184	*Tewsgill*	1857	1872
185	*Garrion*	1857	c1872 (replaced 1874)

O-4-2 Built by Neilson & Co, c1855
DW 5ft 0in, Cyls 16 x 22 O/S.
Purchased from W. Dixon & Co 1857.
Not certain that these locos were identical.

No	Name	Date	Withdrawn
186	*Calder*	1857	1881
187	*Cambusnethan*	1857	1882

O-4-2 Built by Hawthorn's of Leith, works no 47, 1851
DW 5ft 0in, Cyls 17 x 20 O/S.
Purchased from J. Watson & Co, 1858.

No	Name	Date	1866 no	1867 no	1872 no	1876 no	1877 no	Withdrawn
95	*Glencairn*	1858	111	120	123	451	680	1878

O-4-2 Built by Neilson & Co, works nos as below.
            Dubs & Co, works nos as below.
DW 5ft 2in, TW 3ft 9in, Cyls 16½ x 22 O/S (17in), WB 6ft 5in + 7ft 4in, THS
969.27 sq ft, WP 120lbs/sq in, Wt 27 tons 12½ cwts.
Flush topped boilers, bent weather board. Built for coal burning. Steam
brakes. Dome and double Salter safety valve over firebox. First 12 ordered
with steam tenders, but order amended to be fitted with ordinary tenders.
At rebuilding Ramsbottom safety valves were fitted - some on third ring of
boiler casing, some over firebox and dome on boiler centre. THS 980 sq ft,
WP 130lbs/sq in, Cyls increased to 17in diameter, cabs added.
Built by Neilson & Co, works nos 700-711, 1008-1019.
            Tenders, works nos 712-23, 1020-31.

No	Date	1881 no	Duplicate no	year	Rebuilt	Withdrawn
216	1861		216A	1888	1872	
			1272	1898		1900
217	1861		217A	1888	1872	1892
218	1861		218A	1888	1873	1895
219	1861		219A	1888	1870	1892
220	1861		220A	1888	1876	1890
221	1861		221A	1888	1877	1896
222	1861		222A	1888	1871	1893
223	1861		223A	1888	1880	1892
224	1861		224A	1889	1874	1896
225	1861		225A	1889	1872	1890

No	Date		Duplicate no	year	Rebuilt	Withdrawn
226	1861		226A	1889	1876	1893
227	1861		227A	1889	1870	1890
243	1864	**615**	615A	1889	1877	1897
244	1864	**616**	616A	1889	1873	1894
245	1864	**617**	617A	1889	1875	1895
246	1864	**618**	618A	1889	1873	1894
247	1864	**619**	619A	1889	1873	1894
248	1864	**620**	621A	1889	1873	
			1278	1898		
			1620	1901		1901
249	1864		249A	1887	1871	1891
250	1864		250A	1887	1873	1893
251	1864		251A	1887	1873	1892
252	1864		252A	1887	1872	1894
253	1864		253A	1887	1875	1895
254	1864		254A	1887	1872	1894

Built by Dubs & Co, works nos 1-10, 88-107.
WB 6ft 6in + 7ft 4in.

No	Date	Duplicate no	year	Rebuilt	Withdrawn
272	1865	272A	1888	1877	1894
273	1865	273A	1888	1873	1892
274	1865	274A	1888	1874	
		1275	1898		1898
275	1865	275A	1887	1880	1888
276	1865	276A	1887	1879	
		1276	1898		1899
277	1865	1277	1911	1871 7/1886 0-4-2ST	
				Wt 39 tons 15 cwts	1/1912
278	1865	278A	1887	1876	1895
279	1865	279A	1887	1877	1892
280	1865	280A	1887	1879	
		1277	1899		1899
281	1865	281A	1887	1876	1892
387	1866	387A	1888	1879	
		1300	1898		1899
388	1866	388A	1894		1891
389	1866	389A	1890	1873	1894
390	1866	1390	1911	6/1886 0-4-2ST	
				2/1902 New cyls	6/1912
391	1866	391A	1890	1871	
		1301	1899		
		1391	1900		1902
392	1866	392A	1890	1875	1894
393	1866	1393	1911	6/1886 0-4-2ST as 277	
				2/1902 new cyls	
				blr ex 1391, firebox from	
				1395	1/1912
394	1866	394A	1890	1875	1895
395	1866	395A	1890	1877	
		1302	1899		
		1395	1900		1902
396	1866	396A	1890	1878	
		1303	1899		1900
397	1866	1397	1911	5/1886 0-4-2ST as 277	
				10/1901 New cyls	
				firebox ex 1305	6/1912
398	1866	398A	1890	1872	1897
399	1866	399A	1890	1874	
		1304	1899		
		1399	1900		1902

No	Date	Duplicate no	year	Rebuilt		Withdrawn
400	1866	400A	1890	1875		1895
401	1866	401A	1890	1874		1895
402	1866	402A	1890	1875		
		1305	1899			1901
403	1866	403A	1889	1873		
		1306	1899			1899
404	1866	404A	1889	1874		1894
405	1866	1405	1911	1872	6/1886 0-4-2ST	
				as 277 9/1901 New cyls		5/1913
406	1866	406A	1889	1874		1898

Built by Neilson & Co, works nos 1248-57.

No	Date	Duplicate no	year	Rebuilt		Withdrawn
407	1866	407A	1889	1876		
		1307	1899			1899
408	1866	408A	1889	1874		1895
409	1866	409A	1889			
		1308	1899			
		1409	1899			1909
410	1866	410A	1890			
		1309	1899			
		1410	1900			1903
411	1866	411A	1890			
		1310	1899			
		1411	1900			1903
412	1866	412A	1890			
		1311	1899			1899
413	1866	413A	1890	1874		1894
414	1866	414A	1890			1891
415	1866	415A	1890	1874		1891
416	1866	1416	1910	1873, 5/1886 0-4-2ST		
				as 277, 1/1901 New cyls,		
				firebox ex 1303		4/1916

0-4-2 Built by Dubs & Co, works nos as below.
           Neilson & Co, works nos as below
DW 5ft 2in, TW 3ft 9in, Cyls 17 x 24 O/S, WB 6ft 5in + 7ft 4in, THS 798.5 sq ft, WP 130lbs/sq in, Wt 30 tons 2¾ cwts.
Gooch link motion. Some had second-hand tenders (all four-wheel). Similar to rebuilds of 216 class.

Built by Dubs & Co, works nos 410-19, 463-70.

No	Date	Duplicate no	year	Capital no	year	Withdrawn
552	1870	552A	1892	**652**	1902	
		1312	1899			
		1552	1900			1908
553	1870	553A	1892			
		1313	1899			
		1553	1900			1901
554	1870	554A	1892			
		1314	1899			
		1554	1900			1904
555	1870	555A	1892	**382**	1896	
		543A	1897			
		1311	1899			
		1382	1899			
		1555	1900	**664**	1902	
		1555	1907			1914

No	Date	Duplicate no	year	Capital no	year	Withdrawn
556	1870	556A	1892			
		1315	1899	**658**	1901	
		1556	1908			1909
557	1870	557A	1892			
		1316	1899			
		1557	1900			1910
558	1870	558A	1892			
		1317	1899			
		1558	1900			1902
559	1870	559A	1893			
		1318	1899	**632**	1900	1904
560	1870	560A	1893	**651**	1898	1912
561	1870	561A	1893	**655**	1893	1905
562	1871	562A	1893			
		1321	1899	**665**	1900	1907
563	1871	563A	1893			
		1322	1899			
		1563	1900	**645**	1903	
		1563	1905			1908
564	1871	564A	1896			
		1323	1899			1899
565	1871	565A	1896			
		1324	1899			
		1565	1900	**636**	1902	1904
566	1871	566A	1896	**644**	1898	
		1566	1905			1905
567	1871	567A	1896			
		1325	1899			
		1567	1900	**631**	1900	
		1567	1904			1915
568	1871	568A	1896			
		1326	1899	**663**	1900	
		1568	1907			1908
569	1871	569A	1896			
		1327	1899	**647**	1901	
		1569	1905			1909

Built by Neilson & Co, works nos 1610-15, 1626-32.

No	Date	Duplicate no	year	Capital no	year	Withdrawn
570	1871	570A	1896			
		1328	1899			
		1570	1900			1907
571	1871	571A	1896			
		1329	1899			
		1571	1900			1900
572	1871	572A	1896			
		1330	1899			
		1572	1900			1910
573	1871	573A	1896			
		1331	1899			
		1573	1900			1907
574	1871	574A	1896			
		1332	1899			
		1574	1900			1902
575	1871	575A	1896			
		1333	1899			
		1575	1900			1909
576	1871	576A	1896			
		1334	1899	**660**	1900	1905

No	Date	Duplicate no	year	Capital no	year	Withdrawn
577	1871	577A	1896			
		1335	1899			
		1577	1900			1900
578	1871	578A	1896			
		1336	1899			
		1578	1900			1907
579	1871	579A	1896			
		1337	1899			
		1579	1900	**646**	1904	
		1579	1905			1913
580	1871	580A	1896			
		1338	1899			
		1580	1904	**158**	1904	1907
581	1871	581A	1896			
		1339	1899			
		1581	1900			1917
582	1871	582A	1896			
		1340	1899			
		1582	1900			1900

O-4-2 Built by Neilson & Co, works nos as below.
DW 5ft 2in, TW 3ft 8in, Cyls 17 x 24 O/S, WB 6ft 5in + 7ft 4inm THS 1057 sq ft, WP 130lbs/sq in, Wt 34 tons 11¼ cwts.
Four-wheel tenders, dome between second and third rings of boiler casing, Ramsbottom safety valves over firebox.

No	Date	Works no	Duplicate no	year	Capital no	year	Withdrawn
324	1872	1693					1907
325	1872	1694	1325	1909			1910
326	1872	1695	1326	1909			1909
327	1872	1696	1327	1909			1911
328	1872	1697	1328	1909			1909
329	1872	1698	329A	1897			
			1295	1899			
			1329	1900			1909
330	1872	1699	330A	1897			
			1296	1899			
			1330	1900			1909
331	1872	1700	331A	1897			
			1297	1899			
			1331	1900			1909
332	1872	1701	332A	1897			
			1298	1899			
			1332	1900	**610**	1904	
			1332	1910			1910
333	1872	1702	333A	1897			
			1299	1899			
			1333	1900			1909
595	1872	1748	595A	1897			
			1341	1899			
			1595	1901			1910
596	1872	1749	596A	1897			
			1302	1899			
			1596	1901			1911
597	1872	1750	597A	1897			
			1343	1899			
			1597	1901			1907
598	1872	1751	598A	1897			1898*
599	1872	1752	599A	1897			
			1344	1899			
			1599	1901			1909

600	1872	1753	1600	1901			1904
601	1872	1754	1601	1901			1901
602	1872	1755	1602	1901			1904
603	1872	1756	1603	1903	**659**	1904	
			1603	1908			1912
604	1872	1757	1604	1903	**608**	1910	
			1604	1910			1917
605	1873	1819	1605	1903			1910
606	1873	1820	1606	1903			1907
607	1873	1821	1607	1903	**648**	1904	
			1607	1905			1907
608	1873	1822	1608	1910			1910
609	1873	1823	1609	1910			1915
610	1873	1824					1904*
611**	1873	1825	611A	1895			
			1345	1899			
			1611	1901	**642**	1903	1905
612	1873	1826	612A	1895			
			1346	1899			
			1612	1901			1912
613	1873	1827	613A	1895			
			1347	1899			
			1613	1901	**669**	1904	
			1613	1907			1908
614	1873	1828	614A	1895			
			1348	1899			
			1614	1901	**666**	1906	1907
621**	1874	1870	1621	1900	**654**	1905	1908
622	1874	1871	1622	1900	**656**	1904	1908
623	1874	1872	1623	1900			1912
624	1874	1873	1624	1900			1911
625	1874	1874	1625	1900			1921
626	1874	1875	1626	1900	**662**	1904	
			1626	1908			1909
627	1874	1876	1627	1902			1909
628	1874	1877	1628	1902			1911
629	1874	1878	1629	1907			1908
630	1874	1879	1630	1907			1907

```
*598A Withdrawn under scrapping no 566A
 610  Withdrawn under scrapping no 1332
**611 in accident Woodhall 2/6/1880
 621  in accident Woodhall 2/6/1880
```

2-4-0 Built by George England & Co, 1852
DW 5ft 0in, Cyls 15 x 20 O/S.
Purchased from C. Dunlop & Co, 1857.

No	Name	Date	
182	*Cuilhill*	1857	Withdrawn 1870
183	*Monkland*	1857	Withdrawn 1872

2-4-0 Built by CR at St Rollox   (C)
      Neilson & Co, works nos 488-91 (tenders 492-5)   (N)
DW 6ft 2in, LW 3ft 2in, Cyls 18 x 24 O/S, WB 6ft 3in + 8ft 9in, WP 110lbs/sq
in, Wt 32 tons 15 cwts approx.
Connor design of double frame Crewe tyoe, curved running plate, raised
firebox with dome over, bent weatherboard, tall Connor 'stove pipe' chimney,
Salter safety valves. Neilson locos had steam tenders on six wheels with
8 x 18 cyls which were transferred in 1860 to 197 class (below). Rebuilt
with flush boilers, WP 130lbs/sq in and cabs.

No	Date		Rebuilt	Duplicate no	year	Withdrawn
189	1858	C	1869	189A	1891	1894
190	1858	C	1869	190A	1891	
				1232	1899	
				1190	1901	1902
193	1859	N	1870	193A	1891	1898
194	1859	N	1869	194A	1891	
				1233	1899	1899
195	1859	N	1869	195A	1891	1898
196	1859	N	1869	196A	1891	1897
191	1859	C	1869	191A	1891	1894
192	1859	C	1875	192A	1891	1894

2-4-0 Built by CR at St Rollox
     Neilson & Co, works nos as below
     Beyer Peacock & Co, works nos as below
DW 6ft 2in, LW 3ft 7in, Cyls 18 x 24 O/S, WB 6ft 9in + 8ft 9in, WP 120lbs/ sq in, Blr 11ft 2¾in x 4ft 1in, blr pitch 6ft 5½in, THS 947.5 sq ft. Improved 189 class with larger boiler. Rebuilt with similar flush type boiler as fitted to rebuilt 76 class. Dome over firebox as built with Salter safety valves off set to rear of second ring of boiler casing. When rebuilt all but four had Ramsbottom safety valves. Steam tenders ordered but cancelled.

Built by CR at St Rollox. Steam tenders from 193-6 (above) fitted, but very soon converted to ordinary six-wheel tenders.

No	Date	Rebuilt	Duplicate no	year	Withdrawn
197	1860	1869, 1874	197A	1891	
			1234	1899	
			1197	1901	1908
198	1860	1871	198A	1891	
			1235	1899	1899
199	1860	1868	199A	1894	
			1236	1899	
			1199	1901	1903
200	1860	1871	200A	1894	1897

Built by   Neilson & Co, works nos 603-11 (tenders 612-20).

No	Date	Rebuilt	Duplicate no	year	Withdrawn
201	1860	1869	201A	1894	1896
202	1860	1869	202A	1894	1896
203	1860	1868	203A	1894	
			1237	1899	1900
204	1860	1869	204A	1895	1895
205	1860	1868	205A	1894	
			1238	1899	
			1205	1900	1903
206	1861	1869	206A	1895	
			1239	1899	1900
207	1861	1869	207A	1895	1897
208	1861	1869	208A	1895	1897
209	1861	1868,1874	209A	1895	1897

Built by Beyer Peacock & Co, works nos 158-63

No	Date	1862 no	1864 no	Rebuilt	Duplicate no	year	Withdrawn
85	1861	87	256	1869	256A	1894	1895
86	1861	88	257	1868	257A	1894	1895
89	1861		258	1869	258A	1894	1895
90	1861		259	1879	259A	1894	1896

91	1861	**260**	1870	260A	1894	1897
92	1861	**261**	1869	261A	1894	
				1267	1898	1900

Built by CR at St Rollox with 'half cabs' instead of bent weatherboard.

| | | | Duplicate | | |
No	Date	Rebuilt	no	year	Withdrawn
210	1862	1870, 1882	210A	1895	
			1240	1899	
			1210	1900	1902
211	1862	1870, 1882	211A	1895	1897
212	1862	1869	212A	1895	1896
213	1863	1870	312A	1895	
			1241	1899	1899
214	1863	1870	214A	1895	
			1242	1899	1899
215	1863	1870	215A	1895	
			1243	1899	
			1215	1901	1904

2-4-0 Built by Neilson & Co, works nos as below
              Dubs & Co, works nos as below
DW 5ft 2in, LW 3ft 2in, Cyls 17 x 22 O/S, WB 6ft 1in + 8ft 9in, THS 1000.2
sq ft, WP 120lbs/sq in, Wt 28 tons 18 cwts.
Flush top boiler, dome on second ring of boiler casing. Salter safety
valve, cabs.

Built by Neilson & Co, works nos 724-31 (tenders 732-9).

| | | | Duplicate | | |
No	Date	Rebuilt	no	year	Withdrawn
228	1861	1872, 1888	228A	1886	1896
		(Brittain blr)			
229	1861	1872	229A	1886	1888
230	1861	1875	230A	1886	1886
231	1861	1873	231A	1886	1888
232	1861	1871	232A	1887	1889
233	1861	1871	233A	1887	1888
234	1861	1872	234A	1887	1888
235	1861	1882	235A	1887	1888
		(Brittain blr)			

Built by Dubs & Co, works nos 11-16, 29-31.

| | | | Duplicate | | |
No	Date	Rebuilt	no	year	Withdrawn
282	1865		282A	1887	1888
283	1865		283A	1887	1888
284	1865		284A	1887	1890
285	1865				1884 (after accident Holytown 5/1884)
286	1865		286**A**	1887	1888
287	1865		287A	1887	1888
384	1866	1886			1906
385	1866		385A	1887	1888
386	1866	1883	386A	1887	
			1349	1899	
			1386	1901	1909

2-4-0 Built by CR at St Rollox
DW 6ft 8in, LW 3ft 7½in, Cyls 17 x 24 O/S, WB 6ft 10in + 8ft 7in, THS 900
sq ft approx, WP 130lbs/sq in, Wt 32 tons 12½ cwts.
Double frames, raised firebox. Rebuilt with flush boilers, dome on second

ring of boiler casing, Ramsbottom safety valves and cabs.

No	Date	Rebuilt	Duplicate no	Duplicate year	Withdrawn
92	1865	1880	92A	1897	1899
93	1866	1879	93A	1897	1899
94	1866	1878	94A	1897	1899
95	1866	1881	95A	1896	1896
96	1866	1878	23A	1896	1896
97	1866	1881	97A	1897	
			1219	1899	
			1097	1900	1909
103	1867	1879	103A	1897	1898
104	1867	1880	1220	1899	1899
105	1867	1879	7A	1895	1895
106	1867	1878			1896
107	1867	1883 (Brittain blr) (renumbered **54** 1898)	1221	1899	1899

2-4-0 Built by Dubs & Co, works nos 19-**38**.
DW 6ft 2in, LW 3ft 7in, Cyls 18 x 24 O/S, WB 6ft 9in + 8ft 9in, THS 1020 sq
ft, WP 130lbs/sq in, Wt 32 tons 13½ cwts. Raised firebox, Connor chimney.
Built with cab and dome over firebox. Rebuilt with Brittain boilers THS
1011.2 sq ft, WP 140lbs/sq in (later 120lbs/sq in) (except 380 & 288 fitted
with Drummond boilers).

No	Date	Rebuilt	Renumbered no	Renumbered year	Duplicate no	Duplicate year	Withdrawn
288	1865	1880, 10/1886	**155**	1899			1910
289	1865	1880			1216	1899	
					1289	1900	1900
290	1865	1881			1217	1899	
					1290	1900	1908
291	1865	1884					1895
292	1865	1882			1266	1899	1899
293	1865	1880			13A	1898	1898
380	1866	8/1886 Drummond blr					1911
381	1866	1881			542A	1897	
					1273	1898	
					1381	1900	1907
382	1866	1884			555A	1896	1896
383	1866	1884	**241**	1898	1249	1899	
			383*	1900			1909

*Restored to Capital list.
2-4-0 Built by Neilson & Co, works nos 1258-77, 1370-81, 1497-1501.
DW 6ft 2in, LW 3ft 7½in, Cyls 18 x 24 O/S,
WB 7ft 0in + 8ft 6in (417-36)
     6ft 9in + 8ft 9in (474-85, 334-8),
THS 1020.5 sq ft, WP 120lbs/sq in, Wt 35 tons 17 cwts.
Built with flush boilers, dome on second ring of boiler casing, conical cover
over safety valves over firebox, double frames. Completely rebuilt by
Drummond THS 939.02 sq ft, WP 150lbs/sq in for main line work. Drummond
boiler except as noted, Drummond chimney, Stirling pattern cab, closed
leading splashers combined with large sand box on 419-33, 435, 473, 476-7,
479-80, 483. 475, 478 & 484 similar but possibly not fitted with Stirling
cab. Drummond boiler was 4ft 4½in external diameter (as against 4ft 2in on
Connor boiler) and became known as 'Rebuild boiler'. 1870 locos not rebuilt.

No	Date	Rebuilt	Duplicate no	year	Withdrawn
417	1866	1881 Brittain blr	1417	1907	1908
418	1866	1882 Brittain blr	1418	1910	1911
419	1866	5/1885	1419	1907	1908
420	1866	8/1883	1420	1909	1910
421	1866	11/1885	1421	1909	1910
422	1866	7/1884	1422	1907	1908
423	1866	11/1883	1423	1909	1909
424	1866	1/1886	1591	1906	1907
425	1867	7/1885	1425	1907	1907
426	1867	4/1885	1426	1907	1908
427	1867	9/1883	1587	1900	1900
428	1867	9/1884	1590	1900	1901
429	1867	2/1884	1429	1907	1908
430	1867	3/1885	1430	1911	1912
431	1867	7/1884	1245	1899	1899
432	1867	9/1883			1910
433	1867	4/1884	1433	1910	1912
434	1867	1883 Brittain blr	1434	1906	1907
435	1867	4/1884	1588	1900	1900
436	1867	1883 Brittain blr	1436	1910	1912
474	1867	1883 Lambie blr	1474	1910	1913
475	1867	5/1886			1910
476	1867	5/1885	1476	1910	1914
477	1867	2/1886	1477	1910	1912
478	1867	6/1886	1478	1910	1916
479	1867	3/1885	1246	1899	1899
480	1868	12/1885	1247	1903	1903
481	1868	1887 Brittain blr	1481	1910	1913
482	1868	1887 Brittain blr	1482	1900	1905
483	1868	11/1885	1483	1910	1913
484	1868	10/1886	1484	1910	1920
485	1868	1/1886			
(renumbered **473** 1877)					1905
334	1870		334A	1894	
			1268	1899	1899
335	1870		335A	1899	
			1269	1899	1899
336	1870		336A	1894	
			1270	1899	
			1336	1901	1905
337	1870		337A	1894	
			1271	1899	
			1337	1901	1902
338	1870		338A	1894	
			1272	1899	1899

2-4-0 Built by CR at St Rollox
                    Neilson & Co, works nos as below.
DW 7ft 2in, LW 3ft 7in, Cyls 17 x 24 O/S, WB 7ft 1½in + 8ft 7in, WP 140lbs/
sq in, Wt 32 tons 18¾ cwts.
Designed to work in conjunction with 76 class singles on passenger trains.
Raised top firebox with dome over, Salter safety valves (1867 locos only)
rebuilt with flush topped boilers with dome on second ring of boiler casing,
Ramsbottom safety valves, Connors or Brittain boilers.
From 1868, all built with flush boilers 4ft 2in diameter.

Built by CR at St Rollox

No	Date	Rebuilt	Capital no	Capital year	Duplicate no	Duplicate year	Withdrawn
98	1867	1878			98A	1897	
					1222	1899	1899
99	1867	1879			99A	1897	1898
100	1867	1881					1897
101	1867	1884 Brittain blr			101A	1897	
					1223	1898	1898
102	1867	1882	112	1897			1906
108	1867	1879			1224	1898	1898
109	1868	1878, 1885 Brittain blr	56	1899	1225*	1899	
					1109	1902	1907
110	1868	1878			1226	1899	1900
111	1868	1881			1227	1899	
					1111	1900	1900
112	1868	1878			102A	1897	
					1218	1898	1899

*No 109 to Duplicate List 1225, 1899. Restored to Capital List **56** 1899.

Built by Neilson & Co, works nos 1382-7.
Rebuilt with Drummond boilers*. No 117 later fitted with Lambie boiler.

No	Date	1876 no	Rebuilt	Duplicate no	Duplicate year	Withdrawn
466	1868	**117**	1884	1117	1912	1913
467	1868	**118****	1882	1118	1912	1914
468	1868	**119****	1882	1119	1912	1915
469	1868	**120**	1884	1120	1912	1914
470	1868	**121**	1883	1121	1912	1913
471	1868	**122**	1884	1122	1912	1914

*Drummond boilers had dome off centre to rear of middle ring of boiler
 casing, THS 939.02 sq ft, Wt 33 tons 19 cwts.
 **Nos 118 & 119 rebuilt with closed splashers, others retained open type
 as built.

Built by Neilson & Co, works nos 1662-7, 1758-63.
Rebuilt with Drummond boilers as above.
Cylinders increased to 17½in diameter as 42 class (page no 62) becoming then
known as 30 class. Nos 30-5 had Stirling steam reversing gear.

No	Date	Rebuilt	Duplicate no	Duplicate year	Withdrawn
30	1872	1899	1030	1912	1917
31	1872	1895	1031	1912	1914
32	1872	1895	1032	1912	1917
33	1872	1895*	1033	1912	1915
34	1872	1897	1034	1912	1914
35	1872	1895	1035	1912	1921
36	1873	1895	1036	1912	1917
37	1873	1896	1037	1912	1914
38	1873	1896			1912
39	1873	1895	1039	1913	1915
40	1873	1899	1040	1913	1917
41	1873	1896	1041	1913	1913

*No 33 fitted with Steel & McInnes air brake 24/4/1873.

2-4-0 Built by CR at Perth

DW 7ft 2in, LW 3ft 10½in, Cyls 17 x 22 O/S, WB 7ft 6in + 8ft 0in, Blr 10ft
11½in x 4ft 1in, THS 1142.03 sq ft, WP 120lbs/sq in.
Parts made in ex SNE works at Arbroath, assembled at Perth. Raised firebox
with dome over. Pillar safety valves centre of boiler and on dome, cab with
half depth side plate and rear poles. Four-wheel tenders. See note, page

no 27 concerning building date.

No	Date	1876 no	1886 no	Withdrawn
472	1868	123	123A	1888
473	1868	124	124A	1893

2-4-0 Built by Dubs & Co, works nos as below.
          Neilson & Co, works nos as below
DW 6ft 2in, LW 3ft 8in, Cyls 16½ x 22 O/S (17), WB 6ft 6in + 8ft 7in, THS 982.2 sq ft, WP 140lbs /sq in, Wt 34 tons, 19¾ cwts.
Local passenger engine. Flush topped boilers. Dome on second ring of boiler casing. Mostly second-hand tenders. Cyls increased to 17in diameter in 1870s on all locos.

Built by Dubs & Co, works nos 303-8, 390-7.
Naylor and Salter type safety valves later replaced by Ramsbottom type on most locos.

No	Date	Renumbered no	year	Duplicate no	year	Withdrawn
1	1869	61	1881			
		59	1885	22A	1896	1896
2	1869			2A	1893	
				1201	1899	
				1002	1900	1904
3	1869			3A	1893	1898
4	1869			4A	1893	1898
5	1869			5A	1893	1894
6	1869			6A	1893	1896
17	1870			17A	1894	1898
18	1870			18A	1894	
				1207	1899	1899
19	1870			(19A)	1895	1895
20	1870			20A	1895	
				1208	1899	
				1020	1900	1901
21	1870	166	1900*	21A	1895	
				1209	1899	1907
22	1870			22A	1895	1896
23	1870	96	1896*	23A	1895	
				96A	1897	1898
24	1870	59	1896	1204	1902	1906

*Restored to Capital list.

Built by Neilson & Co, works nos 1515-19, 1553-7, 1605-9 1880.
Spring balance safety valves in brass casing over firebox later replaced on most locos by Ramsbottom type.

No	Date	Duplicate no	year	Capital no	year	Withdrawn
7	1870	7A	1893	105	1895	
		1213	1899			
		1105	1900			1900
8	1870	8A	1893			
		1202	1899	54	1900	1905
9	1870	9A	1893			
		1203	1899	55	1899	
		1009	1902			1906
10	1870	10A	1893			
		1204	1899	58	1900	
		1010	1902			1905
11	1870	11A	1893			
		1205	1899			1899

No	Date	Renumbered no	year	no	year	Withdrawn
12	1870	12A	1893			1896
13	1870	13A	1894	**293**	1898	
		1220	1899			
		1013	1900			1901
14	1870	14A	1894			1896
15	1870	15A	1894			
		1206	1900	**162**	1900	1903
16	1870	16A	1894			1896
25	1871	25A	1895			
		1210	1899			
		1025	1902			1908
26	1871	26A	1895			
		1211	1899			
		1026	1902			1913
27	1871	27A	1895			1898
28	1871	28A	1895	**106**	1896	
		1214	1899			
		1028	1902			1903
29	1871	29A	1895			
		1212	1899			
		1029	1902			1910
49	1874	1049	1903			
		1125	1906			1908

Built by Neilson & Co, works nos 1881-5 as above. Rebuilt as 55 class (below) in 1880-5.

		Renumbered		Duplicate		
No	Date	no	year	no	year	Withdrawn
50	1874			1050	1903	1907
51	1874			1051	1903	
				1029	1905	1905
52	1874			1052	1905	1911
53	1874	**464**	**1906***	1053	1905	
				1053	1907	1918
54	1874	**107**	1898	1221	1899	
				1008	1900	1900

*Restored to Capital List

2-4-0 Built by Neilson & Co, works nos 1502-14, 1550-2.
DW 5ft 2in, LW 3ft 2in, Cyls 17 x 24 O/S, WB 6ft 2½in + 8ft 9in, THS 868.8 sq ft, WP 120lbs/sq in, Wt 34 tons 2¾ cwts.
Goods engine with flush boiler, dome on second and third ring of boiler casing with Salter safety valves. Four-wheel tenders.

No	Date	Duplicate no	year	Capital no	year	Withdrawn
372	1870	372A	1891			
		1283	1899			
		1372	1900			1904
373	1870	373A	1891			1893
374	1870	374A	1891			
		1284	1899			
		1374	1900			1902
375	1870	375A	1891			
		1285	1899			
		1375	1900			1908
376	1870	376A	1891			
		1286	1899			1899
377	1870	377A	1891			
		1287	1899			
		1377	1901			1911

No	Date	Dup no	year	Cap no	year	Withdrawn
378	1870	378A	1891			1896
379	1870	379A	1891			1898
544	1870	544A	1892			
		1288	1899			
		1544	1900	**635**	1902	
		1375	1904			
		1544	1905			1905
545	1870	545A	1892			1894
546	1870	546A	1892			
		1289	1899			1900
547	1870	547A	1892			
		1290	1899			
		1547	1900			1905
548	1870	548A	1892			
		1291	1899			
		1548	1900			1905
549	1870	549A	1892			
		1292	1899			
		1549	1900			1901
550	1870	550A	1892			
		1293	1899			
		1550	1900			1910
551	1870	551A	1892			
		1294	1899			
		1551	1900	**639**	1904	
		1551	1904			1908

2-4-0 Built by Dubs & Co, works nos 520-33, 534-44, 690-6
DW 6ft 2in, LW 3ft 9in, Cyls 18 x 24 O/S, WB 6ft 9in + 8ft 9in, THS 731.7
sq ft (1872 series), 741.6 sq ft (1873 series), WP 130lbs/sq in, later
125lbs/sq in, Wt 36 tons 8 cwts.
Goods engine with flush boiler dome and safety valves off set to rear of
middle ring of boiler casing. Some locos later fitted with Westinghouse
brake for working passenger trains.

		1881 no	Duplicate		Capital		
No	Date	no	no	year	no	year	Withdrawn
583	1872		583A	1896			
			1256	1899			
			1583	1901	**431**	1901	
			1583	1908			1909
584	1872		584A	1896			
			1257	1899			1900
585	1872		585A	1896			
			1258	1899			1900
586	1872		586A	1896			
			1259	1899			
			1586	1900	**127**	1905	
			1586	1909			1910
587	1872		587A	1896			
			1260	1899			
			1587	1900	**427**	1901	
			1587	1909			1913
236	1872		236A	1898			
			1244	1898			
			1236	1900	**162**	1903	
			1443	1903			1905
237	1872		237A	1898			
			1245	1898	**431**	1899	1901
238	1872		238A	1898			
			1246	1898			1899

239	1872		239A	1898			
			1247	1898			
			1239	1900			1909
240	1872		240A	1898			
			1248	1898			
			1240	1900	**165**	1902	1908
241*	1872		241A	1898			
			1249	1898	**383**	1898	
			1241	1900			1906
242	1872		242A	1898			
			1250	1898			
			1242	1900			1907
535	1872	**243**	1251	1899			1901
536	1872	**244**	1252	1899			
537	1872	**245**	1253	1899			1899
538	1872	**246**	1254	1899			1900
539	1872	**247**	1255	1899			
			1247	1901	**480**	1903	
			1247	1910			1916
588	1872		588A	1897	**291**	1898	
			291A	1899			
			1218	1899			
			1588	1900	**435**	1901	
			1588	1909			1912
589	1872		589A	1897			
			(1261)	1899			1899
590	1872		590A	1897			
			1262	1899			
			1590	1901	**428**	1901	
			1590	1909			1917
591	1872		591A	1897			
			1263	1899			
			1591	1901	**424**	1906	
			1591	1906			1911
592	1872		592A	1897			
			1264	1899			1900
593	1872		593A	1897			
			(1265)	1899			1899
594	1872		594A	1897			
			1266	1899			
			1594	1901	**466**	1906	
			1594	1906			1910
437	1873		1235	1900			
			1437	1900			1909
438	1873		1241	1900			
			1438	1900	**160**	1904	
			1438	1907			1911
439	1873		1242	1900			
			1439	1900			1908
440	1873		1245	1900	**479**	1900	
			1440	1910			1917
441	1873		1246	1900			
			1441	1900			1907
442	1873		1253	1900			
			1442	1900	**465**	1906	
			1442	1907			1907
443	1873		1261	1900			
			1443	1900	**164**	1904	1912

*Rebuilt Drummond boiler 9/1886

2-4-0 Built by Dubs & Co, works nos 697-703
DW 7ft 2in, LW 3ft 7½in, Cyls 17½ x 24 O/S, WB 7ft 1½in + 8ft 7in, THS
790.4 sq ft, WP 130lbs/sq in, Wt 36½ tons.
Became known as 30 class when 30 series of 98 class (page no .57.) rebuilt as
above. Secondary duty locos, main line traffic. Six-wheel tenders. Flush
topped boilers, dome on second ring. THS when reboilered 1095.76lbs/sq in.

No	Date	Rebuilt	Duplicate no	year	Withdrawn
42	1874	1898	1042	1913	1913
43	1874	1883 Brittain Boiler, 1898*	1043	1913	1913
44	1874	1898			1912
45	1874	1898	1045	1913	1913
46	1874	1896	1046	1913	1917
47	1874	1897	1047	1913	1913
48	1874	1898	1048	1913	1914

*No 43 also fitted with Reikie/McIntosh valve gear in 1903 removed in 1904.

2-4-0 Built by Neilson & Co, works nos 1952-55.
DW 6ft 2in, LW 3ft 8in, Cyls 17 x 22 O/S, WB 6ft 7in + 8ft 7in, THS
992.7 sq ft, WP 130lbs/sq in, Wt 35 tons 14¾ cwts. Nos 49-54 of 1 class
(page no 59) rebuilt to this type. Flush boilers, dome on second ring of
boiler casing.

No	Date	1899 no	Duplicate no	year	Withdrawn
55	1875	108	1203	1899	1900
56	1875	109	1225	1899	1899
57	1875		1057	1902	1906
58	1875		1204	1900	1900

2-4-0 Built by Dubs & Co, works nos as below.
        Neilson & Co, works nos as below.
DW 6ft 2in, LW 3ft 9in, Cyls 18 x 24 O/S, WB 6ft 9in + 8ft 9in, THS 1079.5
sq ft, WP 130lbs/sq in, Wt 37 tons 2 cwts. Goods engine standard pattern
cabs, except no 641 which had Stirling pattern cab. Some had closed
splashers. Westinghouse brake fitted to several for working passenger trains
in McIntosh period.

Built by Dubs & Co, works nos 725-30, 776-83, 965-9

No	Date	1876 no	1881 no	Duplicate no	year	Withdrawn
615	1874		459	1459	1910	1911
616	1874		460			1909
617	1874		461			1911
618	1874		462			1911
619	1874		463	1463		1909
620	1874		464			1906
636	1875	466				1906
637	1875	467		1467	1909	1909
638	1875	468		1468	1909	1910
639	1875	469		1469	1909	1910
640	1875	470		1470	1907	1908
641	1875	471*		1471	1911	1919
642	1875	472		1472	1906	1907
643	1875	473				
	renumbered 465 1877**					1906
444	1877			1444	1900	1911
445	1877			1445	1900	1914
446	1877			1446	1900	1912
447	1877			1447	1900	1905
448	1877			1448	1900	1908

*No 471 rebuilt with Drummond cab and closed splashers and fitted with

```
       spare 418 class boiler (reclassed 418).
**No 465 rebuilt 1885.
```

Built by Neilson & Co, works nos 2229-38.

No	Date	Duplicate no	year	Capital no	year	Withdrawn
449	1878	1449	1900			1912
450	1878	1450	1900			1907
451	1878	1451	1900			1913
452	1878	1452	1900	482	1905	
		1715	1908			1912
453	1878	1453	1900			1908
454	1878	1454	1900			1914
455	1878	1455	1900			1908
456	1878	1456	1909			1910
457	1878	1457	1912			1912
458	1878	1458	1912			1913

4-4-O Built by Neilson & Co, works nos 2126-30.
DW 7ft 2in, LW 3ft 4½in, Cyls 18 x 24 O/S, WB 6ft Oin + 6ft 7½in + 8ft 7in, THS 987.262 sq ft, WP 140lbs/sq in, Blr 4ft 2in inside diam. Centre line of boiler 6ft 9in. Cyls at 6ft 3in centres. Wt 41 tons 7 cwts. Design much under the influence of Brittain due to Connor's illness. Neilson's also collaborated with design work. Copper tubes and firebox. Single frames, slide valves and Gooch fixed link motion. Six-wheel tenders wheels 4ft Oin diam, 1880 gallons, 4 tons coal, Wt 29 tons 7¼ cwts.
Performance against singles on Carlisle road was disappointing due to being underboilered.
Reboilered by Drummond, THS 939.02 sq **ft**, WP 150lbs/ sq in, Wt 41 tons 9¾ cwts. Capacity of tender increased to 4½ tons coal, but still found unsuitable for Carlisle trains. Were put onto working Dundee trains both before and after rebuilding becoming known as 'Dundee bogies'.

No	Date	Duplicate no	year	Withdrawn
125	1877			7/1906
126	1877	1126	1909	8/1910
127	1877	(1586)	1905	3/1905
128	1877			11/1907
129	1877			4/1907

O-4-OPT Built by Neilson & Co, works nos below.
DW 3ft 6in, Cyls 12 x 18, THS 353 sq ft, WP 120lbs/sq in. Standard Neilson industrial design purchased from stock in 1862 (see building dates below).

No	Date	Date built	Works no	1872 no	1877 no	Withdrawn
236	1862	1860	563	141		1873*
237	1862	1861	665	142	517	1879
238	1862	1862	808	143	518	1885
239	1862	1862	809	144		1877**

```
 *Sold 8/1873 to contractor on Oban line.  Scrapped 1880.
**Sold to contractor on Oban line.  Resold 1880 to Jackson & Sons and rebuilt
then resold to Brownside Coal Co.  Scrapped c1895.
```

O-4-OPT Built by A. Barclay & Sons, works nos 31-2.
DW 3ft 6in, Cyls 12 x 20, WB 5ft 6in.
Standard design. Cylinders later made 13 x 20.

No	Date	Withdrawn
270	1865	1884
271	1865	1885

O-4-OST Built by Neilson & Co, works no 1247.
DW 3ft 6in, Cyls 12 x 18, THS 525 sq ft, WP 140lbs/sq in, Wt 20.9 tons,
WB 5ft 6in.

No	Date	
123	1867	
	1872	Renumbered **151**
	1877	Renumbered **521**. Withdrawn 1884

O-4-OST Built by A. Barclay & Co, works nos as below.
DW 3ft 6in, Cyls 12 x 20, WB 5ft 6in.
No 15 (built 1867) and no 16 (1868) became CR stock through bankruptcy of
owners. No 138 built 1870.

No	Date	Works no	1870 no	1877 no	1884 no	Duplicate no	year	Withdrawn
15	1869	71	**135**	**524**				1884
16	1869	81	**136**	**525**	**369**	369A	1887	1888
134	1870	91		**523**	**527**	527A	1888	1896
137	1871	109		**526**				1883
138	1871	103		**527**				1882
131	1872	129		**522**	**539**	539A	1887	1888*

*No 539A sold to A Cowan & Co.

O-4-OST Built by A. Barclay & Co, works nos 124, 149.
DW 3ft 8in, Cyls 14 x 21, WB 5ft 6in.

No	Date	1877 no	1887 no	Withdrawn	
133	1872	**507**	507A	1888	Sold to Merry & Cunningham
					Carnbroe Iron Works. Scrapped 1921
132	1874	**506**		1887	

O-4-OT Built by Dubs & Co, works nos 630-1.
DW 3ft 6in, Cyls 14 x 22, Rebuilt O-4-OST 1890.

No	Date	1877 no	Duplicate no	year	Capital no	year	LMS no	Withdrawn
446	1873	**508**	508A	1888				
			1364	1899				
			1508	1900	**163**	1903		
			1163	1915			(16002)	8/1926
447	1873	**509**	509A	1888				
			1365	1899				
			1509	1900	**162**	1903		
			1162	1915			(16001)	11/1933

O-4-OST Built by Neilson & Co, works nos as below.
DW 3ft 8in, Cyls 14 x 20, WB 7ft 0in, THS 722.5 sq ft, WP 125lbs/sq in. Tank
capacity 800 gallons, Wt 27 tons 3 qrs. Double slide bars. Canopy supported
on four poles as built, later provided with cab in most cases. Progenitor of
CR standard 'pug'. Reboilered by Drummond, THS 683 sq ft, WP 140lbs/sq in.
Some retained Connor chimney.
Works nos 2122-4, 2202.

No	Date	Rebuilt	Duplicate no	year	Capital no	year	LMS no	Withdrawn
502	1876	1898	1505	1912				
			1502	1920				1921
503	1876	1893, 1919	1503	1919			16003	9/1939
504	1876	1895	1504	1916				1919
505	1876	1899, 1912	505A	1895				
			1361	1899				
			1505	1900	**502**	1912		
			1505	1920			16004	1/1939

works nos 2347-50, 2741-6.

No	Date	1916 no	Duplicate no	year	LMS no	Withdrawn
528	1878		1528	1915		1920
529	1878		1529	1915	16005	Transferred to "works" 1925 Withdrawn 1940
530	1878		1530	1915		1917
531	1878		1531	1915		1918
532	1881		1532	1915	16006	1926
533	1881		1533	1918		1921
534	1881		1534	1918	16007	1929
535	1881		1535	1918		1921
536	1881		1536	1918		1922
537	1881	**504**	1537	1920		1922

0-4-4WT Built by Neilson & Co, works nos 1775-6, 1937-8.
DW 4ft 8½in, TW 2ft 8in, Cyls 17 x 22 O/S (18), Length of boiler 10ft 0½in,
THS 779.28 sq ft, Wt 42 tons 3½ cwts.
WB 488-9 5ft 9in + 9ft 3in + 4ft 10½in
   490-1 5ft 9in + 10ft 0in + 5ft 0in
Cylinders increased to 18in diameter about 1882.

No	Date	1881 no	Duplicate no	year	Withdrawn
488	1873	**167**	167A	1899	
			1350	1899	
			1167	1900	1913
489	1873	**168**	168A	1899	
			1351	1899	
			1168	1900	1907
490	1874	**169**	169A	1899	
			1352	1899	
			1169	1900	1902
491	1874	**170**	170A	1899	
			1353	1900	1900

0-6-0ST Built by Neilson & Co, works nos 1559-60.
DW 3ft 8in, Cyls 15 x 20 O/S, WB 4ft 8in + 4ft 6in, WP 130lbs/sq in.

No	Date	1877 no	Duplicate no	year	Withdrawn
139	1870	**510**	510A	1890	
			1362	1899	1899
140	1870	**511**	511A	1890	
			1363	1899	
			1511	1900	1901

0-6-0ST Built by Neilson & Co, works nos as below.
        Dubs & Co, works nos as below.
DW 4ft 2in, Cyls 17 x 20 O/S, WB 5ft 0in + 7ft 9in, THS 728.3 sq ft, WP
140lbs/sq in, Wt 38 tons 3¾ cwts. Sometimes attached to special truck for
carrying extra coal. Trucks marked 'engine tender'.

Built by Neilson & Co, works nos 1601-4, 1933-6.

No	Date	Renumbered no	year	Duplicate no	year	Withdrawn
536	1871	**147**	1872			
		512	1877			
				512A	1890	
				1356	1899	
				1512	1901	1921

537	1871	148	1872			
		513	1877	513A	1890	
				1357	1899	
				1513	1901	
		500	1904*	1537	1910	1919
538	1871	149	1872			
		514	1877	514A	1890	
				1358	1899	
				1514	1901	1918
539	1871	150	1872			
		515	1877	515A	1890	
				1359	1899	
				1515	1901	1911
182	1874	498	1876	1498	1911	1914
183	1874	499	1876	1499	1910	1914
184	1874	500	1876			1904
185	1874	501	1876			1907

No 185 had 17 x 22 cylinders for a period.
*Restored to Capital List

Built by Dubs & Co, works nos 784-9

No	Date	Duplicate no	year	Capital no	year	Withdrawn
492	1875	1492	1903	146	1905	
		1492	1905			1906
493	1875	1493	1903	151	1904	
		1493	1905			1906
494	1875	1494	1903	152	1904	
		1494	1911			1914
495	1875	1495	1903	157	1904	
		1495	1912			1921
496	1875	1496	1903			1905
497	1875	1497	1903			1906

0-6-OST Built by Neilson & Co, works no 1774.
DW 4ft 2in, Cyls 17 x 25 O/S (17 x 20), THS 869 sq ft, close coupled. O/S
valve gear. Possibly originally built for export, but left on maker's
hands, this very powerful loco worked Cuilhill yard on the Monkland canal
for a time and then was used intermittently on the building of the Oban line,
as well as general shunting duties. Cylinders made 17 x 20 1887 or 1889.

		1877	Duplicate		
No	Date	no	no	year	Withdrawn
141	1873	516	1360	1899	
			1516	1901	1907

0-6-0 Built by Neilson & Co, works no 460.
DW 5ft 2in, Cyls 16 x 22 O/S, WB 6ft 3in + 7ft 0in, THS 895 sq ft,
WP 95lbs/sq in.
Purchased by Connor for purposes of comparing performance against four-
coupled types. Rebuilt 2-4-0 1873 WP 125lbs/sq in.

		Rebuilt	1882	
No	Date	2-4-0	no	Withdrawn
188	1858	1873	725	1888

0-6-0 Built by CR at St Rollox
DW 5ft 2in, Cyls 17 x 24, WB 5ft 6in + 8ft 3in, THS 780 sq ft, WP 130lbs/
sq in, Wt 34 tons 14¾ cwts. Double slide bar. Four-wheel tender. Built
for comparison with 0-4-2s.

		1875	Duplicate		
No	Date	no	no	year	Withdrawn
120	1872	367	367A	1887	
			1281	1899	1900

121	1872	**368**	368A	1887	
			1282	1899	
			1368	1901	1905

0-6-0 Built by Dubs & Co, works nos 731-5, 940-7, 949-64, 1024-33.
DW 5ft 2in, Cyls 18 x 24 O/S, WB 5ft 6in + 5ft 6in, Blr 14ft 1¼in x 4ft 2in
inside diam, THS 1083.5 sq ft, WP 140lbs/sq in, Wt 37 tons 3½ cwts. All
wheels in front of firebox. Extensive tests carried out on 1874 locos,
which had circular firehole doors, before remainder ordered. Rather rare
example of six-coupled outside cylinder loco. Six-wheel tenders 1840 gallons
later replaced by four-wheel ones from 0-4-2s on some because of turntable
difficulties.

No	Date	Duplicate no	year	Withdrawn
631	1874	1567	1900	1903
632	1874	1318	1900	1901
633	1874	1633	1904	1908
634	1874	1634	1904	1905
635	1874	1544	1904	
		(1375)	1904	1904
636	1876	1565	1902	1903
637	1876	1637	1904	1905
638	1876	1578	1904	1904
639	1876	1551	1904	1904
640	1876	1600	1904	1904
641	1876	1605	1904	1904
642	1876	1611	1903	1903
643	1876	1643	1905	1905
644	1876	598A	1897	1898
645	1876	1602	1903	1903
646	1876	1579	1900	1904
647	1876	1327	1900	1909
648	1876	1607	1904	1904
649	1876	1637	1904	1904
650	1876	1650	1905	1905
651	1876	(1319)	1899	1899
652	1876	1552	1902	1903
653	1876	282A	1899	1899
654	1876	1621	1905	1905
655	1876	561A	1893	
		(1320)	1899	1899
656	1876	1622	1904	1904
657	1876	283A	1899	1899
658	1876	1315	1900	1901
659	1876	1603	1904	1904
660	1877	1334	1900	1901
661	1877	284A	1899	1900
662	1877	1626	1904	1904
663	1877	1326	1900	1901
664	1877	1555	1902	1902
665	1877	(1321)	1900	1900
666	1877			1901
667	1877	1667	1907	1908
668	1877			1907
669	1877	1613	1904	1904

Brittain Locomotives 1876-82

2-4-0 Built by Dubs & Co. Works nos 1061-70.
DW 6ft 2in, LW 3ft 8in, Cyls 17 x 24 O/S, WB 6ft 7in + 8ft 7in, THS 1071 sq
ft, WP 130 lbs/sq in, Wt 35 tons 14¾ cwts. 6-wheel tenders originally but
later ran with 4-wheel tenders. WP later increased to 140 lbs/sq in. Weight
redistributed by Drummond increasing that on leading axle from 10 tons
16¼ cwts to 10 tons 19¼ cwts, driving axle from 12 tons 19¼ cwts to 13 tons
0¾ cwts and reducing that on the rear coupled axle from 11 tons 18¾ cwts to
11 tons 14¾ cwts.
Date of building given by McEwan in *Loco Mag* Vol 51 (1945) is incorrect.
Blr retained with dome on second ring of casing.

| | | Duplicate list | | |
No	Date	no	year	Withdrawn
130	1878	1130	1912	1912
131	1878	1131	1912	1917
132	1878	1132	1911	1918
133	1878	1133	1911	1917
134	1878	1134	1911	1916
135	1878	1135	1911	1912
136	1878	1136	1910	1913
137	1878	1137	1910	1912
138	1878	1138	1910	1913
139	1878	1139	1910	1916

0-4-2 Built by Dubs & Co. Works nos 1138-47 (1878) 1485-1504 (1881)
DW 5ft 2in, TW 3ft 8in, Cyls 17 x 24 O/S, WB 6ft 5in + 7ft 4in, THS 1118.1
sq ft, WP 140 lbs/sq in, Wt 34 tons 11¼ cwts. Second-hand 4-wheel tenders
originally fitted on 1878 locos, later being provided with 6-wheel tenders.
1881 locos had new 6-wheel tenders, but later ran for a time with 4-wheel
tenders from O.6.Os and other locos being broken up.
Curved running plate, dome on second ring of boiler casing. All reboilered
by 1904, some with immodified Drummond boilers and others with McIntosh
boilers equivalent to 29 class O.6.OT (McIntosh).Fitted with Westinghouse
brake by McIntosh for branch line passenger work. No 706 and one other,
probably 704 retained original 'stove pipe' chimney, the others getting
the standard capped chimney. 1881/2 locos had larger sand boxes. WP when
reboilered 150 lbs/sq in. THS 1085 sq ft, Wt 36tons 1½cwts.

| | | Renumbered | | | Duplicate | | LMS | |
No	Date	no	year	Rebuilt	no	year	no	Withdrawn
670	1878			1910	1670	1919		1922
671	1878			1911	1671	1919		1922
672	1878			1908	1672	1919	(17000)	1925
673	1878			1908	1673	1919	(17001)	1925
674	1878			1907	1674	1919	17007	1930
675	1878			1901				
				1911	1675	1919	17008	1929
676	1878			1902	1676	1919	17002	1930
677	1878			1901	1677	1919	(17009)	1927
678	1878			1911	1678	1919		1922
679	1878			1901	1679	1919	(17010)	1927
700	1881	248	1887	1901				
				1911	1248	1920	(17015)	1923
701	1881	249	1887	1901				
				1911	1249	1920		1922
702	1881	250	1887	1901	1250	1920	(17016)	1923
703	1881	251	1887	1901				
				1911	1251	1920	17017	1928
704	1881	252	1887	1903	1252	1921		1922

705	1881	**253**	1887	1902				
				1912	1253	1921	17003	1932
706	1881	**254**	1887	1912	1254	1920		1920
707	1881	**255**	1887	1909	1255	1921	17004	1927
708	1881	**275**	1887	1904	1275	1921	17018	1930
709	1881	**276**	1887	1909	1276	1921		
					k709	1922		1922
710	1881	**278**	1887	1912			(17012)	1928
711	1881	**279**	1887	1902				
				1914			17013	1928
712	1881	**280**	1887	1901	1280	1919	17019	1926
713	1882	**281**	1887	1901	1281	1919		1922
714	1882	**282**	1887					
		653	1899					
		165	1908	1911			17011	1930
715	1882	**283**	1887					
		657	1899					
		482	1908	1909	1482	1922		1922
716	1882	**284**	1887					
		661	1899	1909	1488	1918		
					1716	1922	(17006)	1926
717	1882	**285**	1887					
					1205	1899		
					1285	1900		
		159	1901	1910				
		487	1915		1717	1922	17020	1932*
718	1882	**286**	1887					
					1207	1899		
					1286	1900		
		161	1901					
		486	1915	1911	1718	1922	17005	1926
719	1882	**287**	1887					
					1215	1899		
					1287	1901		
		164	1901	1902				
		1164	1904					
		164	1912	1913	1164	1918	17014	1928

*Latterly used only for tube cleaning at Edinburgh by connecting tube cleaning rod to brake pipe.

4-4-0 Built by Dubs & Co. Works nos 1672-81.
DW 5ft 2in, LW 3ft 2in, Cyls 18 x 24 O/S, Blr 10ft 0in x 4ft 3in, THS 1146.42 sq ft, WP 130 lbs/Sq in, WB 6ft 0in + 6ft 7in + 8ft 5in, Wt 41 tons 11¾ cwts.
Oban Bogie designed for Oban line to replace 2-4-2Ts of 1880* which were considered to have too heavy a front axle loading. Weight limited to 41½ to 42 tons and length overall limited by size of turntables resulting in 4-wheel high-sided tender being used. Stirling type of direct steam reversing gear. Dome on second ring of boiler casing and 'stovepipe' chimney when built. As rebuilt and reboilered (THS 1085.9 sq ft, Wt 40 tons 17½ cwts, WP 150 lbs/sq in), capped chimney and dome between second and third ring of boiler casing (4ft 4½in diameter) as on 29 class 0-6-0T.
*qv

No	Date	Rebuilt	Duplicate no	year	LMS no	Withdrawn
179	1882	10/1900	1179	1913	14100	1930
180	1882	6/1901	1180	1913	(14101)	1925
181	1882	4/1900	1181	1914	(14102)	1923
182	1882	3/1901	1182	1914	14103	1930

183	1882	3/1900	1183	1914	(14104)	1927
184	1882	12/1900	1184	1914		1922
185	1882	12/1900	1185	1914		1922
186	1882	3/1901	1186	1914	14105	1930
187	1882	5/1900	1187	1914	(14106)	1924
188	1882	7/1898	1188	1914	(14107)	1925

Classified 'IP' by LMS

2-4-0T Built by Dubs & Co. Works nos 1200-11.
    DW 5ft 3in, LW 3ft 9in, Cyls 17 x 22 O/S, THS 1069.5 sq ft, WB 6ft 3in +
8ft 0in, Wt 41 tons 10½ cwts. Intended for branch line work, the leading
axle had lateral displacement of 1in to either side. Side tanks, dome on
second ring of boiler casing.

		Duplicate		
No	Date	no	year	Withdrawn
140	1879	1140	1904	1905
141	1879	1141	1904	1907
142	1879	1142	1904	1905
143	1879	1143	1904	1905
144	1879	1144	1904	1906
145	1879	1145	12/1905	1910
146	1879	(1492)*		1905
147	1879	1147	12/1905	1907
148	1879	1148	12/1905	1907
149	1879	1149	12/1905	1913
150	1879	1150	12/1905	1907
151	1879	(1493)*		1905

*Cut up number

2-2-2WT Built by CR at St Rollox
    DW 5ft 1in, LW & TW 3ft 1in, Cyls 9½ x 15 O/S, THS 386.11 sq ft, WP 110 lbs/
sq in (later 100 lbs/sq in), WB 6ft 6in + 7ft 6in, Wt 26 tons 13½ cwts.
Built as loco for officer's saloon from spare parts ex-nos 77 & 78 but
with new frames and cylinders. Raised firebox casing, dome on middle ring
of boiler casing, Ramsbottom safety valves, Gooch fixed link motion.

		Duplicate		
No	Date	no	year	Withdrawn
1	1881	1A	1893	
		1200	1898	
		1001	1900	1902

2-4-2T Built by Neilson & Co. Works nos 2567-81.
    DW 5ft 8in, LW & TW 3ft 10in, Cyls 17½ x 22 O/S, THS 1091.5 sq ft, WB 6ft
6in + 8ft 0in + 6ft 6in, Wt 51 tons 12 cwts. Radial LW & TW based on
LNW 2-4-2T and intended for the Oban line, these gave repeated trouble
due to derailments thought to be due to a too small radius being used for
the radial axles. They had to be taken off the Oban line and 0-4-2s of
670 class were used until replaced with 179 class 4-4.0s. Used on local
trains and fitted with condensing apparatus for working Glasgow Central
low level section after new axleboxes had been provided in 1882.

		Duplicate			
No	Date	no	year	Withdrawn	
152	3/1880	(1494)*		1904	
153	1880	1153	1911	1921	Latterly used for boiler wash out duties at Carlisle Kingmoor
154	1880	1154	1911	1912	
155	1880	288A	1899	1900	
156	1880	1156	1911	1912	
157	1880	(1495)*		1904	

158	1880	1158	1904	1906	Accident Eglington St Jct 19/3/1883
159	1880	(1285)*		1901	
160	1880	1160	1904	1906	
161	1880	(1286)*		1901	Accident Haughhead Jct 26/12/1899
162	4/1880	15A	1894		
		1206	1899	1899	
163	1880	1508	1903	1903	
164	1880	(1287)*		1901	
165	1880	1240	1902	1903	
166	1880	1209	1900	1901	Accident Haughhead Jct 21/1/89, Quarter Rd 23/12/99

*Cut up number

0-4-0 Crane tank built by Neilson & Co. Works no 2408.
DW 3ft 3in, Cyls 11 x 20, WB 5ft 9in, WP 120 lbs/sq in, THS 439 sq ft,
Wt 17 tons 17 cwts. For use at St Rollox. Crane latterly removed.

		Duplicate		
No	Date	no	year	Withdrawn
485	1878	1368	1899	
		1485	1900	1908

0-6-0ST Built by Neilson & Co. Works nos 2697-2702.
DW 4ft 0in, Cyls 18 x 22 O/S, WB 5ft 0in + 8ft 0in, Blr 9ft 11½in x
4ft 8½in, THS 1050 sq ft, WP 140 lbs/sq in, Wt 41 tons 17½ cwts. Shunting
locos with vertical hand brake wheel which gave them the nickname of
'steam boats' in the Clyde area. Three rebuilt with new boilers and
fireboxes (THS 1090.7 sq ft, WP 150 lbs/sq in, later reduced again to
140 lbs/sq in) and new cabs and capped chimneys with safety valve on
centre dome instead of over firebox.

			Duplicate		
No.	Date	Rebuilt	no	year	Withdrawn or sold
486	1881	1913			Sold 1913 to United Collieries no 10. Scrapped 1935
487	1881	1912			Sold 1913 to United Collieries No 11. Scrapped 1938
488	1881		1488	1918	7/1919
489	1881	3/1913	1489	1922	1928*
490	1881		1490	1918	1921
491	1881				1921

*as LMS (16150)

Drummond Locomotives 1882-1895

4-2-2 Built by Neilson & Co. Works no 3553.
DW 7ft 0in, LW 3ft 6in, TW 4ft 6in, Cyls 18 x 26, WB 6ft 6in + 6ft 7in +
8ft 0in, Blr 10ft 3in x 4ft 4½in, THS 1053.3 sq ft, WP 150 lbs/sq in,
Wt 41 tons 17½cwt. Neilson design for Edinburgh International Exhibition
1886 with CR backing, exhibited with 4.4.0 no 124. Awarded Gold Medal.
The last single-driver loco in use in the UK it was preserved by the LMS
at St Rollox and is now in the Glasgow Museum of Transport. Took part in
1888 'races' London to Edinburgh (relief trains run ahead of main
scheduled train).

		Duplicate			
No	Date	no	year	LMS no	Withdrawn
123	1886	1123	1914	14010	4/1935

4-4-0 Built by Neilson & Co. Works nos 3058-67.
                CR at St Rollox Orders Y, Y21, Y25
DW 6ft 6in, LW 3ft 6in, Cyls 18 x 26, Blr 10ft 3½in x 4ft 5½in, THS 1210.7
sq ft, WP 150 lbs/sq in, WB 6ft 6in + 6ft 7in + 9ft 0in, Wt 45 tons 3 cwts.
New standard design of main line passenger loco. Stephenson valve gear,
Westinghouse brake, lever reverse. Originally intended to run with tenders
identical to 294 class 0-6-0s these were found to have heating problems at
high speed and new tenders were built at St Rollox with improved springing
for all the 1884/5 locos nos 69 and 72 having 2500 gallon tenders,
60-65 having 2800 gallon tenders and the remainder very similar 2840
gallon tenders. These had four small openings in the frames between the
wheels. All later locos were fitted with 3550 gallon tenders with two
large openings between the wheels. Rebuilt as below. Large tenders fitted
to large boiler rebuilds (as 721 class Wt 46 tons 11 cwts).

The following were built by Neilson & Co works nos 3058-67

No	Date	Boilers Transferred	Rebuilt	Duplicate no	year	LMS no	Withdrawn
66	2/1884	7/1895 ex70	3/1901 large blr	1066	1922	14298	1/1930
67	1884	2/1897 ex60	11/1902 1915	1067	1922	14290	1927
68	1884	6/1893 ex75 1922 ex89	2/1902	1068	1922	(14291)	1924
69	1884		5/1902 1911	1069	1922	(14292)	1925
70*	1884	10/1894 ex60	4/1901 large blr	1070	1922	(14299)	1927
71	1884	10/1893 ex68 1917-21 ex1065	7/1898 large blr	1071	1922	(14300)	1927
72	1884		1891 1903**	1072	1920	(14293)	1924
73	1884	10/1896 ex524	2/1902 large blr	1073	1920	14301	1928
74	1884	2/1894 ex71 1922 ex1087	8/1901	1074	1920	(14294)	1923
75*	4/1884	1/1893 ex72 5/1896 ex519 1921 ex1064	5/1901 large blr	1075	1920	14302	10/1929

*ran with bogie tender about 1906
**new cylinders fitted 9/1891. Rebuilt 1903 after accident at Greenloaning

The following were built at St Rollox to Order Y.

No	Date	Boilers Transferred	Rebuilt	1916 no*	Duplicate no	year	LMS no	Withdrawn
60	2/1885	5/1894 ex74 4/1896 ex61 1919 1905blr	12/1901 large blr 1917 new cyls & frames	17	1060 1060	1916 1922	(14303)	10/1929
61	1885	later fitted boiler ex14	12/1895 new blr		1061	1916	(14295)	1925
62	1885	1916 ex87	4/1902 large blr	87	1062 1062	1916 1921	14304	1931
63	1885		4/1902 large blr		1063	1916		11/1916
64	1885		12/1901 large blr		1064	1917		12/1920
65	1885		6/1901 large blr		1065	1916		4/1918

*Restored to capital list.

The following were built at St Rollox to Order Y21, but had redesigned
steam port with short direct steam passages allowing rapid entry of steam
into cylinders necessitating double slide valves. Vertical screw reverse.
WP set at 175 lbs/sq in for no 76 and 200 lbs/sq in for remainder for
trials in high pressure steam. Reduced to 150 lbs/sq in in 1895, except
No 79 reduced to 160 lbs/sq in 11/1891 when new cylinders fitted (possibly
reverting to previous front end steam arrangement).
No 78 took part in London-Aberdeen 'races' 1895.

No	Date	Rebuilt	Duplicate no	year	LMS no	Withdrawn
76	7/1889	6/1905	1076	1920		8/1920
77	1889	8/1891 new cyls 3/1907	1077	1920		8/1922
78	1889	10/1903	1078	1920		8/1921
79*	1889	11/1891 new cyls 11/1899	1079	1920	14297	1928
84	1889	12/1906	1084	1921	(14306)	1927
87	11/1889	10/1903**	1087	1915		1916

*Named *Carbrook* 1895. Withdrawn 7/1922 but reinstated after being fitted
 with boiler ex-1077 12/1922.
**Believed fitted with second-hand large boiler 1915.

The following were built at St Rollox to Order Y25. Original front end
arrangement reverted to steel crank axles, sanding by gravity only.
WP 160 lbs/sq in reduced to 150 lbs/sq in. 83, 88-90 had screw reverse.

No	Date	Boilers transferred	Rebuilt	1922 no*	Duplicate no	year	LMS no	Withdrawn
83	1/1891	Believed 1920-2 ex1087	1909		1083	1921	(14305)	1928
88	1891	1922 ex15	7/1907	15	1088 1015	1921 1922	14309	2/1930
89	1891		8/1899		1089	1921		2/1921
90**	1891	1921 ex1089	9/1906		1090	1921	(14307)	1924
91	1891		5/1902		1091	1921		12/1922
113	3/1891		10/1903		1113	1916		2/1921

*restored to capital list.
**Took part in London-Aberdeen 'races' 1895. Classified '1P' by LMS.

4-4-0 Built by Dubs & Co, Works no 2245
DW 6ft 6in, LW 3ft 6in, Cyls 19 x 26. Other dimensions as 66 class.
Built for Edinburgh International Exhibition 1886. Awarded Gold Medal
along with no 123. Bryce-Douglas valve gear and vertical screw reverse.
Frames extended upwards to cover valve chests, resulting in 1½in higher
pitch of boiler than 66 class, the chimney being correspondingly reduced.
Gravity sanding, Westinghouse brake, 2,840 gallon tender. Rebuilt with
Stephenson link motion, 18 x 26 cylinders, but pitch of boiler not altered.

No	Date	Rebuilt	Duplicate no	year	LMS no	Withdrawn
124	1886	12/1887 18x26 cyls 8/1906	1124	1916	(14296)	1925

Named *Eglinton* 1890.

4-4-0 Built by CR at St Rollox. Orders Y13, Y28.
DW 5ft 9in, LW 3ft 6in, Cyls 18 x 26, Blr 10ft 0in x 4ft 3in, THS 936.95 sq
ft, WP 150 lbs/sq in, WB 6ft 6in + 6ft 7in + 8ft 0in, Wt 42 tons 7¼ cwt.
Smaller version of 66 class, often referred to as Coast Bogie or Gourock
Bogie. Westinghouse brake. Rebuilt with 1898 or 1904 version of rebuild
boiler, except no 85 which had a larger higher pitched boiler, THS 1158 sq ft,
Wt 43 tons 9¼ cwt.

The following were built to Order Y13 and had 2,840 gallon tenders.

No	Date	Rebuilt	Duplicate no	year	LMS no	Withdrawn
80	2/1888	2/1905	1080	1920	(14108)	1927
81	1888	4/1903	1081	1920	(14109)	1930
82	1888	3/1904**	1082	1920	14110	1927
85*	1888	1905				1916
86*	1888		1086	1921		8/1921
116*	4/1888		1116	1916		4/1921

*screw reverse originally. ** Boiler ex 15 in 1916.

The following were built to Order Y28 and had larger boilers designed by
Smellie. THS 1139.6 sq ft, WP 160 lbs/sq in. Drummond 3,130 gallon tender.

No	Date	Rebuilt	Duplicate no	year	LMS no	Withdrawn
114	7/1891	1908	1114	1916	(14111)	1927
115	1891		1115	1916		8/1922
195	1891	1907	1195	1922	(14112)	1923
196	1891	1907	1196	1922	14113	1930
197	1891	1907	1197	1922	14114	1930
198	9/1891	3/1908	1198	1923	14115	1929

Classified 'IP' by LMS

0-4-2ST Built by CR at St Rollox. Order Y1.
DW 3ft 8in, TW 2ft 6in (solid), Cyls 14 x 20 O/S, Blr 10ft 9in x 3ft 7¾in,
THS 684 sq ft, WP 140 lbs/sq in, WB 7ft 0in + 6ft 9in, Wt 31 tons 4cwt.
Designed for working Killin branch. Westinghouse brake added about 1887.
Reversing lever on right-hand side. Trailing axle had side play only and
was not radial. See also 0-4-0ST, 264 class.

No	Date	Duplicate no	year	LMS no	Withdrawn
262	6/1885	1262	1918	(15000)	1928
263	1885	1263	1918	15001	4/1947

0-4-4T Built by CR at St Rollox. Orders SN, Y19, Y26.
DW 5ft 0in, TW 2ft 6in (solid), Cyls 16 x 22, Blr 8ft 8½in x 3ft 10in,
THS 672.3 sq ft, WP 150 lbs/sq in, WB 6ft 4in + 7ft 6in + 5ft 0in, Wt 37
tons 15½ cwt. Designed for light branch line work. Westinghouse brake. Locos
to orders Y19 & Y26 had larger bunkers. Coal rails added later by McIntosh.
Ramsbottom safety valves. Cowcatchers were at first fitted on some locos
working the Warlockhead and Ballachulish branches. Boilers redesigned
2/1908. Nos 1177/8 rebuilt 1924 with new boilers, steel firebox and WP 160
lbs/sq in.

The following were built to Order SN

No	Date	Rebuilt	Duplicate no	year	LMS no	Withdrawn
171	5/1884		1171	1912		11/1921
172	1884		1172	1912	(15100)	1925
173	1884		1173	1912		8/1922
174	1884		1174	1912	(15101)	1924
175	1884		1175	1912	(15102)	1928
176	8/1884		1176	1913		3/1921
177	2/1886	1924	1177	1913	15103	11/1945*
178	1886	1924	1178	1913	15104	6/1933
228	1886		1228	1913		9/1921
229	1886		1229	1913	(15105)	1925
230	1886		1230	1913		10/1922
231	5/1886		1231	1913		9/1922

*Scrapped 8/46

The following were built to Order Y19

No	Date	Duplicate no	year	LMS no	Withdrawn
222	2/1889	1222	1914	(15106)	1924
223	2/1889	1223	1914	15107	1927
224	2/1889	1224	1914	15108	1925
225	2/1889	1225	1914		12/1923
226	2/1889	1226	1914		5/1921
227	2/1889	1227	1914	(15109)	1925

The following were built to Order Y26.

No	Date	Duplicate no	year	LMS no	Withdrawn
189	4/1891	1189	1914		4/1917
190	1891			15110	1928
191	1891	1191	1922	(15111)	1924
192	1891	1192	1922	(15112)	1925
193	1891	1193	1922	(15113)	1924
194	5/1891	1194	12/1922	15114	1930

Classified 'IP' by LMS

0-4-0ST Built by CR at St Rollox. Orders Y1, Y22, Y27.
DW 3ft 8in, Cyls 14 x 20 O/S, WB 7ft 0in, Wt 27 tons 7½ cwts. Other
details as 0-4-2ST 262 class. Basically Neilson design of 1875 as Connor
502 class (page no) but with Drummond chimney, regulator, smokebox and
cab details. Order Y1 included the two 0-4-2STs, 262 class, which were
derived from the same design. These had bunkers, but the 0-4-0STs had
none the lower half of the cab side sheet being extended to form a small
coal space on either side of the firebox. Later, small wooden 'engine
tender' trucks carrying about 1½ tons were attached. Dumb buffers. Water
capacity 800 gallons. Coal 11 cwt. Springs below axle boxes. Improved
boilers and steel fireboxes later fitted. Cylinders redesigned 11/1907.

The following were built to Order Y1

No	Date	Rebuilt	Duplicate no	year	LMS no	BR no	Withdrawn
264	1885		1264	1918	(16012)		1925
265	1885	c1930	1265	1918	16013		12/1934
266	1885				(16008)		1926
267	1885	1921,1929			16009		3/1946
268	1885	1928			16010	(56010)	3/1950
269	1885		1269	1921			c1922
270	1885				16011	56011	1/1959
271	9/1885		1271	1918	(16014)		1925

The following were built to Order Y22

No	Date	Duplicate no	year	LMS no	Withdrawn
615	4/1889			16015	10/1935
616	1889			16016	11/1936
617	1889			(16017)	1925
618	1889			(16018)	2/1924
619	1889				1920
620	7/1889			16019	1/1935 Sold to White Moss Colliery.

The following were built to Order Y27

No	Date	Duplicate no	year	LMS no	Withdrawn
510	4/1890	1510	1920	(16020)	1923
511	1890	1511	1920	(16021)	1924

512	1890	1512	1920	16022	10/1935
513	1890	1513	1920	(16023)	1923
514	1890	1514	1920	(16024)	1927
515	5/1890	1515	1920	16025	9/1939 Reinstated
					11/1939 to Service Stock
					5/1960

Class continued by McIntosh 1895-1908 (Order nos Y43, Y63, Y68, Y88,
page no 90).

0-6-0ST Built by CR at St Rollox. Orders Y14, Y18, Y20, Y24.
DW 4ft 6in, Cyls 18 x 26, Blr 10ft 0in x 4ft 1½in, THS 939.02 sq in,
WP 150 lbs/sq in, Wt 43 tons 16¾ cwt, WB 7ft 6in + 8ft 0in. Boiler similar
to 'rebuild' boiler used on Connor 2-4-0s. Open footplate, Stirling pattern
cab with rear weatherboard, full length saddle tank, steam brakes, lever
reverse. Wheelbase increased to 7ft 6in + 8ft 9in from order Y18 and cab
lengthened, rear splasher omitted. Nicknamed 'Jubilee Pugs'.

The following were built to Order Y14

No	Date	Renumbered no	year	LMS no	Withdrawn
323	8/1887	505	1895	(16205)	1926
385	1887			16204	1930
506	1887			(16206)	1928
507	1887			(16207)	1928
538	1887	384	1918	(16203)	1929
539	9/1887	383	1918	16202	1930

The following were built to Order Y18

No	Date	Duplicate no	year	LMS no	Withdrawn
232	12/1887	1232	1916	16212	1928
233	12/1887	1233	1916	(16213)	1927
234	12/1887	1234	1916		12/1922
235	12/1887	1235	1916	16214	1929
216	1/1888			(16200)	1927
217	1/1888			(16201)	1927

The following were built to Order Y20

No	Date	LMS no	Withdrawn
218	11/1888	(16208)	1928
219	11/1888	(16209)	1933
220	12/1888	(16210)	1930
221	12/1888	16211	1930 (Rebuilt 1/1902)
386	12/1888		by 1923
387	12/1888		by 1923

The following were built to Order Y24

No	Date	Duplicate no	year	LMS no	Withdrawn
388	5/1890			(16215)	1928
389	1890			(16216)	1925
391	1890			(16217)	1925
392	1890			(16218)	1928
394	1890	1394	1922		9/1922
395	1890	1395	1922	(16224)	1925
396	1890	1396	1922		1922
398	1890			(16219)	1927
399	1890			16220	1928
400	1890			16221	1929

401	1890			(16222)	1926
402	8/1890			(16223)	1926

Classified '3F' by LMS

0-6-0ST Built by CR at St Rollox. Order Yl6
DW 3ft 8in, Cyls 14 x 20, WB 7ft 0in + 6ft 0in, Wt 31 tons O½ cwt. Other
details as 0-4-2ST 262 class. Six-coupled version of 0-4-0ST 264 class.

			Duplicate		
No	Date	no	year	LMS no	Withdrawn
272	4/1888	1272	1916		3/1922
273	1888	1273	1916	16100	8/1929
274	1888	1274	1916	16101	1928
508	1888	1508	1913		8/1922
509	1888	1509	1913	(16102)	1928
527	5/1888	1527	1915		12/1921

0-6-0 Built by Neilson & Co. Works nos as below. CR at St Rollox. Orders as
below.
DW 5ft 0in, Cyls 18 x 26, Blr 10ft 3½in x 4ft 5½in, THS 1210.7 sq ft,
WP 150 lbs/sq in, WB 7ft 6in + 8ft 9in, Wt 41 tons 6cwt. Drummond standard
goods engine. Same boilers as 66 class 4-4-0s. Design influenced by
Stroudley designs for LBSC. Dome and Ramsbottom safety valve on second ring
of boiler. Double framed 2,840 gallon tender. Rebuilt with Lambie pattern
boilers and, later, 'pop' safety valves. Nicknamed 'Jumbos'. 2,500 gallon
tenders
The following were built by Neilson & Co. Works nos 3043-57.

		Renumbered		Duplicate			LMS			
No	Date	no	year	no	year	Rebuilt	no	BR no	Withdrawn
294*	11/1883			1294	1919	1915	17249	57249	7/1962
295	1883	262	1918			1918	17232	57232	5/1961
296	1883	263	1918			1914	17233	57233	9/1961
297	1883	264	1918				17234	57234	2/1957
298	1883	539	1918				17246	57246	9/1961
299	1883	259	1918				17230	57230	7/1956
300	1883	260	1918				17231	(57231)	5/1949
301	1883	335	1918				17235	57235	10/1955
302	1883	337	1918				17236	57236	9/1961
303	1883	365	1918			1902	17241	57241	5/1959
304	1883	367	1918			1916	17242	57242	7/1962
305	1883	374	1918				17243	57243	6/1959
306	1883	403	1918			1917	17244	57244	9/1961
307	1883	517	1918				17245	57245	9/1961
308	1/1884	548	1918			1917	17247	57247	7/1959

*Sold to Government 1917. Same number on ROD. Left 11/1917, returned 6/1919
and repurchased.

The following were built at St Rollox to Order RA

No	Date	Rebuilt	LMS no	BR no	Withdrawn
349	11/1883	1902	17237	57237	10/1962
350	1883		17238	57238	9/1961
351	1883	1916	17239	57239	11/1961
352	1883	1918	17240	57240	10/1962
353	1/1884		17250	57250	9/1961
354	1/1884		17251	57251	10/1962

The following were built by Neilson & Co. Works nos 3252-71. 2,800 gallon
tenders.

			Duplicate				
No	Date	Rebuilt	no	year	LMS no	BR no	Withdrawn
517*	7/1884		1517	1918	17269	57269	8/1963
518	1884	1917			17252	57252	11/1962
519	1884				17253	57253	10/1962

No	Date				BR		Withdrawn
520	1884				17254	57254	7/1962
521	1884	1916			17255	(57255)	3/1952
522	1884	1917			17256	57256	9/1961
523	1884	1905			17257	57257	9/1961
524	1884	1906			17258	57258	10/1962
525	1884	1921			17259	57259	10/1962
526	1884	1917			17260	57260	10/1955
680*	1884	1899	1680	1919	17270	57270	11/1963
681	1884	1916			17261	57261	12/1963
682*	1884	1910	1682	1919	17271	57271	9/1961
683	1884	1916			17262	57262	9/1961
684	1884				17263	57263	10/1961
685	1884	1903			17264	57264	9/1961
		1916					
686	1884	1917			17265	57265	7/1962
687	1884	1922			17266	57266	11/1959
688	1884	1907			17267	57267	4/1962
		1920					
689	12/1884	1918			17268	57268	9/1961

*Sold to Government 1917
517 left 9/1917 returned 10/1919 (same number on ROD)
680 left 9/1917 returned 9/1919 (ROD 5680)
682 left 11/1917 returned 7/1919 (ROD 5682)
All repurchased 1919

The following were built at St Rollox to Order SW. 2840 gallon tenders.

		1892	Duplicate			LMS		
No	Date	no	no	year	Rebuilt	no	BR no	Withdrawn
690	12/1885				1905	17276	57276	11/1959
691	12/1885	361				17272	57272	10/1951
692	12/1885	362				17273	57273	2/1960
693	12/1885	363			1916	17274	57274	4/1962
694	12/1885	364			1916	17275	57275	4/1962
695 *	12/1885	365	1365	1919		17294	57294	11/1949

*Sold to Government 1917. Same number on ROD. Left 11/1917, returned 9/1919 and repurchased.

The following were built at St Rollox to Order Y5. 2840 gallon tenders.

		1918	Duplicate			LMS		
No	Date	no	no	year	Rebuilt	no	BR no	Withdrawn
309	6/1886	549				17248		3/1946
310*	1886		1310	1919		17290	(57290)	6/1948
311	1886	553				17283	57283	2/1951
312	1886	558			1907	17284	57284	10/1962
313	1886	680			1916	17285	57285	11/1961
314	1886	682			1914	17286	(57286)	2/1949
315*	1886		1315	1919	1913	17291	57291	8/1963
316	1886	703			1906	17287	57287	1/1961
317	1886	705				17288	57288	11/1961
318*	1886		1318	1919	1910	17292	57292	12/1961
319*	1886		1319	1919		17293		11/1947
320	9/1886	707				17289	57289	10/1951

*Sold to Government 1917 (same numbers on ROD)
310 left 10/1917 returned 7/1919
315 left 10/1917 returned 7/1919
318 left 11/1917 returned 10/1919
319 left 11/1917 returned 10/1919
All repurchased 1919

The following were built at St Rollox to Order Y9. 2840 gallon tenders.

No	Date	Duplicate no	year	Rebuilt	LMS no	BR no	Withdrawn
355	12/1886				17277	57277	4/1951
356	12/1886			1910	17278	57278	6/1963
357	12/1886			1908	17279	57279	10/1959
358	12/1886			1916	17280	(57280)	8/1952
359	12/1886				17281	(57281)	11/1947
360	12/1886			1908	17282	57282	11/1955
366	1887				17304	57304	6/1948
367*	1887	1367	1919	1895	17312	57312	9/1957
368	1887				17305	(57305)	2/1949
369	1887				17306	57306	7/1951
370	1887			1920	17307	57307	9/1959
371	2/1887				17308	(57308)	5/1948

*Sold to Government 1917 (same number on ROD). Left 10/1917, returned 6/1919 and repurchased.

The following were built at St Rollox to Order Y12. 2840 gallon tenders.

No	Date	Renumbered no	year	Duplicate no	year	Rebuilt	LMS no	BR no	Withdrawn
321	5/1887	**708**	1918			1905	17310	57310	12/1949
322	1887	**380**	1918			1917	17309	57309	11/1863
339*	1887	**323**	1895	1323	1919		17311	57311	9/1962
340	1887						17295	57295	6/1962
341	1887					1903	17296	57296	12/1963
342	1887					1899	17297		11/1947
343	1887					1916	17298	57298	4/1950
344	1887					1916	17299	57299	10/1962
345	1887					1913	17300	57300	6/1962
346	1887					1907	17301	(57301)	5/1948
347	1887					1905	17302	57302	10/1963
						1917			
348	8/1887					1906	17303	57303	10/1961

*Sold to Government 1917 (same number on ROD). Left 11/1917, returned 1919 and repurchased.

The following were built at St Rollox to Order Y23. Second hand tenders.

No	Date	Duplicate no	year	Rebuilt	LMS no	BR no	Withdrawn
403*	11/1889	1403	1919		17313		1/1948
404**	1889				17314	57314	3/1962
406	1889			1917	17315	57315	12/1955
407	1889				17316	57316	10/1949
408	1889			1916	17317	57317	11/1961
409	1889				17318	57318	10/1951
410	1890			1915	17319	57319	12/1961
411	1890			1918	17320	57320	3/1956
412	1890				17321	57321	11/1961
413	1890			1912	17322	57322	3/1953
414	1890			1910	17323	57323	6/1951
415	7/1890				17324	57324	5/1961

*Sold to Government 1917 (same number on ROD). Left 11/1917, returned 6/1919 and repurchased. ** No 404 had a new 2500 gallon tender.

The following were built at St Rollox to Order Y29. 2500 gallon tenders.

No	Date	Duplicate no	year	Rebuilt	LMS no	BR no	Withdrawn
372	11/1891			1918	17325	57325	12/1961
373	1891				17326	57326	4/1963
374*	1891	1374	1919	1909	17348	57348	3/1963

375	1891		1909	17327	(57327)	4/1948
376	1891			17328	57328	4/1963
377	1891		1907	17329	57329	10/1962
378	1891			17330	(57330)	6/1948
379	1891		1917	17331	57331	9/1962
540	1892			17332	57332	11/1952
541	1892			17333	(57333)	3/1948
542	1892			17334	57334	3/1951
543	5/1892			17335	57335	10/1961

*Sold to Government 1917 (same number on ROD). Left 10/1917, returned 8/1915
and repurchased.

The following were built at St Rollox to Order Y30 and had Westinghouse
brake fitted and 2,500 gallon tenders.

No	Date	Rebuilt	LMS no	BR no	Withdrawn
691	4/1892		17342	(57342)	7/1950
692	1892		17343	(57343)	4/1948
693	1892		17344	57344	11/1951
694	1892		17345	57345	3/1962
695	1892	1922	17346	57346	8/1957
696	5/1892		17347	57347	3/1962

The following were built at St Rollox to Order Y31. 2,500 gallon tenders.

		Duplicate					
No	Date	no	year	Rebuilt	LMS no	BR no	Withdrawn
544	7/1892				17336	57336	9/1963
545	1892			1921	17337	57337	12/1952
546	1892			1922	17338	57338	3/1962
547	1892			1907	17339	57339	6/1959
548*	1892	1548	1919		17349	57349	7/1961
549*	1892	1549	1919		17350	57350	11/1961
550**	1892				17357	57357	3/1962
551	1892				17340	57340	11/1962
552	1892				17341	57341	7/1962
553*	8/1892	1553	1919		17351	57351	8/1949

*Sold to Government 1917 (same numbers on ROD)
548 left 11/1917 returned 7/1919
549 left 11/1917 returned 7/1919
553 left 1917 returned 1919
All repurchased 1919
**550 was in accident at Pollokshaws South 17/1/1923

The following were built at St Rollox to Order Y32 and had Lambie boilers
with safety valves over the firebox and dome set further forward.
Modified steam and exhaust passages, cab and boiler handrail arrangements,
blower, smoke box door fastening. Tender footplate hand rails and doors
covering gap between cab and tender provided. 2,500 gallon tender.

		Duplicate				
No	Date	no	year	LMS no	BR no	Withdrawn
554	12/1892			17358	57358	5/1949
555	12/1892			17359	57359	3/1962
556	12/1892			17360	57360	3/1963
557	12/1892			17361	57361	12/1959
558*	12/1892	1558	1919	17352	57352	10/1951
559	1/1893			17362	57362	6/1962
560	1/1893			17363	57363	12/1961
561	1/1893			17364	57364	12/1961
562	1/1893			17365	57365	5/1962
563	1/1893			17366	57366	11/1961

*Sold to Government 1917 (same number on ROD). Left 1917, returned 8/1919
and repurchased.

The following were built at St Rollox to Order Y33. Lambie modifications and boiler as above and fitted with Westinghouse brake.

No	Date	Rebuilt	LMS no	BR no	Withdrawn
697	3/1893	1917	17367	57367	12/1961
698	1893	*	17368	57368	5/1958
699	1893	1903**	17369	57369	10/1962
700	1893		17370	57370	3/1962
701	1893		17371	(57371)	7/1948
702	5/1893		17372	57372	1/1952

*698 was later vacuum fitted for working 'foreign' fish traffic from Aberdeen.
**699 had 721 class boiler fitted 1903 experimentally. Removed 12/1906.

The following were built at St Rollox to Order Y36 as orders Y32 and Y33 with Westinghouse brake.

No	Date	Rebuilt	LMS no	BR no	Withdrawn
199	2/1894	1918	17373	57373	7/1961
200	2/1894		17374	(57374)	5/1948
201	2/1894		17375	57375	12/1963
202	2/1894		17376		8/1946

The following were built at St Rollox to Order Y37 and had steam brakes, larger dome covers, curved angle iron to tender handrail plates matching cab 'lean out' and slightly repositioned handrails. 2,800 gallon tender.

No	Date	1895 no	Duplicate no	year	Rebuilt	LMS no	BR no	Withdrawn
256	5/1894					17377	57377	9/1961
257	5/1894				1918	17378	57378	9/1962
258	6/1894					17379	57379	2/1951
259*	7/1894		1259	1919		17389	57389	11/1961
260*	1894		1260	1919		17390	57390	5/1950
261	1894					17380	(57380)	4/1948
334	1894					17381	(57381)	8/1949
335*	1894		1335	1919		17391	57391	10/1950
336¡	1894					17382	(57382)	3/1949
337*	1894		1337	1919		17392	57392	12/1961
203	1894	338			1916	17383	57383	7/1962
204	11/1894	339			1921	17384	57384	1/1863

*Sold to Government 1917 (same numbers on ROD)
259 left 11/1917 returned 5/1919
260 left 11/1917 returned 6/1919
335 left 10/1917 returned 8/1919
337 left 9/1917 returned 6/1919
All repurchased 1919

The following were built at St Rollox to Order Y38 as Order Y37. 709/10 had Westinghouse brake.

No	Date	Duplicate no	year	Rebuilt	LMS no	BR no	Withdrawn
703*	10/1894	1703	1919				
		1704	1920		17353	57353	11/1961
704	1894			1909	17385	57385	6/1962
705*	1894	1705	1919				
		1706	1920		17354	57354	12/1959
706	1894				17386	57386	5/1962
707*	1894	1707	1919		17355	57355	12/1963
708*	1894	1708	1919		17356	57356	6/1961
709	1895				17387	57387	11/1952
710	6/1895				17388	57388	3/1953

*Sold to Government 1917.
703 left 1917 returned 1919 (ROD 5703)

705 left 11/1917 returned 8/1919 (ROD 5705)
707 left 1917 returned 1919 (ROD 5707)
708 left 11/1917 returned 1919 (ROD 5708)
All repurchased 1919
The Drummond 0-6-0s were classified '2F' by the LMS.

Lambie Locomotives 1892-5

4-4-0 Built by CR at St Rollox. Order Y35
   DW 6ft 6in, LW 3ft 6in, Cyls 18 x 26, Blr 10ft 3½in x 4ft 6¼in, THS 1184.12
   sq ft, WP 160 lbs/sq in, WB 6ft 6in + 6ft 7in + 9ft 0in, Wt 45 tons 5¼ cwt.
   Smellie boiler, similar but larger than that provided for Y28 series of 80
   class, otherwise basically to Drummond design with Lambie fittings including
   safety valves over firebox. New design of chimney with flat topped rim.
   Smokebox door had wheel and handle. Bogie pivot 2in in front of centre which
   was perpetuated on all subsequent leading bogie locos. 3,570 gallon tender.
   Cylinders redesigned 11/1904. No 17 was the fastest loco used for the Perth-
   Aberdeen section in the London-Aberdeen 'races' of 1895.

No	Date	Duplicate no	year*	Rebuilt	LMS no	Withdrawn
13	4/1894	1013	1921	1903	14308	1927
14	4/1894			1905		11/1920
15	5/1894	1015	1921	1904		
				1907	14309	1930
16	5/1894	1016	1921	1904		10/1922
17	5/1894			1905		1916
18	5/1894	1018	1921	1917	14310	1930

*Date to Duplicate List not confirmed
Classified 'IP' by LMS.

4-4-OT Built by CR at St Rollox. Order Y34.
   DW 5ft 0in, LW 3ft 2in, Cyls 17 x 24, Blr 10ft 0in x 4ft 4⅛in, THS 1095.76
   sq ft, WP 150 lbs/sq in, WB 6ft 0in + 6ft 10in + 9ft 0in, Wt 50 tons 6¾ cwt.
   Condenser fitted for working Glasgow Central low level.line. Three (including
   no 10) had Gresham and Craven steam sanding. Remainder had gravity sanding.
   Westinghouse brakes. Condensing gear removed from 1917.

No	Date	LMS no	Withdrawn
1	7/1893	15020	1933
2	1893	15021	11/1934
3	1893	15022	12/1933
4	1893	15023	10/1934 Accident Whinknowe 2/1/1906
5	1893	15024	10/1935
6	1893	15025	6/1938
7	1893	15026	1931
8	1893	15027	8/1935
9	1893	15028	8/1926 (rebuilt 1919)
10	1893	15029	1932
11	1893	(15030)	1927
12	1/1894	(15031)	1930 Accident Glasgow Central 24/1/1925

Classified 'IP' by LMS.

0-4-4T Built by CR at St Rollox. Order Y40.
   DW 5ft 9in, TW 3ft 2in, Cyls 18 x 26, WB 7ft 6in + 9ft 0in + 5ft 6in, Wt 53
   tons 16 cwts. Boiler details as 1 class 4-4-OT above. Condenser fitted for
   working on Glasgow Central low level line. Cylinders redesigned 4/1909.
   Condensing apparatus removed from 1917. Westinghouse brake. Coal rails added
   about 1904. Rebuilt by LMS with McIntosh 0-4-4T boilers as below (or
   equivalent).

No	Date	Rebuilt	LMS no	BR no	Withdrawn
19	4/1895	1934	15115		7/1947
20	4/1895		15116	(55116)	5/1948
21	4/1895		15117	(55117)	6/1948
22	4/1895	1933	15118		12/1947
23	4/1895	1933	15119	55119	8/1953
24	4/1895	1932	15120		3/1946
25	5/1895	1932	15121	55121	6/1952

26	5/1895	1935	15122	55122	1/1952
27	5/1895		15123	55123	1/1950
28	5/1895		15124	55124	10/1961

Classified "2P' by LMS.

0-4-0ST Built by Dubs & Co. Works nos 534 & 629.
DW 3ft 7in, Cyls 14 x 22 O/S.
Taken over from Colin Dunlop & Co 1892 and placed on duplicate list.

1892	Date	
No	built	
538A	1872	Withdrawn 1899
539A	1873	Renumbered 1367 1899. Withdrawn 1900. Believed sold and not broken up until 1913.

0-6-0ST Built by CR at St Rollox. Order Y39
DW 4ft 6in, Cyls 18 x 26, WB 7ft 6in + 8ft 9in, Wt 46 tons 5¼cwt. Boiler details as 1 class 4-4-0T. Basically Drummond 323 class with Lambie boiler and full cab and dome further forward. Safety valves over firebox necessitating shortening of saddle tank. Cast iron wheels. Connor buffers. Water capacity 950 gallons.

No	Date	Rebuilt	LMS no	Withdrawn
211	1/1895		16225	1928
212	2/1895		(16226)	1926
213	2/1895		(16227)	1928
214	2/1895	3/1913	16228	8/1929
215	3/1895		16229	1928

Classified '3F' by LMS

McIntosh Locomotives 1895-1914

4-4-0 Built by CR at St Rollox. Order Y44
DW 6ft 6in, LW 3ft 6in, Cyls 18¼ x 26, Blr 10ft 3½in x 4ft 9¼in, THS 1403.23
sq ft, WP 160 lbs/sq in, WB 6ft 6in + 6ft 7in + 9ft 0in, Wt 46 tons 19¾ cwt.
Development of Lambie 13 class with larger, higher pitched boiler, amended
brake layout with Westinghouse reservoir on tender. Bogie as 13 class. 3,750
gallon tender used initially, later 4,125 gall bogie types of 1897 and 1899
were used. Cylinders redesigned 11/1904.

No	Name	Date	Rebuilt	LMS no	Withdrawn
721	*Dunalastair**	1/1896		14311	1931
722		2/1896		14312	11/1933
723	*Victoria***	2/1896		14313	8/1933
724	*Jubilee***	2/1896		14314	1930
725		2/1896		14315	10/1935
726		3/1896	1919***	14316	10/1935
727		3/1896		14317	1932
728		3/1896		14318	12/1934
729		4/1896		14319	4/1932
730		4/1896		14320	1931
731		4/1896		14321	1931
732		4/1896	1908	14322	12/1933
733		5/1896	7/1908	14323	1932
734		5/1896		14324	1930
735		5/1896		14325	1933

   *Name removed 1917
  **Name applied 1897. Removed by 1914. No 724 fitted for oil burning 1912.
***Tender cab 1917.

4-4-0 Built by CR at St Rollox. Order Y51.
DW 6ft 6in, LW 3ft 6in, Cyls 19 x 26, Blr 11ft 1in x 4ft 9¼in, THS 1500
sq ft, WP 175 lbs/sq in, WB 6ft 6in + 7ft 7in + 9ft 0in, Wt 49 tons.
Larger version of 721 class with larger boiler and smokebox and extended
frames. Gresham and Craven steam sanding for forward running. Wider cab.
Sand boxes separated from leading splasher and placed below running plate.
4,125 gallon tenders. Locos rebuilt with superheaters had 19½ x 26 cyls,
THS 1131.1 sq ft, Wt 52 tons and had boiler pitched 3in higher at 8ft,
WP 170 lbs/sq in.

No	Name	Date	Rebuilt		LMS no	Withdrawn
766	*Dunalastair II**	12/1897	10/1914	S'heat	14430	1/1936
767		12/1897	5/1920		14326	11/1939
			1933 812 class blr			
768		1/1898	3/1920		14327	8/1936
769		1/1898	1/1915	S'heat	14431	2/1936
770		2/1898	1923		14328	10/1940
771		2/1898	3/1914	S'heat	14432	3/1935
772		2/1898	7/1914	S'heat	14433	4/1937
			1933 300 class blr			
773		2/1898	11/1920 1930		14329	12/1936
			812 class blr			
774		2/1898	1923		14330	1941
775		3/1898	4/1920		14331	1945
776		3/1898	1924, 1931		14332	7/1946
			812 class blr			
777		3/1898	10/1907, 3/1920		14333	9/1947
778		4/1898	1907, 1920		14334	4/1936
779**	*Breadalbane**	4/1898	1920		14335	10/1939
780		4/1898	1923, 1933		14336	6/1939
			812 class blr			

  *Names removed 1917. *Breadalbane* later reinstated until 1925.
 **No 779 in accident Dinwoodie 25/10/1928.

4-4-0 Built by CR at St Rollox. Order Y57 (900-2), Y62 (remainder).
DW 6ft 6in, LW 3ft 6in, Cyls 19 x 26, Blr as 766 class, THS 1540 sq ft,
WP 180 lbs/sq in, WB 6ft 6in + 7ft 7in + 9ft 6in, Wt 51 tons 14 cwt. Larger
firebox, longer coupled wheelbase, steam reversing, higher pitched boiler
(8ft). Often referred to unofficially as *Dunalastair III*. 4,125 gallon
tenders. Locos rebuilt with super-heaters had cyls 19½ x 26, THS 1150.3 sq
ft, WP 170 lbs/sq in, Wt 54 tons 10 cwts.

No	Date	Rebuilt	LMS no	Withdrawn
900	12/1899	5/1918 S'heat	14435	10/1928*
901	12/1899	3/1914 S'heat	14436	11/1937
902	12/1899	1921	14346	10/1939
887	4/1900	1923	14337	4/1947
888	5/1900	1922	14338	3/1946
889	5/1900	1923	14339	1941
890	6/1900	1919	14340	12/1946
891	6/1900	1919	14341	8/1939
892	7/1900	1922	14342	3/1939
893	7/1900	1911	14343	1932
894	6/1900	4/1916 S'heat	14434	4/1948**
895	6/1900	1919	14344	1941
896	5/1900	1920	14345	1941
897	5/1900	1919, 1930 S'heat and piston valves using blr from 14435	14347	3/1939
898	5/1900	7/1914 S'heat	14437	6/1939
899	4/1900	1/1923 S'heat	14348	1944

*900 scrapped after Dinwoodie accident.
**as BR (54434)

4-4-0 Built by CR at St Rollox. Order no Y72 (140-4), Y76 (145-50), Y85
(923-7), Y92 (137/8, 136).
DW 6ft 6in, LW 3ft 6in, Cyls 19 x 26, Blr 11ft 2in x 5ft 0in, THS 1615 sq
ft, WP 180 lbs/sq in, WB 6ft 6in + 7ft 7in + 9ft 9in, Wt 56 tons 10 cwts.
Coupled wheelbase further extended and larger boiler than 900 class and
boiler pitch increased to 8ft 3in. One engine in Y76 batch was fitted with
compressed air sanding, the others had steam sanding. Steam-assisted lever
reverse. Cabs and splashers as 49 class 4-6-0s. 4,300 gallon bogie tender
(136-8 4,600 gallons). Sometimes referred to, unofficially as *Dunalastair IV*.

No	Date	Rebuilt	LMS no	BR no	Withdrawn
140*	5/1904	1919	14349		1941
141	5/1904	1905	14350		10/1945
142	6/1904	1908	14351		10/1939
143	6/1904	1920	14352		7/1937
144	6/1904		14353		4/1937
145	11/1905	1924	14354		1942
146	12/1905	1921	14355		5/1939
147	12/1905	12/1922 S'heat	14356		1941**
148	12/1905		14357		8/1938
149	12/1905	1919	14358		1940
150	1/1906		14359		10/1938
923	12/1907	1917 S'heat 20½in cyls	14438	54438	5/1955
924	1/1908	5/1915 S'heat 20½in cyls	14439	54439	8/1958
925	1/1908	5/1919 S'heat 20½in cyls	14360		12/1943
926	1/1908	1921	14361		3/1937
927	2/1908	1921	14362		4/1937
137	6/1910	1926	14363	(54363)	10/1948
138	7/1910	1925	14364		3/1939
136	7/1910	1925	14365		10/1939

*140 in Quintinshill accident 22/5/1915
**14356 destroyed by enemy action in air raid at Ladybure 1941.
Unsuperheated locos in above four classes were LMS class '2P'.

Superheated locos were '3P'.

4-4-0 Built by CR at St Rollox. Order Y92 (139), Y97 (132-5), Y101 (117-22)
DW 6ft 6in, LW 3ft 6in, Cyls 19 x 26. As 140 class but fitted with Schmidt
superheater, and piston valves. WP 165 lbs/sq in, Wt 59 tons. Superheater
heating surface 330 sq ft (Y92, 97), 295 sq ft (Y101). THS 1695 sq ft.

No	Date	LMS no	BR no	Withdrawn
139	7/1910	14440	54440	1/1957
132	4/1911	14441	54441	8/1957
133	4/1911	14442		7/1946
134	5/1911	14443	54443	10/1955
135	5/1911	14444	54444	10/1953
117	7/1912	14445	54445	12/1952
118	1912	14446	54446	8/1955
119	1912	14447	54447	6/1953
120	1912	14448	54448	2/1955
121	1912			11/1915*
122	8/1912	14449	54449	11/1953

*Scrapped after Quintinshill accident 22/5/1915

4-4-0 Built by CR at St Rollox. Order Y105 (43-8), Y109 (remainder).
DW 6ft 6in, LW 3ft 6in, Cyls 20½ x 26. As 139 class but with Robinson type
superheaters and larger cylinders. WP 170 lbs/sq in. 4,600 gallon bogie
tenders.

No	Date	LMS no	BR no	Withdrawn
43	5/1913	14450	54450	10/1955
44	1913	14451	54451	9/1955
45	1913	14452	54452	7/1957
46	1913	14453	54453	8/1957
47	1913	14454	54454	10/1955
48	6/1913	14455	54455	7/1954*
39	4/1914	14456	54456	2/1957
40	4/1914	14457	54457	2/1955
41	4/1914	14458	54458	12/1957
42	4/1914	14459	54459	12/1954
123	5/1914	14460	54460	10/1955

*48 in Quintinshill accident 22/5/1915. Withdrawn after accident at Aviemore.
Classified '3P' by LMS.

0-4-4T Built by CR at St Rollox. Order Y48 (92-103), Y59 (879-86), Y60 (437-8).
DW 5ft 9in, TW 3ft 2in, Cyls 18 x 26, Blr 10ft 0in x 4ft 4½in, Wt 55 tons
15 cwt. Other dimensions as Lambie 19 class 0-4-4T. Condenser fitted. Y59/60
which were officially regarded as a separate class had amended tube layout
(206 x 1¾in instead of 224 x 1⅝in) giving THS 1086.4 sq ft. Side tanks as 29
class 0-6-0T Drummond bunker. These locos carried new style number plates
with raised characters. Westinghouse brake. The most successful of the
condensing tank engines. Cylinders redesigned 4/1909. Condensing apparatus
removed from 1917.

No	Date	1922 no	LMS no	BR no	Withdrawn
92	5/1897	13	15125	55125	1/1957
93	5/1897	14	15126	55126	7/1961
94	6/1897	15	15127	(55127)	
95	6/1897	16	15128		5/1946
96	6/1897	17	15129	55129	9/1950
97	6/1897	18	15130	(55130)	9/1948
98	7/1897		15131		7/1946
99	7/1897		15132	55132	10/1951
100	7/1897		15133	(55133)	12/1948
101	7/1897		15134	55134	4/1951
102	7/1897		15135	55135	7/1953

| 103 | 7/1897 | 15136 | 55136 | 2/1953 |

879 class Orders Y59/60 (see above). Wt 56 tons 10¾ cwt.

No	Date	LMS no	BR no	Withdrawn
879	1/1900	15137		10/1947
880	1/1900	15138	55138	7/1951
881	2/1900	15139	55139	8/1952
882	2/1900	15140	55140	9/1952
883	2/1900	15141	55141	7/1958
884	2/1900	15142	55142	12/1952
885	2/1900	15143	55143	5/1953
886	2/1900	15144	(55144)	7/1952
437	3/1900	15145	55145	4/1955
438	3/1900	15146	55146	6/1954

Classified '2P' by LMS

O-4-4T Built by CR at St Rollox. Order no Y56.
DW 4ft 6in, TW 2ft 6in, Cyls 17 x 24, Blr as 879 class, WB 7ft 6in +
8ft 0in + 5ft 0in, Wt 51 tons 2½ cwt. Enlarged cab, lever reverse,
Westinghouse brake. Originally worked Balerno and Cathcart Circle Services.

No	Date	LMS no	Withdrawn
104	3/1899	15147	8/1929
105	3/1899	15148	1931
106	3/1899	15149	4/1936
107	3/1899	15150	8/1935
108	3/1899	15151	3/1937
109	3/1899	15152	10/1934
110	4/1899	15153	4/1938
111	4/1899	15154	1930
167	4/1899	15155	10/1935
168	4/1899	15156	6/1937
169	4/1899	15157	12/1934
170	6/1899	15158	10/1935

Classified '1P' by LMS

O-4-4T Built by CR at St Rollox. Order nos as below.
DW 5ft 9in, TW 3ft 2in, Cyls 18 x 26, Blr as 879 class, WB as Lambie 19
class, Wt 53 tons 19 cwt. Standard O-4-4T for suburban and branch working.
Non condensing version of 879 class. Cylinders redesigned 4/1909.

The following were built to Order Y61 (439-43) and Y64 (remainder)

No	Date	LMS no	BR no	Withdrawn
439	3/1900	15159	55159	12/1949
440	1900	15160	55160	10/1958
441	1900	15161	55161	10/1953
442	1900	15162	55162	5/1956
443	4/1900	15163		3/1946
444	9/1900	15164	55164	2/1959
445	1900	15165	55165	9/1961
446	1900	51566	55166	9/1953
447	1900	15167	55167	6/1961
448	1900	15168	55168	5/1957
449	1900	15169	55169	5/1961
450	1900	15170	55170	10/1952
451	1900	15171	(55171)	10/1951
452	1900	15172	(55172)	11/1952
453	1900	15173	55173	1/1962
454	1900	51574	55174	1/1956
455	12/1900	15175	55175	2/1953

The following were built to Order Y77 (151, 473, 655) and Y78 (remainder).
These and subsequent batches had THS 1104.5 sq ft.

No	Date	1918 no	LMS no	BR no	Withdrawn
151	3/1906		15176	55176	10/1958
473	3/1906		15178	55178	10/1958
655	3/1906	**423**	15177	55177	6/1955
125	4/1906		15180	(55180)	8/1948
384	4/1906	**463**	15182	55182	6/1958
660	4/1906		15186	55186	1/1952
112	12/1906		15179	55179	9/1953
424	1907		15181	55181	10/1951
464	1907		15183	55183	9/1950
465	1907		15184	(55184)	11/1949
466	1907		15185	55185	6/1961
666	2/1907		15187	55187	2/1955

The following were built to Order Y84 (158, 419, 422, 429, 470), Y90
(remainder).

No	Date	LMS no	BR no	Withdrawn
158	11/1907	15188	(55188)	3/1951
419	11/1907	15189	55189	12/1962*
422	11/1907	15190	(55190)	6/1948
429	11/1907	15191	55191	11/1950
470	11/1907	15192	(55192)	10/1950
126	10/1909	15193	55193	4/1955
127	10/1909	15194	55194	3/1955
420	11/1909	15195	55195	6/1961
421	1909	15196	55196	12/1955
427	11/1909	15197	55197	11/1954
428	11/1909	15198	55198	5/1961
456	12/1909	15199	55199	7/1961
467	12/1909	15200	55200	8/1961
468	12/1909	15201	55201	9/1961
469	12/1909	15202	55202	8/1961

*Preserved at Bo'ness as CR 419

The following were built to Order Y94 (155, 160, 459, 461), Y96 (152-4, 156
380, 462), Y102 (remainder).

No	Date	Renumbered no	year	LMS no	BR no	Withdrawn
155	4/1910			15203	55203	12/1961
160	4/1910			15204	55204	12/1962
459	1910			15205	55205	7/1956
461	1/1911			15206	55206	9/1961
152	3/1911			15207	55207	9/1961
153	1911			15208	55208	9/1961
154	1911			15209	55209	6/1961
156	1911			15210	55210	7/1961
380	6/1911	**460**	1918	15211	55211	9/1961
462	1911			15212	55212	12/1958
157	4/1912			15213	55213	6/1958
383	4/1912	**164**	1918	15214	55214	9/1961
457	1912			15215	55215	9/1961
458	7/1912			15216	55216	9/1961

The following were built to Order Y106 (228-31), Y110 (remainder).

No	Date	LMS no	BR no	Withdrawn
228	1913	15217	55217	7/1962
229	1913	15218	55218	1/1960

230	1913	15219	55219	5/1961
231	1913	15220	55220	9/1961
222	8/1914	15221	55221	10/1961
223	1914	15222	55222	9/1961
224	1914	15223	55223	9/1961
225	1914	15224	55224	12/1961
226	1914	15225	55225	1/1962
227	10/1914	15226	55226	9/1961

Class continued by Pickersgill (page no 102). Classified '2P' by LMS.

O-4-OST Built by CR at St Rollox. Order nos below.
DW 3ft 8in, Cyls 14 x 20 O/S, WP 140 lbs/sq in, WB 7ft Oin, Wt 27 tons
7½ cwt. Continuation of Drummond **264 class**。

The following were built to Order Y43 (611-4), Y63 (621-6), Y68 (627-8),
Y88 (remainder).

		Renumbered				
No	Date	no	year	LMS no	BR no	Withdrawn
611	10/1895			16026	(56026)	6/1950
612	10/1895			16027	56027	10/1960*
613	10/1895			16028	56028	5/1957
614	11/1895			16029	56029	12/1962
621	7/1900			16030	56030	6/1958
622	7/1900			16031	56031	4/1962
623	7/1900			16032	56032	10/1960
624	7/1900			16033		10/1935
625	8/1900			16034		10/1935
626	8/1900			16035	56035	8/1960
627	12/1902			(16036)		1925
628	12/1902			16037		12/1935**
431	12/1908	269	1922	16039	56039	10/1962
463	12/1908	265	1918	16038	56038	5/1959

*as Crewe works pilot. ** Sold to Bent Colliery (Cadzow Colliery), Hamilton.
4/1945 to Stewart's & Lloyds, Corby no 27.

O-4-OST Built by A. Barclay & Co 1896. Works no 772.
        Purchased from Lanarkshire Colliery in lieu of debt.
DW 3ft 2in, Cyls 13 x 20 O/S, WP 140 lbs/sq in.

		Duplicate			
No	Date	no	year	LMS no	Withdrawn
781	1897	1781	1912	(16000)	1924

4-6-O Built by CR at St Rollox. Order Y66 (55-9), Y75 (remainder).
DW 5ft Oin, LW 3ft 6in, Cyls 19 x 26, Blr 14ft 0⅛in x 4ft 9¼in, THS 1905 sq
ft (Y66), 1812 sq ft (Y75), WP 175 lbs/sq in, WB 5ft 9in + 6ft 9½in +
5ft 3in + 6ft Oin, Wt 57 tons 8cwt. Lengthened version of 900 class 4-4-O
boiler. 3,000 gallon tender (six wheel). Y66 locos designed for Oban line.
Y75 locos had smoke box tube plate recessed 9in into boiler barrel.

No	Date	LMS no	Withdrawn
55	5/1902	14600	8/1934
56	5/1902	14601	10/1934
57	5/1902	14602	1928
58	6/1902	14603	10/1935
59	6/1902	14604	12/1936
51	8/1905	14605	2/1937
52	9/1905	14606	11/1937
53	9/1905	14607	10/1934
54	9/1905	14608	12/1935

4-6-O Built by CR at St Rollox. Order Y69.
DW 6ft 6in, LW 3ft 6in, Cyls 21 x 26, Blr 17ft 4½in x 5ft Oin, THS 2323 sq
ft, WP 200 lbs/sq in, WB 6ft 6in + 7ft 2in + 7ft 6in + 7ft 6in, Wt 73 tons.

Steam-assisted lever reverse. Boiler modified by recessing tube plate
1ft 7in further. THS 2032 sq ft 7/1904. Balanced slide valves 9/1904.
Rebuilt with Schmidt super-heaters and Cyls 20¼ x 26, WP 175 lbs/sq in
and piston valves 1911. Bogie tender.

No	Date	Rebuilt	LMS no	Withdrawn
49	3/1903	3/1911	14750	1933
50	4/1903*	4/1911	14751	1933

*Named *Sir James Thompson*

4-6-0 Built by CR at St Rollox. Order Y80.
DW 6ft 6in, LW 3ft 6in, Cyls 20 x 26, Blr 17ft 7⅞in x 5ft 3½in, THS 2265.8
sq ft, WP 200 lbs/sq in, WB 6ft 6in + 7ft 6in + 7ft 2in + 7ft 6in, Wt 73 tons.
Superheated as 49 class 1911. Wt 74 tons 5 cwt. Bogie tender.

No	Date	Rebuilt	LMS no	Withdrawn
903	5/1906*	5/1911	14752	1930
904	1906	5/1911	14753	1929
905	1906	7/1911	14754	1927
906	1906	4/1911	14755	1928
907	7/1906	2/1911		1/1916**

*Named *Cardean*. Accident Crawford 2/4/1909.
**Scrapped after Quintinshill accident 22/5/1915.
Above three classes of 4-6-0 classified '4P' by LMS.

4-6-0 Built by CR at St Rollox. Order Y79.
DW 5ft 0in, LW 3ft 6in, Cyls 19 x 26, Blr 14ft 0½in x 5ft 3½in, THS 2023
sq ft, WP 175 lbs/sq in, WB 5ft 9in + 6ft 9½in + 5ft 3in + 6ft 0in, Wt
60 tons 8 cwt. Express goods and mixed traffic duties. Modification of
51-4 series of 55 class, 3, 750 gallon tender.

No	Date	LMS no	Withdrawn
918	7/1906	17900	1930
919	1906	17901	1930
920	1906	17902	1930
921	1906	17903	5/1929
922	9/1906	17904	1930

Classified '3F' by LMS

4-6-0 Built by CR at St Rollox. Order Y81.
DW 5ft 9in, LW 3ft 6in, Cyls 19 x 26, Blr 15ft $8^3/_{16}$in x 5ft 3½in, THS 2178
sq ft, WP 180 lbs/sq in, WB 5ft 9in + 6ft 9½in X 6ft 8in + 6ft 8in, Wt 64
tons. Larger version of 918 class.

No	Name*	Date	LMS no	Withdrawn
908		10/1906	14609	1933
909	*Sir James King*	1906	14610	1933
910		1906	14611	1931
911	*Barochan*	1906	14612	1931
912		1906	14613	1932
913		1906	14614	1930
914		1906	14615	1931
915		1906	14616	1930
916		1906	14617	1930
917		1/1907	14618	2/1935

*Names removed 1917
Classified '4P' by LMS

4-6-0 Built by CR at St Rollox. Order Y107.
DW 5ft 9in, LW 3ft 6in, Cyls 19 x 26, Blr as 908 class. THS 1567 sq ft
+ 403 sq ft superheater, WP 170 lbs/sq in, WB 5ft 9in + 7ft 0½in + 6ft 8in +
6ft 8in, Wt 68 tons 10 cwts.

No	Date	LMS no	Withdrawn
179	12/1913	17905	1945

180	12/1913	17906	2/1936
181	1/1914	17907	11/1935
182	1/1914	17908	2/1946
183	2/1914	17909	11/1936

4-6-0 Built by CR at St Rollox. Order Y112.
DW 5ft 9in, LW 3ft 6in, Cyls 19½ x 26. Other dimensions as 179 class.

No	Date	LMS no	Withdrawn
184	12/1914	17910	5/1936
185	12/1914	17911	4/1935
186	12/1914	17912	6/1937
187	1914	17913	11/1934
188	1914	17914	6/1935
189	3/1915	17915	3/1935

Above two classes of 4-6-0 classified '3F' by LMS

0-6-0 Built by CR at St Rollox. Order nos as below.
DW 5ft 0in, Cyls 18 x 26, Blr as Y38 batch of 294 class, WB as 294 class,
Wt 40 tons 6 cwt, (42 tons 4cwts fitted with condenser), THS 1169.2 sq ft.
Modified form of Drummond 294 class with small footsteps at rear of tender.
Westinghouse brake. Steam heating apparatus from 1911.

The following were built to Order Y41

No	Date	LMS no	BR no	Withdrawn
711	6/1895	17393	(57393)	4/1949
712	1895	17394	57394	11/1951
713	1895	17395	57395	3/1953
714	1895	17396	57396	5/1958
715	1896	17397	57397	3/1953
716	1896	17398	57398	5/1962
717	1896	17399	(57399)	9/1949
718	1896	17400	(57400)	7/1949
719	1896	17401	(57401)	3/1950
720	8/1896	17402	(57402)	8/1949

The following were built to Order Y45

No	Date	LMS no	BR no	Withdrawn
736	9/1896	17403	(57403)	10/1949
737	9/1896	17404	57404	9/1961
738	9/1896	17405	57405	9/1958
739	9/1896	17406		1/1948
740	9/1896	17407	57407	5/1959
741	10/1896	17408		2/1948
742	10/1896	17409	57409	1/1950
743	10/1896	17410	57410	2/1953
744	10/1896*	17411	57411	9/1961
745	10/1896	17412	57412	3/1956
746	11/1896	17413	57413	10/1958
747	11/1896	17414	57414	4/1959
748	11/1896	17415	(57415)	11/1949
749	11/1896	17416	57416	7/1961
750	2/1897	17417	57417	10/1962
751	3/1897	17418	57418	9/1961
752	3/1897	17419	57419	5/1959
753	3/1897	17420	(57420)	10/1949
754	3/1897	17421	(57421)	9/1948
755	3/1897	17422	(57422)	6/1948
756	3/1897	17423	57423	3/1953
757	4/1897	17424	57424	12/1959
758	4/1897	17425	57425	11/1950
759	4/1897	17426	57426	9/1961

760	4/1897	17427	(57427)	7/1949

*Tender cab 1917.

The following were built to Order Y46

No	Date	LMS no	BR no	Withdrawn
564	5/1896	17433	57433	5/1952
565	5/1896	17434	57434	5/1961
566	5/1896	17435	57435	2/1960
567	6/1896	17436	57436	10/1961
568	6/1896	17437	57437	7/1958
569	6/1896	17438	(57438)	4/1953
570	6/1896	17439	57439	2/1953
571	6/1896	17440	(57440)	5/1950
572	6/1896	17441	57441	11/1961
573	6/1896	17442	(57442)	7/1948
574	7/1896	17443	57443	8/1958
575	7/1896	17444	57444	11/1959

The following were built to Order Y47. 583-7 Condenser fitted.

No	Date	LMS no	BR no	Withdrawn
576	11/1896	17445	57445	8/1962
577	12/1896	17446	57446	9/1961
578	12/1896	17447	57447	10/1962
579	12/1896	17448	57448	2/1960
580	12/1896	17449	(57449)	11/1949
581	12/1896	17450	57450	3/1953
582	12/1896	17451	57451	9/1961
583	2/1897	17469	(57469)	11/1948
584	2/1897	17470	57470	9/1961
585	2/1897	17471	(57471)	9/1948
586	2/1897	17472	57472	9/1961
587	2/1897	17473	57473	6/1961

The following were built to Order Y49

No	Date	LMS no	BR no	Withdrawn
761	4/1897	17464	57464	2/1953
762	5/1897	17465	57465	4/1959
763	5/1897	17466	(57466)	4/1949
764	6/1897	17467	57467	2/1950
765	6/1897	17468	57468	2/1952
588	8/1897	17452	(57452)	6/1949
589	8/1897	17453	57453	11/1950
590	9/1897	17454	(57454)	3/1953
591	9/1897	17455	57455	6/1951
592	9/1897	17456	57456	1/1956

The following were built to Order Y50

No	Date	LMS no	BR no	Withdrawn
329	9/1897	17428		8/1947
330	9/1897	17429	57429	9/1961
331	10/1897	17430	57430	9/1957
332	10/1897	17431	57431	6/1961
333	10/1897	17432	57432	9/1961
593	10/1897	17457	57457	2/1956
594	10/1897*	17458	57458	10/1950
595	11/1897	17459	57459	12/1956
596	11/1897*	17460	57460	1/1957
597	11/1897	17461	57461	9/1961
598	11/1897	17462	57462	6/1959
599	11/1897	17463	57463	12/1961

*Tender cab 1917

The above 0-6-0s were classified '2F' by the LMS.

0-6-0 Built by CR at St Rollox. Orders Y54, Y58.
                    Neilson Reid & Co (works nos as below)
                    Sharp Stewart & Co (works nos as below)
                    Dubs & Co (works nos as below)
DW 5ft 0in, Cyls 18½ x 26, Blr as 721 class 4-4-0, WB 7ft 9in + 9ft 0in,
Wt 45 tons 13¾ cwt. Improved design intended as express goods loco
incorporating features of the 711 class 0-6-0s and 721 and 766 class 4-4-0s.
3,000 gallon tender. Batch **Y54** had Westinghouse brakes, the remainder had
steam brakes. Steam heating apparatus from 1911.

The following were built to Order Y54 at St Rollox.

No	Date	LMS no	BR no	Withdrawn
812	5/1899	17550	57550	12/1962
813	5/1899	17551	(57551)	7/1948
814	5/1899	17552	57552	12/1959
815	6/1899	17553	57553	10/1959
816	6/1899	17554	57554	6/1960
817	6/1899	17555	57555	11/1962
818	6/1899	17556	57556	4/1958
819	6/1899	17557	57557	9/1962
820	6/1899	17558	57558	9/1960
821	7/1899	17559	57559	9/1961
822	7/1899	17560	57560	9/1961
823	7/1899	17561	(57561)	7/1949
824	7/1899	17562	57562	5/1962
825	7/1899	17563	57563	12/1961
826	8/1899	17564	57564	9/1961
827	8/1899	17565	57565	12/1962
828	8/1899	17566	57566	8/1963*

*Preserved Boat of Garton, Strathspey Railway.

The following were built to Order Y58 at St Rollox

No	Date	LMS no	BR no	Withdrawn
282	9/1899	17617	57617	9/1962
283	9/1899	17618	57618	3/1962
284	9/1899	17619	57619	6/1961
285	9/1899	17620	57620	6/1962
286	9/1899	17621	57621	4/1962
287	10/1899	17622	57622	7/1962
288	10/1899	17623	57623	11/1961
289	10/1899	17624	(57624)	5/1949
290	10/1899	17625	57625	7/1963
291	10/1899	17626	57626	3/1962
292	11/1899	17627	57627	11/1963
293	11/1899	17628	57628	2/1960

The following were built by Neilson, Reid & Co. Works nos 5613-31

No	Date	LMS no	BR no	Withdrawn
829	12/1899	17567		11/1947 After accident, Beith
830	12/1899	17568	57568	12/1963
831	12/1899	17569	57569	11/1962
832	12/1899	17570	57570	8/1961
833	12/1899	17571	57571	4/1962
834	12/1899	17572	57572	6/1963
835	12/1899	17573	57573	11/1957
836	12/1899	17574	(57574)	6/1948
837	12/1899	17575	57575	9/1959
838	12/1899	17576	57576	9/1961
839	4/1900	17577	57577	7/1962

840	4/1900	17578	(57578)	11/1948
841	4/1900	17579	57579	11/1961
842	4/1900	17580	57580	11/1961
843	4/1900	17581	57581	11/1963
844	4/1900	17582	57582	9/1957
845	4/1900	17583	57583	11/1961
846	4/1900	17584	(57584)	6/1949
847	5/1900	17585	57585	11/1961
848	5/1900	17586	57586	6/1961

The following were built by Sharp Stewart & Co. Works nos 4634-48.

No	Date	LMS no	BR no	Withdrawn
849	8/1900	17587	57587	7/1962
850	8/1900	17588	57588	12/1957
851	8/1900	17589	57589	10/1956
852	8/1900	17590	57590	9/1963
853	8/1900	17591	57591	6/1961
854	8/1900	17592	57592	8/1963
855	8/1900	17593	57593	11/1961
856	8/1900	17594	57594	12/1962
857	8/1900	17595	57595	11/1959
858	8/1900	17596	57596	9/1962
859	8/1900	17597	57597	4/1962
860	8/1900	17598		10/1946
861	8/1900	17599	57599	11/1959
862	8/1900	17600	57600	12/1963
863	8/1900	17601	57601	12/1962

The following were built by Dubs & Co. Works nos 3880-94.

No	Date	LMS no	BR no	Withdrawn
864	4/1900	17602	57602	12/1962
865	4/1900	17603	57603	3/1962
866	5/1900	17604	57604	12/1962
867	5/1900	17605	57605	5/1960
868	5/1900	17606	(57606)	9/1948
869	5/1900	17607	57607	3/1963
870	5/1900	17608	57608	12/1962
871	5/1900	17609	57609	7/1960
872	5/1900	17610		11/1946
873	5/1900	17611	57611	11/1962
874	5/1900	17612	57612	4/1962
875	5/1900	17613	57613	9/1962
876	5/1900	17614	57614	10/1962
877	5/1900	17615	57615	7/1963
878	5/1900	17616	(57616)	5/1948

O-6-O Built by CR at St Rollox. Orders Y87, Y86, Y89.
DW 5ft 0in, Cyls 18½ x 26. Other dimensions as 812 class. Updated version of 812 class with cab based on 900 class.

The following were built to Order Y87. 652-3, 657, 665 were fitted with vacuum ejector.

No	Date	LMS no	BR no	Withdrawn
652	3/1908	17629	(57629)	9/1948
653	3/1908	17630	57630	11/1963
654	3/1908	17631	57631	9/1962
656	3/1908	17633	57633	12/1961
657	3/1908	17634	57634	8/1963
665	6/1908	17640	57640	11/1961

The following were built to Order Y86 (658/9, 662-4), Y89 (remainder).

No 658 was fitted with vacuum ejecter and nos 664, 325-8, 423 and 460
were fitted with spark arresters.

No	Date	1918 no	LMS no	BR no	Withdrawn
658	6/1908		17635	57635	3/1962
659	6/1908		17636	(57636)	12/1948
662	8/1908		17637	57637	12/1961
663	9/1908		17638	57638	10/1959
664	9/1908		17639	(57639)	9/1948
325	6/1909		17641	(57641)	4/1948
326	6/1909		17642	57642	7/1962
327	6/1909		17643	57643	9/1962
328	6/1909		17644	57644	9/1962
423	6/1909	**655**	17632	57632	11/1961
460	6/1909	**661**	17645	57645	11/1962

O-6-O Built by CR at St Rollox. Order Y98.
DW 5ft 0in, Cyls 19½ x 26, Blr 10ft 3½in x 4ft 8½in, THS 1190.1 sq ft
plus superheater 266.9 sq ft, WP 160 lbs/sq in, WB as 812 class, Wt 51 tons
2½ cwt. Superheated version of 652 class with boiler pitched 6in higher
(8ft 3in) and Schmidt superheater. Westinghouse brake.

No	Date	LMS no	Withdrawn
30	7/1912	17646	8/1935
31	1912	17647	9/1946
32	1912	17648	1945
33	11/1912	17649	1945

Above three classes of O-6-O classified '3F' by LMS

2-6-O Built by CR at St Rollox. Order Y103.
DW 5ft 0in, LW 3ft 6in, Cyls 19½ x 26, Blr as 30 class, WB 7ft 3in + 7ft
9in + 9ft 0in, Wt 54 tons 5 cwt. 2-6-O version of 30 class O-6-O with
frames lengthened by 2ft 6in. Steam brake, vacuum ejecter. Superheater
damper omitted. Known as 'converted 30 class'.

No	Date	LMS no	Withdrawn
34	11/1912	17800	11/1936
35	1912	17801	12/1936
36	1912	17802	11/1935
37	1912	17803	9/1936
38	12/1912	17804	6/1937

Classified '3F' by LMS.

O-6-OT Built by CR at St Rollox. Order no Y42.
DW 4ft 6in, Cyls 18 x 26, Blr 10ft 0in x 4ft 4½in (as 879 class O-4-4T,
page no 88), THS 1086.4 sq ft, WB 7ft 6in + 8ft 9in, Wt 49 tons 14½ cwt.
Fitted with condensers for working Glasgow low level line. Side tanks as
879 class (higher than Lambie O-4-4Ts). Westinghouse brake. Cylinders
redesigned 5/1909. Condensing apparatus removed from 1917.

No	Date	LMS no	BR no	Withdrawn
29	11/1895	16231	56231	2/1956
203	11/1895	16232	56232	4/1962
204	11/1895	16233	56233	10/1956
205	11/1895	16234	56234	8/1957
206	12/1895	16235	56235	11/1959
207	12/1895	16236	56236	12/1958
208	12/1895	16237	56237	2/1953
209	1/1896	16238	56238	9/1958
210	1/1896	16239	56239	3/1961

O-6-OT Built by CR at St Rollox. Order nos as below.
DW 4ft 6in, Cyls 18 x 26, Wt 47 tons 15¼ cwt. Other dimensions as 29 class
above. Non condensing version of 29 class. From Y73 firebox strengthened and

WP increased from 150 lbs/sq in to 160 lbs/sq in, cab fittings altered and
small front steps substituted. Cyls redesigned 5/1909.

The following were built to Order Y52

No	Date	LMS no	BR no	Withdrawn
782	6/1898	16254	56254	4/1958
783	6/1898	16255	56255	11/1958
784	6/1898	16256	56256	6/1959
785	6/1898	16257	57257	2/1957
786	7/1898	16258	56258	4/1953
787	7/1898	16259	56259	6/1960
788	7/1898	16260	56260	12/1960

The following were built to Order Y53

No	Date	LMS no	BR no	Withdrawn
789	8/1898	16261	56261	10/1956
790	8/1898	16262	56262	1/1959
791	9/1898	16263	56263	12/1955
792	9/1898	16264	56264	10/1959
793	9/1898	16265	56265	8/1958
794	9/1898	16266	56266	11/1959
795	9/1898	16267	56267	7/1958
796	9/1898	16268	56268	2/1952
797	9/1898	16269	56269	12/1959
798	10/1898	16270	56270	1/1958
799	10/1898	16271	56271	5/1956
800	10/1898	16272	56272	10/1958
801	10/1898	16273	56273	6/1956
802	10/1898	16274	56274	1/1958
803	10/1898	16275	56275	3/1958
804	10/1898	16276	56276	2/1953
805	11/1898	16277	56277	4/1958
806	11/1898	16278	56278	6/1962
807	11/1898	16279	56279	10/1960
808	11/1898	16280	56280	12/1957
809	11/1898	16281	56281	10/1958
810	11/1898	16282	56282	5/1958
811	12/1898	16283	56283	8/1958

The following were built to Order Y55

No	Date	LMS no	BR no	Withdrawn
236	12/1898	16240	56240	6/1961
237	12/1898	16241	56241	1/1960
238	12/1898	16242	56242	6/1961
239	12/1898	16243	56243	1/1957
240	12/1898	16244	56244	5/1958
241	12/1898	16245	56245	3/1959
242	1/1899	16246	56246	4/1961
243	1/1899	16247	56247	1/1959
244	1/1899	16248	56248	1/1955
245	1/1899	16249	56249	9/1956
246	1/1899	16250	56250	2/1954*
247	1/1899	16251	56251	10/1958
485	1/1899	16252	56252	6/1959
516	1/1899	16253	56253	11/1958

*56250 sold to Wemyss Coal company. Scrapped 1/1957

The following were built to Order Y73 (see above). Nos 636-40 had
Westinghouse brakes.

No	Date	LMS no	BR no	Withdrawn
631	10/1904	16285	56285	9/1959

632	10/1904	16286	56286	
633	11/1904	16287	56287	4/1959
634	11/1904	16288	56288	1/1959
635	12/1904	16289	56289	10/1960
636	11/1904	16290	56290	6/1959
637	11/1904	16291	56291	7/1959
638	12/1904	16292	56292	5/1960
639	12/1904	16293	56293	11/1958
640	12/1904	16294	56294	4/1957

The following were built to Order Y74 and had Westinghouse brakes.

No	Date	LMS no	BR no	Withdrawn
641	3/1905	16295	56295	11/1959
642	3/1905	16296	56296	8/1959
643	4/1905	16297	56297	11/1957
644	4/1905	16298	56298	10/1961
645	4/1905	16299	56299	1/1957
646	4/1905	16300	56300	10/1960
647	5/1905	16301	56301	10/1958
648	5/1905	16302	56302	12/1962
649	5/1905	16303	56303	8/1956
650	5/1905	16230	56230	1/1957

The following were built to Order Y82

No	Date	Renumbered no	year	LMS no	BR no	Withdrawn
128	4/1907			16304	56304	3/1960
129	4/1907			16305	56305	12/1961
166	4/1907			16306	56306	12/1958
324	4/1907	271	1919	16307	56307	10/1956
472	4/1907			16311	56311	1/1959
668	5/1907			16317	56317	5/1956
425	4/1907	275	1922	16308	56308	10/1860
434	1907	489	1922	16312	56312	5/1962
501	5/1907			16313	56313	1/1962
630	6/1907			16315	56315	5/1958

The following were built to Order Y83

No	Date	Renumbered no	year	LMS no	BR no	Withdrawn
417	9/1907			16310	56310	11/1960
426	9/1907	276	1922	16309	56309	1/1961
629	10/1907			16314	56314	2/1958
667	10/1907			16316	56316	10/1959
669	10/1907			16318	56318	6/1959

The following were built to Order Y91 (432-3, 475), Y93 (remainder)

No	Date	Renumbered no	year	LMS no	BR no	Withdrawn
432	1/1910	487	1922	16325	56325	12/1962
433	1910	488	1922	16284	56284	6/1958
475	2/1910			16319	56319	5/1956
435	7/1910	490	1922	16326	56326	10/1961
436	7/1910	491	1922	16327	56327	9/1959
476	7/1910			16320	56320	11/1957
477	7/1910			16321	56321	9/1959
478	7/1910			16322	56322	9/1959
479	7/1910			16323	56323	10/1958
480	8/1910			16324	56324	3/1961

The following were built to Order Y95

No	Date	Renumbered no	year	LMS no	BR no	Withdrawn
416	3/1910			16328	56328	9/1958
418	3/1910	**482**	1922	16331	56331	6/1960
481	9/1910			16330	56330	5/1958
474	10/1910			16329	56329	8/1957
483	10/1910			16332	56332	10/1959
484	10/1910			16333	56333	10/1959
500	10/1910			16334	56334	12/1957
608	11/1910			16335	56335	7/1960
609	11/1910			16336	56336	12/1962
610	11/1910			16337	56337	6/1961

The following were built to Order Y99

No	Date	Renumbered no	year	LMS no	BR no	Withdrawn
277	4/1911			16338	56338	4/1961
390	1911			16344	56344	9/1959
393	1911			16339	56339	8/1956
397	1911			16340	56340	10/1959
405	1911			16341	56341	3/1961
430	1911	**486**	1922	16343	56343	11/1960
471	10/1911			16342	56342	3/1957

The following were built to Order Y104. 171-4 had Westinghouse brake.

No	Date	LMS no	BR no	Withdrawn
651	10/1912	16351	(56351)	11/1948
781	1912	16352	56352	5/1959
130	1912	16345	56345	10/1958
131	12/1912	16346	56346	9/1957
171	10/1912	16347	56347	7/1962
172	1912	16348	56348	5/1960
173	1912	16349	56349	3/1960
174	12/1912	16350	56350	7/1957

The following were built to Order Y108

No	Date	LMS no	BR no	Withdrawn
175	9/1913	16353	56353	7/1958
176	1913	16354	56354	2/1958
177	1913	16355	56355	11/1956
178	1913	16356	56356	12/1961
508	1913	16357	56357	12/1957
509	10/1913	16358	56358	9/1956

Class continued by Pickersgill, page no 105.
Classified '3F' by LMS

0-6-OT Built by CR at St Rollox. Order Y100
DW 4ft 0in, Cyls 17 x 22 O/S, Blr 9ft 2½in x 4ft 4⅛in, THS 860 sq ft, WP 160 lbs/sq in, WB 5ft 0in + 5ft 0in, Wt 47 tons 15 cwt. Intended for working lines too sharply curved for 782 class, where a more powerful loco than 0-4-OST was required.

No	Date	LMS no	BR no	Withdrawn
498	1/1912	16151	56151	9/1961
499	1/1912	16152	56152	3/1959

Class continued by Pickersgill, page no 106.
Classified '2F' by LMS

0-8-O Built by CR at St Rollox. Orders Y65 (600-1), Y67 (602-3), Y70 (604-7)
DW 4ft 6in, Cyls 21 x 26, Blr 10ft 11⅞ x 4ft 9½in, THS 2008 sq ft, WP 175 lbs/

sq in, WB 8ft 6in + 5ft 4in + 8ft 6in, Wt 60 tons 12¼ cwt. Second (driving)
pair of wheels flangeless. Boiler was extended version of 900 class 4-4-0.
3,570 gallon tenders. Westinghouse brake. Mineral engine.

No	Date	LMS no	Withdrawn
600	7/1901	17990	1929
601	7/1901	17991	1929
602	1/1903	17992	1927
603	2/1903	17993	1928
604	2/1903	17994	1928
605	5/1903	17995	1930
606	6/1903	17996	1928
607	6/1903	17997	1928

Classified '4F' by LMS

0-8-OT Built by CR at St Rollox. Order Y71
DW 4ft 6in, Cyls 19 x 26, Blr 10ft 3½in x 4ft 6½in, THS 1189 sq ft, WP 175
lbs/sq in, WB 7ft 9in + 5ft 7½in + 5ft 7½in, Wt 62 tons 15¼ cwt. Mineral
tank engine. Second (driving) pair of wheels flangeless. Boiler was a
modified form of those fitted to McIntosh 0-6-0s but pitch was 8ft 4½in,
1ft 1½in higher. Large cab with doors, Westinghouse brake.

No	Date	1923 LMS no	1926 LMS no	Withdrawn
492	11/1903	16500	16950	9/1936
493	12/1903	16501	16951	1932
494	12/1903	16502	16952	1936
495	12/1903	16503	16953	7/1935
496	1/1904	16504	16954	1932
497	1/1904	16505	16955	3/1939

Classified '4F' by LMS

The 'Connel Bus'

This was a converted road motor charabanc which had previously been used for
a connecting road service linking Clarkston railway station with Eaglesham in
Renfrewshire.
From 6/1909 until 1913, when a roadway was constructed on Connel Bridge in
addition to the railway line, this vehicle was fitted with flanged wheels and
operated ten trips per day over the bridge to North Connel on the Ballachulish
branch (including Sundays) and augmented the normal service. Four trips were
extended to Benderloch and on these journeys cars could be carried, two
carriage trucks being provided.
The charabanc was converted at St Rollox including altering the reverse gear
to give a higher speed as it had no means of turning. It ran in reverse on
the down journey propelling one or both carriage trucks as required and ran
forwards hauling the trucks on the up journey. See also Vol 25, p177 (1949).
The make of the charabanc is not recorded, but was possibly a Thorneycroft.
It had a 30hp petrol engine and carried twenty seats arranged in tiers under
a high canopy supported by metal poles with a glass screen behind the driver.
Photographs of this strange vehicle can be seen in *The Callender and Oban
Railway* by John Thomas and *Railway Magazine* Vol 25 (1909). The former is
probably an official photograph bearing the legend 'Caledonian Railway Rail
Motor Service Connel Ferry & Benderloch' on the side of the vehicle*. *The
Railway Magazine* photograph, although posed, shows the bus in traffic.
*Reproduced in Model Railways Vol 4, p22 (1975).

Pickersgill Locomotives 1914-23

4-4-0 Built by CR at St Rollox. Order Y113. North British Locomotive Co. Works
nos below.
DW 6ft 6in, LW 3ft 6in, Cyls 20 x 26, Blr 11ft 2in x 4ft 11½in, THS 1329 sq
ft + superheater 200 sq ft, WP 175 lbs/sq in, WB 7ft 0in + 7ft 7in + 9ft 9in,

Wt 61 tons 5 cwt, 4,200 gallon tender. New chimney casting. St Rollox locos had Ross pop safety valves later adopted as standard by LMS. Smokebox wing plates dispensed with.

The following were built to Order Y113 at St Rollox

No	Date	LMS no	BR no	Withdrawn
113	2/1916	14461	54461	5/1959
114	1916	14462	54462	5/1960
115	1916	14463	54463	12/1962
116	1916	14464	54464	10/1961
121	1916	14465	54465	9/1962
124	5/1916	14466	54466	3/1962

The following were built by North British Locomotive Co works nos 21442-51

No	Date	LMS no	BR no	Withdrawn
928	1916	14467	54467	10/1959
929	1916	14468	54468	10/1959
930	1916	14469	54469	11/1959
931	1916	14470	54470	12/1959
932	1916	14471	54471	10/1959
933	1916	14472	54472	10/1959
934	1916	14473	54473	10/1959
935	1916	14474	54474	10/1959
936	1916	14475	54475	6/1961
937	1916	14476	54476	3/1960

4-4-0 Built by CR at St Rollox. Order Y124.
                Armstrong-Whitworth & Co. Works nos below.
                North British Locomotive Co. Works nos below.
DW 6ft 6in, LW 3ft 6in, Cyls 20½ x 26. Otherwise as 113 class.

The following were built to Order Y124 at St Rollox

No	Date	LMS no	BR no	Withdrawn
72	5/1920	14477	54477	5/1960
73	5/1920	14478	54478	7/1961
74	6/1920	14479	54479	10/1959
75	7/1920	14480	54480	8/1960
76	7/1920	14481	54481	6/1953*
77	7/1920	14482	54482	3/1962
78	8/1920	14483	54483	6/1961
79	9/1920	14484	54484	11/1959
80	9/1920	14485	54485	10/1961
81	9/1920	14486	54486	3/1962

*54481 scrapped on site after Gollanfield collision 9/6/1953

The following were built by Armstrong-Whitworth & Co. Works nos 111-20

No	Date	LMS no	BR no	Withdrawn
82	2/1921	14487	54487	3/1961
83	3/1921	14488	54488	2/1961
84	3/1921	14489	54489	12/1961
85	4/1921	14490	54490	5/1960
86	4/1921	14491	54491	12/1961
87	4/1921	14492	54492	11/1961
88	5/1921	14493	54493	11/1961
89	5/1921	14494	54494	8/1960
90	6/1921	14495	54495	3/1962
91	6/1921	14496	54496	10/1959

The following were built by North British Locomotive Co. Works nos 22943-54.

No	Date	LMS no	BR no	Withdrawn
66	11/1922	14497	54497	10/1959
67	11/1922	14498	54498	5/1960
68	11/1922	14499	54499	5/1960
69	12/1922	14500	54500	3/1962
70	12/1922	14501	54501	12/1961
71	12/1922	14502	54502	9/1962
92	12/1922	14503	54503	10/1959
93	12/1922	14504	54504	10/1959
94	12/1922	14505	54505	4/1961
95	12/1922	14506	54506	11/1961
96	12/1922	14507	54507	11/1961
97	12/1922	14508	54508	12/1959

Classified '3P' by LMS

O-4-4T Built by CR at St Rollox. Orders Y114 (1915), Y130 (1922).
DW 5ft 9in, TW 3ft 2in, Cyls 18 x 26, WB 6ft 0in + 8ft 0in + 8ft 0in,
Wt 57 tons 12 cwt. Otherwise as **439 class** (page no 90) Continuation of
standard O 4 4T but with bogie and coupled wheelbase extended. Steam
sanding. Locos to Y130 had WP increased from 150 lbs/sq in to 160 lbs/sq
in and Ross pop safety valves.

No	Date	LMS no	BR no	Withdrawn
159	8/1915	15227	55227	12/1961
161	1915	15228	55228	9/1961
162	1915	15229	55229	9/1961
163	10/1915	15230	55230	9/1961
418	1922	15231	55231	6/1961
425	1922	15232	55232	9/1961
426	1922	15233	55233	9/1961
430	1922	15234	55234	12/1962
435	1922	15235	55235	5/1961
436	1922	15236	55236	9/1961

O-4-4T Built by CR at St Rollox. Order Y130
DW 5ft 9in, TW 3ft 2in, Cyls 18¼ x 26, Wt 57 tons 17½ cwt. Otherwise as 159-
436 above, but with special cast iron buffers and 18¼ diam cylinders for
banking duties at Beattock.

No	Date	LMS no	BR no	Withdrawn
431	1922	15237	55237	7/1961
432	1922	15238	55238	9/1961
433	1922	15239	55239	7/1961
434	1922	15240	55240	11/1961

Above two classes of O-4-4T classified '2P' by LMS.
10 more locos built by LMS 1925 Nos 15260-9

4-6-O Built by Hawthorn Leslie & Co. Works nos 3095-3100.
DW 6ft 0in, LW 3ft 3in, Cyls 21 x 28 O/S, Blr 5ft 1 3/16in x 14th 4½in, THS
1599.6 sq ft + superheater 350 sq ft, WP 160 lbs/sq in, Wt 72 tons 6 cwt,
WB 6ft 6in** + 5ft 7½in + 6ft 3in + 8ft 0in. Ordered by Highland Railway
but sold by them to CR after delivery of first loco HR no 70 *River Ness*.
939 (intended as HR 71 *River Spey*) - 943 delivered direct to CR (nos 938 &
939 in Highland green) after HR civil engineer had ruled that they exceeded
weight limits. This brought about the resignation of HR Loco Supt F.G. Smith
who had ordered them. Steam reverse Walschaerts valve gear. Continuous
splasher. Belpaire firebox. Ross pop safety valves. Westinghouse brake
added in addition to vacuum ejectors originally fitted for HR which were
retained. Nicknamed 'Hielmen'. Usually known as 'River' class.
**bogie had centre pivot.

No	Date	LMS no	Withdrawn
938	11/1915	14756	11/1939
939	11/1915	14757	12/1936

940	11/1915	14758	9/1945
941	12/1915	14759	2/1939
942	12/1915	14760	12/1946*
943	12/1915	14761	11/1939

*14760 withdrawn 4/1939; reinstated 9/1940
Classified '4P' by LMS

4-6-0 Built by CR at St Rollox. Order Yll5 (no 60), Yll6 (remainder).
DW 6ft 1in, LW 3ft 6in, Cyls 20 x 26 O/S, Blr 15ft 9in x 5ft 3½in, THS 1676
sq ft + superheater 258.3 sq ft, WP 175 lbs/sq in, WB 7ft 0in + 6ft 0in +
7ft 0in + 7ft 6in, Wt 75 tons. Shortened version of 903 class 4-6-0 boiler.
Cab slightly smaller than 903 class. Steam-assisted lever reverse. Westinghouse brake and vacuum ejectors. Bogie pivot 2in in front of bogie centre.

No	Date	LMS no	BR no	Withdrawn
60	11/1916	14650	(54650)	9/1953 Accident Gretna
				5/11/1940
61	12/1916	14651	(54651)	3/1950
62	1/1917	14652	(54652)	11/1948
63	2/1917	14653	(54653)	7/1949
64	3/1917	14654	(54654)	1/1952
65	4/1917	14655		1/1944

Classified '3P' by LMS

A further twenty similar locos with 20½ x 26 O/S cylinders were built by the
LMS in 1925-6, numbered 14630-49.

4-6-0 Built by CR at St Rollox. Order Yl25.
DW 6ft 1in, LW 3ft 6in, Cyls (3) 18½ x 26 (2 O/S), Blr 16ft 3in x 5ft 9in,
THS 2370 sq ft + superheater 270 sq ft, WP 180 lbs/sq in, WB 7ft 0in +
6ft 8in + 7ft 0in + 8ft 0in, Wt 81 tons. Steam assisted lever reverse.
Piston valves, Walschaerts valve gear, Ross pop safety valves. Vacuum and
Westinghouse brakes fitted. 4,200 gallon tender slightly widened, increasing
capacity to 4,500 gallons (six wheel). Steam sanding.

No	Date	LMS no	Withdrawn
956	6/1921	14800	1931
957	7/1921	14801	3/1934
958	7/1921	14802	1/1935
959	8/1921	14803	1933

Classified '5P' by LMS

4-6-0 Built by North British Locomotive Co. Works nos 22955-62.
DW 5ft 6in, LW 3ft 6in, Cyls 19½ x 26 O/S, Blr 14ft 0in x 4ft 8⅛ in, THS
1823 sq ft, WP 185 lbs/sq in, WB 7ft 0in + 5ft 5in + 6ft 2in + 6ft 2in,
Wt 62 tons 15½ cwt. Built to replace Oban bogies on Oban line. Walschaerts
valve gear. Non superheated.

No	Date	LMS no	Withdrawn	
191	12/1922	14619	11/1940	
192	12/1922	14620	12/1939	
193	12/1922	14621	12/1945	
194	12/1922	14622	11/1943	
195	12/1922	14623	12/1939	Scrapped 1943
196	12/1922	14624	2/1940	
197	12/1922	14625	2/1939	Scrapped 12/1939
198	12/1922	14626	4/1943	

Classified '3P' by LMS

0-6-0 Built by CR at St Rollox. Orders as below.
DW 5ft 0in, Cyls 18½ x 26, Blr 10ft 3½in x 4ft 9¼in, THS 1451.7 sq ft, WP
170 lbs/sq in, WB 7ft 9in + 9ft 0in, Wt 49 tons 5 cwt. New design based on
McIntosh 30 class. Non superheated. First twelve locos originally had steel

fireboxes, copper being substituted 1920-2. Smoke box 5 in shorter than 30 class, steam sanding. 3,000 gallon tender with coal rails. Steam brakes. 17661 was vacuum fitted by LMS.

The following were built to Order Y119

No	Date	Rebuilt superheated	LMS no	BR no	Withdrawn
300	2/1918	1930	17656		7/1936
301	2/1918		17657		11/1934
302	2/1918	12/1927	17658	57658	12/1962
303	3/1918	9/1927	17659	57659	11/1961
304	3/1918		17660		1/1936
305	4/1918		17661	57661	9/1963
306	4/1918		17662		1945*
307	4/1918	4/1928	17663	57663	11/1961
308	1918		17664		2/1939
309	6/1918	1924	17665	57665	11/1961

*17662 withdrawn 7/1939; reinstated 1940

The following were built to Order Y120
17673 was vacuum fitted by LMS

No	Date	Rebuilt superheated	LMS no	BR no	Withdrawn
310	7/1918	5/1929	17666	57666	7/1962
311	1918		17667	57667	7/1962
312	12/1918	1924	17668	57668	1/1963
313	12/1918		17669	57669	11/1961
314	12/1918		17670	57670	3/1963
315	1/1919		17671	57671	7/1962
316	2/1919		17672	57672	10/1962
317	3/1919		17673	57673	3/1962
318	3/1919		17674	57674	11/1962
319	4/1919		17675		11/1937
320	4/1919		17676		12/1937
321	5/1919		17677		11/1936

The following were built to Order Y122

No	Date	Rebuilt superheated	LMS no	BR no	Withdrawn
294	6/1919	1929	17650	57650	11/1961
295	6/1919	1927	17651	57651	11/1961
296	6/1919	6/1932	17652	57652	11/1963
297	7/1919		17653	57653	1/1961
298	7/1919		17654	57654	12/1962
299	7/1919		17655	57655	4/1962
322	1919		17678		6/1937
323	5/1919		17679	57679	12/1963
324	9/1919		17680		6/1935

The following were built to Order Y123 and had slide valves instead of piston valves.

No	Date	Rebuilt superheated	LMS no	BR no	Withdrawn
280	10/1919	8/1929	17681	57681	10/1962
281	11/1919	3/1929	17682	57682	5/1962
670	11/1919		17683		6/1937
671	11/1919	1931	17684	57684	11/1962
672	11/1919		17685		6/1937
673	12/1919		17686	57686	3/1962
674	12/1919		17687		9/1946*

675	12/1919		17688	57688	12/1963
676	1/1920	2/1930	17689	57689	8/1963
677	1/1920		17690	57690	8/1963
678	2/1920	9/1930	17691	57691	7/1962
679	1/1920		17692		6/1936

*17687 withdrawn 3/1939; reinstated 1940.
Classified '3F' by LMS

4-6-2T Built by North British Locomotive Co. Works nos 21480-91
DW 5ft 9in, LW & TW 3ft 6in, Cyls 19½ x 26, Blr 14ft 11in x 4ft 9¼in, THS
1516 sq ft + 200 sq ft superheater, WP 170 lbs/sq in, WB 7ft 0in + 5ft 10in
+ 6ft 7½in + 6ft 7½in + 7ft 0in, Wt 91 tons 13 cwt. Steam-assisted reverse.
Westinghouse brake. Vacuum ejector. Steam sanding for either direction of
running. Sometimes referred to as 'Wemyss Bay Tanks'.

No	Date	LMS no	BR no	Withdrawn
944	3/1917	15350	55350	3/1952
945	1917	15351	(55351)	12/1948
946	1917	15352	55352*	3/1952
947	1917	15353	55353	6/1951
948	1917	15354	(55354)	8/1949
949	1917	15355		1/1948
950	1917	15356	55356	7/1950
951	1917	15357		7/1946
952	1917	15358		5/1946
953	1917	15359	55359	10/1953
954	1917	15360	55360	2/1952
955	1917	15361	(55361)	6/1952

*15352 carried prefix 'M' 1948-5/1950.
Classified '4P' by LMS

0-6-0T Built by CR at St Rollox. Order nos below.
DW 4ft 0in, Cyls 17 x 22 O/S. As McIntosh 498 class of which it was a
continuation.

The following were built to Order Y111

No	Date	LMS no	BR no	Withdrawn
527	4/1915	16153	56153	6/1959
528	1915	16154	56154	7/1959
529	1915	16155	56155	9/1958
530	1915	16156	56156	10/1959
531	1915	16157	56157	12/1958
532	6/1915	16158	56158	1/1961

The following were built to Order Y121

No	Date	LMS no	BR no	Withdrawn
533	8/1918	16159	56159	3/1962
534	1918	16160	56160	7/1959
535	1918	16161	56161	12/1958
536	1918	16162	56162	2/1959
537	1/1918	16163	56163	6/1959
538	10/1918	16164	56164	10/1958

The following were built to Order Y126

No	Date	LMS no	BR no	Withdrawn
502	1920	16165	56165	1/1960
503	1920	16166	56166	6/1959
504	1920	16167	56167	3/1961
510	1920	16168	56168	5/1961
511	1920	16169	56169	3/1961
512	1921	16170	56170	2/1960
513	1921	16171	56171	2/1961

| 514 | 1921 | 16172 | 56172 | 10/1960 |
| 515 | 1921 | 16173 | 56173 | 5/1961 |

Classified '2F by LMS

0-6-0T Built by CR at St Rollox. Orders Y117 (1916), Y127 (1921-2)
DW 4ft 6in, Cyls 18 x 26. As McIntosh **782 class** of which it was a
continuation.

No	Date	LMS no	BR no	Withdrawn
232	6/1916	16359	56359	5/1959
233	1916	16360	56360	8/1961
234	1916	16361	56361	11/1960
235	1916	16362	56362	8/1961
272	1916	16363	56363	6/1960
273	1916	16364	56364	12/1960
274	9/1916	16365	56365	5/1959
248	7/1921	16366	56366	10/1956
249	7/1921	16367	56367	2/1960
250	8/1921	16368	56368	12/1961
251	8/1921	16369	56369	11/1957
252	4/1922	16370	56370	2/1961
253	4/1922	16371	56371	1/1960
254	5/1922	16372	56372	5/1961
255	5/1922	16373	56373	10/1959
394	5/1922	16374	56374	10/1959
395	6/1922	16375	56375	8/1958
396	6/1922	16376	56376	3/1961

Classified '3F' by LMS

Locomotives from Ministry of Transport 1919-21

Fifty ex-ROD type 2-8-0s were hired between 8/1919 until Government control
of the railways ceased on 15/8/1921. Built to Government order in 1917-19 the
sixteen locomotives to 1994 (inclusive, but excluding no 1745) had seen
service in Europe. 1745 and all the locos in the 2000 series came direct from
the makers. On their return they were placed in store at Gretna until disposed
of as below. On the CR they carried the letters 'CR' on the tenders but no
numbers were allotted. Nicknamed 'Froggies', they were not very popular with
CR enginemen due to their 'right-hand drive'.

2-8-0 Built*by Kitson & Co Ltd (K)
              Nasmyth Wilson & Co Ltd (NW)
              Robert Stephenson & Co Ltd (RS)
              North British Locomotive Co (NBL)
DW 4ft 8in, LW 3ft 6in, WB 8ft 4in + 5ft 8½in + 5ft 8½in + 5ft 11in, Cyls
21 x 26, Blr 15ft 0in x 5ft 0in, THS 1758 sq ft (including superheater
255 sq ft).

ROD no	Date built	Builder	Date to CR where known	Disposal
1615	6/1918	K		To J&A Brown NSW 3/1927
1701	12/1917**	NW		To LNER 6554 2/1927
1702	12/1917**	NW		To Shanghai Nanking 7/1925
1703	12/1917**	NW		To Shanghai Nanking 7/1925
1705	1/1918**	NW		To Kailan Mining 10/1926
1710	2/1918**	NW		To Shanghai Nanking 7/1925
1711	2/1918**	NW		To Armstrong Whitworth(spares)12/1926
1712	2/1918**	NW		To LNER 6555 2/1927
1745	12/1919	RS	3/1920	To Shanghai Nanking 7/1925
1808	9/1917	NBL		To Armstrong Whitworth(spares)12/1926
1812	9/1917	NBL		To LNER 6566 2/1927
1816	10/1917	NBL		To LNER 6568 2/1927

1817	10/1917	NBL		To LNER 6569 2/1927
1824	11/1917	NBL		To LNER 6572 2/1927
1834	12/1917	NBL		To LNER 6575 2/1927
1846	1/1918**	NBL		To Shanghai Nanking 7/1925
1994	1/1919	NBL		To Peking-Mukden 10/1926
2077	8/1919	NBL	9/1919	To Peking-Mukden 10/1926
2078	8/1919	NBL	9/1919	To LNER 6623 2/1927
2079	8/1919	NBL	9/1919	To LNER 6624 2/1927
2080	8/1919	NBL	9/1919	To Shanghai Nanking 7/1925
2081	8/1919	NBL	9/1919	To LNER 6625 2/1927
2082	8/1919	NBL	9/1919	To LNER 6626 2/1927
2083	9/1919	NBL	10/1919	To Shanghai Nanking 7/1925
2084	9/1919	NBL	10/1919	To LNER 6627 2/1927
2086	10/1919	NBL	10/1919	To Shanghai Nanking 7/1925
2087	10/1919	NBL	10/1919	To LNER 6628 2/1927
2125	8/1919	NBL	10/1919	To Peking-Mukden 10/1926
2126	8/1919	NBL	10/1919	To LNER 6633 2/1927
2127	8/1919	NBL	10/1919	To Kailan Mining 10/1926
2128	8/1919	NBL	11/1919	To Peking-Mukden 10/1926
2129	9/1919	NBL	11/1919	To Peking-Mukden 10/1926
2130	9/1919	NBL	11/1919	To Kailan Mining 10/1926
2131	9/1919	NBL	11/1919	To Kailan Mining 10/1926
2132	9/1919	NBL	12/1919	To LNER 6634 2/1927
2133	9/1919	NBL	12/1919	To LNER 6635 2/1927
2134	9/1919	NBL	12/1919	To LNER 6636 2/1927
2135	9/1919	NBL	10/1919	To LNER 6637 2/1927
2136	9/1919	NBL	10/1919	To LNER 6638 2/1927
2137	9/1919	NBL	10/1919	Scrapped 1926
2158	10/1919	NBL	11/1919	To Kailan Mining 10/1926
2159	10/1919	NBL	11/1919	To Kailan Mining 10/1926
2160	10/1919	NBL	11/1919	To LNER 6640 2/1927
2161	10/1919	NBL	11/1919	To Shanghai Nanking 7/1925
2162	11/1919	NBL	12/1919	To LNER 6641 2/1927
2163	11/1919	NBL	12/1919	To Shanghai Nanking 7/1925
2164	11/1919	NBL	12/1919	To Shanghai Nanking 7/1925
2165	12/1919	NBL	12/1919	To LNER 6642 2/1927
2166	12/1919	NBL	12/1919	To Peking-Mukden 10/1926
2167	12/1919	NBL	12/1919	To Shanghai Nanking 7/1925

*For full description and listing see Vol 8
**Calculated date.

Caledonian Railway
Number Index

Number	Year	Description
1	1847	2-2-2 ex GP&G
	1869	2-4-O 1 class
	1881	2-2-2WT
	1893	4-4-OT 1 class
2	1847	2-2-2 ex GP&G
	1859	2-2-2WT ex 77
	1869	2-4-O 1 class
	1893	4-4-OT 1 class
3	1847	2-2-2 ex GP&G
	1869	2-4-O 1 class
	1893	4-4-OT 1 class
4	1847	2-2-2 4 class
-6	1869	2-4-O 1 class
	1893	4-4-OT 1 class
7	1847	2-2-2 4 class
-12	1870	2-4-O 1 class
	1893	4-4-OT 1 class
13	1847	2-2-2 4 class
-14	1870	2-4-O 1 class
	1894	4-4-O 13 class
	1922	O-4-4T ex 92/3
15	1847	2-2-2 4 class
	1869	O-4-OST 15 class
	1870	2-4-O 1 class
	1894	4-4-O 13 class
	1922	4-4-O ex 1088
	1922	O-4-4T ex 94
16	1847	2-2-2 4 class
	1859	2-2-2WT ex 78
	1869	O-4-OST 15 class
	1870	2-4-O 1 class
	1894	4-4-O 13 class
	1922	O-4-4T ex 95
17	1847	2-2-2 4 class
	1870	2-4-O 1 class
	1894	4-4-O 13 class
	1916	4-4-O ex 1060
	1922	O-4-4T ex 96
18	1847	2-2-2 4 class
	1870	2-4-O 1 class
	1894	4-4-O 13 class
	1922	O-4-4T ex 97
19	1847	2-2-2 4 class
-22	1870	2-4-O 1 class
	1895	O-4-4T 19 class
23	1847	2-2-2 4 class
	1868	2-2-2 ex 26
	1870	2-4-O 1 class
	1895	O-4-4T 19 class
24	1847	2-2-2 4 class
	1870	2-4-O 1 class
	1895	O-4-4T 19 class
25	1847	2-2-2 4 class
	1869	Blank
	1871	2-4-O 1 class
	1895	O-4-4T 19 class
26	1847	2-2-2 4 class
	1869	2-2-2 ex 8
	1871	2-4-O 1 class
	1895	O-4-4T 19 class
27	1847	2-2-2 4 class
	1869	2-2-2 ex 11
	1871	2-4-O 1 class
	1895	O-4-4T 19 class
28	1848	2-2-2 4 class
	1871	2-4-O 1 class
	1895	O-4-4T 19 class
29	1848	2-2-2 4 class
	1869	2-2-2 ex 21
	1871	2-4-O 1 class
	1895	O-6-OT 29 class
30	1848	2-2-2 4 class
	1872	2-4-O 98/30 class
	1912	O-6-O 30 class
31	1848	2-2-2 4 class
	1869	2-2-2 ex 38
	1872	2-4-O 98/30 class
	1912	O-6-O 30 class
32	1848	2-2-2 4 class
	1869	2-2-2 ex 31
	1872	2-4-O 98/30 class
	1912	O-6-O 30 class
33	1849	2-2-2 4 class
	1872	2-4-O 98/30 class
	1912	O-6-O 30 class
34	1849	2-2-2 4 class
-35	1872	2-4-O 98/30 class
	1912	2-6-O 34 class
36	1849	2-2-2 4 class
-37	1873	2-4-O 98/30 class
	1912	2-6-O 34 class
38	1849	2-2-2 4 class
	1869	2-2-2 ex 12
	1873	2-4-O 98/30 class
	1912	2-6-O 34 class
39	1849	2-2-2 4 class
	1869	2-2-2 ex 13
	1873	2-4-O 98/30 class
	1914	4-4-O 43 class
40	1849	2-2-2 4 class
	1870	2-2-2 ex 22
	1873	2-4-O 98/30 class
	1914	4-4-O 43 class
41	1849	2-2-2 4 class
	1869	2-2-2 ex 14
	1871	2-2-2 ex 26
	1873	2-4-O 98/30 class
	1914	4-4-O 43 class
42	1847	2-2-2 4 class
	1869	2-2-2 ex 6
	1872	2-2-2 ex 38
	1874	2-4-O 42/30 class
	1914	4-4-O 43 class
43	1847	2-2-2 4 class
	1874	2-4-O 42/30 class
	1913	4-4-O 43 class
44	1847	2-2-2 4 class
	1870	2-2-2 ex 9
	1872	2-2-2 ex 36
	1874	2-4-O 42/30 class
	1913	4-4-O 43 class

45	1848	2-2-2 4 class
	1872	2-2-2 ex 39
	1874	2-4-O 42/30 class
	1913	4-4-O 43 class
46	1848	2-2-2 4 class
	1872	2-2-2 ex 35
	1873	2-2-2 ex 37
	1874	2-4-O 43/30 class
	1913	4-4-O 43 class
47	1848	2-2-2 4 class
	1874	2-4-O 42/30 class
	1913	4-4-O 43 class
48	1848	2-2-2 4 class
	1869	2-2-2 ex 7
	1870	2-2-2 ex 19
	1872	2-2-2 ex 33
	1874	2-4-O 42/30 class
	1913	4-4-O 43 class
49	1848	2-2-2 4 class
	1870	2-2-2 ex 24
	1871	2-2-2 ex 27
	1872	2-2-2 ex 31
	1874	2-4-O 1 class
	1903	4-6-O 49 class
50	1848	2-2-2 4 class
	1870	2-2-2 ex 48
	1874	2-4-O 1 class
	1903	4-6-O 50 class
51	1848	2-2-2 4 class
-52	1874	2-4-O 1 class
	1905	4-6-O 55 class
53	1848	2-2-2 4 class
	1869	2-2-2 ex 56
	1874	2-4-O 1 class
	1905	4-6-O 55 class
54	1848	2-2-2 4 class
	1874	2-4-O 1 class
	1898	2-4-O ex 107
	1900	2-4-O ex 1202
	1905	4-6-O 55 class
55	1848	2-2-2 4 class
	1869	2-2-2WT ex 2
	1874	2-4-O 55 class
	1899	2-4-O ex 1203
	1902	4-6-O 55 class
56	1848	2-2-2 4 class
	1869	2-2-2 ex 16
	1874	2-4-O 55 class
	1899	2-4-O ex 1225
	1902	4-6-O 55 class
57	1848	2-2-2 4 class
	1869	2-2-2 ex 1
	1869	2-2-2 ex 41
	1870	2-2-2 ex 20
	1875	2-4-O 55 class
	1902	4-6-O 55 class
58	1848	2-2-2 4 class
	1869	2-2-2 ex 3
	1875	2-4-O 55 class
	1900	2-4-O ex 1204

	1902	4-6-O 55 class
59	1849	2-2-2/2-4-O 59 class
	1885	2-4-O ex 61
	1896	2-4-O ex 24
	1902	4-6-O 55 class
60	1849	2-2-2/2-4-O 59 class
	1885	4-4-O 66 class
	1916	4-6-O 60 class
61	1852	2-2-2/2-4-O 59 class
	1881	2-4-O ex 1
	1885	4-4-O 66 class
	1916	4-6-O 60 class
62	1852	2-2-2/2-4-O 59 class
	1883	Blank
-64	1885	4-4-O 66 class
	1917	4-6-O 60 class
65	1848	ex GP&G
	1852	Blank
	1854	2-2-2 65 class
	1882	Blank
	1885	4-4-O 66 class
	1917	4-6-O 60 class
66	1848	ex GP&G
-69	1854	2-2-2 65 class
	1884	4-4-O 66 class
	1922	4-4-O 72 class
70	1848	ex GP&G
-71	1855	2-2-2 65 class
	1882	Blank
	1884	4-4-O 66 class
	1922	4-4-O 72 class
72	1848	ex GP&G
-75	1855	2-2-2 65 class
	1882	Blank
	1884	4-4-O 66 class
	1920	4-4-O 72 class
76	1848	ex GP&G
	1855	2-2-2 65 class
	1859	2-2-2 76 class
	1889	4-4-O 66 class
	1920	4-4-O 72 class
77	1848	ex GP&G
	1851	2-2-2WT 77 class
	1859	2-2-2 76 class
	1889	4-4-O 66 class
	1920	4-4-O 72 class
78	1848	ex GP&G
	1851	2-2-2WT 77 class
	1860	Blank
	1861	2-2-2 76 class
	1889	4-4-O 66 class
	1920	4-4-O 72 class
79	1848	ex GG&C
	1851	Blank
	1861	2-2-2 76 class
	1889	4-4-O 66 class
	1920	4-4-O 72 class
80	1848	ex GG&C
	1854	2-4-OT 80 class
	1861	2-2-2 76 class

	1888	4-4-0 80 class
	1920	4-4-0 72 class
81	1848	ex GG&C
	1850	Blank
	1854	2-4-0T 80 class
	1861	2-2-2 76 class
	1888	4-4-0 80 class
	1920	4-4-0 72 class
82	1848	ex GG&C
	1850	Blank*
	1861	2-2-2 76 class
	1888	4-4-0 80 class
	1921	4-4-0 72 class
83	1848	ex P&G
	1852	Blank
	1854	0-4-0ST
	1863	2-2-2 76 class
	1891	4-4-0 66 class
	1921	4-4-0 72 class
84	1848	ex P&G
	1852	Blank
	1854	0-4-2 ex 87
	1864	2-2-2 76 class
	1889	4-4-0 66 class
	1921	4-4-0 72 class
85	1848	ex P&G
	1854	0-4-2 ex 88
	1861	2-4-0 197 class
	1864	2-2-2 76 class
	1887	Blank
	1888	4-4-0 80 class
	1916	Blank
	1921	4-4-0 72 class
86	1848	ex W&C
	1861	2-4-0 197 class
	1864	2-2-2 76 class
	1888	4-4-0 80 class
	1921	4-4-0 72 class
87	1848	ex W&C
	1854	0-4-2ST 87 class
	1862	2-4-0 ex 85
	1865	2-2-2 76 class
	1889	4-4-0 66 class
	1916	4-4-0 ex 1062
	1921	4-4-0 72 class
88	1848	ex W&C
	1854	0-4-2ST 87 class
	1864	2-2-2 88 class
	1891	4-4-0 66 class
	1921	4-4-0 72 class
89	1848	ex W&C
-91	1861	2-4-0 197 class
	1864	2-2-2 88 class
	1891	4-4-0 66 class
	1921	4-4-0 72 class
92	1848	ex W&C
	1861	2-4-0 197 class
	1865	2-4-0 92 class
	1897	0-4-4T 92 class

*see GP&G no 16
page no 17

	1922	4-4-0 72 class
93	1848	ex W&C
-94	1864	ex GT
	1866	2-4-0 92 class
	1897	0-4-4T 92 class
	1922	4-4-0 72 class
95	1848	ex W&C
	1864	0-4-2
	1866	2-4-0 92 class
	1896	Blank
	1897	0-4-4T 92 class
	1922	4-4-0 72 class
96	1849	0-6-0/0-4-2 96 class
	1866	2-4-0 92 class
	1896	2-4-0 ex 23A
	1897	0-4-4T 92 class
	1922	4-4-0 72 class
97	1849	0-6-0/0-4-2 96 class
	1866	2-4-0 92 class
	1897	0-4-4T 92 class
	1922	4-4-0 72 class
98	1849	0-6-0/0-4-2 96 class
-100	1867	2-4-0 98 class
	1897	0-4-4T 92 class
101	1848	0-4-2 101 class
-102	1867	2-4-0 98 class
	1897	0-4-4T 92 class
103	1848	0-4-2 101 class
	1867	2-4-0 92 class
	1897	0-4-4T 92 class
104	1848	0-4-2 101 class
	1867	2-4-0 92 class
	1899	0-4-4T 104 class
105	1848	0-4-2 101 class
	1867	2-4-0 92 class
	1895	2-4-0 ex 7A
	1899	0-4-4T 104 class
106	1849	0-4-2 106 class
	1867	2-4-0 92 class
	1896	2-4-0 ex 28A
	1899	0-4-4T 104 class
107	1849	0-4-2 106 class
	1867	2-4-0 92 class
	1898	2-4-0 ex 54
	1899	0-4-4T 104 class
108	1849	0-4-2 106 class
	1868	2-4-0 98 class
	1899	2-4-0 ex 55
	1899	0-4-4T 104 class
109	1849	0-4-2 106 class
	1868	2-4-0 98 class
	1899	2-4-0 ex 56
	1899	0-4-4T 104 class
110	1849	0-4-2 106 class
	1868	2-4-0 98 class
	1899	0-4-4T 104 class
111	1847	0-4-2 111 class
	1866	0-4-2 ex 95
	1867	0-4-2 ex 98
	1868	2-4-0 98 class
	1899	0-4-4T 104 class

	1899	O-6-OT 782 class	280	1865	O-4-2 216 class
248	1864	O-4-2 216 class	-281	1887	O-4-2 ex 712/3
	1882	2-2-2 ex 303		1919	O-6-O 300 class
	1887	O-4-2 ex 700	282	1865	2-4-O 228 class
	1921	O-6-OT 782 class	-287	1887	O-4-2 ex 714-9
249	1864	O-4-2 216 class		1899	O-6-O 812 class
-251	1887	O-4-2 ex 701-3	288	1865	2-4-O 288 class
	1921	O-6-OT 782 class	-290	1899	O-6-O 812 class
252	1864	O-4-2 216 class	291	1865	2-4-O 288 class
-254	1887	O-4-2 ex 704-6		1896	Blank
	1922	O-6-OT 782 class		1898	2-4-O ex 588A
255	1864	O-4-2 ex 241		1899	O-6-O 812 class
	1874	O-4-2 ex 132	292	1865	2-4-O 288 class
	1877	O-4-2 ex 264		1899	O-6-O 812 class
	1880	2-4-O ex 158	293	1865	2-4-O 288 class
	1886	Blank		1898	2-4-O ex 13A
	1887	O-4-2 ex 707		1899	O-6-O 812 class
	1922	O-6-OT 782 class	294	1865	ex SC
256	1864	2-4-O ex 87	-299	1883	O-6-O 294 class
	1894	O-6-O 294 class		1919	O-6-O 300 class
257	1864	2-4-O ex 86	300	1865	ex SC
	1894	O-6-O 294 class	-308	1883	O-6-O 294 class
258	1864	2-4-O ex 89		1918	O-6-O 300 class
	1894	O-6-O 294 class	309	1865	ex SC
259	1864	2-4-O ex 90/1		1886	O-6-O 294 class
-260	1894	O-6-O 294 class		1918	O-6-O 300 class
	1918	O-6-O ex 299-300	310	1865	ex SC
261	1864	2-4-O ex 92	-311	1877	2-2-2 ex 460/1
	1894	O-6-O 294 class		1886	O-6-O 294 class
262	1864	ex Portpatrick		1918	O-6-O 300 class
-263	1885	O-4-2ST 262 class	312	1865	ex SC
	1918	O-6-O ex 295/6	-314	1877	2-2-2 ex 456-8
264	1864	ex Portpatrick		1886	O-6-O 294 class
	1875	O-4-2 ex 114		1918	O-6-O 300 class
	1877	O-4-OWT ex 454	315	1865	ex SC
	1884	Blank		1877	2-2-2 ex 459
	1885	O-4-OST 264 class		1886	O-6-O 294 class
	1918	O-6-O ex 297		1919	O-6-O 300 class
265	1864	ex Portpatrick	316	1865	ex SC
	1885	O-4-OST 264 class		1867	Blank
	1918	O-4-OST ex 463		1876	O-4-2T ex 119
266	1864	ex Portpatrick		1877	2-2-2 ex 462
-268	1885	O-4-OST 264 class		1886	O-6-O 294 class
269	1864	ex Portpatrick		1919	O-6-O 300 class
	1885	O-4-OST 264 class	317	1865	ex SC
	1922	O-4-OST ex 431	-319	1877	2-2-2 ex 463-5
270	1865	O-4-OPT 270 class		1886	O-6-O 294 class
	1885	O-4-OST 264 class		1919	O-6-O 300 class
271	1865	O-4-OPT 270 class	320	1865	ex SC
	1885	O-4-OST 264 class		1875	2-2-2 ex 57
	1919	O-6-OT ex 324		1879	Blank
272	1865	O-4-2 216 class		1880	2-4-O ex 159
-274	1888	O-6-OST 272 class		1886	O-6-O 294 class
	1916	O-6-OT 782 class		1919	O-6-O 300 class
275	1865	O-4-2 216 class	321	1865	ex SC
-276	1887	O-4-2 ex 708/9		1886	Blank
	1922	O-6-OT ex 425/6		1887	O-6-O 294 class
277	1865	O-4-2/O-4-2ST 216 class		1919	O-6-O 300 class
	1911	O-6-OT 782 class	322	1865	ex SC
278	1865	O-4-2 216 class		1877	O-4-2 ex 452
-279	1887	O-4-2 ex 710/11		1887	O-6-O 294 class

	1919	0-6-0 300 class
323	1865	ex SC
	1877	0-4-2 ex 453
	1887	0-6-0ST 323 class
	1895	0-6-0 ex 339
	1918	Blank
	1919	0-6-0 300 class
324	1865	ex SC
	1872	0-4-2 324 class
	1907	0-6-0T 782 class
	1919	0-6-0 300 class
325	1865	ex SC
-328	1872	0-4-2 324 class
	1909	0-6-0 652 class
329	1865	ex SC
-332	1872	0-4-2 324 class
	1897	0-6-0 711 class
333	1865	ex SC
	1867	2-2-2 ex 316
	1872	0-4-2 324 class
	1897	0-6-0 711 class
334	1865	ex SC
	1870	2-4-0
	1894	0-6-0 294 class
335	1865	ex SC
	1870	2-4-0
	1894	0-6-0 294 class
	1918	0-6-0 ex 301
336	1865	ex SC
	1870	2-4-0 417 class
	1894	0-6-0 294 class
337	1865	ex SC
	1870	2-4-0 417 class
	1894	0-6-0 294 class
	1918	0-6-0 ex 302
338	1865	ex SC
	1870	2-4-0 417 class
	1895	0-6-0 ex 203
339	1865	ex SC
	1887	0-6-0 294 class
	1895	0-6-0 ex 204
340	1865	ex SC
-348	1887	0-6-0 294 class
349	1865	ex SC
-350	1883	0-6-0 294 class
351	1865	ex SC
	1880	2-4-0 ex 162
	1882	Blank
	1883	0-6-0 294 class
352	1865	ex SC
	1883	0-6-0 294 class
353	1865	ex SC
-354	1884	0-6-0 294 class
355	1865	ex SC
-359	1886	0-6-0 294 class
360	1865	ex SC
	1880	2-4-0 ex 163
	1884	2-4-0 ex 354A
	1886	0-6-0 294 class
361	1865	ex SC
- 362	1886	Blank

363	1865	ex SC
-364	1888	Blank
	1892	0-6-0 ex 693/4
365	1865	ex SC
	1886	Blank
	1892	0-6-0 ex 695
366	1865	ex SC
	1887	0-6-0 294 class
367	1865	ex SC
	1875	0-6-0 ex 120
	1887	0-6-0 294 class
	1918	0-6-0 ex 304
368	1865	ex SC
	1875	0-6-0 ex 121
	1887	0-6-0 294 class
369	1865	ex SC
	1868	0-4-2WT ex 469
	1877	Blank
	1880	2-4-0 ex 164
	1884	0-4-0ST ex 525
	1887	0-6-0 294 class
370	1865	ex SC
	1876	0-4-2 ex 118
	1879	Blank
	1880	2-4-0 ex 165
	1887	0-6-0 294 class
371	1865	ex SC
	1877	0-4-2T ex 316
	1887	0-6-0 294 class
372	1865	ex SC
-373	1870	2-4-0 372 class
	1891	0-6-0 294 class
374	1865	ex SC
	1870	2-4-0 372 class
	1891	0-6-0 294 class
	1918	0-6-0 ex 305
375	1865	ex SC
-379	1870	2-4-0 372 class
	1891	0-6-0 294 class
380	1866	2-4-0 288 class
	1911	0-4-4T 439 class
	1918	0-6-0 ex 322
381	1866	2-4-0 288 class
	1897	0-6-0 ex 542A
382	1866	2-4-0 288 class
	1896	0-6-0 ex 555A
	1897	0-6-0 ex 543A
383	1866	2-4-0 288 class
	1898	2-4-0 ex 1249
	1900	2-4-0 ex 1249
	1910	Blank
	1912	0-4-4T 439 class
	1918	0-6-0ST ex 539
384	1866	2-4-0 228 class
	1906	0-4-4T 439 class
	1918	0-6-0ST ex 538
385	1866	2-4-0 228 class
	1887	0-6-0ST 323 class
386	1866	2-4-0 228 class
	1888	0-6-0ST 323 class

At top of second column:

| 1892 | 0-6-0 ex 691/2 |

387	1866	O-4-2 216 class
	1888	O-6-OST 323 class
388	1866	O-4-2 216 class
-389	1890	O-6-OST 323 class
390	1866	O-4-2 216 class
	1912	O-6-OT 782 class
391	1866	O-4-2 216 class
-392	1890	O-6-OST 323 class
393	1866	O-4-2 216 class
	1911	O-6-OT 782 class
394	1866	O-4-2 216 class
-396	1890	O-6-OST 323 class
	1922	O-6-OT 782 class
397	1866	O-4-2 216 class
	1911	O-6-OT 782 class
398	1866	O-4-2 216 class
-402	1890	O-6-OST 323 class
403	1866	O-4-2 216 class
	1889	O-6-O 294 class
	1918	O-6-O ex 306
404	1866	O-4-2 216 class
	1889	O-6-O 294 class
405	1866	O-4-2 216 class
	1911	O-6-OT 782 class
406	1866	O-4-2 216 class
-409	1889	O-6-O 294 class
410	1866	O-4-2 216 class
-415	1890	O-6-O 294 class
416	1866	O-4-2 216 class
	1910	O-6-OT 782 class
417	1866	2-4-O 417 class
	1907	O-6-OT 782 class
418	1866	2-4-O 417 class
	1910	O-6-OT 782 class
	1922	O-4-4T 439 class
419	1866	2-4-O 417 class
	1907	O-4-4T 439 class
420	1866	2-4-O 417 class
-421	1909	O-4-4T 439 class
422	1866	2-4-O 417 class
	1907	O-4-4T 439 class
423	1866	2-4-O 417 class
	1909	O-6-O 652 class
	1918	O-4-4T ex 655
424	1866	2-4-O 417 class
	1906	2-4-O ex 1591
	1907	O-4-4T 439 class
425	1867	2-4-O 417 class
-426	1907	O-6-OT 782 class
	1922	O-4-4T 439 class
427	1867	2-4-O 417 class
	1901	2-4-O ex 1587
	1909	O-4-4T 439 class
428	1867	2-4-O 417 class
	1901	2-4-O ex 1590
	1909	O-4-4T 439 class
429	1867	2-4-O 417 class
	1907	O-4-4T 439 class
430	1867	2-4-O 417 class
	1911	O-6-OT 782 class
	1922	O-4-4T 439 class

431	1867	2-4-O 417 class
	1899	2-4-O ex 1245
	1901	2-4-O ex 1583
	1908	O-4-OST 264 class
	1922	O-4-4T 431 class
432	1867	2-4-O 417 class
-433	1910	O-6-OT 782 class
	1922	O-4-4T 431 class
434	1867	2-4-O 417 class
	1907	O-6-OT 782 class
	1922	O-4-4T 431 class
435	1867	2-4-O 417 class
	1901	2-4-O ex 1588
	1910	O-6-OT 782 class
	1922	O-4-4T 439 class
436	1867	2-4-O 417 class
	1910	O-6-OT 782 class
	1922	O-4-4T 439 class
437	1866	ex SNE
-438	1873	2-4-O 583 class
	1900	O-4-4T 879 class
439	1866	ex SNE
-443	1873	2-4-O 583 class
	1900	O-4-4T 439 class
444	1866	ex SNE
-445	1874	2-2-2WT ex 55/6
	1877	2-4-O 615 class
	1900	O-4-4T 439 class
446	1866	ex SNE
-447	1873	O-4-OT 446 class
	1877	2-4-O 615 class
	1900	O-4-4T 439 class
448	1866	ex SNE
	1877	2-4-O 615 class
	1900	O-4-4T 439 class
449	1866	ex SNE
	1876	O-4-2 ex 122
	1878	2-4-O 615 class
	1900	O-4-4T 439 class
450	1866	ex SNE
	1868	O-4-OT ex 468
	1878	2-4-O 615 class
	1900	O-4-4T 439 class
451	1866	ex SNE
	1870	2-2-2 ex 452
	1873	Blank
	1876	O-4-2 ex 123
	1878	2-4-O 615 class
	1900	O-4-4T 439 class
452	1866	ex SNE
-453	1870	ex Solway
	1878	2-4-O 615 class
	1900	O-4-4T 439 class
454	1866	ex SNE
	1868	O-4-OWT ex 466
	1878	2-4-O 615 class
	1900	O-4-4T 439 class
455	1866	ex SNE
	1868	O-4-OST ex 467
	1878	2-4-O 615 class
	1900	O-4-4T 439 class

456	1866	ex SNE		1868	2-4-0 472 class
	1878	2-4-0 615 class		1876	2-4-0 ex 643
	1909	0-4-4T 439 class		1877	2-4-0 ex 485
457	1866	ex SNE		1906	0-4-4T 439 class
-458	1878	2-4-0 615 class	474	1866	ex SNE
	1912	0-4-4T 439 class	-478	1867	2-4-0 417 class
459	1866	ex SNE		1910	0-6-OT 782 class
	1877	0-6-0 ex 661	479	1866	ex SNE
	1881	2-4-0 ex 615		1867	2-4-0 417 class
	1910	0-4-4T 439 class		1900	2-4-0 ex 1245
460	1866	ex SNE		1910	0-6-OT 782 class
	1871	2-2-2	480	1866	ex SNE
	1877	0-6-0 ex 662		1868	2-4-0 417 class
	1881	2-4-0 ex 616		1900	2-4-0 ex 1247
	1909	0-6-0 652 class		1910	0-6-OT 782 class
	1918	0-4-4T ex 380	481	1866	ex SNE
461	1866	ex SNE		1868	2-4-0 417 class
	1877	0-6-0 ex 663		1910	0-6-OT 782 class
	1881	2-4-0 ex 617	482	1866	ex SNE
	1911	0-4-4T 439 class		1868	2-4-0 417 class
462	1866	ex SNE		1905	2-4-0 ex 1452
	1877	0-6-0 ex 666		1908	0-4-2 ex 657
	1881	2-4-0 ex 618		1922	0-6-OT ex 418
	1911	0-4-4T 439 class	483	1866	ex SNE
463	1866	ex SNE	-484	1868	2-4-0 417 class
	1877	0-6-0 ex 667		1910	0-6-OT 782 class
	1881	2-4-0 ex 619	485	1866	ex SNE
	1908	0-4-OST		1868	2-4-0 417 class
	1918	0-4-4T ex 384		1878	0-4-0 Crane Tank
464	1866	ex SNE		1899	0-6-OT 782 class
	1877	0-6-0 ex 668	486	1866	ex SNE
	1881	2-4-0 ex 620		1872	2-2-2 ex 451
	1906	2-4-0 ex 1053		1878	2-2-2WT ex 530
	1907	0-4-4T 439 class		1881	0-6-OST 486 class
465	1866	ex SNE		1914	Blank
	1877	2-4-0 ex 473		1915	0-4-2 ex 161
	1906	2-4-0 ex 1442		1922	0-6-OT ex 430
	1907	0-4-4T 439 class	487	1866	ex SNE
466	1866	ex SNE		1877	2-2-2 ex 444
	1868	2-4-0 98 class		1880	0-4-2 ex 255
	1876	2-4-0 ex 636		1881	0-6-OST 486 class
				1914	Blank
	1906	2-4-0 ex 1594		1915	0-4-2 ex 159
	1907	0-4-4T 439 class		1922	0-6-OT ex 432
467	1866	ex SNE	488	1866	ex SNE
-469	1868	2-4-0 98 class		1873	0-4-4WT 488 class
	1876	2-4-0 ex 637-9		1881	0-6-OST 486 class
	1909	0-4-4T 439 class		1919	Blank
470	1866	ex SNE		1922	0-6-OT ex 433
	1868	2-4-0 98 class	489	1866	ex SNE
	1876	2-4-0 ex 640		1873	0-4-4WT 488 class
	1907	0-4-4T 439 class		1881	0-6-OST 486 class
471	1866	ex SNE		1922	0-6-OT ex 434
	1868	2-4-0 98 class	490	1866	ex SNE
	1876	2-4-0 ex 641	-491	1874	0-4-4WT 488 class
	1911	0-6-OT 782 class		1881	0-6-OST 486 class
472	1866	ex SNE		1922	0-6-OT ex 435/6
	1868	2-4-0 472 class	492	1866	ex SNE
	1876	2-4-0 ex 642	-497	1875	0-6-OST 536 class
	1907	0-6-OT 782 class		1903	0-8-OT
473	1866	ex SNE	498	1866	ex SNE

544	1870	2-4-0 372 class	621	1874	0-4-2 324 class
-547	1892	0-6-0 294 class	-626	1900	0-4-0ST 264 class
548	1870	2-4-0 372 class	627	1874	0-4-2 324 class
-549	1892	0-6-0 294 class	-628	1902	0-4-0ST 264 class
	1918	0-6-0 ex 308/9	629	1874	0-4-2 324 class
550	1870	2-4-0 372 class	-630	1907	0-6-0T 782 class
-551	1892	0-6-0 294 class	631	1874	0-6-0 631 class
552	1870	0-4-2 552 class		1900	0-4-2 ex 1567
	1892	0-6-0 294 class		1904	0-6-0T 782 class
553	1870	0-4-2 552 class	632	1874	0-6-0 631 class
	1892	0-6-0 294 class		1900	0-4-2 ex 1318
	1918	0-6-0 ex 311		1904	0-6-0T 782 class
554	1870	0-4-2 552 class	633	1874	0-6-0 631 class
-557	1892	0-6-0 294 class	-634	1901	Blank
558	1870	0-4-2 552 class		1904	0-6-0T 782 class
	1892	0-6-0 294 class	635	1874	0-6-0 631 class
	1918	0-6-0 ex 312		1901	Blank
559	1870	0-4-2 552 class		1902	2-4-0 ex 1544
-561	1893	0-6-0 294 class		1904	0-6-0T 782 class
562	1868	2-2-2 ex 454/5	636	1875	2-4-0 615 class
-563	1870	0-4-0ST ex 139/40		1876	0-6-0 631 class
	1871	0-4-2 552 class		1902	0-4-2 ex 1565
	1893	0-6-0 294 class		1904	0-6-0T 782 class
564	1871	0-4-2 552 class	637	1875	2-4-0 615 class
-582	1896	0-6-0 711 class	-638	1876	0-6-0 631 class
583	1872	2-4-0 583 class		1904	0-6-0T 782 class
-589	1897	0-6-0 711 class	639	1875	2-4-0 615 class
590	1871	0-4-0ST ex 562/3		1876	0-6-0 631 class
-591	1872	2-4-0 583 class		1904	2-4-0 ex 1551
	1897	0-6-0 711 class		1905	0-6-0T 782 class
592	1871	0-4-0ST ex 141	640	1875	2-4-0 615 class
	1872	2-4-0 583 class		1876	0-6-0 631 class
	1897	0-6-0 294 class		1904	0-6-0T 782 class
593	1872	2-4-0 583 class	641	1875	2-4-0 615 class
-594	1897	0-6-0 294 class		1876	0-6-0 631 class
595	1872	0-4-2 324 class		1905	0-6-0T 782 class
-599	1897	0-6-0 294 class	642	1875	2-4-0 615 class
600	1872	0-4-2 324 class		1876	0-6-0 631 class
-601	1901	0-8-0 600 class		1903	0-4-2 ex 1611
602	1872	0-4-2 324 class		1905	0-6-0T 782 class
	1902	Blank	643	1875	2-4-0 615 class
	1903	0-8-0 600 class		1876	0-6-0 631 class
603	1872	0-4-2 324 class		1905	0-6-0T 782 class
-607	1903	0-8-0 600 class	644	1876	0-6-0 631 class
608	1872	0-4-2 324 class		1898	0-4-2 ex 566A
	1910	0-4-2 ex 1604		1905	0-6-0T 782 class
	1910	0-6-0T 782 class	645	1876	0-6-0 631 class
609	1872	0-4-2 324 class		1903	0-4-2 ex 1563
	1910	0-6-0T 782 class		1905	0-6-0T 782 class
610	1872	0-4-2 324 class	646	1876	0-6-0 631 class
	1904	0-4-2 ex 1332		1901	Blank
	1910	0-6-0T 782 class		1904	0-4-2 ex 1579
611	1872	0-4-2 324 class		1905	0-6-0T 782 class
-614	1895	0-4-0ST 264 class	647	1876	0-6-0 631 class
615	1873	2-2-2 ex 54		1901	0-4-2 ex 1327
	1874	2-4-0 615 class		1905	0-6-0T 782 class
	1881	0-4-2 ex 243	648	1876	0-6-0 631 class
	1889	0-4-0ST 264 class		1904	0-4-2 ex 1607
616	1874	2-4-0 615 class		1905	0-6-0T 782 class
-620	1881	0-4-2 ex 244-8	649	1876	0-6-0 631 class
	1889	0-4-0ST 264 class	-650	1905	0-6-0T 782 class

651	1876	0-6-0 631 class
	1898	0-4-2 ex 560A
	1912	0-6-0T 782 class
652	1876	0-6-0 631 class
	1902	0-4-2 ex 1552
	1908	0-6-0 652 class
653	1876	0-6-0 631 class
	1899	0-4-2 ex 282
	1908	0-6-0 652 class
654	1876	0-6-0 631 class
	1905	0-4-2 ex 1621
	1908	0-6-0 652 class
655	1876	0-6-0 631 class
	1893	0-4-2 ex 561A
	1906	0-4-4T 439 class
	1918	0-6-0 ex 423
656	1876	0-6-0 631 class
	1904	0-4-2 ex 1622
	1908	0-6-0 652 class
657	1876	0-6-0 631 class
	1899	0-4-2 ex 283
	1908	0-6-0 652 class
658	1876	0-6-0 631 class
	1901	0-4-2 ex 1315
	1908	0-6-0 652 class
659	1876	0-6-0 631 class
	1904	0-4-2 ex 1603
	1908	0-6-0 652 class
660	1873	0-6-0 ex 488
	1877	0-6-0 631 class
	1900	0-4-2 ex 1334
	1906	0-4-4T 439 class
661	1874	0-6-0 ex 490
	1877	0-6-0 631 class
	1899	0-4-2 ex 284
	1918	0-6-0 ex 460
662	1874	0-6-0 ex 491
	1877	0-6-0 631 class
	1904	0-4-2 ex 1626
	1908	0-6-0 652 class
663	1874	0-6-0 ex 492
	1877	0-6-0 631 class
	1900	0-4-2 ex 1326
	1908	0-6-0 652 class
664	1875	0-6-0 ex 497
	1877	0-6-0 631 class
	1902	0-4-2 ex 1555
	1908	0-6-0 652 class
665	1875	0-6-0 ex 500
	1877	0-6-0 631 class
	1900	0-4-2 ex 1321
	1908	0-6-0 652 class
666	1875	0-6-0 ex 493
	1877	0-6-0 631 class
	1902	Blank
	1906	0-4-2 ex 1614
	1907	0-4-4T 439 class
667	1875	0-6-0 ex 494/5
-668	1877	0-6-0 631 class
	1907	0-6-0T 782 class
669	1875	0-6-0 ex 496

	1877	0-6-0 631 class
	1904	0-4-2 ex 1613
	1907	0-6-0T 782 class
670	1876	0-6-0 ex 498/9
-671	1877	0-4-2 ex 674/5
	1878	0-4-2 670 class
	1919	0-6-0 300 class
672	1876	2-4-0 ex 501
	1878	0-4-2 670 class
	1919	0-6-0 300 class
673	1876	2-4-0 ex 502
	1877	2-2-2 ex 311
	1878	0-4-2 670 class
	1919	0-6-0 300 class
674	1876	0-4-2 ex 504
	1877	2-2-2 ex 315
	1878	0-4-2 670 class
	1919	0-6-0 300 class
675	1876	0-4-2 ex 505
	1877	2-2-2 ex 319
	1878	0-4-2 670 class
	1919	0-6-0 300 class
676*	1875	0-4-0ST ex 116/7
-677	1877	2-2-2 ex 322/3
	1878	0-4-2 670 class
	1919	0-6-0 300 class
678	1877	0-4-0ST ex 455
	1878	0-4-2 670 class
	1919	0-6-0 300 class
679	1877	0-4-0T ex 450
	1878	0-4-2 670 class
	1919	0-6-0 300 class
680	1877	0-4-2 ex 451
	1879	Blank
	1880	2-4-0 ex 166
	1881	2-4-0 ex 167
	1884	0-6-0 294 class
	1918	0-6-0 ex 313
681	1877	0-4-2 ex 511
	1884	0-6-0 294 class
682	1877	0-4-2 ex 512
	1881	2-4-0 ex 168
	1884	0-6-0 294 class
	1918	0-6-0 ex 314
683	1877	0-4-2 ex 513
	1884	0-6-0 294 class
684	1877	0-4-2 ex 515
	1884	0-6-0 294 class
685	1877	0-4-2 ex 522
	1884	0-6-0 294 class
686	1877	0-4-2 ex 516-9
-689	1884	0-6-0 294 class
690	1877	0-4-2 ex 520
	1884	Blank
	1885	0-6-0 294 class
691	1877	0-4-2 ex 521
	1885	0-6-0 294 class
	1892	0-6-0 294 class

* see page no 37 regarding 676/7

692	1877	0-4-2 ex 523-6
-695	1885	0-6-0 294 class
	1892	0-6-0 294 class
696	1877	0-4-2 ex 527
	1886	Blank
	1892	0-6-0 294 class
697	1876	0-4-2 ex 506
	1886	Blank
	1893	0-6-0 294 class
698	1877	0-4-2 ex 449
	1880	Blank
	1881	2-4-0 ex 169
	1882	0-4-2 ex 180
	1890	Blank
	1893	0-6-0 294 class
699	1877	0-4-2 ex 507
	1882	0-4-2 ex 183
	1887	Blank
	1893	0-6-0 294 class
700	1877	0-4-2 ex 508-10
-702	1881	0-4-2 670 class
	1888	Blank
	1893	0-6-0 294 class
703	1877	2-2-2 ex 314
	1881	0-4-2 670 class
	1888	Blank
	1894	0-6-0 294 class
	1918	0-6-0 ex 316
704	1878	0-4-2 ex 670
	1881	0-4-2 670 class
	1888	Blank
	1894	0-6-0 294 class
705	1878	0-4-2 ex 671
	1881	0-4-2 670 class
	1888	Blank
	1894	0-6-0 294 class
	1918	0-6-0 ex 317
706	1878	2-4-0 ex 672
	1880	Blank
	1881	0-4-2 670 class
	1888	Blank
	1894	0-6-0 294 class
707	1878	0-4-2 ex 528/9
-708	1881	0-4-2 670 class
	1888	Blank
	1894	0-6-0 294 class
	1918	0-6-0 ex 320/1
709	1878	0-4-2 ex 531
	1881	0-4-2 670 class
	1888	Blank
	1895	0-6-0 294 class
710	1878	2-2-2 ex 673
	1880	Blank
	1881	0-4-2 670 class
	1888	Blank
	1895	0-6-0 294 class
711	1878	2-2-2 ex 674/5
-712	1881	0-4-2 670 class
	1888	Blank
	1895	0-6-0 711 class
713	1878	2-2-2 ex 676/7
-714	1882	0-4-2 670 class
	1888	Blank
	1895	0-6-0 711 class
715	1878	0-4-0ST ex 678
	1882	0-4-2 670 class
	1888	Blank
	1896	0-6-0 711 class
716	1878	0-4-0T ex 679
	1882	0-4-2 670 class
	1888	Blank
717	1896	0-6-0 711 class
-718	1882	0-4-2 670 class
	1888	Blank
	1896	0-6-0 711 class
719	1881	0-4-0T ex 716
	1882	0-4-2 670 class
	1888	Blank
	1896	0-6-0 711 class
720	1881	0-4-2 ex 705
	1888	Blank
	1896	0-6-0 711 class
721	1881	2-2-2 ex 713 allotted
	1881	0-4-2 ex 704
	1886	Blank
	1896	4-4-0 721 class
722	1881	2-2-2 ex 714
	1881	0-4-2 ex 708
	1887	Blank
	1896	4-4-0 721 class
723	1881	2-2-2 ex 712 allotted
	1881	0-4-2 ex 709
	1883	Blank
	1896	4-4-0 721 class
724	1881	0-4-2 ex 700
	1882	0-4-2 ex 179
	1885	Blank
	1896	4-4-0 721 class
725	1881	0-4-2 ex 701
	1882	2-4-0 ex 188
	1889	Blank
	1896	4-4-0 721 class
726	1896	4-4-0 721 class
-735		
736		
-749		
750	1897	0-6-0 711 class
-765		
766	1897	4-4-0 766 class
-767		
768	1898	4-4-0 766 class
-780		
781	1897	0-4-0ST
	1912	0-6-0T 782 class
782	1898	0-6-0T 782 class
-811		
812	1899	0-6-0 812 class
-838		

839	1900	0-6-0 812 class
-878		
879	1900	0-4-4T 879 class
-886		
887	1900	4-4-0 900 class
-899		
900	1899	4-4-0 900 class
-902		
903	1906	4-6-0 903 class
-907		
908	1906	4-6-0 908 class
-917		
918	1906	4-6-0 918 class
-922		
923	1907	4-4-0 140 class
924	1908	4-4-0 140 class
-927		

928	1916	4-4-0 113 class
-937		
938	1915	4-6-0 938 class
-943		
944	1917	4-6-2T
-955		
956	1921	4-6-0 956 class
-959		
960	Blank	
-1000		

From 1898 numbers above 1000 were used
for the duplicate list, replacing the
previous 'A' suffix system.
Initially the numbering was at random
but from roughly 1900 the system was
gradually introduced whereby 1000 was
added to the Capital list numbers.

GLASGOW AND SOUTH WESTERN RAILWAY

INTRODUCTION

As already mentioned with reference to the Caledonian, the G&SW started as the Glasgow, Paisley, Kilmarnock and Ayr Railway which absorbed the former plate tramway from Kilmarnock to Troon and the Paisley and Renfrew Railway.

In 1846, after failing in the previous Session due to Caledonian opposition, the Glasgow, Dumfries and Carlisle Railway was authorised to join an extension of the GPK&A's Kilmarnock branch with the Caledonian line at Gretna. The Act provided that when the line was complete the GD&C and the GPK&A would amalgamate to form the G&SW which duly took effect on 28 October 1850.

In 1854 the railway from Kilwinning to Ardrossan, which had been constructed by the Glasgow, Paisley and Ardrossan Canal, was vested in the railway company. The canal, which had been open since 1811, ended at Johnstone and in 1827 obtained an Act authorising the building of a railway from the canal to Ardrossan where it had originally intended the canal should terminate. The scheme was overtaken however by the GPK&A, over a similar route and only the above section of railway was built. Since 1840 it had been separated from the canal management and had been run as a subsidiary company of the GPK&A. The canal, which offered considerable competition to the railway for both passenger and goods traffic, was to play a significant part in the formation of the G&SW system.

By a succession of small, originally independent companies which had working agreements with the G&SW, the coast line was extended from Ayr to Maybole in 1856, Girvan in 1860 and a connection made with the Portpatrick railway at Challoch Junction in 1877, giving access to Portpatrick and Stranraer.

As with the Portpatrick railway the main object of these extensions through sparsely populated country was the Irish traffic which was originally expected to concentrate on Portpatrick. However because of physical difficulties, after a great deal of money had been spent by the government and the LNWR, the packet service was switched to Stranraer in 1874.

Considerable traffic was generated from England for the Stranraer-Larne packet service and the Portpatrick Railway (after a period being worked by the Caledonian) was amalgamated with the Wigtownshire Railway in 1885 under a joint board of the Caledonian, G&SW, Midland and LNWR as the Portpatrick and Wigtownshire Joint Railway.

Irish traffic from Glasgow was not much attracted to the Stranraer route however. With the establishment of steam ships the shorter sea crossing (the original reason for the GP&A canal) no longer seemed so attractive and the direct sailings from Glasgow continued to be more popular.

Consequently the coast route south of Ayr was hardly profitable and the Girvan and Portpatrick Junction had to be rescued from insolvency by a consortium of bankers as the Ayrshire and Wigtownshire Railway before being finally absorbed into the G&SW in 1892.

The line from Dumfries to Castle Douglas, where the Portpatrick began, was completed under G&SW auspices in 1859 and continued to Kirkudbright in 1864. The route from Dumfries through Castle Douglas to Portpatrick, completed in 1861, was known as 'the Port Road'.

In 1869 the G&SW opened an independent line to Greenock and Gourock in competition with the Caledonian and in 1888 G&SW territory was invaded by the Lanarkshire and Ayrshire, an associated company of the Caledonian, with its line to Ardrossan.

The Glasgow, Barrhead and Kilmarnock Joint line was completed in 1873 and shortened the Glasgow-Dumfries route by 10 miles. From 1 May 1876 through trains were worked from the Midland Railway at Carlisle to Glasgow via this route following the completion of the MR Settle and Carlisle line. The old route to Carlisle via Paisley became known as 'the Long Road', a term mostly used by engine men to describe goods trains by this route.

Meanwhile the GP&A canal changed its name to Glasgow, Paisley and Johnstone and continued stiff opposition to the railway. An agreement was reached that the canal would cease to carry passengers in return for a guaranteed annual payment of £1358 and a rate-fixing agreement which favoured the carrying of coal by canal, but the railway found this agreement disadvantageous and in 1850 were successful in having it legally set aside. The canal was purchased by the railway in 1868 and in 1881 powers were obtained to convert the canal into a railway, the new 'canal line' being opened in 1885.

Various loop lines and branches were opened in Ayrshire and Renfrewshire between 1856 and 1906 and the Ardrossan line was extended up the coast to Largs. In the south the Cairn Valley Light Railway from Dumfries to Moniaive was opened in 1905.

Having experimented in the 1870s with Westinghouse brakes the G&SW eventually adopted automatic vacuum brakes as standard but, no doubt due to the proximity of the Westinghouse-fitted Caledonian Railway, many locomotives were dual fitted. London trains were Westinghouse to work with NB stock.

Except for locomotives designed by Drummond the driver's position on the footplate was on the right.

Passenger stock was of a high standard, not only the joint stock with the Midland for the through service between St Enoch (opened 1876) and St Pancras, but on other services also. On minor services the G&SW tended to offer a greater comfort than the equivalent on the Caledonian.

Locomotives were painted green from the time of Patrick Stirling, although the shade and lining changed at different periods. Manson adopted a dark olive green, Drummond a light olive green. A 'wine' colour tried out by Patrick Stirling on one or more of the 40 class 2-2-2s was not perpetuated. The 2 and 40 class singles had metal number plates, but his other locomotives had numbers painted on the cab sides. Under James Stirling numbers were painted on the butter beams with 'No' to the left of the coupling. Smellie painted the buffer beam vermilion and repeated the number on the tender surrounded by a garter. Manson put the company's initials on the tender and the number on the cab side except 8 class 4-4-0s and 306 class 0-6-0s. Footplate valances and steps were crimson lake. In 1897 the buffer beam number was transferred to the tender without 'No'. In 1920 it was decided to paint goods engines black, but only fifty were so treated by 1922 when green was reverted to until the introduction of LMS livery.

Passenger stock was painted dark green from 1847 until 1884 when a dark red very similar to the Midland red was adopted and the Company Coat of Arms added. Goods wagons were light grey with black metal work and white on black lettering.

Passenger traffic was heaviest between Glasgow and the coast, with many evening and weekend excursions at very cheap fares. Coal from the Ayrshire collieries accounted for a large proportion of the freight tonnage.

The 'Sou West' was very much a railway of character with a high degree of loyalty amongst its staff and many colourful individuals especially the enginemen. No doubt this was true of many railways at the time but it is due to the various books and magazine articles by David L. Smith that these have been so well and vividly recorded on the G&SW.

Locomotive Superintendents

Peter Robertson	1850-53	ex GPK&A since 1840. Resigned
Patrick Stirling	1853-66	Resigned
James Stirling	1866-78	Resigned
Hugh Smellie	1878-90	Resigned
James Manson	1890-1912	Retired
Peter Drummond	1911-1918	Died
Robert Harben Whitelegg	1918-1923	Formation of LMS
(Chief Mechanical Engineer from 1/1/1919)		

Peter Robertson had been with the GPK&A since 1840 and was succeeded by a man destined to become a very famous name in locomotive history though he is more normally associated with his next company, the Great Northern.

Patrick Stirling was apprenticed under his uncle, James Stirling at Dundee

Foundry then went to Neilson & Co at their Hyde Park works in Glasgow, becoming a shop foreman. After a period as Locomotive Superintendent of the Caledonian and Dumbartonshire Railway he went to work for Lawrence Hill at Port Glasgow on marine work and from there to R&W Hawthorn at Newcastle-on-Tyne.

In 1853 he was appointed to the G&SW at the age of thirty three having been recommended by Hawthorns. From 1860 he adopted the domeless boiler and much of his work on the G&SW foreshadows his even greater achievements on the Great Northern.

He was responsible for planning and opening Kilmarnock works in 1856.

James Stirling was Patrick's younger brother and had been apprenticed on the G&SW under Patrick Stirling. After a year spent working as a fitter at Sharp Stewart & Co in Manchester he returned to the drawing office at Kilmarnock, later becoming Works Manager.

He continued the basic designs of his brother, in particular the domeless boiler and in 1874 perfected a steam reversing gear which was widely used on G&SW locos. He resigned in 1878 to take up a similar position on the South Eastern.

Hugh Smellie had also worked his way up with the company and had succeeded James Stirling as Works Manager.

In 1870 he was appointed Locomotive Engineer to the Maryport and Carlisle Railway and returned from there to the G&SW to replace Stirling. He was concerned with the experiments with continuous brakes, eventually adopting automatic vacuum.

He built up a reputation for sound economic design in his locomotives, continuing the Stirling tradition of domeless boilers. He fitted his 22 class six-coupled goods engines with steam brakes.

After his departure to the Caledonian, James Manson was the man most associated with the company. He, too, was a Kilmarnock-trained man. During 1870-8 he served with the Bibby Line, sailing between the Mersey and the Mediterranian, rising from Third Engineer to Chief Engineer. In 1878 he returned to the G&SW as Works Manager at Kilmarnock leaving again when appointed Locomotive Superintendent of the Great North of Scotland in 1883.

On his return to take charge at Kilmarnock, his final and longest appointment, he set about producing some of the company's most successful designs with domed boilers and, later, superheaters.

He introduced the automatic tablet exchanger and in the interests of saving injury to engine men in hand exchanging refused to patent it.

Although a courteous and humane man he was not always just with his discipline of subordinates, being inclined to order drastic demotions not always fairly deserved. Drummond was said to be so appalled when he took over that he ordered some to be reversed.

Peter Drummond was the younger brother of Dugald Drummond and was steeped in his brother's locomotive designs having worked under him in turn on the LBSC, NB and Caledonian. In 1896 he became Locomotive C&W Superintendent on the Highland Railway (qv).

On his appointment to the G&SW he introduced a complete change of policy, designing some very large and powerful locomotives. Although the superheated ones were better these designs cannot be regarded as entirely successful, being sluggish and heavy on coal.

He also, unaccountably, changed the driver's position from right to left-hand side of the footplate.

Whitelegg, who had designed the 4-6-4Ts on the London, Tilbury and Southend, resigned from the railway when the LT&S was taken over by the Midland and entered into a partnership in an agricultural engineering firm and also did some consultative work. In 1917 he joined the Admiralty.

Taking up his appointment with the G&SW he found its locomotives and works like many other railways at the time, were very run down after the war. He intended to completely reboiler all the locomotives built before Drummond, reducing the number of boiler types in use from 37 to 10 which were to include those designed by Drummond. Only three had been produced however by 1923, designated X1-X3 and the scheme was not completed, although boilers built were fitted by the LMS.

The 4-6-4T design he produced was a larger version of the LTSR design intended for the fast trams from Glasgow to the coast. He had designs in hand for a 4-4-4T and a 4-6-6T, but these plans were overhauled by the amalgamation of the G&SW into the Northern Division of the LMS on 1 January 1923. Whitelegg then left railway service once again to become General Manager of Beyer Peacock & Co in Manchester.

The rebuilds of the Manson locos were not a great success and in fact the general impression in retrospect is that good locomotives had been spoiled and Manson, still living in retirement, is said to have been saddened by the spectacle.

This and the fact that the G&SW boilers did not fit readily into the standardisation schemes introduced by the LMS led to the early scrapping of G&SW locos and by 1948 when British Railways took over, only one was left, itself scrapped only four months later.

Duplicate List

Until 1878 locomotives on the Duplicate List literally duplicated the numbers of their replacements.

Smellie introduced the 'R' list (R1-R49). The last locomotives to be given R numbers were 0-4-0s 92/3 in 1/1890 (R47/8) and 0-4-2s 147/8 (R8 and R49) in 7/1890.

From 11/1890 Manson changed to an 'A' list system for duplicates but did not renumber the locomotives on Smellie's 'R' list, which was allowed to fall out of use gradually as locos were broken up.

Under the 1919 renumbering scheme when locos were given groups of numbers according to wheel arrangement the duplicate stock was kept separate from the capital stock being given groups of numbers from 560 up. At this date two locos, both 0-4-0s still survived in the 'R' list (R12 and R39) and were given numbers 732/3. The whole of the 1919 renumbering was carried out between March and June of that year.

GLASGOW AND SOUTH WESTERN RAILWAY

CONSTITUENT COMPANIES

Glasgow, Paisley, Kilmarnock and Ayr

Incorporated 1837. Opened Ayr to Irvine 3 August 1839, to Kilwinning 23 March 1840, Glasgow to Paisley 14 July 1840, to Howood (temporary station) 21 July 1840, Kilwinning to Beith 21 July 1840, throughout Glasgow to Ayr 12 August 1840, Dalry to Kilmarnock branch 4 April 1843, extension to Auchinleck 9 August 1848, to Cumnock 20 May 1850. Line from Glasgow Bridge Street to Paisley joint with Glasgow, Paisley and Greenock.

45 locomotives as under: Not numbered until 1847 and numbers probably not carried.

2-2-0 Built by Stark & Fulton (SF)
        Bury & Co (B)
DW 5ft 6in, LW 4ft 0in, Cyls 12 x 18*, Wt 10 tons. Four-wheel tenders. Bury type with inside bar frames ordered against the stated preference of John Miller, the engineer, for Stephenson type six-wheel locos. He disclaimed all liability for the consequences of the decision but they gave good service in fact. *SF locos sometimes recorded as 13 x 18.

No	Name	Date		G&SW no 1850	
1	*Mercury*	7/1839	SF	1	Sold 6/1860
2	*Mazeppa*	7/1839	SF	2	Scrapped 1855/6
3	*Marmion*	9/1839	B	3	Scrapped 1855/6
4	*Cutty Sark*	2/1840	B	4	Scrapped 1855/6

Nos 1 and 3 extensively renewed 1846
No 4 hauled inaugral train from Glasgow to Ayr with no 5 11/8/1840.

2-2-2 Built by Kinmond, Hutton & Steel (KHS)
        Thomas Edington & Sons (E)
        Stark & Fulton (SF)
DW 5ft 6in, TW 3ft 6in, Cyls 13 x 18, Stephenson sandwich frame type to Miller's specification, dome on first ring of boiler cover with spring balance safety valve on top. Raised firebox with second valve over it. Minor details probably differed between the makers and Edington locos had a second dome with safety valve over firebox. Delivery much delayed and criticism of workmanship resulted in arbitration between the company and Stark & Fulton, carried out by Murdoch Aitken & Co, settled in the latter's favour. Dugald Bannatyne Stark had been appointed Locomotive Superintendent on 10/6/1840 but was suspended as a result of the above dispute. Miller resigned 7/10/1840 and Peter Robertson took over. Committee minutes also record criticism of Edington locos.

No	Name	Date		G&SW no 1850	
5	*Wallace*	8/1840	KHS*	5	Scrapped 1855/6
6	*Bruce*	9/1840	KHS	6	Scrapped 1855/6
7	*Phoenix*	9/1840	E	7	Replaced 1872
		1852			Rebuilt 0-4-0 or 2-4-0 Cyls 15 x 20
8	*Dunlop***	1840	E	8	Sold 7/1847
	Possibly renamed *Prince Albert*				
9	*Kelburne*	1840	SF*	9	Scrapped 1855/6
10	*Garnock*	1841	SF*	10	Sold 1851
11	*Eglinton*	1841	KHS	11	Replaced 1860

12	*Portland*	1841 KHS	12	Withdrawn 11/1857
13	*Ailsa*	1841 SF	13	
		1852/3		Rebuilt. Sold 6/1860
14	*Loudoun*	1841 SF	14	Replaced 1857
15	*Blair***	1841 E	15	Sold 2/1847
16	*Daldowie***	1841 E*	16	Sold 2/1847
	Possibly renamed			
	Queen			

*Lowe records no 5 as SF, no 9 as KHS, no 10 as E and no 16 as SF. C/f MacLennan Steel *Dundee's Iron Horses* p26 for KHS locos which agrees with above listing and with Smith.

**Lowe and SLS (1950) give *Prince Albert* as original name for no 8. Lowe states sold 7/1847 to L&NW and renamed *Dunlop* but this is not confirmed by L&NW records and as several of the other locos have local names it seems more likely that it was named after the Ayrshire town of that name. Lowe and SLS (1950) give the name *Kyle* for no 15 instead of *Blair* which is given by Smith. Lowe and SLS (1950) give *Queen* as the original name for no 16 instead of *Daldowie* as given by Smith.

2-2-0 Built by E. Bury & Co.
DW 5ft 6in, Cyls 13 x 18, Cylinders of no 18 were given as 14in diameter in 1844. Lowe records both these locos as built by Stark & Fulton in 1839, but Smith quotes Board minutes that they were ordered in 1840 after a meeting in August 1840 attended by James Kennedy, E. Bury's foreman.

			G&SW	
No	Name	Date	no 1850	
18	*Stuart*	1/1841	18	Rebuilt 7/1853. Sold 6/1860
19	*Bute*	1/1841	19	Rebuilt 1852
				Replaced 1858

0-4-0 Built by E. Bury & Co.
DW 5ft 0in, Cyls 13 x 18, Cylinders recorded as 13 x 20 in 1845. Goods engines.

			G&SW	
No	Name	Date	no 1850	
17	*Clairmont*	2/1841	17	Replaced 1857
20	*Arran*	7/1841	20	Sold 8/1849 to Sykes & Wardrop after being on loan to contractor named Strap. S&W were contractors for GD&C but must have resold the loco back to company as resold 17/3/1855 by G&SW

2-2-2 Built by Kinmond Hutton & Steel
DW 5ft 6in, LW & TW 3ft 6in, Cyls as below. Purchased from stock and said to be as 5 class.

		Date	Date		G&SW	
No	Name	built	to stock	Cyls	no 1850	
21	*Burns*	1843	3/1843	14x18	21	Replaced 1859
26	*Mars*	1845	1845	13x18	26	Sold 6/1860

Nos 21 & 12 headed opening train on Kilmarnock branch 4/4/1843.

0-4-0 Built by E. Bury & Co.
DW 5ft 0in, Cyls 14 x 22. Mineral engines for Glangarnock Ironworks traffic.

No	Name	Date	G&SW no 1850	
22	*Logie*	1843	22	Replaced 1860
23	*Miller*	1843	23	Withdrawn 12/1857

0-4-0 Built by Bury, Curtis & Kennedy
DW 5ft 0in, Cyls 14 x 20. Further engines for mineral traffic.

No	Name	Date	G&SW no 1850	
24	*Milo*	1845	24	Withdrawn 12/1857
25	*Pluto*	1845	25	Sold 6/1860

2-2-2 Built by GPK&A at Cook St, Glasgow
DW 5ft 6in, LW & TW 3ft 6in, Cyls 13½ x 18 O/S, THS 455.5 sq ft. Said to be to Peter Robertson's design. Inside frames, dome on centre of boiler with spring balance safety valve. D.K. Clarke *Railway Machinery* gives Cyls 14 x 18 for no 31.

No	Name	Date	G&SW no 1850	
27	*Thunderbolt*	10/1845	27	Sold 1866
28	*Lightning*	4/1846	28	Replaced 1864
29	*Firebrand*	10/1846	29	Replaced 1864
31	*Orion*	3/1847	31	Replaced 1864

No 31 headed opening train on Muirkirk branch 9/8/1848

2-2-2 Built by Caird & Co in 1840
DW 5ft 0in, Cyls 13 x 18. Purchased from stock.

No	Name	Date	G&SW no 1850	
30	*Wasp*	3/1846	30	Withdrawn 3/1855

0-4-0 Built by Bury, Curtis & Kennedy
DW 5ft 0in, Cyls 13 x 20. Mineral engines.

No	Name	Date	G&SW no 1850	
32	*Victoria*	4/1846	32	Withdrawn 11/1857
33	*Vulcan*	5/1846	33	Replaced 1857
34	*Cyclops*	10/1846	34	Withdrawn 11/1857
35	*Minerva*	10/1846	35	Sold 6/1860
36	*Saturn*	1/1847	36	Replaced 1858
37	*Jupiter*	1/1847	37	Sold 6/1860

2-2-2 Built by Kinmond, Hutton & Steel
DW 5ft 6in, Cyls 13 x 18 O/S. Said to be similar to 27 class.

No	Name	Date	G&SW no 1850	
38	*North Star*	1846	38	Withdrawn 11/1857
39	*Meteor*	1846	39	Replaced 1861
40	*Planet*	1846	40	Replaced 1860
41	*Comet*	1846	41	Sold 6/1860

0-4-0 Built by Neilson and Mitchell. Works nos 8 & 9
DW 5ft 0in, Cyls 13 x 18. Probably maker's design of goods engine.

No	Name	Date	G&SW no 1850	
42	*Nimrod*	1846	42	Replaced 1862
43	*Actaeon*	1846	43	Replaced 1862

2-2-2 Built by GPK&A at Cook St, Glasgow
DW 5ft 6in, Cyls 14 x 18. Larger boiler than 27 class.

No	Name	Date	G&SW no 1850	
44	*Altas*	1847	**44**	Sold 6/1865
45	*Vesuvius*	1848	**45**	Replaced 1865

Some singles were fitted with Robertson design of steam brake.

Kilmarnock and Troon 4ft 0in gauge

Incorporated 1808. Opened 6 July 1812 as plate tramway. Leased to GPK&A 16 July 1846 and converted to standard gauge conventional railway for locomotive haulage. Conversion completed 1 March 1847. Prior to conversion horse haulage only was used. A Stephenson locomotive is reputed to have been tried out on the plateway in about 1816/17, but found too heavy for the track. After conversion the line was worked by the GPK&A/G&SW but in 1851 the following locomotives were acquired purely for the purpose of shunting at Troon Harbour.

2 locomotives as under, not taken into G&SW stock.

0-4-0T Built by Neilson & Co. Works nos 48/9
  DW 4ft 0in, Cyls 14 x 20

  Dates of withdrawal not known.

Paisley and Renfrew 4ft 6in gauge

Incorporated 1835. Opened 3 April 1837. Company sold to GPK&A 22 July 1847 and powers granted to alter the line to standard gauge (carried out in 1866).

3 locomotives as under: All out of use from March 1842 when horse haulage was adopted in preference.

2-2-0 Built by Robert Stephenson & Co 1831
      Purchased from Glasgow, Garnkirk & Coatbridge for £350

  DW 4ft 6in, Cyls 10 x 14. See page no 14
  Name
  St Rollox Sold by auction 12/1848

2-2-2 Built by Murdoch Aitken & Co.
  Dimensions not known
  Name
  Paisley   Sold by auction 12/1848
  Renfrew   Sold by auction 12/1848

Glasgow, Dumfries and Carlisle

Incorporated 1846. Opened Dumfries to Gretna Junction (connection with Caledonian) 23 August 1848, Dumfries to Closeburn 15 October 1849, Cumnock to Old Cumnock (connection with Cumnock extension of GPK&A) 20 May 1850, throughout 28 October 1850. The Act of incorporation provided that when complete the company would amalgamate with the GPK&A to form the G&SW. The locomotives were ordered by the GPK&A on behalf of the GD&C and GPK&A worked the uncompleted portions as they were opened. The G&SW therefore came into existence on 28 October 1850 and the GD&C locos were numbered from 46 to 85 following the GPK&A numbers which were retained.

40 locomotives as under: All ordered 9/1847 but 3 Bury and several Hawthorn
locos had their delivery deferred at the request of the GPK&A. This caused
much confusion in Hawthorn's works with locos being switched to other orders,
in particular Great Northern nos 51-6, and making exact building dates and
works numbers difficult to ascertain.

0-4-2 Built by Bury, Curtis & Kennedy
   DW 5ft 0in, TW 3ft 4in, Cyls 16 x 24, WB 8ft 0in + 6ft 9in, THS 1028 sq ft,
   Wt 22½ tons. 6-wheel version of standard Bury locomotive with bar frames,
   raised firebox (c/f LNW (S Div) 6 class, Vol 2A, p70). Used on goods trams
   but not found very satisfactory.

Date	1850 no	
1848	46	Replaced 1862
1848	47	Replaced 1862. Sold for scrap 8/1865
1848	48	Replaced 1863
1848	49	Replaced 1863. Sold for scrap 8/1865
1848	50	Replaced 1863. Sold for scrap 8/1865
1848	51	Replaced 1863
1848	52	Withdrawn 8/1865 and sold for scrap
1848	53	Withdrawn 8/1865 and sold for scrap
1848	54	Withdrawn 8/1865 and sold for scrap
1848	55	Replaced 1865
1849	56	Built 1848 delivery held back. Replaced 1865
1849	57	Built 1848 delivery held back. Replaced 1865
1849	58	Built 1848 delivery held back. Replaced 1866

2-2-2 Built by Kinmonds & Co
   DW 6ft 0in, LW & TW 3ft 6in, Cyls 15 x 20, WB 5ft 4in + 7ft 0in, Wt 19 tons.

Name	Date	1850 no	Replaced
Dumfries	1848	77	1869
Glasgow	1848	78	1870
Carlisle	1848	79	1868
Solway	1848	80	1869
Afton	1848	81	1868
Queen	1848	82	1869
Albert	1848	83	1869
Princess	1848	84	1868
Nith	11/1848	85	1869

   later renamed
   Nithsdale

2-4-0 Built by R & W Hawthorn. Works nos 691-6
   DW 5ft 0in, LW 3ft 6in, Cyls 15 x 21, WB 6ft 0½in + 7ft 9½in, WP 80lbs/sq
   in. Central dome.

Date	1850 no	Replaced
1848	59	1870
1848	60	1870
1848	61	1868
1848	62	1871
1849	63	1870
1849	64	1871

2-2-2 Built by R & W Hawthorn. Delivery deferred.
   DW 6ft 0in, LW & TW 3ft 6in, Cyls 15 x 21, WB 7ft 0in + 6ft 10in, THS 907
   sq ft, WP 80 lbs/sq in. Central dome, outside frames 1,200 gallon tenders.

No	Date	Replaced
71	1850	1870
72	1850	1870

73	1851	1869
74	1851	1870
75	1851	1870
76	1851	1870

0-4-0 Built by R & W Hawthorn. Delivery deferred.
DW 5ft 0in, Cyls as below, WP 80 lbs/sq in, four-wheel 800 gallon tenders.
Possibly had domeless boilers.

No	Date	Cyls	Replaced
65	1850	15x18	1871
66	1851	15x21	1871
67	1852	15x21	1872
68	1852	15x21	1873
69	1852	15x21	1871
70	1852	15x20	1872

Ardrossan and Johnstone 4ft 6in gauge

Incorporated 1827. Opened 1831. Constructed by Glasgow, Paisley and Ardrossan
Canal from Kilwinning to Ardrossan for horse haulage. Section from Kilwinning
to end of canal at Johnstone, although authorised, never built. Act of 23
July 1840 separated railway from Canal Company and name changed to **Ardrossan**
as virtually a subsidiary company of the GPK&A. Altered to standard gauge and
double tracked for locomotive haulage by 8/1840 and connected to GPK&A at
Kilwinning. Company vested in G&SW by Act of 24 July 1854.

6 locomotives as under: (two unidentified)*

0-4-0 Built by Barr & Mcnab, Paisley
  DW not known, Cyls 12 x 18, Bury type.

Name	Date	
Firefly	7/1840	Possibly renamed *Fire King*
King Cole	8/1840	

0-4-0 Builders unknown
  Dimensions unknown. Bury type goods engine.
  Possible

Name	Date	
Tam o'Shanter	1841	To G&SW **10** 1854. Replaced 1861

2-2-2 Built by Neilson & Co. Works nos 22/3 c1848
  DW 5ft 6in, Cyls 13 x 18.

  Names and subsequent history of these two locomotives are obscure. See note
  below*

0-4-0 Builder unknown
  Dimensions unknown

  One locomotive acquired c1854. See note below*

*David L. Smith carried out exhaustive research on these locomotives in all
the available records and he indicated in his book (p20) that the published
histories (Ahrons *Loco Mag*, April 1922, *SLS Journal* June 1934, and the SLS
history of the G&SW, 1950) do not tally with the contemporary reports in
their account of these locos. All the above histories give the names of the
two Neilson singles as *Tam o'Shanter* and *Soutar Johnny* taken into G&SW
stock as nos 10 and 16 and refer to two further Bury type 0-4-0s named
Eglinton and *Blair*. However a report on 31/1/1855 after the takeover
recommends that only *Tam o'Shanter* which it describes as a goods engine be

taken into stock at a valuation of £500. This must therefore refer to one of
the 0-4-Os. Two other locos are identified in the report, *Fire King* (which
may be a renaming of *Firefly*) and *King Cole*, valued at £200 each, the other
three being valued only at a combined scrap value of £165. The Company's half
yearly reports make it clear that from 31/12/1841 there were three four-wheel
locomotives and from 12/12/1848 the number of locomotives is reported to be
five which would include the two Neilson locos. In a later report there is a
reference to a locomotive being rebuilt in December 1852. There is no record
of the acquisition of the sixth locomotive although the SLS (1950) makes
reference to a mysterious 'steam car' being operated in the 1840s. It is
possible to speculate that the 1852 rebuild was to one of the Neilson locos
and that this is the *Tam o'Shanter* referred to in 1855 but this seems
unlikely and still does not explain why the other Neilson loco should be
considered as scrap after only seven years service. Similarly it is tempting
to suggest that the GPK&A *Eglinton* and *Blair* (pages 127-8)found their way
onto the Androssan at second or third-hand, but again this seems most unlikely
as they were Stephenson-type singles not Bury-type 0-4-Os.

Wigtownshire

Incorporated 1872. Opened Newton Stewart to Wigtown 3 April 1875, to Millisle
2 August 1875, Garlieston branch 3 April 1876, throughout to Whithorn 9 July
1877. Laid with flat bottom rails. Transferred to Portpatrick and Wigtownshire
Joint by Act 6 August 1885. Locomotives provided by Thomas Wheatley as
contractor and subsequently his son W.T. Wheatley. Light green livery (except
no 3), Coaches (ex LNW) had oak graining.

8 locomotives as under:

2-2-2WT Built by North British at St Margarets 1856.
        Purchased by Wheatley 1875/7
  DW 5ft 6in, Cyls 13 x 18. Overhauled Cowlairs works on purchase. (See Vol 6,
  NBR) Lettered *Wigtownshire Railway no 1*. Weatherboard only. Dome on first
  ring of boiler casing. Wheatley 'stove pipe' chimney.

No	Date purchased	
1	1875	ex-NB 32. Front weather board only. Rebuilt c1883 2-4-OWT DW 4ft 6in (supplied by Cowlairs), Cyls 13¼ x 20 and cab at Wigtown. Later fitted with Westinghouse brake. Withdrawn 1903.
5	4/1877	ex-NB 31A. Front and rear weatherboards. Rebuilt 1885 by Shanks, Arbroath 0-6-OWT, DW 3ft 4in, Cyls 13½ x 18. Withdrawn 1903

0-4-2PT Built by R & W Hawthorn in 1847 as 0-4-2 for Edinburgh and Northern
        (no 36) (see Vol 6 NBR) Purchased by Wheatley 1870.
  DW 5ft 0in, Cyls 14½ x 21. Outside frames. Rebuilt 0-4-2PT at Cowlairs on
  purchase with Wheatley chimney and dome in centre. Tank extended from
  smokebox to firebox. Two injectors and front and rear weatherboards.

No	Date to stock	
2	1875	ex NB 146. Withdrawn c1891

0-4-2 Built by Sharp Stewart. Works no 1233 in 1860 for Fleetwood, Preston &
      West Riding Jct (see Vol 3B, p19). Purchased by Wheatley 1876.
  DW 5ft 0in, Cyls 15 x 20. Blr 10ft 0in x 3ft 4in (incorrectly recorded in
  Loco Mag, Vol 49 1953). Four-wheel tender. Central dome. Small weatherboard.
  Tender weatherboard fitted later. Black livery with red boiler bands, brass
  funnel, brass rims on splashers with name on rear driving splasher.

No	Name	Date purchased	
3	*Addison*	5/1876	ex L&Y/LNW Jt. Withdrawn 1894

0-4-0 Built by Beyer Peacock, Works no 42, in 1856 as 0-4-0ST for FP & WR Jct.
(see Vol 4A, P19). Purchased by Wheatley 1876.
DW 4ft 0in, Cyls 14 x 20. Rebuilt by L&Y on purchase as 0-4-0 with ex L&Y
four-wheel tender. Domeless boiler, safety valve over firebox in conical
casing. Small weatherboard.

No	Name	Date purchased	
4	*Gardner*	5/1876	ex-L&Y/LNW Jt. Rebuilt 0-4-2ST with extended frames and cab at Wigtown 1882/3. Cyls later 14¼ x 20. Withdrawn 1894.

0-6-0ST Built by Fletcher Jennings. Works no 155.
DW 4ft 0in, Cyls 14 x 20.

Delivered 1875/6 but returned to Fletcher Jennings owing to dispute over
payment. Ultimately sold to Wright Butler & Co, Swansea 1/1883.

0-6-0ST Built by Manning Wardle & Co. Works no 196, 1866. To Solway Junction
     1868/9 (see page no   ). Purchased by Wheatley 1/1872.
DW 3ft 0in, Cyls 11 x 16. Cab fitted before 1882.

No	Name	Date to stock	
6	*Bradby*	1882	ex CR 539. Withdrawn 1894

Tram Engine (probably 0-4-0). Built by Yorkshire Engine Co, Sheffield 1883.
     Purchased 1885.
Dimensions not known. Possibly intended for proposed tramway extension to
Isle of Whithorn which was not built.

Loco not numbered. Out of use from 1886 until sold for stationary work at
George Hotel, Stranraer, 1895. Not taken over by Joint Committee.

Girvan and Portpatrick Junction

Incorporated 1865. Opened 5 October 1877. Connection at Girvan with G&SW
(by Ayr and Maybole, opened 1856, and Maybole and Girvan, opened 1860, both
worked by G&SW) and at Challoch Junction with Portpatrick. Worked by G&SW
until 1886. From 12 April 1886 traffic was worked by W.T. Wheatley as
contractor. New company incorporated 1887 to purchase G&PJ and rolling stock
as the *Ayrshire and Wigtownshire*. Vested in G&SW by Act 26/6/1892.

8 locomotives as under: (Nos 1-5 taken over by A&W 1 August 1887)

4-4-0T Built by Slaughter Gruning & Co for the North London in 1861 (see
     Vol 2A, p57). Purchased by W.T. Wheatley 1886.
DW 5ft 3in, LW 3ft 2in, Cyls 15½ x 22, THS 969 sq ft, WP 120 lbs/sq in,
Wt 37 tons, O/S frame bogies.

Nos 1-3 introduced to G&PJ by W.T. Wheatley. Most accounts state that these
were ex-NL nos 31, 32 and 34 as stated in Vol 2A but Smith, *Little Railways
of South West Scotland* quotes North London Railway minutes which indicate
that the three locomotives were not purchased until 1886 and that they were
nos 33/6/7 not 31/2/4. This would probably mean that nos 31/2/4 were the
three that went to the Marquis of Bute's railway. Smith further records
that it is not certain in what order they were numbered on the G&PJ. Nos 2

& 3 were withdrawn in 1891, no 1 in 1892. All were scrapped in 1893 without being taken into G&SW stock.

0-4-OST Built by Hughes & Co, Loughborough, c1864.
DW 3ft 0in, Cyls 10 x 15.
Worked on Potteries, Shrewsbury and North Wales 1873-7 when sold to Walker Bros, Wigan. Sold to W.T. Wheatley by I.W. Boulton 1886.

Not numbered and dismantled soon after purchase.

0-6-0 Built by Neilson & Co. Works no 3584/5 (N)
            Clyde Locomotive Co. Order E5 (C)
DW 5ft 1½in, Cyls 17 x 26, Blr 4ft 3in max diam, THS 1,065.19 sq ft, WP 140 lbs/sq in (N), 160 lbs/sq in (C), WB 7ft 5in + 7ft 10in, Wt 36 tons 18¾ cwt (N), 2,200 gallon tender. Central dome, Ramsbottom safety valves over firebox, Stephenson link motion, left-hand lever reverse, tender footboards and hand rails. N locos originally ordered by Wheatley came lettered *G&PJn Ry* on tender and originally had steam brakes later altered to Westinghouse and steam sanding with Stirling cabs. C locos were lettered *A & WR* and were Westinghouse fitted with steam sanding. They had a different shape of cab with rearward projection similar to CR Connor design. N locos later had WP increased to 150 lbs/sq in. Westinghouse brakes removed from all except 303 in 1895.

		G&SW	Duplicate		
No	Date	no 1892	no	date	Withdrawn
4	1886 N	302*	302A	6/1913	1914
5	1886 N	303	303A	6/1913	1917
6	1887 C	304	304A	6/1913	1914
7	1887 C	305	305A	6/1913	1917

*No 302 later had tender weatherboard fitted

Glasgow, Barrhead and Kilmarnock Joint

Incorporated 12 July 1869 setting up joint CR/G&SW Committee for Glasgow, Barrhead and Kilmarnock line (opened 1871-3).

1 locomotive as under: (for working Beith branch)

0-4-4T Built by Dubs & Co. Works no 892.
DW 5ft 7in, TW 3ft 0in, Cyls 18 x 24, THS 1165 sq ft, WP 130 lbs/sq in, WB 7ft 6in + 10ft 3in + 5ft 0in, Wt 42 tons approx. Dark brown livery, yellow lining, lettered *Jt Ln No 1*. Brass dome, copper top on chimney.
Date
1875   Believed given CR boiler in 1907. Admitted to G&SW stock 1913 but not given number until 1921 when believed no 537 allotted.

Glasgow and Paisley Joint

4 locomotives as under: (for shunting at Paisley Greenlaw goods station). Dark red livery with black lining.

0-4-OST Built by Dubs & Co. Works no 64.
DW 3ft 6in, Cyls 12 x 22, THS 540 sq ft, Wt 17 tons 8 cwt.
No   Date
1   1866 Sold 1887

0-4-OST Built by Dubs & Co, Works no 644.
DW 3ft 6in, Cyls 14 x 22, THS 651 sq ft, Wt 20 tons 11 cwt.

```
No      Date
2       1873 Sold 1887
```

O-4-OST Built by Neilson & Co. Works nos 3616/7
DW 3ft 6in, Cyls 14 x 20, THS 685 sq ft, Wt 28 tons 14 cwt.

```
No      Date
1       1887 Believed allotted G&SW 736 in 1919. To LMS (16050). Withdrawn
             3/1924
2       1887 Believed allotted G&SW 737 in 1919. To LMS (16051). Withdrawn
             3/1924
```

GLASGOW AND SOUTH WESTERN

Robertson Locomotives 1850-3

2-2-2 Built by G&SW Cook Street, Glasgow.
DW 6ft 0in, LW & TW 3ft 6in, Cyls 15 x 20 O/S, WB 5ft 4in + 7ft 0in, Wt
19 tons. Built 1850/1 as a replacement for ex-GPK&A no 8 sold in 1847 and
possibly originally taking the same name *Dunlop*.

No	Date
8	1851 Replaced 1868

2-2-2 Built by Kinmonds & Co.
Assumed dimensions DW 6ft 6in, Cyls 15 x 20.

No	Date
16	1851 Replaced 1868

0-4-0 Built by R & W Hawthorn. Works nos 780-7, 840/1
DW 5ft 0in, Cyls 15 x 20, WP 95 lbs/sq in. Domeless boilers.

No	Date	1854 no	Replaced
86	8/1852		1872
87	8/1852		1872
88	10/1852		1872
89	10/1852		1872
90	12/1852		1872
91	12/1852		1873
92	7/1853		1872
93	8/1853		1872
94	12/1853	5	1873
95	12/1853	6	1873

Patrick Stirling Locomotives 1855-69

2-2-2 Built by Neilson & Co. Works nos 77-80 1854/5.
DW 6ft 0in, Cyls 15 x 20 O/S. Dome on centre of boiler, column type safety
valve above firebox. Four-wheel tender.

No	Date	Replaced
95	3/1855	1874
96	3/1855	1875
97	3/1855	1874
98	8/1855	1874

2-2-2 Built by G&SW Kilmarnock. Works nos as below.
DW 6ft 6in, LW & TW 3ft 6in, Cyls 16 x 21 O/S. Main line passenger duties.
First locomotives built at Kilmarnock works, opened 1856. Most had domes
in boiler centre with safety valves over firebox in a conical casing with
extended base, but some may have been domeless. Report on derailment of no
11 on 29/5/1861 gives cyls 16 x 22, WB 6ft 5in + 6ft 7in.

No	Date	Works no	Replaced
2	1857	1	1879
3	1/1858	2	1877
4	1/1858	3	1877
12	1858	4	1878
19	1858	5	1876
21	1/1859	6	1874
26	1859	9	1880
38	1/1859	7	1879
41	1859	8	1878
1	1/1860	10	1879
18	1/1860	11	1880
11	1860	12	1877
13	1860	13	1877

2-2-2 Built by G&SW Kilmarnock. Works nos as below.
DW 6ft 6in, LW & TW 3ft 6in, Cyls 16 x 21 O/S, THS 927.7 sq ft, WB 6ft 0in
+ 7ft 4in, Wt 24¾ tons, 1,200 gallon tenders, four and six-wheel. Domeless
boilers. Canopy supported on poles fitted later to no 40 and, possibly, to
others. Stirling cabs fitted to some later still, including 44.

No	Date	Works no		Replaced
40	1860	14	Giffard injector on right Ramsbottom safety valves boiler centre by 1877/8	1881
39	1/1861	15		1877
27	1861	16		1880
10	1861	17	Thought to have had 15x21 cyls later probably increased to 16x22	1877
43	1/1862	18		1877
42	1/1862	19	Giffard injector on left	1881
28	1864	26		1880
29	1864	27		1880
31	1864	28		1880
44	1864	29		1876

2-2-2 Built by G&SW, Kilmarnock. Works nos as below.
DW 7ft 0in, LW & TW 3ft 7in, Cyls 16 x 24 O/S, WB 7ft 6in + 7ft 6in, WP
125 lbs/sq in, THS 870 sq ft, Wt 28 tons 9¾ cwt. Domeless boiler, safety
valves over firebox replaced by Ramsbottom type over boiler centre.
Stirling cab. Open fan-like splashers. Six-wheel tenders. P. Stirling's

last G&SW express passenger design with strong resemblance to his later
designs for the Great Northern. They were built, however, before the
introduction of continuous brakes on passenger trains and never had them
fitted.

No	Date	Works no	Duplicate no	date	Withdrawn
45	3/1865	32	R31	1/1886	5/1887
151	4/1866	39			1884
152	6/1866	40			1885
153	1/1867	43	R33	5/1886	3/1888
154	1/1867	44	R34	5/1886	5/1887
155	10/1867	47			1884
156	11/1867	48			1884
84	3/1868	50	R32	2/1886	4/1887
61	4/1868	51	R30	12/1885	10/1886
16	6/1868	52			1885
79	7/1868	53	R35	9/1886	12/1886

0-(2-2)-0 Built by R & W Hawthorn. Works nos 894-7.
DW 5ft 0in, Cyls 15 x 20, Blr 3ft 11¾in max diam, WB 12 ft 1in with
crankshaft axle.

No	Date	Replaced
99	4/1855	1866
100	5/1855	1866
101	6/1855	1867
102	8/1855	1867

2-4-0 Built by Neilson & Co.
DW 5ft 0in, Cyls 15 x 21. Purchased from stock.

No	Date
94	1854/5 Replaced 1866

2-4-0 Built by Beyer Peacock & Co. Works no 72.
DW 5ft 0in, LW 3ft 6in, Cyls 16 x 24 O/S, Blr 4ft 0in max diam, THS 814
sq ft, WB 6ft 5in + 8ft 3in. Beattie patent coal burning firebox. Allan
straight link motion. Beyer Peacock design of tender with O/S springs and
axle boxes. Name removed after short period. Nicknamed 'The Bloomer'.
Similar to *Medusa* class on L&SW.

No	Name	Date
109	*Galloway*	2/1858 Replaced 1874

0-4-2 Built by R & W Hawthorn. Works nos 950-3.
DW 5ft 0in, TW 3ft 6in, Cyls 16 x 22 O/S, Blr 4ft 0in max diam, WB 6ft 10½in
+ 6ft 2½in. Four-wheel tender 800 gallons. Dome on centre of boiler, safety
valves over firebox, curved continuous splasher.

No	Date	Replaced
105	1/1856	1876
106	2/1856	1875
107	5/1856	1875
108	5/1856	1875

0-4-2 Built by Neilson & Co. Works nos 398-404.
Dimensions as 105 class, except WB 7ft 2½in + 6ft 5in, THS 1026.5 sq ft.

No	Date	Replaced
9	11/1857	1874
14	11/1857	1876
15	11/1857	1876
17	12/1857	1877
20	12/1857. Exploded Springhill Jct. 28/3/76	1876
	See note below.	
30	12/1857 Accident Dalbeattie 20/6/1874	1874

33   12/1857   1874

Note. The explosion of number 20 in 1876 had far reaching consequences.
Although the subsequent enquiry did not implicate the safety valves it
was decreed that all existing safety valves then carried over the firebox
should be replaced by Ramsbottom type over the boiler centre and this was
carried out by 1878 on most locomotives.
The explosion itself was very dramatic. The engine was travelling tender
first, hauling a van and a coach carrying workmen, when it occurred and it
somersaulted right over the van behind it, which passed underneath it,
crashing down on the coach. The tender was propelled forward with
considerable force and travelled 1½ miles before coming to rest. (Smith
Locomotives of the Glasgow & South Western, p55)

0-4-2 Built by R & W Hawthorn. Works nos 1034-43.
DW 5ft 0in, TW 3ft 6in, Cyls 16 x 22 O/S, WB 7ft 2½in + 6ft 6in, THS 1,005
lbs/sq in, Wt 26 tons 16 cwt. Centre dome safety valve in conical casing
over firebox.

No	Date	Replaced
34	7/1858	1874
36	7/1858	1875
32	8/1858	1875
25	8/1858	1874
110	10/1858	1874
111	10/1858	1876
112	1/1859	1876
113	1/1859	1875
114	1/1859	1876
115	1/1859	1874

0-4-2 Built by Sharp Stewart & Co. Works nos as below.
DW 5ft 0in, TW 3ft 6in, Cyls 16 x 22, WB 7ft 2in + 8ft 10in, WP 120 lbs/sq
in, THS 1043.7 sq in, Wt 27 tons 2 cwts. Four-wheel tender capacity 1,150
gallons. Domeless boiler. Auxiliary buffers between standard ones for
working chaldron wagons (also provided on some earlier goods locos) but on
this class both were spring pattern. Copper fireboxes caused some
difficulties. Original weatherboard replaced by small Stirling cabs on some.
1860 locos had boiler feed by two pumps as hitherto, but 1861 locos had one
pump and one Giffard injector. Original safety valves over firebox replaced
by Ramsbottom type over boiler centre. 0-4-2T rebuilds were vacuum fitted
with cabs.

No	Date	Works no	Rebuilt 0-4-2T	Duplicate no	date	Withdrawn
23	7/1860	1196		R15	6/1881	1889
35	7/1860	1197		R10	7/1881	1893
37	7/1860	1198		R11	11/1881	1883
116	7/1860	1199	1886	R26	8/1885	1904
117	7/1860	1200	1880/1	R27	8/1885	
118	7/1860	1201		R14	12/1881	1883
119	8/1860	1202		R20	6/1882	1883
120	8/1860	1203		R3	6/1882	1888
121	9/1860	1204	1880/1	R28	6/1885	1890
122	9/1860	1205	1880/1	R25	6/1885	
22	6/1861	1264		R12	6/1881	1888
24	6/1861	1265		R13	6/1881	1884
123	7/1861	1266				1882
124	7/1861	1267				1882
125	9/1861	1270				1882
126	9/1861	1271				1882
127	9/1861	1272	1885	R24	3/1885	1898

128	9/1861	1273	1880/1	R25	3/1885	1893	
129	10/1862	1359	1885	R21	2/1883		
130	10/1862	1360	1885	R11	2/1883		

0-4-2 Built by R & W Hawthorn. Works nos 1222-31.
DW 5ft 0in, TW 3ft 6in, Cyls 16 x 22, Blr 4ft 0½in max diam, THS 930 sq ft,
WP 120 lbs/sq in, WB 7ft 2in + 7ft 1in. Domeless boiler. Stirling cab with
circular side window. Slide valve type regulator with double arm vertical
pull-out handle. One pump and one injector, pump later removed. No engine
or train brakes, but no 137 fitted with Stirling steam reversing gear.
Safety valves altered to Ramsbottom type as previously noted.

		Duplicate		
No	Date	no	date	Withdrawn
131	1864			1883
132	1864	R14	5/1883	1888
133	1864	R20	7/1883	1888
134	1864	R1	7/1883	1888
135	1864	R2	11/1883	1893
136	1864	R18	11/1883	1895
137	1864	R13	1/1884	1891
138	1864	R22	1/1884	1889
139	1864	R23	5/1884	1889
140	1864			1884

0-4-2 Built by Neilson & Co. Order no 306. Works nos 1226-35
DW 5ft 1in, TW 3ft 7in, Cyls 17 x 24, THS 1127 sq ft, Blr 4ft 3½in max diam,
WP 120 lbs/sq in, WB 7ft 4in + 8ft 2in, Wt 29 tons 10½ cwts, 1,500 gallons
six-wheel tender (as 58 class O-6-O) with 3 tons coal capacity. Allan
straight-link motion. No engine or continuous brake. O-4-2T rebuilds had
no rear bunker. Safety valves altered to Ramsbottom type as previously noted.
Load class G.

		Rebuilt	Duplicate		
No	Date	O-4-2T	no	date	Withdrawn
141	9/1866	1887	141A	6/1891	1900
142	9/1866	1887	142A	6/1891	1904
143	9/1866		143A	12/1890	1904
144	9/1866	1886	144A	7/1891	1913
145	9/1866		145A	12/1890	1903
146	9/1866	1886	146A	7/1891	1905
147	10/1866		R8	7/1890	1909
148	10/1866		R49	7/1890	1902
149	10/1866		149A	2/1891	
			100A	6/1917	
			656	1919	12/1923*
150	10/1866		150A	2/1891	
			162A	6/1917	
			657	1919	6/1924*

*No 656 was allotted LMS no 17021
No 657 was allotted LMS no 17022

O-4-O Built by G&SW, Kilmarnock. Works nos as below.
DW 5ft 0in, Cyls 16 x 22, THS 945.7 sq ft, WB 8ft 0in, Wt 26 tons 4 cwt,
four-wheel 1,200 gallon tenders. Built to replace earlier engines. Original
weatherboard replaced with Stirling cab. Safety valves replaced by
Ramsbottom type as previously noted.

		Duplicate		
No	Date	no	year	
52	12/1864	R36	1886	
56	1865	R32	1886/7	All withdrawn by 1903
57	1865	R31	1886/7	

```
53     1865     R30  1886
54     1866     R37  1886  All withdrawn by 1903
55     1866     R35  1887
```

Class continued by J. Stirling, page no 148.

0-6-0 Built by R & W Hawthorn. Works nos 934/4.
DW 4ft 6in, Cyls 16 x 21 O/S, THS 770.75 sq ft, WB 6ft 2in + 6ft 2in. Four-
wheel tenders 1,150 gallons. Centre dome, safety valve over firebox in
cylindrical cover with elongated base. Curved continuous splasher.

No	Date	Replaced
103	11/1855	1871
104	12/1855	1871

0-6-0 Built by G&SW, Kilmarnock. Works nos 20-5
DW 5ft 0in, Cyls 16 x 22, THS 929 sq ft, WP 125 lbs/sq in, Wt 30 tons
6 cwts. Domeless boilers, regulator in smokebox. Tall safety valve casing
over firebox. Weatherboard.

No	Date	Duplicate no	date	Withdrawn
46	1862	R4	7/1878	8/1888
47	1862	R5	7/1878	1893
48	1863	R7	11/1878	8/1888
49	1863	R8	11/1878	6/1890
50	1863	R9	12/1878	1893
51	1863	R6	10/1878	1892

0-6-0 Built by G&SW, Kilmarnock. Works nos as below.
                Neilson & Co. Works nos as below.
DW 5ft 1in, Cyls 17 x 24, Blr 4ft 4in max diam, THS 1103.3 sq ft, WP 120
lbs/sq in, WB 7ft 4in + 8ft 2in, Wt 31 tons 9¼ cwts. Stirling cab.
Giffard injector. Originally had no engine brakes. Steam brakes fitted
about 1908. Safety valves altered to Ramsbottom type as previously noted.
WP increased to 130 lbs/sq in. Six-wheel tenders 1,500 gallons. Load
class G.

The following were built at Kilmarnock. Works nos below.

No	Date	Works no	Duplicate no	date	
58	5/1866	37			Replaced 1890
94	8/1866	38			Replaced 1890
99	11/1866	41	99A	12/1891	Withdrawn 1912
100	12/1866	42	100A	12/1891	Accident Carlisle
					24/12/1902. Withdrawn 3/1915
101	5/1867	45	101A	2/1892	Withdrawn 1909
102	7/1867	46	102A	2/1892	Restored to Capital list
					163 1896
			163A	11/1898	Withdrawn about 1909

The following were built by Neilson & Co with mid feathers in fireboxes.
Works nos 1317-26

No	Date	Renumbered no	date	Duplicate no	date	1919 no	Withdrawn
160	4/1867			160A	12/1897	617	1920
161	4/1867			161A	12/1897	618	1922
162	4/1867			162A	12/1897		1917
163	4/1867						1896
164	5/1867			164A	1/1898	619	1923*
165	5/1867	49	2/1898	165A	1898		1910
166	5/1867			166A	5/1898	620	5/1922
167	5/1867			167A	5/1898	621	4/1922

168	5/1867	168A	6/1898		1909
169	5/1867	169A	6/1898		about 1920

*No 619 allotted LMS no 17100

The following were built by Neilson. Works nos 1443-52, but without mid feather fireboxes and had tube arrangement altered giving THS 1066 sq ft. (order no 351).

No	Date	Duplicate no	date	1919 no	Withdrawn
172	1869	172A	8/1898		6/1917
173	1869	173A	8/1898		3/1915
174	1869	174A	12/1898	623	4/1922
175	1869	175A	12/1898		1910
176	1869	176A	12/1898	624	about 1920
177	1869	177A	2/1899		6/1917
178	1869	178A	2/1899		1910
179	1869	179A	2/1899		7/1917
180	1869	180A	9/1900		3/1915
181	1869	181A	11/1900		6/1917

James Stirling Locomotives 1866-78

2-2-2WT Built by Neilson & Co. Order no 329. Works no 1316.
DW 6ft 0½in, LW & TW 3ft 6½in, Cyls 15 x 20, Blr 3ft 9½in max diam, THS
640.9 sq ft, WB 6ft 4½in + 7ft 4½in, WP 130 lbs/sq in. First G&SW tank
engine built for working Renfrew branch. Domeless boiler, safety valve in
brass cover over firebox. Tank extended round bunker at rear. Weatherboards
only.

No	Date	
159	3/1867	Withdrawn 1877

2-4-0 Built by G&SW, Kilmarnock. Works nos 49, 54-67
DW 6ft 6in, LW 3ft 7in, Cyls 17 x 24, THS 861 sq ft, WP 130 lbs/sq in, WB
7ft 4in + 8ft 2in, Wt 31 tons 4¼ cwt. Domeless boiler, safety valves over
firebox, open fan-tail splashers. Cut away cab with small circular window.
Plainer chimney without brass top fitted later. Lever reverse. Safety
valves altered to Ramsbottom type as previously noted. Vacuum ejectors and
train pipes fitted 1887/8. Also fitted with Westinghouse brake on loco and
tender with train pipe.

No	Date		Duplicate no	date	Withdrawn
8	2/1868		8A	5/1892	1905
80	7/1868		80A	11/1893	
73	10/1868		73A	1/1893	1900
170	12/1868		170A	8/1892	1901
171	1/1869		171A	1892	1903
82	5/1869		82A	1/1894	1903
81	6/1869		81A	11/1893	1900
83	6/1869 Rebuilt 1877		83A	1/1894	1905
85	7/1869		85A	1892	1917
182	11/1869		182A	5/1894	1902
183	11/1869		183A	5/1894	1901
77	12/1869		77A	1893	1904
78	2/1870		78A	7/1893	1904
72	4/1870		72A	12/1892	1913
74	5/1870		74A	1/1893	1904

2-4-0 Built by G&SW, Kilmarnock. Works nos 68-77.
DW 6ft 0in, LW 3ft 7in, Cyls 17 x 24, Wt 32½ tons, WB & WP as 8 class.
Outward appearance as 8 class except for smaller DW. Westinghouse brake
fitted after 1876 had cylinders beneath the footplate instead of between
coupled wheels. Vacuum ejectors and train pipes fitted in 1888. Ramsbottom
safety valves substituted as previously noted.

No	Date	Duplicate no	date	1919 no	Withdrawn
75	7/1870	75A	5/1893		1904
76	7/1870	76A	5/1893		1900
771	9/1870	71A	12/1892	727	1923*
59	9/1870	59A	11/1890		1898
60	12/1870	60A	11/1894		1904
63	12/1870	63A	2/1895		1906
62	3/1871	62A	12/1894	726	1919
64	3/1871	64A	2/1895		1908
103	6/1871	103A	7/1894		1909
104	6/1871	104A	7/1894		1905

*No 727 was allotted LMS no 14000

0-4-2 Built by Neilson & Co. Orders nos as below.
DW 5ft 7½in, TW 3ft 7¼in, Cyls 17 x 24, THS 939.9 sq ft, Blr 4ft 2in max
diam, WP 130 lbs/sq in, WB 7ft 6in + 7ft 2in, Wt 29½ tons. Domeless boiler.
Cut away cab without side windows. Solid splashers. Six-wheel 1,500 gallon

tender. Ramsbottom safety valves substituted as previously noted, but no 204 still not altered in 1900. In the list below W = later fitted with Westinghouse brakes and vacuum ejectors. Others later fitted with all vacuum equipment.

Order no 365. Works nos 1564-73. Fitted with lever reverse.

No	Date	Rebuilt O-4-2T	Duplicate no	date	Capital no	date	Renewed*	Withdrawn
187	12/1870		187A	3/1897				1917
188	12/1870		188A	7/1897			3/1901	
189	12/1870 W		(renumbered)		199	1897		
			199A	1899			6/1900	
190	12/1870 W		190A	7/1897	203	1/1899		
			203A	9/1900				1917
191	12/1870		191A	7/1899			11/1900	
192	1/1871 W		192A	7/1899			6/1900	
193	1871		193A	7/1899				1913
194	2/1871		194A	5/1899			6/1900	
195	2/1871	1889	195A	5/1899				1912
196	2/1871	1889	196A	5/1899				1912

*See page no 156

Order no 373. Works nos 1616-25. Fitted with vertical screw reverse.

No	Date	Rebuilt O-4-2T	Duplicate no	date	Renewed*	Withdrawn
197	1871	1889	197A	10/1899		1908
198	1871	2/1889	198A	10/1899		1913
199	1871 W					7/1897
200	1871	8/1888	200A	1/1900		1907
201	1871	5/1888	201A	1/1900		1907
202	1871	10/1888	202A	1/1900		1906
203	1871 W					1/1899
204	1871 W				11/1900	
205	1871 W				11/1900	
206	1871	2/1888	206A	2/1901		1908

*See page no 156

O-4-2 Built by Dubs & Co. Works nos 615-24.
DW 5ft 7in, TW 3ft 7in, Cyls 18 x 24, THS 1049.4 sq ft, Wt 29 tons 1 cwt, 1,500-gallon tenders. Mixed traffic loco with outward appearance similar to 187 class. Screw reverse. No 212-4 fitted with Westinghouse automatic brake after 1876 with train pipe. Others given vacuum equipment in late 1880s and 212-4 had vacuum ejectors and train pipes added. Load Class F.

No	Date	Duplicate no	date	1919 no	Allotted LMS no	Withdrawn
208	5/1873	208A	5/1903	651	(17023)	1923
209	5/1873	209A	5/1903			1913
210	5/1873	210A	6/1903			1913
211	6/1873	211A	6/1903	652	(17024)	1923
212	6/1873	212A	7/1903	653	(17025)	1923
213	6/1873	213A	7/1903			1913
214	6/1873	214A	12/1903	654	(17026)	1923
215	6/1873	215A	1/1904			1904
216	6/1873	216A	1/1904			1913
217	6/1873	217A	5/1904	655		1923

O-4-2 Built by Neilson & Co as below.
Dubs & Co as below.
DW 5ft 7in, TW 3ft 7in, Cyls 18 x 26, Blr 4ft 4in max diam, THS 1155.41 sq ft, WP 130 lbs/sq in, WB 7ft 6in + 7ft 2in, Wt 33 tons 5 cwts, 1,800-gallon

tenders. Domeless boiler. Salters spring balance safety valves specified
but Ramsbottom type fitted above firebox without cover later transferred
to third ring of boiler cover. Locos not renewed by Manson were reboilered
with domeless boilers 4ft 5in max diam, THS 1043.5 sq ft. Load class F.

Built by Neilson & Co. Order no 420. Works nos 1886-95. Fitted with vertical
screw reverse.

No	Date	Renewed*
221	1874	1902
222	1874	1902
223	1874	1904
224	1874	1901
225	1874	1903
226	1874	1901
227	1874	1901
228	1874	1902
229	1874	1903
230	1874	1904

*See page no 156

Built by Neilson & Co. Order no 435. Works nos 1956-65. Fitted with vertical
screw reverse.

No	Date	Duplicate no	date	1919 no	Renewed*	LMS no	Withdrawn
231	1875				1903		
232	1875				1901		
233	1875				1903		
234	1875				1901		
235	1875				1904		
236	1875				1902		
237	1875				1902		
238	3/1875	238A	5/1904	635		17035	1/1926
239	3/1875	239A	6/1904	636		(17036)	10/1923
240	4/1875	240A	11/1904	637		17037	8/1929

*See page no 156

Built by Neilson & Co. Order no 437. Works nos 1970-9. Fitted with Stirling
steam reverse.

No	Date	Duplicate no	date	1919 no	Renewed*	LMS no	Withdrawn
241	4/1875	241A	11/1904	638			1919
242	4/1875	242A	11/1904	639		17038	1/1925
243	1875				1901		
244	1875	244A	3/1905				1915
245	1875				1902		
246	5/1875	246A	3/1905	640			1922
247	5/1875				1901		
248	5/1875				1902		
249	5/1875	249A	3/1905				1914
250	5/1875	250A	6/1905				1914

*See page no 156

Built by Dubs & Co. Order no 970. Works nos 970-9. Fitted with Stirling
steam reverse.

No	Date	Duplicate no	date	1919 no	Renewed*	LMS no	Withdrawn
251**	1876	251A	6/1905				1913
252**	11/1876	252A	6/1905				7/1917
253**	11/1876	253A	10/1905	641		(17039)	10/1923
254**	1876				1902		
255**	1876				1902		

256	1876			1902			
257	1876			1901			
258	1876			1902			
259	12/1876	295A	11/1905				7/1914
260	12/1876			1903			

*See page no 156
**Fitted vacuum brake about 1891

Built by Neilson & Co. Order no 465. Works nos 2205-14. Fitted with Stirling
steam reverse.

		Duplicate		1919	LMS		
No	Date	no	date	no	Renewed*	no	Withdrawn
261	1877				1902		
262	5/1877	262A	12/1905	**642**			1919
263	6/1877	263A	11/1906				1917
264	6/1877	264A	12/1906				1915
265	7/1877	265A	12/1906				7/1917
266	7/1877	266A	5/1906				3/1915
267	7/1877	267A	5/1906	**643**			1919
268	7/1877	268A	6/1906	**644**		(17040)	10/1923
269	7/1877	269A	6/1906	**645**		(17041)	10/1923
270	7/1877	270A	7/1906	**646**		(17042)	5/1924

*See page no 156

Built by Neilson & Co. Order no 481. Works nos 2337-46. Fitted with Stirling
steam reverse and Ramsbottom safety valves on third ring of boiler cover as
built.

		Duplicate		1919	LMS		
No	Date	no	date	no	Renewed*	no	Withdrawn
271	5/1878	271A	7/1906				3/1915
272	5/1878	272A	1/1907	**647**		(17043)	11/1923
273	5/1878	273A	1/1907				1913
274	5/1878	274A	12/1908	**648**		(17044)	5/1924
275	5/1878	275A	1/1909	**649**		17045	1/1925
276	1878				1901		
277	1878	277A	4/1909				2/1911
278	6/1878	278A	5/1909	**650**			1919
279	6/1878	279A	4/1913				7/1917
280	1878				1901		

*See page no156

4-4-0 Built by G&SW, Kilmarnock. Works nos 95, 101-11, 116-7, 120-7.
DW 7ft 1in, LW 3ft 7in, Cyls 18 x 26, Blr 4ft 3in x 10ft 1in, THS 111.8 sq ft,
WP 140 lbs/sq in, WB 4ft 10in + 7ft 2¾in + 8ft 3in, Wt 39 tons, 1,800-gallon
tenders. Built to work the Midland express trains between Carlisle and
Glasgow using the newly completed joint line via Barrhead. Bogie pivot one
inch in front of centre, domeless boiler, cut-away cab with no side windows,
fan-tail splashers, horizontal pull-out regulator, tenders had footboards
and handrails along the sides. No 6 built with spring balance safety valves
all the others Ramsbottom type, but all on the firebox. All later had
Ramsbottom type on second ring of boiler cover. All built with Stirling steam
reverser. Westinghouse brake and train pipe fitted from 1876. Vacuum ejectors
and train pipe fitted 1886/7.

		Duplicate			
No	Date	no	year	Renewed*	Withdrawn
6	7/1873				1/1895
95	5/1874	95A	5/1896	5/1899	
98	6/1874	98A	5/1895		1895
115	8/1874	115A	1897	1/1900	
97	10/1874	97A	5/1896	10/1899	
110	11/1874	110A	12/1896	5/1899	

30	12/1874				6/1895
96	2/1875	96A	5/1896	7/1899	
36	3/1875	36A	11/1896	10/1899	
108**	4/1875				1894
106	6/1875	106A	6/1896	1/1901	
107	7/1875	107A	8/1895	7/1899	
20	4/1876	20A	11/1895	1/1900	
112	4/1876	112A	12/1896	2/1901	
15	10/1876	15A	10/1895	12/1900	
111	11/1876	111A	12/1896	7/1899	
44	12/1876	44A	1/1896	10/1899	
3	1/1877	3A	6/1897	1/1900	
10	5/1877	10A	4/1895		5/1895
39	5/1877	39A	1/1896	5/1899	
4	7/1877	4A	7/1897	9/1900	
11	7/1877				6/1896

*See page no 159. **No 106 exhibited at Darlington Exhibition 1875.

0-4-0 Built by G&SW, Kilmarnock. Works nos 78-100.
DW 5ft 0in, Cyls 16 x 22, THS 938 sq ft, WB 8ft 0in, Wt 26½ tons. Domeless boiler. Renewals of earlier 0-4-0s considered necessary for working mineral branches. Four-wheel tenders (despite drawing in *Loco Mag*, Oct 1922, showing six-wheel tender) with 1,400-gallon capacity. Shallow cabs. Conversion of safety valves to Ramsbottom type was long drawn out and some may not have been converted. Those remaining in 1910 had steam brakes fitted. These locos were the last goods engines to have the lower second pair of buffers between the standard ones.

		Duplicate		1919	
No	Date	no	date	no	Withdrawn
65	9/1871	R34	6/1887		1903-7
66	9/1871	R38	8/1887		9/1915
69	11/1871	R41	12/1887		1909-11
86*	1/1872	R33	3/1888		By 1903
92	1/1872	R47	1/1890		7/1917
89	2/1872	R22	7/1889		By 1903
88	2/1872	R20	6/1889		7/1917
90	4/1872	R45	12/1889		1903-7
67*	7/1872	R39	12/1887	733**	1919
7	8/1872	R12	6/1888	732	4/1922
87	9/1872	R15	6/1889		1903-7
70	9/1872	R42	2/1888		By 1903
93	12/1872	R48	1/1890		By 1903
207*	1/1873	R7	1/1889		1907-11
68	3/1873	R40	12/1887		By 1903
91	3/1873	R46	12/1889		By 1903
5	6/1873	R3	6/1888		By 1903
9	2/1874	R43	7/1888		By 1903
25	3/1874	R44	7/1888		By 1903
33	3/1874	R1	12/1888		1903-7
109	4/1874	R23	7/1889		By 1903
34	5/1874	R4	12/1888		1907-11

*Nos 86, 67 and 207 had vertical screw reverse instead of lever reverse.
**No 733 possibly not carried

0-4-0ST Built by A. Barclay & Co, Kilmarnock. Works nos as below.
DW 3ft 6in, Cyls 12 x 20 O/S, THS 430 sq ft, Wt 22 tons 5 cwt. Not certain that no 184 which was obtained second hand had the same dimensions.

		Works	Duplicate		
No	Date	no	no	date	Withdrawn
157	1866	54	R1	1879	1881
158	1867	56	R2	1879	1881

184*	1869	85	R19	1882	
185	1870	95	R10	1879	1881
186	6/1870	96	R11	1879	1881

*Purchased from Hugh Kennedy, contractor for £650. Built earlier the same year.

0-4-0ST Built by Allen Andrews & Co, Kilmarnock. Works nos 3/4
DW not known, Cyls 14 x 20 O/S.

		Duplicate		
No	Date	no	year	
218	1873	R16	1881	Withdrawal dates not known.
219	1873	R17	1881	Probably still on R list 1889

0-4-0ST Built by A. Barclay & Co in 1873. Works no 239.
        Purchased from Glamorgan Coal Co.
DW 3ft 0in, Cyls 10 x 18 O/S, THS 293 sq ft, Wt 17½ tons.

No	Date	
220	1874	To Duplicate list R18 1881. To Kilmarnock works 1884 designated *Works* as works shunter. Given number 220B in 1894. Reboilered 1898. To War Department c1917 for use at Gretna munitions factory. Sold to Brownside Quarries, Airdrie. Scrapped 1930.

0-4-0ST Built by G&SW, Kilmarnock. Works nos 112-115, 118-19.
DW 4ft 7in, Cyls 16 x 22, WB 7ft 6in, WP 120 lbs/sq in, THS 829 sq ft.
Based on standard 0-4-0 locos, 800-gallon tank extending from front of firebox to front of smokebox. Shallow cab on square coal boxes, no rear bunker. Spring balance safety valves over firebox. Vertical screw reverse on left side to suit conditions at College Yard, Glasgow. Rebuilt c1885 with side tanks extending from front of smokebox to rear DW with cut away for access to motion and Ramsbottom safety valves on third ring of boiler casing. New cabs and lever reverse.

		Duplicate		
No	Date	no	date	Withdrawn
113	9/1875	113A	6/1900	
32	12/1875	32A	10/1896	1911
14	1/1876	14A	7/1896	
114	2/1876	114A	6/1900	
19	7/1876	19A	7/1896	1911
105	7/1876	105A	11/1896	

0-6-0 Built by G&SW, Kilmarnock. Works nos 128-39.
DW 5ft 1in, Cyls 18 x 26, WB 7ft 6in + 7ft 3in, WP 130 lbs/sq in, Wt 35 tons 12 cwts, 1,800-gallon tenders. Domeless boiler. Ramsbottom safety valves on third ring of boiler casing. Single injector, steam reverse. Steam brakes fitted c1907 acting on two pairs of wheels only. Some received Manson chimneys. Load class E, LMS class 1F.

		Duplicate		1919	LMS	
No	Date	no	date	no	no	Withdrawn
13	12/1877	13A	7/1910	563	(17103)	1923
43	12/1877	43A	7/1910	573	17104	1926
41	1/1878	41A	7/1910	572	(17106)	1923
12	1/1878	12A	7/1910			3/1915
17	5/1878	17A	7/1910	565	(17105)	1923
159	5/1878 renumbered					
49	1898	49A	9/1910	577	17109	7/1928
46	7/1878	46A	7/1910	575	17107	8/1927
47	7/1878	47A	7/1910			7/1914
51	10/1878	51A	9/1910	584	17111	9/1925

48	11/1878	48A	9/1910	576	17108	1926
49	11/1878					2/1898*
50	12/1878	50A	9/1910	578	17110	3/1926

*Scrapped after Barrassie Jct accident 4/2/1898

Smellie Locomotives 1879-91

2-4-0 Built by G&SW, Kilmarnock. Works nos 144-55.
DW 6ft 9½in, LW 4ft 4½in, Cyls 18 x 26, Blr 4ft 3in x 10ft 6¼in, THS 1206 sq ft, WP 140 lbs/sq in, WB 8ft 0in + 8ft 3in, Wt 38½ tons. 2,100-gallon tenders. Domeless boiler, Ramsbottom safety valves on third ring of boiler cover. Two injectors. Stephenson link motion. Stirling steam reverser, cab and chimney. Smokebox wing plates, closed splashers, Westinghouse brake with train pipe. Vacuum ejector with front and rear train pipes fitted 1886-9. New design of tender. Load class V.

No	Date	Duplicate no	date	1919 no	LMS no	Withdrawn
157	12/1879	157A	11/1908			9/1913
158	12/1879	158A	6/1909	725		7/1921
185	12/1879	185A	7/1909			1912
186	12/1879	186A	11/1909			1914
26	1/1880	26A	6/1907	721		1919
27	1/1880	27A	7/1907			1912
28	2/1880	28A	11/1907	722		7/1921
29	2/1880	29A	11/1907			7/1914
18	12/1880	18A	6/1907	720	(14001)	9/1923
31	12/1880	31A	1/1908			2/1912
40	1/1881	40A	5/1908	723	(14002)	12/1923
42	1/1881	42A	7/1908	724		7/1921

4-4-0 Built by G&SW, Kilmarnock. Works nos 164-87.
DW 6ft 1½in, LW 3ft 0½in, Cyls 18¼ x 26, Blr 4ft 3in x 10ft 5¼in, THS 1045 sq ft, WP 140 lbs/sq in, WB 5ft 9in + 7ft 3in + 8ft 3in, Wt 41½ tons. Designed for Greenock line and originally known as Greenock Bogies but later, as their distribution spread, the Wee Bogies. Domeless boilers. Nos 139/40 had automatic vacuum brake, the others Westinghouse brake with vacuum ejector and train pipes. Whitelegg X3 boilers and cabs fitted as below. 4ft 8¼in max diam, THS 1139 sq ft, WP 160 lbs/sq in, Wt 44½ tons. Load class T, LMS class 1P (rebuilds 2P).

No	Date	Duplicate no	date	1919 no	Rebuilt	LMS no	Withdrawn
119	6/1882	119A	1/1910	700		14116	12/1931
120	6/1882	120A	1/1910	701	3/1922 Whitelegg X3 boiler	14117	1932
123	7/1882	123A	5/1910				5/1914
124	7/1882	124A	6/1910	702	8/1921* X3 blr	14118	6/1934
125	12/1882	125A	12/1910	703	7/1921* X3 blr	14119	1932
126	12/1882	126A	1/1911	704	10/1921 X3 blr	14120	6/1934
129	2/1883	129A	7/1911	706	2/1922 X3 blr	14121	1932
130	2/1883	130A	1/1912	707		14122	1930
131	2/1883	131A	6/1913	708	7/1922 X3 blr	14123	6/1934
132	5/1883	132A	6/1913	709	1909 Domed blr**	14124	4/1927
133	7/1883	133A	6/1913	710		14125	2/1925
134	7/1883	134A	6/1913	711	12/1921 X3 blr	14126	9/1931
135	11/1883	135A	6/1913	712		14127	5/1930
136	11/1883	136A	6/1913	713	1909 Domed blr 12/1921 X3 blr	14128	1930
137	1/1884	137A	7/1915	714	4/1922 X3 blr	14131	1931
138	1/1884	138A	2/1915	715	***	14132	1931
139	5/1884	139A	2/1915	716	2/1922 X3 blr	14133	1930
140	6/1884	140A	8/1915	717		14134	1930
155	7/1884			467	4/1922 X3 blr	14129	12/1933
156	7/1884			468	11/1921 X3 blr	14130	10/1932

151	12/1884	151A	6/1915	718	7/1922 X3 blr	14136	1930
152	12/1884	152A	9/1915	719	3/1922 X3 blr	14137	12/1933
127	3/1885	127A	2/1911				3/1915
128	3/1885	128A	7/1911	705		14135	1930

*Rebuilt by Beardmore & Co.
**The two 1909 domed boilers were also used on other unrebuilt locos.
***No 716 dual fitted vacuum and Westinghouse 2/1922.

4-4-0 Built by G&SW, Kilmarnock. Works nos 196-211, 220-3.
DW 6ft 9½in, LW 3ft 7½in, Cyls 18¼ x 26, Blr 4ft 3in x 10ft 5¼in, THS 1198 sq ft, WP 120lbs/sq in. WB 5ft 9in + 7ft 3in + 8ft 6in, Wt 43 tons. Built for main line expresses. Layout based on 119 class. 2,500 gallon tenders. Domeless boiler of Siemans steel. Some fitted with removable extended smoke boxes stated by Ahrons to be the first such application in the UK. These included 57/67/70/89 all removed by 1906 Automatic vacuum brake and train pipes now adopted as standard. X3 boiler rebuilds as 119 class. Wt 46 tons 3 cwts. No 69 originally fitted with feed-water heater. Load class T, LMS class 1P.

No	Date	1919 no	Rebuilt	LMS no	Withdrawn
153	5/1886	465	1923 X3 boiler	14142*	7/1932
154	5/1886	466	1923 X3 boiler	14143*	11/1935
79	7/1886	459		14141	11/1927
52	7/1886	448		14138	4/1925
53	12/1886	449	12/1922 X3 boiler	14139	12/1934
54	12/1886	450	1923 X3 boiler	14140	8/1932
55	2/1887	451	1909 Domed blr		
			11/1922 X3 boiler	14144	9/1933
56	4/1887	452	1923 X3 boiler	14145	9/1934
57	6/1887	453	11/1922 X3 boiler	14146	4/1931
65	6/1887				1898**
66	6/1887	454	1923 X3 boiler	14147*	11/1932
67	12/1887	455		14148	6/1926
68	12/1887	456	1923 X3 boiler	14149	1932
69	12/1887	457	1909 Domed blr		
			1923 X3 boiler	14150	3/1929
70	2/1888	458		14151	1/1926
86	3/1888	460		14152	9/1925
87	6/1889	461	1909 Domed blr	14153	1930
88	6/1889	462		14154	3/1927
89	7/1889	463	1923 X3 boiler	14155	1930
109	7/1889	464		14156	11/1927

*Nos 454/65/6 were Westinghouse fitted by LMS for working Lockerbie branch with CR stock.
**No 65 scrapped after accident Barassie Jct 4/2/1898.

0-4-4T Built by G&SW, Kilmarnock. Works nos 140-3.
DW 5ft 7in, TW 3ft 0in, Cyls 18 x 26, Blr 4ft 5in in max diam, WP 130lbs/sq in, WB 7ft 6in + 8ft 6in + 5ft 0in, Wt 46tons 6cwt. Designed by Stirling but completed by Smellie with several of his modifications. Adams radial bogie, Ramsbottom safety valves on third ring of boiler cover, Stirling steam reverser and Westinghouse brake. Stirling cab except on no 2 which had boiler pitched 4¾in higher at 7ft 6in and had overall roof on cab, but not certain if built in this form. Vacuum ejectors and train pipes fitted c1888-90. Rebuilt 1920 with larger tanks (1,200 gallons instead of 1,000 gallons) longer frames, new cast iron chimneys but with original boiler casing. WP increased to 140lbs/sq in, Wt 49tons 6cwt. No 2 continued to have higher pitched boiler. Load class W.

No	Date	Duplicate no	Duplicate date	1919 no	Rebuilt	LMS no	Withdrawn
1	5/1879	1A	2/1914	728	1920	15241	1/1926
2	6/1879	2A	2/1914	729	9/1920	15242	10/1925

| 21 | 7/1879 | 21A | 2/1914 | **730** | 11/1920 | 15243 | 3/1925 |
| 38 | 7/1879 | | 3/1914 | **731** | 11/1920 | 15244 | 2/1925 |

O-4-OT Built by A. Barclay & Co. Works no 258
    in 1883 for Ireland & Co. Purchased 1885.
DW 3ft 6in, Cyls 13 x 20m THS 435 sq ft, Wt 23¼tons.

No	Date	
291	1885	To Duplicate list R14 1888
		To Kilmarnock works shunter by 1894
		designated *'Works'*. Given no 734 in 1919.
		Scrapped 7/25

O-4-OST Built by Andrews, Barr & Co. Works nos 29/30.
DW 3ft 6in, Cyls 14 x 22 O/S.
Replacements for 1873 locos, same numbers

		Duplicate		1919	LMS	
No	Date	no	year	no	no	
218	1881	218A	1900	**658**	16041	To departmental stock 1925.
						Withdrawn 1928.
219	1881	219A	1900	**659**	16040	Withdrawn 12/1932

O-6-O Built by G&SW Kilmarnock as below
            Neilson & Co as below
            Dubs & Co as below
DW 5ft 1½in, Cyls 18 x 26, Blr 4ft 3in x 10ft 6¼in, THS 1061.2 sq ft, WP
140lbs/sq in, WB 7ft 6in + 8ft 3in, Wt 37tons 8cwt. Steam brakes, boiler
and fittings similar to 157 class 2-4-0. Load class E, LMS class 1F (rebuilds
2F).
The following were built at Kilmarnock, Works nos 156-63. Nos 22/3/35/24 had
2,100 gallon tenders, the others had 2,200 gallon tenders. X3 boiler rebuild
4ft 7¾in max diam, THS 1193 sq ft, WP 160lbs/sq in, Boiler pitched at 7ft 6in.

		Duplicate		1919		LMS	With-
No	Date	no	date	no	Rebuilt	no	drawn
22	6/1881	22A	10/1910	**566**		17112	8/1926
23	6/1881	23A	10/1910				3/1915
35	7/1881	35A	10/1910	**570**		17114	5/1924
24	6/1881	24A	10/1910	**567**		17113	7/1927
37	11/1881	37A	11/1910	**571**		17115	1/1926
118	12/1881	118A	9/1910	**592**	*Domed blr	17116	5/1924
184	1/1882	184A	3/1914	**605**	1923 X3 blr	17118	8/1933
220	2/1882			**139**	c1901-3		
					Domed boiler	17117	12/1931

*Date of rebuilding of no 118 not known. Boiler exchanged with one of the
1901-3 rebuilds.

The following were built by Neilson & Co, Works nos 2968-77 and had 2,200
gallon tenders.

		Duplicate		1919		LMS	With-
No	Date	no	date	no	Rebuilt	no	drawn
281	1883				Renewed 7/1911*		
282	1883				Renewed 6/1911*		
285	1883				Renewed 7/1911*		
284	9/1883	284A	1/1916	**606**	c1901-3		
					Domed blr	17119	5/1927
283	1883				Renewed 6/1912*		
286	1883				Renewed 6/1911*		
287	1883				Renewed 12/1912*		
288	1883				Renewed 11/1912*		
289	1883				Renewed 11/1912*		
290	1883				Renewed 7/1912*		

*See page no 165

The following were built at Kilmarnock, works nos 188-95, 212-19 and had 2,200 gallon tenders.

No	Date	Duplicate no	date	1919 no	Rebuilt	LMS no	With-drawn
121	6/1885	121A	11/1915	593		17124	8/1927
122	6/1885	122A	1/1916	594		17125	1/1927
116	8/1885	116A	11/1915	590	*Domed blr	17122	8/1931
117	8/1885	117A	11/1915	591	c1901-3 Domed blr	17123	7/1926
16	12/1885	16A	12/1915	564		17120	3/1928
61	12/1885	61A	12/1915	579	c1901-3 Domed boiler	17121	1/1926
45	1/1886	45A	12/1915	574		17126	3/1925
84	2/1886	84A	12/1915	580		17127	7/1927
5	6/1888	5A	11/1917	560		17129	1930
7	6/1888	7A	11/1917	561		17130	11/1925
9	7/1888	9A	11/1917	562	c1901-3 Domed blr	17131	1930
25	7/1888			135		17128	12/1926
33	11/1888	33A	1/1916	568		17132	2/1926
34	11/1888	34A	1/1916	569		17133	1930
207	1/1889			138		17134	2/1926
291	1889				Renewed 7/1912**		

*Date of rebuilding not known. Boiler exchanged with one of the 1901-3 rebuilds
**See page no 165.

The following were built by Dubs & Co, works nos 2452-61 and had 2,500 gallon tenders. THS 936.5 sq ft, Wt 37tons 5½cwt. Total engine and tender WB 1¼in shorter. X3 boiler rebuilds as no 605 (ex 184 22 class above).

No	Date	Duplicate no	date	1919 no	Rebuilt	LMS no	With-drawn
292	2/1889	292A	4/1913	607		17137	7/1927
293	2/1889	293A	4/1913	608	1/1924 X3 blr	17138	10/1934
294	2/1889	294A	4/1913	609		17139	3/1927
295	2/1889	295A	4/1913	610	*Domed blr	17140	1928
296	2/1889	296A	5/1913	611	11/1924 X3 blr	17141	6/1932
297	2/1889	297A	5/1913	612		17142	1930
298	3/1889	298A	5/1913	613		17143	11/1925
299	3/1889	299A	5/1913	614	7/1924 X3 blr	17144	1932
300	3/1889	300A	5/1913	615		17145	10/1926
301	3/1889	301A	6/1913	616	1924 X3 blr	17146	1932

*Date of rebuilding not known. Boiler exchanged with 1901-3 rebuilds.

The following were built at Kilmarnock, works nos 224-43 and had 2,500 gallon tenders. X3 boiler rebuilds as no 184

No	Date	Duplicate no	date	1919 no	Rebuilt	LMS no	With-drawn
90	12/1889	90A	12/1915	581	c1901-03 Domed blr	17135	8/1926
91	12/1889	91A	12/1915	582	c1901-03 Domed blr 1923 X3 blr	17136	11/1934
92	1/1890	92A	1/1916	583		17148	2/1926
93	1/1890	93A	1/1916	585		17149	9/1926
58	6/1890			136		17147	1930
94	6/1890	94A	1/1916	586	c1901-03 Domed blr	17150	3/1928
147	7/1890	147A	6/1917	601	c1901-03 Domed blr	17153	1930
148	7/1890	148A	6/1907	602	6/1924 X3 blr	17154	1932
143	12/1890	143A	6/1917	597		17151	8/1926
145	12/1890	145A	6/1917	599		17152	2/1926
149	2/1891	149A	6/1917	603		17161	10/1925
150	2/1891	150A	6/1917	604		17162	10/1925
141	6/1891	141A	6/1917	595		17157	2/1926

142	6/1891	142A	6/1917	596		17158	1930
144	7/1891	144A	6/1917	598		17159	9/1926
146	7/1891	146A	6/1917	600		17160	10/1925
99	12/1891	99A	1/1916	587	11/1924 X3 blr	17156	1932
100	12/1891			137	3/1925 X3 blr	17155	1932
101	2/1892	101A	5/1917	588	1924 X3 blr	17163	10/1935
102	2/1892	102A	5/1917	589		17164	10/1926

Manson Locomotives 1890-1912

0-4-2 Built by G&SW, Kilmarnock. Works nos **329-31**, 334-6, 338
DW 5ft 7½in, TW 3ft 7½in, Cyls 17 x 24, Blr 4ft 5in max diam, THS 1027 sq ft,
WP 140 lbs/sq in, WB 7ft 6in + 7ft 2in, Wt 32tons 2cwt. Renewals of James
Stirling locos. Manson cab, screw reverse, **domeless boiler**. In the list
below W = Westinghouse brake and vacuum ejectors, others all vacuum fitted.
Load class G, LMS class 1F.

New No	Date	Old no	1919 no	LMS no	Withdrawn
113*	6/1990 W	192	**268**	17028	1927
114*	6/1900 W	189	**269**	17029	1930
218	6/1900	194	**273**	17033	1/1926
180	11/1900 W	204	**270**	17030	1927
181	11/1900 W	205	**271**	17031	1930
219	11/1900	191	**274**	17034	6/1926
159	3/1901	188	**272**	17032	1930

*tender cabs fitted.

0-4-2 Built by G&SW, Kilmarnock. Works nos 341-64, 371-6.
DW 5ft 7½in, TW 3ft 7½in, Cyls 18 x 26, Blr 4ft 4in, max diam THS 1193 sq ft,
WP 140lbs/sq in, WB 7ft 6in + 7ft 2in, Wt 34tons 16cwts. Renewals of James
Stirling 221 class (same numbers) with new domed boilers pitched 3in higher
at 7ft 3in, two Gresham & Craven injectors steam reversing gear and full
vacuum equipment, and steam sanding to front of leading DW. Modified Manson
cab. Original Stirling tenders retained. Load class F. LMS class 1F.

No	Date	1919 no	LMS no	Withdrawn
224	1901	**241**	17046	11/1927
227	1901	**244**	17048	1930
232	1901	**249**	17049	6/1926
257*	1901	**262**	17053	1930
247	1901	**257**	17052	9/1925
243	1901	**255**	17051	8/1925
276	1901	**266**	17054	1930
280	1901	**267**	17055	1930
226	1901	**243**	17047	5/1927
234	1901	**251**	17050	6/1926
254	1902	**259**	17063	7/1925
258	1902	**263**	17066	1931
222	1902	**239**	17057	1930
228	1902	**245**	17058	3/1928
256	1902	**261**	17065	11/1928
236	1902	**253**	17059	6/1928
237	1902	**254**	17060	11/1929
248	1902	**258**	17062	2/1928
255	1902	**260**	17064	8/1929
261	1902	**265**	17067	1931
245*	1902	**256**	17061	9/1927
221**	1902	**238**	17056	1930
231	1903	**248**	17070	5/1927
260	1903	**264**	17072	4/1928
225	1903	**242**	17068	7/1925
229	1903	**246**	17069	7/1925
233	1903	**250**	17071	9/1928
223	1904	**240**	17073	11/1927
230	1904	**247**	17074	11/1926
235	1904	**252**	17075	6/1925

*Ran with Smellie tender from 1921. Probably others too
**No 221 in accident St Enoch 27/7/1903.

4-4-0 Built by G&SW, Kilmarnock. Works nos as below.
DW 6ft 9½in, LW 3ft 7½in, Cyls 18¼ x 26, Blr 4ft 3in x 10ft 6in, THS 1,203
sq ft, WP 150lbs/sq in, WB 5ft 6in + 7ft 5in + 8ft 3in, Wt 45tons 1cwt.
Based on Q class 4-4-0 of GN of S. Domed boiler. Conventional cab with
seperate roof and semi-circular cut out. Stephenson link motion, slide
valves, Stirling steam reverser, steam sanding, swing link bogie. 2,500
gallon tender. Two eight-wheel tenders (two front pair of wheels a bogie,
rear two pairs fixed) with a capacity of 3,200 gallons were built for this
class and used with the locos assigned to working 'The Diner' (1.30pm ex St
Enoch and 1.30pm ex St Pancras) between Glasgow and Carlisle. In 1892 these
were nos 77/8, 1895 107/8, 1897 189/90. Xl boiler rebuilds 4ft 11½in max
diam. THS 1318 sq ft, WP 170lbs/sq in, Wt 49tons 17cwt. Whitelegg valve
motion substituted on most locos. Load class T, LMS class 1P (rebuilds 2P).

No	Date	Works no	1919 no	Rebuilt Xl blr	Renewed	LMS no	Withdrawn
8	5/1892	244	399			14157	11/1927
85	1892	245			4/1912		
170	8/1892	246	446	11/1920		14160	10/1932
171	1892	247			12/1911		
71	12/1892	248	412	3/1920		14158	11/1932
72	12/1892	249	413			14159	1930
73	1/1893	250	414			14161	12/1931
74	1/1893	251	415			14162	11/1926
75	5/1893	252	416	4/1921		14163	10/1927
76	5/1893	253	417			14164	4/1927
77*	7/1893	254			11/1911		
78	7/1893	255	418			14165	1930
80	11/1893	256	419			14166	6/1926
81	11/1893	257	420			14167	1930
82	1/1894	258	421			14172	10/1931
83	1/1894	259	422	10/1920		14173	6/1931
182	5/1894	260	434	4/1921		14175	10/1931
183	5/1894	261	435			14176	1928
103	7/1894	262	377	3/1910		14168	1928
104	7/1894	263	427			14174	9/1925
59	11/1894	264	406	4/1920		14169	12/1931
60	11/1894	265	407	8/1921		14170	7/1933
62	12/1894	266	408	8/1920		14171	12/1932
63	2/1895	267	409			14181	1/1926
64	2/1895	268	410			14182	1929
6	4/1895	269	398			14177	1930
10**	4/1895	270	400			14178	8/1929
98	6/1895	271	426	11/1920		14183	5/1933
107	8/1895	272	429			14184	10/1931
108	8/1895	273	430	6/1920		14185	9/1932
15	10/1895	274	401			14179	1932
20	11/1895	275	402			14180	12/1927
30	11/1895	276	447	6/1921		14186	12/1931
36	1/1896	277	403			14187	10/1925
39	1/1896	278	404			14188	1931
44	1/1896	279	405			14189	2/1927
95	5/1896	280	423			14190	6/1926
96	5/1896	281	424			14191	11/1925
97	5/1896	282	425	6/1920		14192	4/1931
106	6/1896	283	428			14193	9/1925
110	12/1896	288	431			14194	11/1932
111	12/1896	289	432			14195	12/1932
112	12/1896	290	433			14196	10/1931
115	1897	291			11/1911		
3	6/1897	293	396			14197	1930
4	7/1897	294	397			14198	2/1929

No	Date					
187	6/1897	295	436		14199	11/1931
188	7/1897	296	437	6/1920	14200	9/1931
189	7/1897	297	438	2/1920	14201	4/1929
190	7/1897	298	439		14202	4/1927
65***	9/1900	333	411	9/1920	14244	10/1927
214	12/1903	377	440		14245	1930
215	1/1904	378	441		14249	1/1926
216	1/1904	379	442		14250	2/1928
217	5/1904	380	443		14251	1930
238	5/1904	381	444	6/1920	14252	11/1928
239	6/1904	382	445		14253	2/1928

*No 77 was in accident Pollokshaws 11/12/1899.
**No 10 was fitted with exhaust steam injector.
***No 65 replaced the 153 class 4-4-0 lost in the Barassie Jct accident 4/2/1898 but had the original tender which survived the accident. See page no 160 for renewals.

4-4-0 Built by Dubs & Co. Works nos 3239-48, 3731-45.
DW 6ft 1½in, LW 3ft 7½in, Cyls 18¼ x 26, Blr 4ft 3in x 10ft 6in, THS 1062 sq ft, WP 165lbs/sq in, WB 5ft 6in + 7ft 5in + 8ft 9in, Wt 44tons 14cwt. 2,500 gallon tenders. Xl boiler rebuilds 4ft 11½in max diam, THS 1318 sq ft, WP 170lbs/sq in. All were altered to Whitelegg's motion design. Load class S, LMS class 2P.

No	Date	1919 no	Rebuilt Xl blr	LMS no	Withdrawn
336	5/1895	350		14203	3/1927
337	5/1895	351	2/1921	14204	4/1932
338	5/1895	352		14205	6/1926
339	6/1895	353		14206	1929
340	6/1895	354		14207	5/1927
341	6/1895	355	9/1920*	14208	1930
342	6/1895	356		14209	6/1926
343	6/1895	357		14210	11/1926
344	6/1895	358	10/1920**	14211	9/1932
345	6/1895	359		14212	4/1931
346	3/1899	360***	10/1920	14213	9/1932
347	3/1899	361	2/1921	14214	11/1932
348	3/1899	362		14215	3/1931
349	3/1899	363		14216	7/1926
350	3/1899	364		14217	7/1932
351	3/1899	365		14218	1928
352	3/1899	366		14219	1/1927
353	3/1899	367		14220	12/1931
354	3/1899	368		14221	1928
355	3/1899	369		14222	2/1928
356	4/1899	370	4/1921	14223	1930
357	4/1899	371		14224	1928
358	4/1899	372		14225	10/1927
359	4/1899	373		14226	8/1931
360	4/1899	374		14227	1930

*No 341 was rebuilt by Beardmore & Co.
**No 344 had Drummond cross water-tubes fitted in firebox 1902, removed 1913. In 1920 it was rebuilt by Beardmore & Co.
***No 360 was in accident St Enoch 31/7/1925.

4-4-0 Built by G & SW, Kilmarnock. Works no 292.
DW 6ft 9½in, LW 3ft 7½in, Cyls (4) 14½ x 26 (2), 12½ x 24 O/S (2), Blr 4ft 3in x 10ft 6in, THS 1,206 sq ft, WP 165lbs/sq in, WB 6ft 0in + 7ft 2in+ 8ft 9in, Wt 48tons 10cwt. Inside pair of cylinders had steam chests between them, valves driven by Stephenson link motion on leading coupled axle. O/S cylinders had steam chests on top, valve gear driven from the inside motion

by rocking shafts passing through openings in the frames. All four
cylinders drove the leading coupled axle, the two pairs of cranks being
diametrically opposed. Steam reverse, 2,500 gallon tender. Load class R.

No	Date	
11	4/1897	Accident Border Union Junction 19/1/1898
	11/1915	Rebuilt 240 class boiler (treated as a renewal Works no 457), Wt 50tons 17cwt
	1919	Renumbered **394**
	12/1922	Extensively rebuilt by Whitelegg. Cyls (4) 14 x 26(2), 14 x 24 O/S (2), Blr 5ft 4½in max diam, pitched at 9ft 0½in, THS 1591 sq ft, plus superheater 211 sq ft, WP 180lbs/sq in, WB 6ft 6in + 8ft 0in + 10ft 0in, Wy 61tons 9cwt. New cylinders with two 10in piston valves operating all four cylinders by means of crossed ports. Righthand drive substituted. Drummond type steam reverser. Robinson superheater. Tender exchanged with 18 class 4-4-0 no 341, which was rebuilt with higher sides giving 3,260 gallons and 5 tons coal. Work amounted to a renewal but not treated as such, probably because the 1915 rebuilt had been so treated. Named *Lord Glenarthur*.
	1923	To LMS 14509 (class 3P)
	6/1925	LMS red livery applied, name retained.
	11/1934	Withdrawn

4-4-0 Built by G&SW, Kilmarnock. Works nos 317-28, 332/7/9/40
DW 7ft 1in, LW 3ft 7in, Cyls 18 x 26, Blr 4ft 3in x 10ft 1in, THS 963.5 sq ft,
WP 150lbs/sq in, WB 4ft 10in + 7ft 2¾in + 8ft 3in, Wt 40tons. Renewals of
James Stirling 6 class with rebuilt boilers, reputedly using original casing
(domeless), Manson chimney and cab, closed splashers, shallower valance, two
injectors instead of one, steam sanding. Known as *Aul Bogies* some latterly
had Smellie tenders. Load class V, LMS class 1P.

New		Old	1919	LMS	
No	Date	no	no	no	Withdrawn
194	5/1899	95A	**472**	14231	11/1926
195	5/1899	110A	**473**	14232	10/1927
196	5/1899	39A	**474***	14233	9/1929
191	7/1899	111A	**469**	14228	11/1925
192	7/1899	96A	**470**	14229	12/1925
193	7/1899	107A	**471**	14230	12/1925
197	10/1899	36A	**475***	14234	1930
198	10/1899	97A	**476**	14235	8/1929
199	10/1899	44A	**477**	14236	1930
200	1/1900	3A	**478**	14237	3/1927
201	1/1900	115A	**479**	14238	12/1925
202	1/1900	20A	**480**	14239	1930
203	9/1900	4A	**481**	14240	2/1927
204	12/1900	15A	**482**	14241	10/1929
205	1/1901	106A	**483**	14242	4/1928
206	2/1901	112A	**484**	14243	12/1925

*Two of the boilers were domed and at different times were fitted to
various locos. In 1923 they were fitted to nos 474/5.

4-4-0 Built by G&SW, Kilmarnock. Works nos 383-94, 401-3, 435/6.
DW 6ft 9½in, LW 3ft 7½in, Cyls 18¼ x 26, Blr 4ft 9¼in diam, THS 1434 sq ft,
WP 170lbs/sq in, WB 5ft 6in + 7ft 5in + 8ft 9in, Wt 50tons 8cwt. Larger
boiler pitched 9in higher than 8 class at 8ft 3in, swing link bogie,
Stephenson link motion, Stirling steam reverser. Boiler casing had three
equal diameter rings, butt and strap jointed. Capuchon on chimney, higher
cab otherwise as 8 class. The single bogie eight-wheel tenders built for the
8 class were transferred to this class being first fitted to nos 241/2 then
244/52 and latterly 240/2. Xl boiler rebuilds as rebuilds of 8 class with

which they then became identical, capuchon fitted chimney being replaced
with plain cast iron one. Load class R. LMS class 2P.

No	Date	1919 no	Rebuilt Xl blr	LMS no	Withdrawn
240	10/1904	379	12/1920	14246	1932
241	10/1904	380		14247	1930
242	10/1904	381		14248	1932
244	2/1905	382		14245	11/1925
246	2/1905	383		14255	1928
249	2/1905	384		14256	1932
250	5/1905	385		14257	1929
251	6/1905	386		14258	1931
252	6/1905	387		14259	1929
253	10/1905	388	5/1920	14260	10/1934
259	11/1905	389		14261	8/1931
262	12/1905	390		14262	11/1931
263	11/1906	391		14263	5/1931
264*	12/1906	392		14264	1930
265	12/1906	393		14265	10/1931
77**	11/1911	375		14266	7/1926
115**	11/1911	378		14267	1932

*No 264 had Westinghouse pumps and trainpipes.
**Nos 77 and 115 were renewals of 8 class 4-4-Os (same numbers).

4-4-0 Built by G&SW, Kilmarnock. Works nos 406-14, 419-21, 437-9.
DW 6ft 9½in, LW 3ft 7½in, Cyls 18¼ x 26, THS 1407.6 sq ft, Wt 51tons 14cwts,
Other dimensions as 240 class. As 240 class but with new long, shallow
firebox (106 sq ft as against 119 sq ft on 240 class) necessitating a
rearward extension of the frames. Safety valves unusually far forward on
firebox. New design of 2,900 gallon tender with vertical sides. Reversing
rod curved over splasher. Some had Whitelegg motion fitted. Load class R,
LMS class 2P.

No	Date	1919 no	LMS no	Withdrawn	
18*	6/1907	337	14366	10/1932	
26*	6/1907	338	14367	11/1928	
27**	7/1907	339	14368	3/1928	
28	11/1907	340	14369	1931	
29	11/1907	341	14370	8/1929	
31	1/1908	342	14371	3/1929	
40	5/1908	343	14372	4/1929	Accident Hurlford 13/1/1913
42	7/1908	344	14373	9/1925	
157	11/1908	346	14374	10/1932	
158	6/1909	347	14375	2/1928	
185	7/1909	348	14376	1931	
186	11/1909	349	14377	10/1932	
171***	12/1911	395	14268	1930	
85***	4/1912	376	14269	1930	Accident St Enoch 31/7/1925
130	1/1912	345	14378	10/1927	

*Nos 18/26 fitted with the single bogie tenders during summer of 1908.
**No 27 fitted with Weir pump and feed water heater c1913 removed 1919.
***Nos 171 and 85 were renewals of 8 class 4-4-0 (same numbers).

0-4-4T Built by Neilson & Co. Works nos 4646-55.
DW 5ft 2in, TW 3ft 1in, Cyls 17½ x 24, Blr 4ft 3in x 10ft 1½in, THS 1169.5 sq
ft, WP 150lbs/sq in, WB 7ft 6in + 8ft 9in + 5ft 6in, Wt 51tons 9cwts.
Balanced slide valves on top of cyls. Stephenson link motion. One of class
(unidentified) fitted with air tubes in the firebox. Rebuilt by Whitelegg
with extended frames increasing tank capacity by 100 gallons to 1,100 gallons

and from 1¾tons of coal to 3tons and with short parallel chimneys. Some
had motion altered by replacing rocking shaft with an arm joining
intermediate and valve spindles. Built for suburban services. Load class
W, LMS class 1P.

No	Date	1919 no	Rebuilt	LMS no	Withdrawn
326	10/1893	520	1922	15245	1930
327	10/1893	521	1924	15246	9/1931
328	10/1893	522		15247	1931
329	10/1893	523	1921	15248	1932
330	10/1893	524	1926	15249	1930
331	10/1893	525	1923	15250	6/1931
332	10/1893	526	1923	15251	1930
333	10/1893	527	1924	15252	1930
334	11/1893	528	1921	15253	1932
335	11/1893	529	1922	15254	12/1931

O-4-4T Built by G&SW, Kilmarnock. Works nos 395-400.
DW 4ft 7½in, TW 2ft 6½in, Cyls 16 x 22, Blr 4ft 2in max diam, THS 890 sq ft,
WP 140lbs/sq in, WB 6ft 8in + 5ft 4in + 5ft 0in, Wt 42tons 8cwt. O/S frame
bogie, vacuum brake and trainpipes. Oval buffers, steam sanding and
reverser. Load class J.

No	Date	1919 no	LMS no	Withdrawn
266	5/1906	305	16080	11/1925
267	5/1906	306	16081	11/1932
268	6/1906	307	16082	1932
269*	6/1906	308	16083	1930
270	7/1906	309	16084	1930
271	7/1906	310	16085	12/1931

*No 269 in collision Irongray 1911.

O-4-OWT Rail Motor. Built by G&SW, Kilmarnock.
DW 3ft 6in, Cyls 9 x 15 O/S, THS 440 sq ft, WP 180lbs/sq in, WB 8ft 0in.
Tall dome with dpring balance safety valve on top. Frames were 57ft 2in
with coach section mounted on a carriage bogie. Loco fitted between the
frames and could be removed by dismantling the buffer beam. Coach was in
two sections seating 50 passengers. Gas lighting. Guard's compartment next
to coach end driving compartment. Both were painted in coaching stock red,
the loco being unlined. Numbers were carried on brass plates on the bunker
side. In addition to the loco well tank a second tank was carried under the
coach. Regulator and reverser were operated by the fireman when running
coach forward. One bogie coach or two four-wheel vehicles could be hauled.
Numbered 1-3 on the following dates.

No	Date	
1	9/1904	No works number
2	11/1905	All withdrawn 12/1916
3	11/1905*	All scrapped 1922

*No 3 was separated from the coach section which was given a second bogie
and the frames shortened. It was then attached to the loco in conventional
manner, the loco being then painted standard loco green. This was an attempt
to prevent oscillation from the outside cylinders being transmitted to the
coach.

O-4-OT Built by G&SW, Kilmarnock. Works nos 404/5/15-18.
DW 4ft 7½in, Cyls 16 x 24, Blr 4ft 4in max diam, THS 885.5 sq ft, WP 140lbs/
sq in, WB 7ft 6in, Wt 39tons 12cwt (heaviest O-4-OT in the UK). Drive to
second axle. Stephenson link motion on leading axle driving slide valves on
top of cylinders through a rocking shaft in front of the cylinders. Steam
brake, reverser and sanding. Load class K.

No	Date	1919 no	LMS no	Withdrawn
272	1/1907	316	16044	1930
273	1/1907	317	16045	1930
274	12/1908	318	16046	1930
275	1/1909	319	16047	1930
277	4/1909	320	16048	1930
278	5/1909	321	16049	12/1931

4-6-0 Built by North British Locomotive Co as below
            G&SW, Kilmarnock as below
DW 6ft 6in, LW 3ft 3in, Cyls 20 x 26 O/S, Blr 4ft 9¼in x 15ft 5in, THS 1852
sq ft, WP 180lbs/sq in, WB 6ft 6in + 6ft 2in + 6ft 9in + 8ft 3in, Wt 67tons
2cwt, 4,100 gallon double bogie tender. Swing link bogie, balanced slide
valves on top of cylinders. Stephenson link motion. Stirling steam reverser.
Boiler casing in three equal diamater rings butt and strap jointed. Belpaire
firebox. Cast iron chimney, steam sanding. Built to eliminate double
heading on main line. Extended smokeboxes fitted from 1919. Load class N,
LMS class 3P.

The following were built by North British Locomotive Co. Works nos 15734-43.

No	Date	1919 no	LMS no	Withdrawn
381	5/1903	495	14656	2/1931
382	5/1903	496	14657	1928
383	5/1903	497	14658	1930
384	5/1903	498	14659	1933
385	6/1903	499	14660	9/1927
386	6/1903	500	14661	4/1928
387	6/1903	501	14662	1930
388	6/1903	502	14663	10/1932
389*	6/1903	503	14664	6/1931
390	6/1903	504	14665	1930

*No 389 had Weir fee-water heating from about 1913, removed about 1919.

The following were built by G&SW, Kilmarnock. Works nos 422-5, 428-30 and
had higher cab cut-away and correspondingly raised tender sides. They had
the brake shoes in front of the DW instead of behind. Nos 125-7 had six-
wheel tenders. Nos 510/11 rebuilt by Whitelegg were given similar boilers
with new fireboxes 8ft 9in long instead of 8ft 0in. Smokeboxes were
extended from 4ft 1½in to 5ft 1½in, THS 1880 sq ft, WP 175lbs/sq in, Wt 67tons
19cwt. The boilers were said to be of Drummond's design.

No	Date	1919 no	Rebuilt	LMS no	Withdrawn
119	1/1910	505		14666	12/1931
120	1/1910	506		14667	9/1931
123	5/1910	507		14668	1/1928
124	6/1910	508		14669	1930
125	12/1910	509		14670	8/1931
126	1/1911	510	2/1920	14672	11/1932
127	2/1911	511	6/1920	14671	10/1931

4-6-0 Built by North British Locomotive Co. Works nos 19504/5.
DW 6ft 6in, LW 3ft 8in, Cyls 21 x 26, Blr 4ft 9¾in diam, THS 1560 sq ft +
superheater 445 sq ft, WP 160lbs/ sq in, WB 7ft 0in + 5ft 11in + 6ft 9in +
8ft 3in. Schmidt superheater. No 129 also built with Weir feed-water
heater. NBL recorded wt of no 128 as 71tons 7cwt, but Ahrons in Loco Mag,
March 1924, and the LMS Northern Division Diagram book give 69tons 2cwt.
4,100 gallon double bogie tenders. Load class M, LMS class 3P.

No	Date	1919 no	LMS no	Withdrawn
128	7/1911	512	14673	12/1933
129	7/1911	513	14674	11/1934

O-6-O Built by Dubs & Co. Works nos 2998-3017.
   DW 5ft 1½in, Cyls 18 x 26, Blr 4ft 5in max diam, THS 1,193 sq ft, WP 150lbs/
   sq in, WB 7ft 6in + 8ft 3in, Wt 39½tons. 2,500 gallon tender. Steam
   reverse, gravity sanding, Stirling pattern cab, Manson dome and double beat
   regulator, smoke box wing plates. Automatic vacuum brake. X3 boiler
   rebuilds as Smellie 22 class. Load class D, LMS class 1F (rebuilds 2F).

No	Date	1919 no	LMS no	Rebuilt X3 blr	Withdrawn
306	11/1892	178	17165		6/1926
307	11/1982	179	17166		1930
308	11/1892	180	17167	6/1925	11/1932
309	12/1892	181	17168		1927
310	12/1892	182	17169		1930
311	12/1892	183	17170	12/1925	12/1931
312	12/1892	184	17171		1928
313	12/1892	185	17172		8/1929
314	12/1892	186	17173		11/1932
315	12/1892	187	17174		8/1929
316	12/1892	188	17175		4/1928
317	12/1892	189	17176	4/1925	11/1932
318	1/1893	190	17177		1930
319	1/1893	191	17178		11/1925
320	1/1893	192	17179		11/1927
321	2/1893	193	17180		6/1926
322	2/1893	194	17181		5/1927
323	3/1893	195	17182		7/1925
324	3/1893	196	17183		10/1932
325*	3/1893	197	17184		7/1925

*No 325 had a domeless boiler for a period in the early 1900s.

O-6-O Built by G&SW, Kilmarnock. Works nos 299-316.
   DW 5ft 1½in, Cyls 18 x 26. Dimensions as 306 class. Manson cab and chimney
   as on 4-4-Os. Steam reverse and sanding. X3 boiler rebuilds as above.
   Load class D, LMS class 1F (rebuilds 2F).

No	Date	1919 no	LMS no	Rebuilt X3 blr	Withdrawn
160	12/1897	160	17185		12/1931
161	12/1897	161	17186		1925
162	12/1897	162	17187		12/1931
163	1/1898	163	17188		1930
164	1/1898	164	17189		1930
165	1/1898	165	17190	12/1925	1932
166	5/1898	166	17191		2/1928
167	5/1898	167	17192		1930
168	6/1898	168	17193		4/1933
169	6/1898	169	17194		4/1928
172	8/1898	170	17195	1926	9/1932
173	8/1898	171	(17196)		6/1926*
174	12/1898	172	17197		1930
175	12/1898	173**	17198		1928
176	12/1898	174	17199		12/1931
177	2/1899	175	17200		1925
178	2/1899	176	17201	7/1925	6/1931
179	2/1899	177	17202	7/1926	8/1929

   *No 171 sold 10/1926 to J Stewart Eastern & Co and subsequently named
   Edmund. To Ministry of Fuel and Power 1942.
   To NCB 1947 No 8, fitted LNE J21 class chimney. Scrapped 9/1953. (Smith
   Locomotives of the G&SW Rly, p95).
   **No 173 in accident Pinmore Tunnel 15/1/1922.

0-6-0 Built by Neilson Reid & Co as below
             North British Locomotive Co as below
             G&SW, Kilmarnock as below
DW 5ft 1½in, Cyls 18 x 26, Blr 4ft 5in max diam, THS 1208 sq ft, WP 150lbs/
sq in, WB 8ft 0in + 8ft 10in, Wt 44 tons, 2,500 gallon tenders. Steam
reverse, tool box in front of tender. 21 rebuilt by Whitelegg/LMS with X2
boilers, 4ft 11½in max diam, THS 1,361 sq ft, WP 170lbs/sq in, Wt 47¾tons.
Load class D (rebuilds C), LMS class 2F (rebuilds 3F).

The following were built by Neilson Reid & Co. Works nos 5655-74 (Order no
E833)

No	Date	1919 no	Rebuilt X2 blr	LMS no	Withdrawn
361	5/1900	115		17474	1932
362	5/1900	116	7/1922*	17489	11/1934
363	5/1900	117		17475	10/1931
364	5/1900	118		17476	11/1931
365	5/1900	119		17477	3/1928
366	5/1900	120	4/1922	17490	10/1932
367	5/1900	121		17478	5/1935
368	5/1900	122	11/1920*	17486	9/1937
369	6/1900	123	6/1922	17491	10/1931
370	5/1900	124	4/1924	17479	7/1934
371	6/1900	125	10/1920*	17487	1/1934
372	6/1900	126		17480	7/1931
373	6/1900	127		17481	5/1929
374	6/1900	128	10/1922	17492	5/1935
375	6/1900	129	3/1925	17482	11/1933
376	6/1900	130	11/1920*	17488	4/1937
377	6/1900	131	5/1925	17483	2/1935
378	6/1900	132	9/1922*	17493	11/1933
379	6/1900	133		17484	11/1933
380	6/1900	134	1924	17485	11/1936

*Rebuilt by Vickers & Co, Barrow.

The following were built by North British Locomotive Co. Works nos 17884-95
(Order L226).

No	Date	1919 no	Rebuilt X2 blr	LMS no	Withdrawn
391	4/1907	103	6/1921	17497	12/1937
392	4/1907	104	10/1920*	17498	7/1932
393	4/1907	105		17494	10/1928
394	4/1907	106	12/1920*	17499	9/1932
395	4/1907	107	10/1920*	17500	1931
396	4/1907	108	5/1921	17501	8/1936
397	4/1907	109	9/1922	17502	2/1935
398	4/1907	110		17495	1930
399	4/1907	111	7/1921	17503	11/1932
400	4/1907	112		17496	8/1931
401	4/1907	113	4/1921	17504	11/1936
402	4/1907	114	7/1922	17505	9/1935

*Rebuilt by Vickers & Co, Barrow.

The following were built by G&SW, Kilmarnock. Works nos 426-7 and had
2,900 gallon tenders and higher cab as 17 class.

No	Date	1919 no	LMS no	Withdrawn
12	7/1910	101	17506	10/1934
13	7/1910	102	17507	1932

O-6-O Built by North British Locomotive Co. Works nos 19244-58.
DW 5ft 1½in, Cyls 18 x 26, Blr 4ft 9½in diam, THS 1400 sq ft, WP 160lbs/sq
in, WB 8ft 0in + 8ft 10in, Wt 46tons 15cwts, 2,900 gallon tender. Development of 361 class with larger boiler similar to 240 class 4-4-0 but pitched
9in lower. X2 boiler rebuild as above. Load class C, LMS class 2F (rebuild
3F).

No	Date	1919 no	Rebuilt X2 blr	LMS no	Withdrawn
17	7/1910	86		17508	10/1931
41	7/1910	92		17514	2/1934
43	7/1910	93		17515	5/1935
46	7/1910	94		17516	1930
47	7/1910	95		17517	4/1931
48	9/1910	96		17518	1930
49	9/1910	97		17519	9/1936
50	9/1910	98		17520	1930
51	9/1910	99		17521	1/1937
118	9/1910	100		17522	10/1931
22	10/1910	87	10/1920	17509	6/1934
23	10/1910	88		17510	1930
24	10/1910	89		17511	10/1931
35	10/1910	90		17512	5/1936
37	11/1910	91		17513	12/1931

O-6-O Built by G&SW, Kilmarnock. Works nos 431-4, 440-5.
DW 5ft 1½in, Cyls 18 x 26, Blr 4ft 5in max diam, THS 1193 sq ft, WP 150lbs/sq
in, WB 7ft 6in + 8ft 3in, Wt 37tons 8cwt. Boiler similar to 306 class above,
Stirling cab, Manson's steam brake. Load class D, Lms class 2F.
Renewals of Smellie 22 class (same numbers).

No	Date	1919 no	LMS no	Withdrawn
281	7/1911	140	17203	1930
282	6/1911	141	17204	11/1927
283	6/1912	143	17205	1930
286	6/1912	144	17206	1930
285	7/1911	142	17207	1930
290	7/1912	148	17211	1928
291	7/1912	149	17212	10/1927
287	12/1912	145	17208	1930
288	11/1912	146	17209	1930
289	11/1912	147	17210	1930

O-6-OT Built by G&SW, Kilmarnock. Works nos 284-7, 365-70.
DW 4ft 7½in, Cyls 16 x 22, Blr 4ft 2in max diam, THS 890 sq ft, WP 140lbs/ sq
in, WB 6ft 8in + 6ft 10in, Wt 40tons 3cwts. Shunting loco. Automatic vacuum
brakes, but first four had no train pipes. Front and rear sanding. Steam
reverser. Two rebuilt with frames extended by 1 foot for larger bunkers
increasing coal capacity by 7cwt to 2½tons and tanks extended to front of
smokebox increasing capacity by 460 gallons to 1,110 gallons with shorter
cast iron chimneys. Wt 43tons 13cwts. Load class I.

No	Date	1919 no	Rebuilt	LMS no	Withdrawn
14	7/1896	277		16103	1928
19	7/1896	278		16104	1930
32	10/1896	280	1921	16105	1931
105	11/1896	282		16106	1930
208	5/1903	284		16107	1930
209	5/1903	285		16108	10/1932
210	6/1903	286	1922	16109	8/1931
211	6/1903	287		16110	12/1931
212	7/1903	288		16111	11/1932
213	7/1903	289		16112	1930

Class continued by Drummond page no 167.

Drummond Locomotives 1913-17

4-4-0 Built by North British Locomotive Co. Works nos 20128-33.
DW 6ft 0in, LW 3ft 6in, Cyls 19½ x 26, Blr 5ft 3in x 12ft 0in, THS 1884 sq ft,
WP 180lbs/sq in, WB 6ft 6in + 8ft 3in + 10ft 0in, Wt 61tons 17cwt. Completely
new style of design similar to LSW D15 class. Driving position changed to
letf-hand side. Six-wheel outside frame 3,800 gallon tender. Inside
Walschaerts valve gear. Smoke box steam drier and tender water-feed heater on
the Dugald Drummond system. Piston valves. Safety valves over firebox.
Vacuum brake and train pipe and also fitted with Westinghouse equipment.
Injectors substituted for feed-water heating and pumps in 1915. Steam driers
removed in 1919, Wt then being recorded as 61tons. All but one fitted with
superheaters by LMS. Load class P, LMS class 3P.

No	Date	1919 no	Rebuilt S'heat	LMS no	Withdrawn
131	6/1913	331	7/1923	14510	9/1936
132	6/1913	332		14511	10/1934
133	6/1913	333	1/1931	14512	10/1934
134	6/1913	334	2/1926	14513	12/1937
135	6/1913	335	9/1926	14514	7/1936
136*	6/1913	336	9/1926	14515	6/1937

*No 136 was originally fitted with a domed firegrate. Later, as no 336, it
was fitted with 'pop' safety valves in 1920.

4-4-0 Built by G&SW, Kilmarnock. Works nos 451-6.
DW 6ft 0in, LW 3ft 6in, Cyls 19½ x 26, THS 1,592 sq ft + 330.61 sq ft
superheater, Wt 64tons 1cwt (assumed). Other dimensions as 131 class.
Superheater version of 131 class with Schmidt superheater (22 elements),
Wakefield mechanical lubricator, double acting Weir feed pumps (removed by
Whitelegg). Marine-type big ends, replaced by cottered type. Left-hand
drive. Heaviest 4-4-0 in UK. Load class P, LMS class 3P.

No	Date	1919 no	LMS no	Withdrawn
137	1/1915	325*	14516	9/1936
138	2/1915	326	14517	5/1937
139	2/1915	327	14518	12/1934
140	8/1915	328	14519	11/1936
151	8/1915	329	14520	11/1935
152	9/1915	330	14521	8/1937

*No 325 was reboilered 1923 with boiler similar to the rebuilt No 394 (ex 11)
with Robinson superheater, THS 1591 sq ft + superheater 211 sq ft. Reversing
gear moved to right-hand side.

0-6-0 Built by North British Locomotive Co. Works nos 20113-27.
DW 5ft 0in, Cyls 19½ x 26, Blr 5ft 4½in max diam, THS 1784 sq ft, WP 180lbs/
sq in, WB 8ft 1in + 9ft 0in, Wt 57tons 15½cwt. Six-wheel outside frame
3,800 gallon tenders. Left-hand drive, lock up safety valves over firebox,
smoke box steam drier, Stephenson Link motion, piston valves placed above
cylinders. Smoke box wing plates. Drummond steam reverser and tender-water
heater. Gravity sanding and vacuum brake with train pipe. Known as
'pumpers' because of the feed water pumps. Tender heaters, smokebox driers
and smoke box wing plates removed by Whitelegg. Marine type big ends
replaced by cottered type. Load class A, LMS class 4F.

No	Date	1919 no	LMS no	Withdrawn
279	4/1913	71	17750	9/1931
292	4/1913	72	17751	1930
293	4/1913	73	17752	11/1931
294	4/1913	74	17753	12/1932
295	4/1913	75	17754	8/1931

296	5/1913	**76**	17755	1930		
297	5/1913	**77**	17756	11/1932		
298	5/1913	**78**	17757	1930		
299	5/1913	**79**	17758	9/1933		
300	5/1913	**80**	17759	4/1933	Accident Pinwherry	
301	6/1913	**81**	17760	1930		2/7/1928
302	6/1913	**82**	17761	1930		
303	6/1913	**83**	17762	10/1931		
304	6/1913	**84**	17763	10/1931		
305	6/1913	**85**	17764	1930		

2-6-0 Built by North British Locomotive Co. Works nos 21172-82.
DW 5ft 0in, LW 3ft 6in, Cyls 19½ x 26, Blr 5ft 4½in max diam, THS 1491 sq ft
+ superheater 211 sq ft, WP 180lbs/sq in, WB 6ft 6in + 8ft 1in + 9ft 0in, Wt
62tons 0½cwt. Six-wheel outside frame 3,970 gallon tender. Eight-wheel
version of 279 class 0-6-0 with Robinson superheater and lengthened smokebox.
Mechanical lubricator, no feedwater heating. Vacuum brakes and train pipes.
Tender carried two lifting jacks. Known as *Austrian goods* due to wholly
unfounded story about an Austrian order frustrated by the war. Load class A,
LMS class 4F.

		Renumbered		1919	LMS	
No	Date	no	date	no	no	Withdrawn
403	9/1915	**33**	1/1916	**52**	17821*	9/1946
404	9/1915	**34**	1/1916	**53**	17822	4/1944
405	9/1915	**92**	1/1916	**55**	17824	9/1935
406	9/1915	**93**	1/1916	**56**	17825	11/1936
407	9/1915	**94**	1/1916	**57**	17826	11/1945
408	9/1915	**99**	1/1916	**58**	17827*	4/1938
409	11/1915	**16**	12/1915	**51**	17820*	1/1938
410	10/1915	**61**	12/1915	**54**	17823	12/1936
116**	11/1915			**59**	17828	12/1935
117**	11/1915			**60**	17829	1/1939
					reinstated 1942	
					finally w'drawn 3/1947	
121**	11/1915			**61**	17830*	11/1938

*LMS 17820/1 reboilered 1931 and 17827/30 in 1934 with boilers built at St
 Rollox.
**Nos 116/7 & 121 were intended to be 411-3.

0-6-0T Built by G&SW Kilmarnock. Works nos 446-50.
DW 4ft 7½in, Cyls 16 x 22. Continuation of Manson class 14 (page no   ).

		1919		LMS	
No	Date	no	Rebuilt	no	Withdrawn
1	2/1914	**275**	1922	16113	1931
2	2/1914	**276**		16114	1932
21	2/1914	**279**		16115	1932
38	3/1914	**281**		16116	10/1932
184	3/1914	**283**	2/1923	16117	9/1931

0-6-0T Built by North British Locomotive Co. Works nos 21519-21.
DW 4ft 2in, Cyls 17 x 22, Blr 3ft 11⅞in max diam, THS 838 sq ft, WP 160lbs/
sq in, Wt 40tons. Richardson balanced slide valves, Walschaerts valve gear,
lever reverse. Drive was to centre wheels which were flangeless, vacuum brake
without train pipe. Load class H, LMS class 2F.

		1919	LMS	
No	Date	no	no	
5	11/1917	**322**	16277	Withdrawn 4/1932
				Reinstated 5/1932
				Finally withdrawn 4/1934
7	11/1917	**324**	16378	Sold 4/1934 to Hatfield Colliery No 5.

9	11/1917	**324**	16379	Sold 4/1934 to Hatfield Colliery no 7 (later NCB) Preserved Glasgow Museum of Transport.	

O-6-2T Built by North British Locomotive Co. Works nos 21242-7, 21507-18.
DW 5ft 0in, TW 4ft 0in, Cyls 18¼ x 26, Blr 4ft 6¼in max diam, THS 1254 sq ft,
WP 180lbs/sq in, WB 7ft 6in + 7ft 6in + 7ft 9in, Wt 66tons 5¼cwt.   Eddlewood
mechanical lubricator.   Drummond steam reverser.   Vacuum brake and train
pipe.   Radial TW gave 2in play either side of centre.   Load class B, LMS
class 3F.

No	Date	1919 no	LMS no	1926 no	Withdrawn
45*	12/1915	**23**	16422	16922	12/1945
84*	12/1915	**24**	16423	16923	1/1938
90*	12/1915	**25**	16424	16924	5/1936
91*	12/1915	**26**	16425	16925	3/1936
122*	1/1916	**11**	16410	16910	11/1936**
284*	1/1916	**22**	16421	16921	12/1945
101	5/1917	**27**	16426	16926	12/1945
102	5/1917	**28**	16427	16927	2/1938
141	6/1917	**12**	16411	16911	3/1946
142	6/1917	**13**	16412	16912	6/1938
143	6/1917	**14**	16413	16913	1/1938
144	6/1917	**15**	16414	16914	6/1937
145	6/1917	**16**	16415	16915	3/1938
146	6/1917	**17**	16416	16916	2/1936
147	6/1917	**18**	16417	16917	8/1940
148	6/1917	**19**	16418	16918	5/1936
149	6/1917	**20**	16419	16919	11/1937
150	6/1917	**21**	16420	16920	11/1947

*1915/16 locos were intended to be nos 16/61/116/7/21/2
**LMS 16910 sold to Robert McAlpine & Son (No 80).

Whitelegg Locomotives 1919-22

4-4-0 Built by G&SW, Kilmarnock (no works no).
DW 6ft 9½in, LW 3ft 7½in, Cyls 18¼ x 26. Replacement of earlier locomotive
not identified. As Whitelegg rebuild of Manson 8 class (page no 157) with X1
boiler.

No	Date	LMS no	Withdrawn
485	7/1921	14270	12/1933

0-6-0 Built by G&SW, Kilmarnock (no works no).
DW 5ft 1½in, Cyls 18 x 26. Replacement of earlier locomotive not identified.
As Whitelegg rebuilds of Manson 361 class (page no 164) with X2 boilers.

No	Date	LMS no	Withdrawn
150	7/1921	17523	1931
151	12/1921	17524	4/1935

0-6-2T Built by North British Locomotive Co. Works nos 22070-9.
DW 5ft 0in, TW 4ft 0in, Cyls 18¼ x 26, Wt 66tons 19cwts. Other dimensions as
Drummond 45 class (page no 168). Ordered by Drummond but amended before
completion by Whitelegg in certain details. Water capacity increased to
1910 gallons (as against 1800 gallons. 45 class). Controls arranged for
right-hand drive. Load class B, LMS class 3F.

No	Date	LMS no	1926 no	Withdrawn	
1	5/1919	16400	16900	12/1939	
2	5/1919	16401	16901	2/1944	
3	5/1919	16402	16902	12/1938	
4	5/1919	16403	16903	11/1936*	
5	5/1919	16404	16904	2/1937**	
6	6/1919	16405	16905	4/1948	Allotted BR 56905
7	6/1919	16406	16906	6/1938	
8	6/1919	16407	16907	11/1945	
9	6/1919	16408	16908	6/1937**	
10	6/1919	16409	16909	6/1936	

*LMS 16903 Sold to Robert McAlpine & Son (no 81)
**LMS 16904/8 Sold to Ashington Coal Co (Nos 1&2)

0-4-0ST Built by Peckett & Co. Works no 977 in 1904. Purchased from Ayr
          Harbour Commissioners on taking over Ayr Harbour in 1919.
DW 3ft 2½in, Cyls 14 x 20, WP 150lbs/sq in, WB 5ft 6in, Wt 24½tons. Brass
covered dome with spring safety valves on dome.

No	Date	LMS no	
735	1919	16043	Was Kilmarnock works shunter in 1928.
			Withdrawn 1930

4-6-4T Built by North British Locomotive Co. Works nos 22886-91.
DW 6ft 0in, LW & TW 3ft 6in, Cyls 22 x 26 O/S, Blr 5ft 6⅜in x 14ft 11in,
THS 1730 sq ft + 255 sq ft superheater, WP 180lbs/sq in, WB 7ft 0in + 5ft
8in + 6ft 7in + 6ft 7in + 6ft 2in + 7ft 0in, Wt 99tons 1½cwts. Robinson
21 element superheater. Boiler clothing plates were of blue planished steel
and were originally unpainted. Flat topped dome cover and safety valves
(over firebox) painted black. Walschaerts valve gear, piston valves, steam
reverser, swing link bogies with coil springs. Vacuum brake on coupled
wheels. Large cab and footplate. An updated version of Whitelegg's 4-6-4T
design for the LT&SR (Volume 3A). Load class 0, LMS class 5p. LMS red
livery applied.

No	Date	LMS no	Withdrawn
540	3/1922	15400	1/1935
541	3/1922	15401	4/1935
542	3/1922	15402	3/1935
543	4/1922	15403	12/1935
544	4/1922	15404	9/1936
545	4/1922	15405	8/1936

1	1850	ex GPK&A
	1860	2-2-2 20 class
	1879	O-4-4T 1 class
	1914	O-6-OT 14 class
	1919	O-6-2T 1 class
2	1850	ex GPK&A
	1857	2-2-2 2 class
	1879	O-4-4T 1 class
	1914	O-6-OT 14 class
	1919	O-6-2T 1 class
3	1850	ex GPK&A
-4	1858	2-2-2 2 class
	1877	4-4-O 6 class
	1897	4-4-O 8 class
	1919	O-6-2T 1 class
5	1850	ex GPK&A
	1854	O-4-O ex 94
	1873	O-4-O 65 class
	1888	O-6-O 22 class
	1917	O-6-OT 5 class
	1919	O-6-2T 1 class
6	1850	ex GPK&A
	1854	O-4-O ex 95
	1873	4-4-O 6 class
	1895	4-4-O 8 class
	1919	O-6-2T 1 class
7	1850	ex GPK&A
	1872	O-4-O 65 class
	1888	O-6-O 22 class
	1917	O-6-OT 5 class
	1919	O-6-2T 1 class
8	1850	ex GPK&A
	1851	2-2-2
	1868	2-4-O 8 class
	1892	4-4-O 8 class
	1919	O-6-2T 1 class
9	1850	ex GPK&A
	1857	O-4-2 9 class
	1874	O-4-O 65 class
	1888	O-6-O 22 class
	1917	O-6-OT 5 class
	1919	O-6-2T 1 class
10	1850	ex GPK&A
	1854	ex Ardrossan
	1861	2-2-2 40 class
	1877	4-4-O 6 class
	1895	4-4-O 8 class
	1919	O-6-2T 1 class
11	1850	ex GPK&A
	1860	2-2-2 2 class
	1877	4-4-O 6 class
	1897	4-4-O
	1919	O-6-2T ex 122
12	1850	ex GPK&A
	1858	2-2-2 2 class
	1878	O-6-O 13 class
	1910	O-6-O 361 class
	1919	O-6-2T ex 141
13	1850	ex GPK&A
	1860	2-2-2 2 class
	1877	O-6-O 13 class
	1910	O-6-O 361 class
	1919	O-6-2T ex 142
14	1850	ex GPK&A
	1857	O-4-2 9 class
	1876	O-4-OST 113 class
	1896	O-6-OT 14 class
	1919	O-6-2T ex 143
15	1850	Blank
	1857	O-4-2 9 class
	1876	4-4-O 6 class
	1895	4-4-O 8 class
	1919	O-6-2T ex 144
16	1850	Blank
	1851	2-2-2
	1868	2-2-2 45 class
	1885	O-6-O 22 class
	1915	2-6-O ex 409
	1919	O-6-2T ex 145
17	1850	ex GPK&A
	1857	O-4-2 9 class
	1877	O-6-O 13 class
	1910	O-6-O 17 class
	1919	O-6-2T ex 146
18	1850	ex GPK&A
	1860	2-2-2 2 class
	1880	2-4-O 157 class
	1907	4-4-O 18 class
	1919	O-6-2T ex 147
19	1850	ex GPK&A
	1858	2-2-2 2 class
	1876	O-4-OST 113 class
	1896	O-6-OT 14 class
	1919	O-6-2T ex 148
20	1850	ex GPK&A
	1857	O-4-2 9 class
	1876	4-4-O 6 class
	1895	4-4-O 8 class
	1919	O-6-2T ex 149
21	1850	ex GPK&A
	1859	2-2-2 2 class
	1874	O-4-4T 1 class
	1914	O-6-OT 14 class
	1919	O-6-2T ex 150
22	1850	ex GPK&A
	1861	O-4-2 23 class
	1881	O-6-O 22 class
	1910	O-6-O 17 class
	1919	O-6-2T ex 284
23	1850	ex GPK&A
	1860	O-4-2 23 class
	1881	O-6-O 22 class
	1910	O-6-O 17 class
	1919	O-6-2T ex 45
24	1850	ex GPK&A
	1861	O-4-2 23 class

	1878	O-6-O 13 class
	1898	O-6-O ex 165
	1898	O-6-O ex 159
	1910	O-6-O 17 class
	1919	Blank
50	1850	ex GD&C
	1863	O-6-O 46 class
	1878	O-6-O 13 class
	1910	O-6-O 17 class
	1919	Blank
51	1850	ex GD&C
	1863	O-6-O 46 class
	1878	O-6-O 13 class
	1910	O-6-O 17 class
	1919	2-6-O ex 16
52	1850	ex GD&C
	1864	O-4-O 52 class
	1886	4-4-O 153 class
	1919	2-6-O ex 33
53	1850	ex GD&C
	1865	O-4-O 52 class
	1886	4-4-O 153 class
	1919	2-6-O ex 34
54	1850	ex GD&C
	1866	O-4-O 52 class
	1886	4-4-O 153 class
	1919	2-6-O ex 61
55	1850	ex GD&C
	1866	O-4-O 52 class
	1887	4-4-O 153 class
	1919	2-6-O ex 92
56	1850	ex GD&C
-57	1865	O-4-O 52 class
	1887	4-4-O 153 class
	1919	2-6-O ex 93/4
58	1850	ex GD&C
	1866	O-6-O 58 class
	1890	O-6-O 22 class
	1919	2-6-O ex 99
59	1850	ex GD&C
	1870	2-4-O 75 class
	1891	Blank
	1894	4-4-O 8 class
	1919	2-6-O ex 116
60	1850	ex GD&C
	1870	2-4-O 75 class
	1894	4-4-O 8 class
	1919	2-6-O ex 117
61	1850	ex GD&C
	1868	2-2-2 45 class
	1885	O-6-O 22 class
	1915	2-6-O ex 410
	1919	2-6-O ex 121
62	1850	ex GD&C
	1871	2-4-O 75 class
	1894	4-4-O 8 class
	1919	Blank
63	1850	ex GD&C
	1870	2-4-O 75 class
	1895	4-4-O 8 class
	1919	Blank

64	1850	ex GD&C
	1871	2-4-O 75 class
	1895	4-4-O 8 class
	1919	Blank
65	1850	ex GD&C
	1871	O-4-O 65 class
	1887	4-4-O 153 class
	1899	Blank
	1900	4-4-O 8 class
	1919	Blank
66	1850	ex GD&C
	1871	O-4-O 65 class
	1887	4-4-O 153 class
	1919	Blank
67	1850	ex GD&C
	1872	O-4-O 65 class
	1887	4-4-O 153 class
	1919	Blank
68	1850	ex GD&C
	1873	O-4-O 65 class
	1887	4-4-O 153 class
	1919	Blank
69	1850	ex GD&C
	1871	O-4-O 65 class
	1887	4-4-O 153 class
	1919	Blank
70	1850	ex GD&C
	1872	O-4-O 65 class
	1888	4-4-O 153 class
	1919	Blank
71	1850	ex GD&C
	1870	2-4-O 75 class
	1892	4-4-O 8 class
	1919	O-6-O ex 279
72	1850	ex GD&C
	1870	2-4-O 8 class
	1892	4-4-O 8 class
	1919	O-6-O ex 292
73	1851	ex GD&C
	1868	2-4-O 8 class
	1893	4-4-O 8 class
	1919	O-6-O ex 293
74	1851	ex GD&C
	1870	2-4-O 8 class
	1893	4-4-O 8 class
	1919	O-6-O ex 294
75	1851	ex GD&C
-76	1870	2-4-O 75 class
	1893	4-4-O 8 class
	1919	O-6-O ex 295/6
77	1851	ex GD&C
	1869	2-4-O 8 class
	1893	4-4-O 8 class
	1911	4-4-O 240 class
	1919	O-6-O ex 297
78	1851	ex GD&C
	1870	2-4-O 8 class
	1893	4-4-O 8 class
	1919	O-6-O ex 298
79	1851	ex GD&C
	1868	2-2-2 45 class

	1886	4-4-0 153 class
	1919	0-6-0 ex 299
80	1851	ex GD&C
	1868	2-4-0 8 class
	1893	4-4-0 8 class
	1919	0-6-0 ex 300
81	1851	ex GD&C
	1869	2-4-0 8 class
	1893	4-4-0 8 class
	1919	0-6-0 ex 301
82	1851	ex GD&C
-83	1869	2-4-0 8 class
	1894	4-4-0 8 class
	1919	0-6-0 ex 302/3
84	1851	ex GD&C
	1868	2-2-2 45 class
	1886	0-6-0 22 class
	1915	0-6-2T 45 class
	1919	0-6-0 ex 304
85	1851	ex GD&C
	1869	2-4-0 8 class
	1892	4-4-0 8 class
	1912	4-4-0 18 class
	1919	0-6-0 ex 305
86	1852	0-4-0 86 class
	1872	0-4-0 65 class
	1888	4-4-0 153 class
	1919	0-6-0 ex 17
87	1852	0-4-0 86 class
-89	1872	0-4-0 65 class
	1889	4-4-0 153 class
	1919	0-6-0 ex 22-4
90	1852	0-4-0 86 class
	1872	0-4-0 65 class
	1889	0-6-0 22 class
	1915	0-6-2T 45 class
	1919	0-6-0 ex 35
91	1852	0-4-0 86 class
	1873	0-4-0 65 class
	1889	0-6-0 22 class
	1915	0-6-2T 45 class
	1919	0-6-0 ex 37
92	1853	0-4-0 86 class
	1872	0-4-0 65 class
	1890	0-6-0 22 class
	1916	2-6-0 ex 405
	1919	0-6-0 ex 41
93	1853	0-4-0 86 class
	1873	0-4-0 65 class
	1890	0-6-0 22 class
	1916	2-6-0 ex 406
	1919	0-6-0 ex 43
94	1853	0-4-0 86 class
	1855	2-4-0
	1866	0-6-0 58 class
	1890	0-6-0 22 class
	1916	2-6-0 ex 407
	1919	0-6-0 ex 46
95	1853	0-4-0 86 class
	1855	2-2-2 95 class
	1874	4-4-0 6 class

96	1896	4-4-0 8 class
	1919	0-6-0 ex 47
96	1855	2-2-2 95 class
	1875	4-4-0 6 class
	1896	4-4-0 8 class
	1919	0-6-0 ex 48
97	1855	2-2-2 95 class
	1874	4-4-0 6 class
	1896	4-4-0 8 class
	1919	0-6-0 ex 49
98	1855	2-2-2 95 class
	1874	4-4-0 6 class
	1895	4-4-0 8 class
	1919	0-6-0 ex 50
99	1855	0-(2-2)-0 99 class
	1866	0-6-0 58 class
	1891	0-6-0 22 class
	1916	2-6-0 ex 408
	1919	0-6-0 ex 51
100	1855	0-(2-2)-0 99 class
	1866	0-6-0 58 class
	1891	0-6-0 22 class
	1919	0-6-0 ex 118
101	1855	0-(2-2)-0 99 class
-102	1867	0-6-0 58 class
	1892	0-6-0 22 class
	1917	0-6-2T 45 class
	1919	0-6-0 ex 12/13
103	1855	0-6-0 103 class
-104	1871	2-4-0 75 class
	1894	4-4-0 8 class
	1919	0-6-0 ex 39/2
105	1856	0-4-2 105 class
	1876	0-4-0ST 113 class
	1896	0-6-0T 14 class
	1919	0-6-0 ex 393
106	1856	0-4-2 105 class
	1875	4-4-0 6 class
	1896	4-4-0 8 class
	1919	0-6-0 ex 394
107	1856	0-4-2 105 class
-108	1875	4-4-0 6 class
	1895	4-4-0 8 class
	1919	0-6-0 ex 395/6
109	1858	2-4-0
	1874	0-4-0 65 class
	1889	4-4-0 153 class
	1919	0-6-0 ex 397
110	1858	0-4-2 34 class
	1874	4-4-0 6 class
	1896	4-4-0 8 class
	1919	0-6-0 ex 398
111	1858	0-4-2 34 class
	1876	4-4-0 6 class
	1896	4-4-0 8 class
	1919	0-6-0 ex 399
112	1859	0-4-2 34 class
	1876	4-4-0 6 class
	1896	4-4-0 8 class
	1919	0-6-0 ex 400
113	1859	0-4-2 34 class

	1875	0-4-OST 113 class		1883	4-4-0 119 class
	1900	0-4-2 113 class (ex 192)		1913	4-4-0 131 class
	1919	0-6-0 ex 401		**1919**	0-6-0 ex 25
114	1859	0-4-2 34 class	136	1864	0-4-2 131 class
	1876	0-4-OST 113 class		1883	4-4-0 119 class
	1900	0-4-2 113 class (ex 189)		1913	4-4-0 131 class
	1919	0-6-0 ex 402		**1919**	0-6-0 ex 58
115	1859	0-4-2 34 class	137	1864	0-4-2 131 class
	1874	4-4-0 6 class		1884	4-4-0 119 class
	1897	4-4-0 8 class		1915	4-4-0 137 class
	1911	4-4-0 240 class		**1919**	0-6-0 ex 100
	1919	0-6-0 ex 361	138	1864	0-4-2 131 class
116	1860	0-4-2 23 class		1884	4-4-0 119 class
-117	1885	0-6-0 22 class		1915	4-4-0 137 class
	1915	2-6-0 403 class		**1919**	0-6-0 ex 207
	1919	0-6-0 ex 362/3	139	1864	0-4-2 131 class
118	1860	0-4-2 23 class		1884	4-4-0 119 class
	1881	0-6-0 22 class		1915	4-4-0 137 class
	1910	0-6-0 17 class		**1919**	0-6-0 ex 220
	1919	0-6-0 ex 364	140	1864	0-4-2 131 class
119	1860	0-4-2 23 class		1884	4-4-0 119 class
-120	1882	4-4-0 119 class		1915	4-4-0 137 class
	1910	4-6-0 381 class		**1919**	0-6-0 ex 281
	1919	0-6-0 ex 365/6	141	1866	0-4-2 141 class
121	1860	0-4-2 23 class		1891	0-6-0 22 class
	1885	0-6-0 22 class		1917	0-6-2T 45 class
	1915	2-6-0 403 class		**1919**	0-6-0 ex 282
	1919	0-6-0 ex 367	142	1866	0-4-2 141 class
122	1860	0-4-2 23 class		1891	0-6-0 22 class
	1885	0-6-0 22 class		1917	0-6-2T 45 class
	1916	0-6-2T 45 class		**1919**	0-6-0 ex 285
	1919	0-6-0 ex 368	143	1866	0-4-2 141 class
123	1861	0-4-2 23 class		1890	0-6-0 22 class
-125	1882	4-4-0 119 class		1917	0-6-2T 45 class
	1910	4-6-0 381 class		**1919**	0-6-0 ex 283
	1919	0-6-0 ex 369-71	144	1866	0-4-2 141 class
126	1861	0-4-2 23 class		1891	0-6-0 22 class
	1882	4-4-0 119 class		1917	0-6-2T **45** class
	1911	4-6-0 381 class		**1919**	0-6-0 ex 286
	1919	0-6-0 ex 372	145	1866	0-4-2 141 class
127	1861	0-4-2 23 class		1890	0-6-0 22 class
	1885	4-4-0 119 class		1917	0-6-2T 45 class
	1911	4-6-0 381 class		**1919**	0-6-0 ex 287
	1919	0-6-0 ex 373	146	1866	0-4-2 141 class
128	1861	0-4-2 23 class		1891	0-6-0 22 class
	1885	4-4-0 119 class		1917	0-6-2T 45 class
	1911	4-6-0 128 class		**1919**	0-6-0 ex 288
	1919	0-6-0 ex 374	147	1866	0-4-2 141 class
129	1862	0-4-2 23 class	-148	1890	0-6-0 22 class
	1883	4-4-0 119 class		1917	0-6-2T 45 class
	1911	4-6-0 128 class		**1919**	0-6-0 ex 289/90
	1919	0-6-0 ex 375	149	1866	0-4-2 141 class
130	1862	0-4-2 23 class		1891	0-6-0 22 class
	1883	4-4-0 119 class		1917	0-6-2T **45** class
	1912	4-4-0 18 class		**1919**	0-6-0 ex 291
	1919	0-6-0 ex 376	150	1866	0-4-2 141 class
131	1864	0-4-2 131 class		1891	0-6-0 22 class
-134	1883	4-4-0 119 class		1917	0-6-2T 45 class
	1913	4-4-0 131 class		**1919**	Blank
	1919	0-6-0 ex 377-80		1921	0-6-0 361 class
135	1864	0-4-2 131 class	151	1866	2-2-2 45 class

	1884	4-4-0 119 class
	1915	4-4-0 137 class
	1919	Blank
	1921	0-6-0 360 class
152	1866	2-2-2 45 class
	1884	4-4-0 119 class
	1915	4-4-0 137 class
	1919	Blank
153	1867	2-2-2 45 class
-154	1886	4-4-0 153 class
	1919	Blank
155	1867	2-2-2 45 class
-156	1884	4-4-0 119 class
	1919	Blank
157	1866	0-4-0ST 157 class
	1879	2-4-0 157 class
	1908	4-4-0 18 class
	1919	Blank
158	1866	0-4-0ST 157 class
	1879	2-4-0 157 class
	1909	4-4-0 18 class
	1919	Blank
159	1867	2-2-2WT
	1878	0-6-0 13 class
	1899	Blank
	1900	0-4-2 113 class (ex 188)
	1919	Blank
160	1867	0-6-0 58 class
-162	1897	0-6-0 160 class
	1919	retained same no.
163	1867	0-6-0 58 class
	1896	0-6-0 ex 102A
	1898	0-6-0 160 class
	1919	retained same no
164	1867	0-6-0 58 class
-169	1888	0-6-0 160 class
	1919	retained same no
170	1868	2-4-0 8 class
	1892	4-4-0 8 class
	1919	0-6-0 ex 172
171	1869	2-4-0 8 class
	1892	4-4-0 8 class
	1912	4-4-0 18 class
	1919	0-6-0 ex 173
172	1869	0-6-0 58 class
-176	1898	0-6-0 160 class
	1919	0-6-0 ex 174-8
177	1869	0-6-0 58 class
	1899	0-6-0 160 class
	1919	0-6-0 ex 179
178	1869	0-6-0 58 class
-179	1899	0-6-0 160 class
	1919	0-6-0 ex 306/7
180	1869	0-6-0 58 class
-181	1900	0-4-2 113 class (ex 204/5)
	1919	0-6-0 ex 308/9
182	1869	2-4-0 8 class
-183	1894	4-4-0 8 class
	1919	0-6-0 ex 310/11
184	1869	0-4-0ST 157 class

185	1882	0-6-0 22 class
-186	1914	0-6-0T 1 class
	1919	0-6-0 ex 312
	1870	0-4-0ST 157 class
	1879	2-4-0 157 class
	1909	4-4-0 18 class
187	1919	0-6-0 ex 313/4
-190	1870	0-4-2 187 class
	1897	4-4-0 8 class
	1919	0-6-0 ex 315-8
191	1870	0-4-2 187 class
	1899	4-4-0 194 class
	1919	0-6-0 ex 319
192	1871	0-4-2 187 class
-197	1899	4-4-0 194 class
	1919	0-6-0 ex 320-5
198	1871	0-4-2 187 class
	1899	4-4-0 194 class
	1919	Blank
199	1871	0-4-2 187 class
	1897	0-4-2 ex 189
	1899	4-4-0 194 class
	1919	Blank
200	1871	0-4-2 187 class
-202	1900	4-4-0 194 class
	1919	Blank
203	1871	0-4-2 187 class
	1899	0-4-2 ex 190A
	1900	4-4-0 194 class
	1919	Blank
204	1871	0-4-2 187 class
	1900	4-4-0 194 class
	1919	Blank
205	1871	0-4-2 187 class
-206	1901	4-4-0 194 class
	1919	Blank
207	1873	0-4-0 65 class
	1889	0-6-0 22 class
	1919	Blank
208	1873	0-4-2 208 class
-213	1903	0-6-0T 14 class
	1919	Blank
214	1873	0-4-2 208 class
	1903	4-4-0 8 class
	1919	Blank
215	1873	0-4-2 208 class
-217	1904	4-4-0 8 class
	1919	Blank
218	1873	0-4-0ST 218 class
	1881	0-4-0ST 218 class
	1900	0-4-2 113 class (ex 194)
	1919	Blank
219	1873	0-4-0ST 218 class
	1881	0-4-0ST 218 class
	1900	0-4-2 113 class (ex 191)
	1919	Blank
220	1874	0-4-0ST
	1882	0-6-0 22 class
	1919	Blank
221	1874	0-4-2 221 class
-222	1902	0-4-2 224 class

No.	Year	Class
	1901	0-4-2 224 class
	1919	0-6-0T ex 32
281	1883	0-6-0 22 class
-282	1911	0-6-0 281 class
	1919	0-6-0T 38/105
283	1883	0-6-0 22 class
	1912	0-6-0 281 class
	1919	0-6-0T ex 184
284	1883	0-6-0 22 class
	1916	0-6-2T 45 class
	1919	0-6-0T ex 208
285	1883	0-6-0 22 class
-286	1911	0-6-0 281 class
	1919	0-6-0T ex 209/10
287	1883	0-6-0 22 class
-289	1912	0-6-0 281 class
	1919	0-6-0T ex 211-13
290	1883	0-6-0 22 class
	1912	0-6-0 281 class
	1919	Blank
291	1883	0-4-0T
	1889	0-6-0 22 class
	1912	0-6-0 279 class
	1919	Blank
292	1889	0-6-0 22 class
-301	1913	0-6-0 279 class
	1919	Blank
302	1892	ex G&PJ/A&W
-304	1913	0-6-0 279 class
	1919	Blank
305	1892	ex GP&J/A&W
	1913	0-6-0 279 class
	1919	0-4-4T ex 266
306	1892	0-6-0 306 class
-310	**1919**	0-4-4T ex 267-71
311	1892	0-6-0 306 class
-315	**1919**	Blank
316	1892	0-6-0 306 class
-317	**1919**	0-4-0T ex 272/3
318	1893	0-6-0 306 class
-321	**1919**	0-4-0T ex 274/7/8/5
322	1893	0-6-0 306 class
-324	**1919**	0-6-0T ex 5/7/9
325	1893	0-6-0 306 class
	1919	4-4-0 ex 137
326	1893	0-4-4T 326 class
-330	**1919**	4-4-0 ex 138/9/40/51/2
331	1893	0-4-4T 326 class
-335	**1919**	4-4-0 ex 131-5
336	1895	4-4-0 336 class
	1919	4-4-0 ex 136
337	1895	4-4-0 336 class
-341	**1919**	4-4-0 ex 18/26-9
342	1895	4-4-0 336 class
-345	**1919**	4-4-0 31/40/2/130
346	1899	4-4-0 336 class
-349	**1919**	4-4-0 ex 157/8/185/6
350	1899	4-4-0 336 class
-360	**1919**	4-4-0 ex 336-46
361	1900	0-6-0 361 class
-374	**1919**	4-4-0 ex 347-60
375	1900	0-6-0 361 class
-378	**1919**	4-4-0 ex 77/85/103/115
379	1900	0-6-0 361 class
-380	**1919**	4-4-0 ex 240/1
381	1903	4-6-0 381 class
-383	**1919**	4-4-0 ex 242/4/6
384	1903	4-6-0 381 class
-390	**1919**	4-4-0 ex 249-53/9/60
391	1907	0-6-0 361 class
-393	**1919**	4-4-0 ex 263-65
394	1907	0-6-0 361 class
-395	**1919**	4-4-0 ex 11/171
396	1907	0-6-0 361 class
-402	**1919**	4-4-0 ex 3/4/6/8/10/5/20
403	1915	2-6-0 403 class
-410	**1919**	4-4-0 ex 36/9/44/59/60/2-4
411	**1919**	4-4-0 ex 65/71-6/8/80-3/
-430		95-8/104/6-8
431	**1919**	4-4-0 ex 110-12/182/3/
-445		7-90/214-7/38/9
446	**1919**	4-4-0 ex 170
447	**1919**	4-4-0 ex 30/52-7/66-70/
-468		79/86-9/109/153-6
469	**1919**	4-4-0 ex 191-206
-484		
485	**1919**	Blank
	1921	4-4-0 8 class
486	**1919**	Blank
-494		
495	**1919**	4-4-0 ex
-504		381-90
505	**1919**	4-6-0 ex
-513		119/20/3-9
514	**1919**	Blank
-519		
520	**1919**	0-4-4T ex
-529		326-35
530	**1919**	Blank
-536		
537	**1919**	Blank
	1921	Allotted GB&K Joimt
538	**1919**	Blank
-539		
540	**1919**	Blank
-545	1922	4-6-4T 540 class
546	**1919**	Blank
-559		
560	**1919**	Duplicate stock
-624		0-6-0s
625	**1919**	Blank
-634		
635	**1919**	Duplicate stock
-657		0-4-2s
658	**1919**	Duplicate stock
-659		0-4-0STs
660	**1919**	Blank
-699		
700	**1919**	Duplicate stock
-719		4-4-0s
720	**1919**	Duplicate stock
-727		2-4-0s

728	**1919**	Duplicate stock
-731		stock O-4-4Ts
732	**1919**	Duplicate stock
-733		O-4-Os
734	**1919**	Blank
735	**1919**	O-4-OST
736	**1919**	Allotted
-737		G&P Joint

HIGHLAND RAILWAY

INTRODUCTION

Running through the stupendous scenery of what is now a major tourist area with its locomotives bearing their romantic Gaelic place names, this was a railway of strong character with an individuality all of its own.

As the northern part of the mainland railway system its main trunk routes remain intact to this day despite the remote areas through which they pass, because of their strategic importance and the difficult terrain which make the construction of modern roads difficult and expensive and their cost effectiveness for an essentially seasonal traffic flow, low.

In fact of all the Scottish railways the lines of the Highland have retained a greater proportion of their mileage despite many threats of closures. Only the branch lines and the old main line between Aviemore and Forres have been closed. The railway connected Inverness with Perth in the South and Aberdeen in the East. From Inverness to the North stretched the Northern main line 161¼ miles long to Wick and Thurso. At Dingwall the Kyle of Lochalsh line connected the railway to the Isle of Skye and the Western Isles.

It is important to remember that it was the railway which popularised the area as a tourist attraction, which grew steadily from the 1890s with heavy sleeping cars to be hauled over the 1,484 ft summit at Druimnachdar requiring the construction of large locomotives.

Another feature of the Highland was the fact that of the 506 route miles only about 47 miles were double track, including the passing loops.

The Great North of Scotland obtained an Act in 1846 for a railway from Aberdeen to Inverness, but capital for railways in the Highlands was not easy to raise, the expectations of profits being low and it was only opened to Huntly in 1854 and Keith in 1856 after the passing of two further Acts.

Inverness interests, impatient at the delay for the much needed link to Aberdeen, principally supported by the Earls of Grant and Seafield obtained powers in 1854 for a railway from Inverness to Nairn which was opened in 1855. A second company, the Inverness and Aberdeen Junction, was formed in 1856 to complete the line to Keith and to take over the Inverness and Nairn and this was opened in 1857-8, linking Inverness with Aberdeen.

The route was circuitous however with the inconvenience of having to change stations in Aberdeen with frequent lost connections and in 1861 the Inverness and Perth Junction was formed to provide a direct connection to the South over the already open Perth and Dunkeld railway. The I&PJ was opened in 1863 and with the P&D with which it amalgamated was worked by the I&AJ which it joined at Forres. The line joined the Scottish Midland Junction at Stanley Junction 7¼ miles from Perth with running powers into the station there.

Meanwhile the Inverness and Ross-shire was absorbed by the I&AJ on its opening to Dingwall in 1862 and reached Invergordon in 1863, Mickle Ferry and Bonar Bridge in 1864.

In 1865 the I&AJ and the I&PJ amalgamated and adopted the title of Highland Railway.

The line to the North was constructed by three companies all worked by the Highland. Two of these companies, the Sutherland (opened Bonar Bridge to Golspie 1868) and the Sutherland and Caithness (opened from Helmsdale to Wick and Thurso 1874) were heavily subscribed to by the HR, but the section of line from Golspie to Helmsdale was entirely financed by the Duke of Sutherland who put up £355,000. It was opened with its own locomotive and borrowed HR coaches as an isolated section between Dunrobin and Gartymore in 1870, being linked with the Sutherland at Golspie eight months later in 1871.

It would be accurate to say that this was a public spirited gesture by the Duke to promote employment rather than for a purely profit motive and in return he was accorded the right to run his locomotive and private saloon whenever he wished over the Highland system, as well as using it on his private line at Dunrobin Castle.

These three companies were amalgamated with the HR in 1884.

The Dingwall and Skye railway was authorised in 1868 and opened to Strome Ferry
on Loch Carron in 1870 passing through Strath Conon and Strath Bran and over the
watershed into Strath Carron. Unfortunately objections by a land owner caused
the line to by-pass Strathpeffer which was later served by a branch line (closed
1951).
The D&S was subscribed to by the Caledonian and the Highland railways and was
worked by the HR being amalgamated in 1880. In 1897 it was extended from Strome
Ferry to Kyle of Lochalsh.
By the 1890s the Company, with careful management, had become a reasonably
profitable undertaking and the tourist traffic was beginning to grow. Threats of
new, more direct, railway promotions to Inverness caused the Highland to obtain
powers to construct the present main line to Inverness from Aviemore over
Culloden Moor and the 1,315ft summit at Slochd Mhuic, cutting out the old route
via Forres which then became a secondary line. This shortened the Perth-
Inverness mileage by 25¼ miles and saved an hour on journey times. It was opened
in 1898.
Possible competition was staved off but with the expensive extension to Kyle of
Lochalsh (with some Government aid on strategic grounds) the resources of the
company were strained to the limit and many economies had to be made.
There were branches to Aberfeldy, Strathpeffer, Hopeman, Fort George, Fortrose,
Fochabers, Portessie, Dornoch and Lybster, the last two being light railways,
nominally independent, constructed under the Light Railways Act and worked 'one
engine in steam' without signalling. Branches to Inverness Harbour and Muirtown
were used only by goods trains.
The HR also worked the Invergarry and Fort Augustus railway from 1903 to 1907.
A Highland Bill to connect this line from Spean Bridge on the North British West
Highland line to Inverness through the Great Glen failed in the House of Lords
in 1897, but the HR was still interested in obtaining powers to operate steamers
on Loch Ness to make the connection. This Bill also failed in 1905 due to
opposition from David MacBrayne and in 1907 they withdrew in favour of the North
British.
Schemes for branches to Ullapool, Gairloch, Lochinver, Loch Laxford, Portskerra,
Scrabster, Gill's Bay, Cromarty, Portmahomak, an extension from Lybster to
Dunbeath and light railways in the Isle of Skye did not materialise.
A proposal for a merger with the Great North of Scotland put to a meeting in 1907
got a vote in favour, but was deemed not to have enough support due to the small
number of shareholders who voted.
In the 1914-18 war there was very heavy traffic on the HR to Admiralty bases at
Invergordon, Kyle of Lochalsh and to Thurso for Scapa Flow, the base of the Home
Fleet. In 1918 when stores for American tropps were being landed at Kyle the
public service was limited to one train each way a day for passengers and goods
had to go by sea from Glasgow.
To work all this traffic and indeed, prevent the complete failure of the system
due to lack of maintenance twenty locomotives from other companies were directed
to the HR by the war-time Railway Executive Committee. These were not the same
twenty all the time, however and the SLS History (1955) lists the following known
to have worked on the Highland and stipulates that the list is not necessarily
exhaustive.

GNSR	0-4-4T	No 84 and another.
LSWR	4-4-2T	0480, 0481, 0485, 0487
NER	0-6-0	162, 202, 262, 636, 1396, 1404, 264, 488, 79
	0-6-0T	1386 and another
	0-4-4T	951
NBR	0-6-0	614, 672, 30
	4-4-0	Two of 729 class
	0-6-0T	One of 1289 class
CR	0-6-0	560, 314, 555
	4-6-0	56 (retained until 1922)
	0-4-4T	1174
	4-4-0	770, 774, 70, 73, 75, 76, 89, 91
	0-6-0ST	One

```
LNWR      2-4-0      1173 (Precedent class The Auditor)
          0-6-0ST    3051, 3160
          0-6-0      3082
```

Locomotive Superintendends

Inverness and Aberdeen Junction

William Barclay	1856-65 Resigned

Highland Railway

William Stroudly	1856-9 Resigned
David Jones	1870-96 Retired
Peter Drummond	1897-1911 Resigned
Frederick Smith	1912-15 Resigned
Christopher Cumming	1915-22 Retired
David Chalmers Urie	1922-3 Formation of LMS

The Inverness and Nairn Railway appointed Alexander Allan of the Scottish Central as consulting engineer and it was he who laid down the specifications for all the locomotives on the I&N and I&AJ. He was also asked to make suitable appointments and he engaged, as Locomotive Superintendent, his nephew William Barclay, who had served his apprenticeship at Dundee and had been some time with George Forrester & Co in Liverpool.

David Jones was also engaged as a driver.

It has been stated (O.S. Nock Steam Railways in Retropspect, pps 33-5 that Barclay's personal contribution to locomotive development on the I&AJ was minimal and that he regarded his position as somewhat of a sinecure leaving everything to Jones whom he appointed as his assistant on 17/4/1858.

Certainly the I&AJ's locomotives were of Allan design, 'Crew' type singles and 2-4-Os of modest power.

It was under Barclay, however, that the locomotive works at Inverness was established in the triangle between the through lines and the North and South station lines where once had been a lake called Loch Gorm.

The I&AJ locos were painted dark green with black lining on the borders and boiler bands.

In 1865 the Board decided to appoint a new Superintendent and Barclay resigned.

His successor was William Stroudley, former works manager at Cowlairs on the Edinburgh and Glasgow railway.

A brilliant locomotive designer, as his famous work on the LBSC proves, Stroudley must have found his experience at Lochgorm frustrating. He was still only 32, keen and enthusiastic, yet the company having obtained the Allan locomotives for the Perth line had no money to spare for further loco building.

Only towards the end of his period was he able to undertake the rebuilding of I&N no 1 as a 2-4-0 and to design the 0-6-0T no 56 Balmain a design which he was to perfect on the LBSC as the famous Terrier tanks. Two more were produced after he left.

He also introduced the yellow colour which he termed 'improved engine green' on the HR with crimson framing and red and white lining for passenger locos, the green being retained for goods engines.

Jones, now 35 and Running Superintendend was appointed in 2/1870 to succeed him after a brief period when Dugald Drummond then Lochgorm Works Manager was in charge.

Jones came from Manchester and had trained on the NE Division of the LNWR at Longsight under Johm Ramsbottom and had acquired a very practical working knowledge of steam locomotives.

It is to Jones that the credit must go for building up the locomotive fleet during the years of the HR's expansion producing the five 4-4-0 designs, culminating in the Strath and Loch class and also introducing the first 4-6-0 locomotives to run in this country.

All of his designs were sound and practical and it is his work that we most associate with the traditional Highland practice.

Unfortunately he suffered an accident when testing one of the new 4-6-Os, badly scalding his left leg, and although the limb was saved he never really recovered and retired on 31/10/1896. It had been his life's work.
He reintroduced green livery in 1874 for passenger locos and this remained the livery until the Grouping although the shade of green varied at different periods and lining was omitted from 1903.
Smith painted the boilers of some engines black and changed the lettering from H.R. to *Highland Railway* (later adding *The*) and removed the number plates but these were only temporary changes and the green, letters H.R. and number plates returned with Cumming. Latterly buffer beams were red.
Coaches were green with varnished teak for the sleeping cars introduced in 1907. Two colour painting of coaches was adopted in 1896, the lower panels bronze green and upper panels white. This was discontinued in 1907.
During Jones period of office the vacuum brake was adopted as standard after trials with Westinghouse on 4-4-O no 64. Some locos were dual fitted however to work Caledonian and other Westinghouse fitted stock. The drivers position on the footplate was on the left.
Drummond came from the Caledonian where he had been works manager at St Rollox under his elder brother Dugald and latterly McIntosh.
As with his later designs for the Glasgow and South Western he was much influenced by the designs of the elder Drummond and broke with HR tradition by designing inside cylinder 4-4-Os, O-6-4Ts and O-6-Os, the latter being a comparative late comer to the Highland.
The *Castle* class 4-6-Os had already been designed by Jones and Drummond only amended it in details. The small and large *Ben* classes were introduced by him and he re-organised the Lochgorm works as he had St Rollox on the **Caledonian**
His status was raised to CME in 1906 with Smith, who had joined the company in 1903 as Works Manager as his assistant. When he left however, Smith was appointed under the old title of Locomotive, Carriage and Wagon Superintendent.
The tragic affair of Smith and the *River* class locomotives was largely a personal one as the design work on the loco was excellent and they were thoroughly modern, efficient machines.
Smith and the Civil Engineer Alexander Newlands had already clashed over a new turntable which Smith had ordered for Inverness without consulting anyone. It was the wrong length to fit the geometry of the track layout and had to be altered.
He arranged for the design work on the new locos to be done at Cowlairs on the NBR as there was only one draughtsman at Inverness and, once again, consultation with other departments was lacking.
Newlands declared the first loco no 70 *River Ness* too heavy for Highland routes and the Board demanded his immediate resignation.
The justification of Newlands decision remains debatable on technical grounds and with only a limited amount of bridge strengthening work they returned to the Highland section of the LMS only ten years later after their spell on the Caledonian.
Board minutes recorded that two had been delivered, but this may have meant ex-works and only no 70 may actually have arrived at Inverness.
Cumming came to the HR from the North British where he was DLS at Burntisland and it was to him that fell the task of coping with the tremendous upheaval of coping with the war traffic.
His superheater goods and *Clan* class 4-6-Os however were very successful and were judged to be the best of the locos taken over by the LMS in Scotland. It was the Highland, the smallest of the three Scottish companies in the LMS group where the locomotive department was in the best order.
Urie, the son of Robert Wallace Urie, the last CME of the LSWR came from the Midland Great Western in Ireland where was was assistant Locomotive Superintendent, but had only a watching brief on the Highland for seven months before the LMS took over on 1/1/1923 when he was appointed Assistant CME to Pickering of the Caledonian on the new Northern Division.

Duplicate List

An A suffix system was used for locos in revenue earning traffic, the suffix being changed to B if the locomotive was put onto Departmental duties.

HIGHLAND RAILWAY: Constituent Companies

Inverness and Nairn
Incorporated 1854. Opened 5 November 1855 (passenger) 1 December 1855 (goods).
Amalgamated with Inverness and Aberdeen Junction as below.

2 locomotives as under:

2-2-2 Built by Hawthorns, Leith. Works nos 129/30.
DW 6ft 0in, LW & TW 3ft 6in, Cyls 15 x 20 O/S, WP 100lbs/sq in, Wt 27tons
(approx).
Crewe type domeless boiler, two spring balance safety valves, one on boiler
and one on raised firebox casing. Allan link motion, weatherboards only.
Four wheel tender.

No*	Name	Date	Rebuilt	Withdrawn
1	Raigmore	9/1855	1869 2-4-0 Cyls 15½ x 20,	1873
			WB 6ft 10in + 6ft 11in and	(Blr to no 16
			cab (wheels from no 3)	
2	Aldourie	10/1855		2/1871

*Same numbers retained by L&AJ, 1857 and HR 1865.

Inverness and Aberdeen Junction
Incorporated 1856. Opened Nairn to Dalvey (temporary station) 22 December
1857, to Elgin 25 March 1858, throughout to Keith (junction with Great North
of Scotland) 18 August 1858. Leased **Inverness and Nairn** from 30 June 1857.
Amalgamated with I&N 17 May 1861. Worked Inverness and Perth Junction from
its opening. Dunkeld (junction with Perth and Dunkeld, opened 7 April 1856 and
amalgamated with I&PJ 8 June 1863) to Pitlochry 1 June 1863, Forres (junction
with I&AJ) to Aviemore 3 August 1863, throughout 9 September 1863. Absorbed
Inverness and Ross-shire 30 June 1862 (opened to Dingwall 11 June 1862, to
Invergordon 23 May 1863, to Mickle Ferry 1 June 1864, to Bonar Bridge 1 October
1864). Amalgamated with I&PJ 1 February 1865 adopting title **Highland Railway**
29 June 1865.

52 locomotives as under:

2-2-2 Built by Hawthorns, Leith. Works nos 146, 161.
DW 6ft 0in, LW & TW 3ft 6in, Cyls 15 x 20 O/S. As Inverness and Nairn 1
class above.

No	Name	Date	Withdrawn
3	St Martins	8/1856	1869 (Boiler to no 56 wheels to no 1)
4	Ardross	9/1857	1872 (Boiler to no 57, wheels to no 3
			1877)

2-2-2 Built by Hawthorn's, Leith. Works nos 258/9.
DW 6ft 0in, Cyls 16 x 20 O/S, WP 120lbs/sq in, Wt 29tons. Otherwise similar
to 1 class but built with cabs which formed the basis on which Stroudley
derived his pattern.

No	Name	Date	Rebuilt	Withdrawn
12	Belladrum (removed 1864)	5/1862	12/1871	9/1898
	renamed Breadalbrane	1871	2-2-2T	
	renamed Strathpeffer	1885		
	name removed	1890		
13	Lovat	7/1862		5/1890
	renamed Thurso	1874		(Blr to no 13)

2-2-2 Built by Hawthorn's, Leith. Works nos 299/300.
DW 6ft 1½in, LW & TW 3ft 7½in, Cyls 17 x 22 O/S, Blr 3ft 11in x 9ft 9½in,
THS 1079.2 sq ft, WP 120lbs/sq in, WB 6ft 9in + 7ft 9in, Wt 31tons. Crewe
type with domeless boiler and raised firebox with longnitudinal mid feather
and two firedoors. WP later raised to 160lbs/sq in. Six wheel 1800 gallon
tenders. Rebuilt 2-4-0, Cyls 18 x 24, Wt 35½tons, 1871/2. Further rebuilt
with larger boiler THS 1186 sq ft and thicker tyres (DW 6ft 3in) increasing

Wt to 37½tons, 1896.

No	Name	Date	Rebuilt	Withdrawn
28	Glenbarry	9/1863	8/1872 2-4-0	
	renamed Grantown		2/1896 new blr	
			(by Sharp Stewart)	
			5/1896 DW 6ft 3in	1905
29	Highlander	10/1863	8/1871 2-4-0	
	renamed Forres		5/1896 new blr	
	to duplicate list	1898	(Sharp Stewart)	
	29A and name		DW 6ft 3in	1905
	removed			

2-2-2 Built by Neilson & Co. Works nos below.
DW 6ft 1½in, Cyls 16½ x 22, other dimensions as 28 class above. Rebuilds as
below.

The following (Works nos 966-71) had mid feather fireboxes as 28 class above.
Names may not all have been carried continuously.

No	Name	Date	Rebuilt	Withdrawn
30	Prince	10/1863	9/1891 2-4-0 Cyls 17 x 22	
	to duplicate list		(later 18 x 22) large	
	30A	1898	blr DW 6ft 3in	1898
31	Princess	10/1863	9/1891 as 30	
			1895 18 x 24 cyls blr	Sold
			ex no 34	1899
32	Sutherland	10/1863	remained 2-2-2	
	renamed Cluny	1874	cyls increased to	
	to duplicate list		17 x 22	9/1898
	32A	1897		
33	Atholl	10/1863	11/1881 blr ex no 50	
	renamed Birnam		3/1883 2-4-0 Cyls	
			17 x 24 (later 18 x 24)	4/1899
34	Seafield	11/1863	12/1883 2-4-0 cyls 17 x 22	4/1897
	renamed Perthshire	c1889	(later 18 x 24)	(laid up
			1890 blr ex no 51	up 9/1893)
35	Kingsmills	11/1863	7/1892 as 30	
	renamed Isla Bank			
	to duplicate list			
	35A	1910		
	renumbered 35B	1920		8/1923*

*No 35 had Drummond chimney top before 7/1923

The following (works nos below) had Cyls 17 x 22 and transverse mid-feather
in firebox except no 55 which had an ordinary firebox. All were rebuilt
2-4-0 with 18 x 24 cylinders, nos 46/7/55 being further rebuilt with large
boilers and thicker tyres as 28 class above

No	Name*	Date	Works no	Rebuilt	Withdrawn
46	Clachnacuddin	6/1864	1055	5/1880 2-4-0 18 x 24	
	renamed Kingussie	1883		12/1895 DW 6ft 3in	
				large blr	1906
47	Bruce	6/1864	1057	6/1880 2-4-0 18 x 24	1906
	renamed Lovat	c1874		6/1895 DW 6ft 3in	Scrapped
	renamed Beauly			large blr	1907
48	Cadboll	6/1864	1056	1/1881 2-4-0 Cyls	
	renamed Dingwall	1886		18 x 24	
	to duplicate list				
	48A	1901			1904
49	Belladrum	7/1864	1058	4/1879 2-4-0 Cyls	
	renamed Helmsdale			18 x 24	
	to duplicate list				
	49A	1899		1894 blr ex no 53	1899

50	*Aultnaskiah*	7/1864	1059	4/1878 2-4-0 18 x 24	
	renamed **Badenoch**			5/1881 blr ex no 33	4/1897
51	*Caithness*	7/1864	1054	7/1875 2-4-0	1900
	renamed *Blair Atholl*	1874		cyls 18 x 24	(laid
	to duplicate list 51A	1899			up 4/1896)
52	*Dunphail*	9/1864	1060	2/1876 2-4-0 18 x 24	1899
53	*Stafford*	10/1864	1061	11/1873 2-4-0 18 x 24	
	renamed *Golspie*	1886		1892 blr ex no 50	1900
	to duplicate list 53A	1898			
54	*Macduff*	10/1864	1062	8/1873 2-4-0 cyls	Sold
	to duplicate list 54A	1900		18 x 24	11/1903
					for scrap
55	*Cluny*	10/1864	1063	9/1874 2-4-0 cyls	
	renamed *Sutherland*	1874		18 x 24	
	renamed *Invergordon*	1884		1/1895 large blr	
				DW 6ft 3in	1906

*Names may not all have been carried continuously.

2-4-0 Built by Hawthorn's, Leith. Works nos below.
   DW 5ft 0in, Cyls 16 x 22 O/S, THS 1188.75 sq ft, Blr 4ft 1in x 10th 9in,
   WB 5ft 11in + 8ft 4in, Wt 28.47tons. Crewe type with raised firebox cover
   and dome over it. Safety valves on firebox and boiler. Four wheel tenders.
   Nos 7 and 10 were rebuilt 4-4-0 for working the Dingwall and Skye railway
   (opened to Strome Ferry 19 August 1870).

No	Name	Date	Works no	Rebuilt	Withdrawn
5	*Seafield*	2/1858	163	7/1870 cyls 16 x 24	5/1897
	name removed by	1863			
	Renamed *Tain*				
	at later period				
6	*Bruce*	5/1858	164	1874 cyls 16 x 23	11/1893
	name removed by	1864		later 16 x 24	
	renamed *Helmsdale*	c1874			
7	*Fife* name removed	8/1858	165	5/1875 4-4-0	5/1899
	later. Renamed			cyls 17 x 24	
	Dingwall at later				
	period from	5/1875			
	to duplicate list 7A	1898			
8	*Altyre*	8/1858	175	later cyls 16 x 24	9/1891
	name removed later				Scrapped
	renamed *Beauly*				11/1893
	at later period				
9	*Aultnaskiah*	8/1858	176	later cyls 16 x 24	11/1893
	name removed later				
	Renamed *Golspie*				
	at later period				
10	*Westhall*	9/1858	177	6/1873 4-4-0	5/1897
	Renamed *Duncraig*	6/1873		cyls 17 x 24	
	name removed later				
11	*Stafford*	10/1859	209	5/1878 Cyls 16 x 24	
	name removed by	10/1864			
	Renamed *Skibo*				
	renumbered 9	11/1893			6/1897

2-4-0 Built by Hawthorn's Leith. Works nos 264/5.
   DW 5ft 0in, LW 3ft 0in, Cyls 16 x 22 O/S, Wt 30½tons. Similar to 7 class
   above but provided with cabs and Beattie patent firebox and transverse mid-
   feather. Rebuilt with cyls 17 x 24 and thicker tyres DW 5ft 2½in, LW 3ft
   2½in.

No	Name	Date	Rebuilt	Withdrawn
14	*Loch* (removed later)	9/1862	2/1872	
	renamed *Evanton*		as above	9/1901
	renumbered **6**	11/1893	1894 blr	Sold
	renumbered **32**	11/1897	ex no 8	1902
	renumbered **49**	2/1899		
15	*Sutherland*	10/1862	1875 as above	11/1893
	name removed	1863		
	renamed *Dunkeld*			
	renamed *Foulis*			

2-4-0 Built by Sharp Stewart & Co. Works nos below.
DW 5ft 1½in, LW 3ft 7½in, Cyls 17 x 22 O/S, Blr 4ft 1in max diam, THS 1164 sq ft, WP 150lbs/sq in, WB 6ft 0in + 9ft 0in, Wt 32tons. Six-wheel 1800 gallon tenders as 28 & 30 class 2-2-2s. Two injectors. Intended for goods traffic. Rebuilt by Jones with new boilers (THS 1078 sq ft) 18 x 24 cylinders and thicker tyres (DW 5ft 3½in, LW 3ft 9½in) increasing Wt to 35½tons. Also Jones design of cab (he used the term 'house') with rounded corners replaced original canopy supported on poles. Boilers similar to nos 14/15.
Names may not have been carried continuously and were all removed latterly.

No	Name	Date	Works no	Rebuilt	Withdrawn
18	*Inverness*	8/1863	1416	7/1887 as above	
	renumbered **36**	1902			1906
19	*Dingwall*	8/1863	1417	8/1879 as above	1896
	renamed *Golspie*			Stationery work until 1903	
20	*Birnam*	8/1863	1426	1/1882 as above	
	renumbered **38**	8/1902			
	to duplicate list 38A	1906		1893 blr ex no 22	1908
21	*Forres*	8/1863	1427	1872 reboilered after explosion	
	renumbered **39**	8/1902		1/1872 near Fochabers	
				4/1874 as above	1909
22	*Aviemore*	9/1863	1436	1/1878 as above	
	(name transferred to 39)			2/1892	1896
23	*Murthly*	10/1863	1437	12/1890 as above	1902
	renamed *Dalcross*				
24	*Invergordon*	10/1863	1438	12/1878 as above	1904
	renamed *Lairg*				
25	*Novar*	10/1863	1439	2/1890 as above	1905
26	*Beauly*	11/1863	1440	5/1893 as above	1913*
27	*Conon*	11/1863	1441	9/1890 as above	
	to duplicate list 27A	1913			
	renumbered 27B	1916			
	renumbered 27A	1918			
	renumbered 27B	1920			1923

*No 26 was laid up from 1910.

2-4-0 Built by Sharp Stewart & Co. Works nos 1506-13/19/20.
DW 5ft 1½in, LW 3ft 7½in, Cyls 17 x 22 O/S, THS 1348.25 sq ft, WP 150lbs/sq in (later 160lbs/sq in), WB 6ft 3in + 9ft 3in, Wt 33tons. Domeless boilers with raised firebox as previously and tenders as 18 class. Rebuilt by Jones with same modifications as applied to 18 class (THS 1138 sq ft, Wt 36½tons). Names may not all have been carried continuously and were all removed latterly.

No	Name	Date	Rebuilt	Withdrawn
36	*Nairn*	4/1864	9/1876 as above	1902
37	*Struan*	4/1864	12/1885 as above	
	to duplicate list 37A	1921	c1926 blr ex no 55	
			1915 blr ex no 42	
			Drummond chimney latterly 8/1923	

38	*Kincraig*	4/1864	8/1879 reboilered	
			9/1891 as above	8/1902
39	*Aviemore*	5/1864	4/1884 as above	8/1902
40	*Keith*	5/1864	5/1885 as above	1905
41	*Kingussie*	5/1864	4/1887 as above	1906
42	*Lentran*	5/1864	12/1882 as above	
	to duplicate list 42A	1911	(by Neilson)	
	renumbered 42B	1920	1915 blr ex no 37	
			Drummond chimney top	1923
43	*Dava*	6/1864	5/1880 as above	1912
44	*Brodie*	6/1864	3/1879 as above	Sold
	to duplicate list 44A	1911		1912
45	*Dalcross*	6/1864	2/1889 as above	1905

0-4-0ST Built by Hawthorn's Leith. Works no 275.
DW 4ft 0in, Cyls 13 x 18, THS 478 sq ft, WP 100lbs/sq in, Wt 16tons 8cwt.
Inside cylinders to Hawthorn standard.

No	Name	Date	
17	*Hopeman*	5/1863	
		1867	Rebuilt 0-4-2T, TW 3ft 1in.
		1879	to duplicate list 17A
	renamed *Needlefield*	1880	to Carriage Works, Inverness
	(and no removed)	1886-96	Stationery work
		1896	renumbered 1A
		1902	Sold.

Findhorn

Incorporated 1859. Opened 16 April 1860 to Kinloss Jct (on I&AJ) from
Findhorn village (3 miles). Leased by I&AJ 4 March 1862 who took over working
of line 31 March 1862 under guarantee. Line closed 1 January 1869.

1 locomotive as under:

0-4-0ST Built by Neilson & Co. Works no 422 1859.
DW 3ft 6in, Cyls 12 x 18 O/S, THS 392 sq ft, WP 120lbs/sq in, Wt 16tons
(approx). Square top saddle tank to Neilson's standard design and their
pattern of indirect motion. Supplied from stock (built 1859).

Date
   1860   Named *Findhorn*
4/1862   Sold by HR to contractor of Sutherland and Caithness railway.

Duke of Sutherland's

Incorporated 1870 as extension of Sutherland railway (incorporated 1865 from
Inverness and Ross-shire at Bonar Bridge to Golspie, opened 18 April 1868).
Opened from Dunrobin to temporary station at Gartymore (but called Helmsdale)
1 November 1870 and throughout Golspie to present station at Helmsdale 16 May
1871 (goods) 19 June 1871 (passenger). Temporary terminus at Dunrobin became
a private station for the duke with private line to Dunrobin Castle.
Locomotive obtained by the duke for working the isolated section 1870-1 and
retained by him for working private line after completion, when HR took over
the working of the main line. With the Sutherland and the Sutherland and
Caithness (incorporated 1871, opened 28 July 1874 completing the line from
Helmsdale to Wick and Thurso) the three companies, all worked by the HR were
amalgamated with the Highland under the Highland Railway (Northern Lines)
Amalgamation Act on 1 September 1884.

2 locomotives as under:

2-4-0T Built by Kitson & Co. Works no 1706.
DW 4ft 0in, Cyls 10 x 18 O/S, THS 379 sq ft, WP 140lbs/sq in, WB 6ft 0in +
5ft 9in, Wt 21tons. Stephenson gear.

```
Name              Date
Dunrobin          1870    Purchased by HR 1895 no 118 Gordon Castle*
                  5/1896  Rebuilt by Sharp Stewart with larger boiler
                          (THS 552.4 sq ft) Cyls 12 x 18, Wt 24tons.
                  1923    Sold as duplicate no 118A

     *name removed by 1900
```

O-4-4T Built by Sharp Stewart & Co.   Works no 4085.
DW 4ft 6in, TW 2ft 6in, Cyls 13 x 18.

Designed by Jones for the son of the above mentioned duke who succeeded him in 1892, to replace the original loco sold to HR.   Remained the private property of the duke and his heirs, but not used after about 1920.

```
Name              Date
Dunrobin          7/1895
                  1952    Exhibited at New Romney
                  1965    Purchased by Imperial Pagents Ltd (Victoria) and
                          preserved at Fort Steel Museum Cranbrooke, British
                          Columbia.
```

HIGHLAND RAILWAY

Stroudley Locomotives 1869-74

0-6-OT Built by HR Lochgorm works, Inverness.
DW 3ft 7in, Cyls 14 x 20, THS 671.25 sq ft, WP 120lbs/sq in, Wt 23½tons.
Utilised boilers from 1 class 2-2-2s, shortened to 7ft 9½in on no 56 and to
7ft 9½in on 57 & 16. Probably provided Stroudley with the prototype for
his 'Terrier' tanks on the LBSC. Nos 57 & 16 added by Jones. Stephenson
link motion rather than Allan straight link. Latterly THS 641.6 sq ft, Wt
26tons. No 56 had pressure raised to 130lbs in 1902.

No	Name	Date	Duplicate no	year	Rebuilt	LMS no	With-drawn
56*	*Balnain*	2/1869	56A	1920	11/1895 new blr		
	renamed *Dornoch*	1902	56B	1922	DW 3ft 8in	16118	1926
57*	*Lochgorm*	11/1872	57A	1920	8/1897 new blr		
	name removed	8/1898	57B	1921	DW 3ft 8in	16119	1932
16*	*St Martins*	10/1874	49A	1912	6/1896 DW 3ft 8in		
	renamed *Fort George*	1899					
	renumbered **49**	2/1901				16383	1928
	to duplicate list 49A	1912					

*No 56 had boiler ex-no 3 and was later fitted with a Jones chimney.
Drummond chimney fitted c1920. No 57 had boiler ex-no 4 and was later fitted
with a Jones chimney. c1926 the boiler ex-16118 was fitted and c1928 the
modified Stroudley chimney ex 16383 was fitted.
No 16 had boiler ex no 1.
Names were removed when LMS livery applied c1925.

Jones Locomotives 1871-1901

2-4-0 Built by HR, Lochgorm.
DW 6ft 0in, Cyls 15½ x 22 O/S, THS 906 sq ft, Wt 27½tons. Renewal of 1855
I&N loco with larger domed boiler and raised firebox. Boiler provided by
Dubs & Co, frames by Hawthorn's.

No	Name	Date	Rebuilt	Withdrawn
2	*Aldourie*	2/1871	1896 blr ex no 32	1903
	name removed	1898		
	and to duplicate list 2A			

2-4-0 Built by HR, Lochgorm
DW 6ft 3½in, LW 3ft 9½in, Cyls 16 x 22 O/S, Blr 4ft 1in x 9ft 5½in, THS
1097 sq ft, WP 160lbs/sq in, WB 6ft 2in + 8ft 4in, Wt 35tons.

No	Name	Date		Withdrawn
3	*Ballindalloch*	7/1877	New tubes & firebox	
	renumbered **30**	7/1898	by Neilson & Co 10/1895	1910
1	*Raigmore*	11/1877		
	renumbered **29**	7/1898	To duplicate list 29A 1910	c1914

4-4-0 Built by Dubs & Co. Works nos below
                HR, Lochgorm
DW 6ft 3½in, LW 3ft 9½in, Cyls 18 x 24 O/S, Blr 4ft 2in x 10ft 8½in, THS
1228 sq ft, WP 140lbs/sq in, WB 6ft 0in + 6ft 9in + 8ft 9in, Wt 41tons.
Jones cabs with rounded corners and square fronts. Crewe type fore end
framing, Adams bogie, brass side valves, Allan link motion, spark arrester
in chimney. Centre dome on boiler. Fitted with counter pressure brake.
Chimney with double casing and louvres on outside which became a standard
feature. No 64 was fitted experimentally with Westinghouse brake and no 4

with automatic vacuum. When latter adopted as standard, no 64 altered and all the remainder vacuum brake fitted increasing weight to 42tons. 6 wheel 1800 gallon tenders.

Duke class
The following were built by Dubs & Co. Works nos 714-23. On reboilering at dates below all except no 63 had WP increased to 150lbs/sq in. No 67 had amended THS 1151 sq ft.

No	Name	Date	Capital no	year	Duplicate no	year	Reboilered	Withdrawn
60	*Bruce*	6/1874					8/1898	Sold*
	renamed *Sutherland*	1884						1909
61	*Sutherlandshire*	6/1874					12/1898**	Sold*
	renamed *Duke*	1/1877						11/1907
62	*Perthshire*	6/1874					5/1899	Sold*
	renamed *Stemster*	1889						1909
	renamed *Huntingtower*	1899						
	renamed *Aultwherrie*	1903						
63	*Inverness-shire*	7/1874					4/1899	11/1907
	renamed *Inverness*							
64	*Morayshire*	7/1874					11/1898	Sold*
	renamed *Seafield*	c1889						1909
65	*Nairnshire*	7/1874					7/1899	Sold*
	renamed *Dalraddy*							1909
66	*Ross-shire*	7/1874					4/1900	11/1907
	renamed *Ardvuela*							
67	*The Duke*	8/1874			67A	1918	12/1897	
	renamed *Cromartie*	1/1877			70A	1923	1913 blr	
			67	1923			ex no 74	1923
68	*Caithness-shire*	8/1874					5/1898	11/1907
	renamed *Caithness*							
	renamed *Muirtown*							
69	*The Lord Provost*	8/1874					8/1898	1909
	renamed *Sir James*							
	renamed *Aldourie*							

*Locos sold were for scrap
**No 61 had Smith water feed heater for a time.

The following were built by HR at Lochgorm, No 4 was reboilered 10/1895 with 150lbs/sq in WP and 1151 sq ft THS. Nos 71-5, 84 were built with above WP & THS. No 84 had larger 2250 gallon tender.

No	Name	Date	Capital no	year	Duplicate no	year	Reboilered	Withdrawn
4	*Ardross*	7/1876	31	1899	31A	1911	10/1895	1913
	renamed *Auchtertyre*	1901						
71	*Clachnacuddin*	12/1883			71A	1912		1915
72	*Bruce*	6/1884			72A	1915	1912*	Sold**
	renamed *Grange*	c1886						1923
73	*Thurlow*(later remvd	2/1885			73A	1916		1923
	renamed *Rosehaugh*	1898						
74	*Beaufort*	9/1885						1913
	(later removed)							
75	*Breadalbone*	10/1886			75A	1917	*	1923
84	*Dochfour*	12/1888			84A	1917	*	

*Nos 72A & 75A had Drummond chimney top by 1923
No 84 had Drummond chimney top before 1916 and a Drummond chimney by 1923.
**Sold for scrap.

4-4-0 Built by HR, Lochgorm.

DW 5ft 3in, LW 3ft 3in, Cyls 18 x 24 O/S, Blr 4ft 2in x 10ft 7½in, THS 1216 sq ft, WP 150lbs/sq in, WB 6ft 0in + 6ft 9in + 8ft 9in, Wt 42tons. Built for the Dingwall and Skye Railway to Strome Ferry following successful conversion of 2-4-0s 7 and 10 and known as *Skye Bogies*. Cylinders, frames and motion were as 60 class. Regarded as mixed traffic locomotives and not named. The last four were completed by Drummond and had Drummond chimneys and no compensating levers between the coupled wheels. LMS class 1P.

No	Date	Duplicate no	Duplicate year	Capital no	Capital year	LMS no		With- drawn
70	5/1882	70A	1916	67	1923	14277	Blr ex no 74 fitted 1923	6/1930
85	8/1892	85A	1919				Sold for scrap	8/1923
86	3/1893					14279	Drummond chimney top after 1923	10/1927
87	12/1893					(14280)	Drummond chimney top c1920	8/1926
88	4/1895					(14281)	Drummond chimney top c1920	1926
5	8/1897			32	1899	14282		1929
6	11/1897			33	1899	14283	Blr ex no 70A 1921 & Jones chimney	1929
7	7/1898			34	1899	14284		6/1930
48	12/1901					14285		1928

4-4-0 Built by Clyde Locomotive Co. Works nos 1-8.

DW 6ft 3in, LW 3ft 9½in, Cyls 18 x 24 O/S, Blr 4ft 2in x 9ft 9½in, THS 1140 sq ft, WP 160lbs/sq in, WB 6ft 0in + 6ft 9in + 8ft 9in, Wt 43tons. Cylinders, motion and frames as 60 class but shorter boilers. Larger 2250 gallon tenders with vacuum brake on engine and tender as well as counter pressure brake 'Lock up' safety valves instead of Adams patent. Tender had both inside and outside bearings.

No	Name	Date	Duplicate no	Duplicate year		With- drawn
76	*Bruce*	12/1886	76A	1917	Drummond chimney top by 1923	1923
77	*Lovat*	5/1886	77A	1917	Withdrawn but reinstated 1915. Latterly had Drummond top. Sold	1918*
78	*Lochalsh*	6/1886	78A	1917	Drummond chimney top before 1923. Sold	1923*
79	*Atholl*	6/1886	79A	1917		1923
80	*Stafford*	7/1886	80A	1919	Sold	1923*
81	*Colville*	7/1886	81A	1919	Blr used at Inverness	1923
82	*Fife*	9/1886	82A	1917	Drummond chimney top before 1916	
	renamed *Durn*	1908				
	name removed	1917			To LMS 14278 Drummond chimney by 1928	6/1930
83	*Cadboll*	10/1886	83A	1917	Drummond chimney top	
	renamed *Monkland*	1902			latterly. Sold	8/1923*

*Nos 77A, 78A, 80A and 83A were sold for scrap but no 77A was still at Culloden in 8/1923.
No 76 *Bruce* was exhibited at the 1886 Edinburgh Exhibition.

4-4-0 Built by Neilson & Co. Works nos 4428-38.

DW 6ft 3in, LW 3ft 9½in, Cyls 18 x 24 O/S, Blr 4ft 6in x 9ft 9½in, THS 1242 sq ft, WP 160lbs/sq in, WB 6ft 0in + 6ft 9in + 8ft 9in, Wt 45tons. *Strath* class. Cylinders, frames and wheels as previous 4-4-0s but with larger diameter boiler. LMS class 1P.

No	Name	Date	Duplicate no	year		LMS no	Withdrawn
89	*Sir George*	5/1892			Drummond chimney top by 1922	14271	8/1930
90	*Tweedale*	5/1892	90A	1919			
	renamed *Grandtully*	1897			Sold for scrap		1923
91	*Strathspey*	6/1892	91A	1919	Steel firebox		
					Loco 1916. Drummond chimney top by 1915		1923
92	*Strathdearn*	6/1892	92A	1921	Steel firebox by North British Loco 1916	14272	6/1930
93	*Strathnairn*	6/1892	93A		Steel firebox by Hawthorn 1918 Sold for scrap		1923
94	*Strathtay*	6/1892			Drummond chimney(14273) top by 1923		1924
					Scrapped		1925
95	*Strathcarron*	6/1892			Steel firebox by 14274 Beardmore 1921 Drummond chimney top by 1913		1930
96	*Glentilt*	6/1892	96A	1922	Steel firebox by Hawthorn 1918 Sold for scrap		1923
97	*Glenmore**	6/1892	97A	1922	Drummond chimney top by c1916 Sold for scrap		1923
98	*Glenbruim*	6/1892			New steel blr 14275 by Hawthorn 1920 short Jones chimney from 1920		1930
99	*Glentromie*	6/1892	99A	1922	Sold for scrap		1923
100	*Glenbruar**	6/1892			Steel blr by Hawthorn 1921 & short Jones chimney		1930

*No 97 was to have been named Glenbruar and no 100 Glenmore.

4-4-0 Built by Dubs & Co. Works nos 3392-3406.
  DW 6ft 3½in, LW 3ft 3in, Cyls 19 x 24 O/S, Blr 4ft 4⅞in x 10ft 6⅜in, THS
  1295 sq ft, WP 175lbs/sq in, WB 6ft 6in + 7ft 0in + 9ft 0in, Wt 49tons.
  Loch class. Amongst the most powerful 4-4-Os at the time comparable with
  Adams 577 class on LSW. Same tenders as 4-6-Os, **six** wheel 3000 gallon.
  Originally fitted with Smith patent piston valves but these replaced by
  Drummond with Richardsom type balanced slide valves. N51 (ex Caledonian)
  boilers fitted by LMS as below (4ft 8in diameter). LMS class 2P.

No	Name	Date		LMS no	Withdrawn
119	*Loch Insh*	7/1896	Drummond chimney by 1903.	14379	
	name removed	8/1944	Jones chimney with Drummond top by 1920		
	name replaced	1946	N51 blr 1925		3/1948*
120	*Loch Ness*	7/1896	N51 blr 1928	14380	
			Drummond chimney top c1923		12/1940
121	*Loch Ericht*	8/1896	N51 blr 1924. McIntosh chimney, later Pickersgill	14381	3/1940
122	*Loch Moy*	8/1896	N51 blr 1926	14382	12/1940
123	*Loch An Dorb*	8/1896	N51 blr 1928	14383	2/1934

124	*Loch Laggan*	8/1896	Rebuilt by Hawthorn 1920-3	14384	9/1938
125	*Loch Tay*	8/1896	N51 blr 1928	14385	4/1950*
126	*Loch Tummel*	7/1896	Slide valves 1921		
			N51 blr 1928	14386	8/1938
127	*Loch Garry*	7/1896		14387	1930
128	*Loch Luichart*	8/1896	Drummond chimney by 1930	14388	1930
129	*Loch Maree*	9/1896		14389	1931
130	*Loch Fannich*	9/1896	Dual brake fitted		
			Drummond chimney c1915		
			N51 blr 1925	14390	2/1937
131	*Loch Shin*	9/1896	N51 blr 9/1924	14391	8/1941
			Scrapped 10/1942		
132	*Loch Naver*	9/1896	N51 blr 1927	14392	
			Ramsbottom safety valves		
			by 1944		4/1947
133	*Loch Laoghal*	9/1896	Rebuilt by Hawthorn	14393	
	renamed		1920-3. Short Jones		
	Loch Laochal		chimney		12/1934

*14379 allotted BR 54379
14385 allotted BR 54385
class continued by Cumming (page no 201)

2-4-0T Built by HR, Lochgorm.
DW 4ft 9in, LW 3ft 9½in, Cylw 16 x 24 O/S, THS 913 sq ft, WP 140lbs/sq in,
WB 5ft 9in + 8ft 4in, Wt 36tons 11cwt. Originally intended for station
duties these were soon pressed into services on the Aberfeldy and Burghead
branches and rebuilt 1881/2 as 4-4-0T LW 2ft 7½in, WB 5ft 6in + 6ft 1½in +
8ft 4in, Wt 39½tons.

			Capital		Duplicate		Rebuilt**	LMS	With-
No	Name*	Date	no	year	no	year	4-4-0T	no	drawn
58	*Burghead*	12/1878			58A	1912	1882	15011	1928
					58B	1920			
59	*Highlander*	6/1879			59A	1912	1881	15010	1933
					59B	1920			
17	*Breadalbane*	12/1879	50	2/1901	50A	1912	1882	15012	1929
	renamed *Aberfeldy*	1886			50B	1920			

*Names removed 1900
**All these locos had Drummond chimney tops by 1919.

0-4-4ST Built by HR, Lochgorm.
DW 4ft 3in, TW 2ft 7½in, Cyls 14 x 20, THS 640 sq ft, WP 100lbs/sq in, WB
6ft 0in + 6ft 6in + 5ft 0in, Wt 32tons. Inside cylinders. Built to replace
original no 12 on Strathpeffer branch with boiler off no 13 2-2-2 cut down
in length and dome fitted on firebox casing. Rebuilt with side tanks and
capacity increased from 820 gallons to 900 gallons (THS 690.5 sq ft, WP
140lbs/sq in, Wt 34tons). Renamed when put to work on Wick and Lybster Light
Railway.

No	Name	Date	
13	*Strathpeffer*	5/1890	Boiler ex no 13
		12/1899	Renumbered **53**
		10/1901	Rebuilt 0-4-4T new boiler
	renamed *Lybster*	1903	
	(later removed)	1919	to Duplicate list 53A
		1923	to LMS 15050
		1929	Withdrawn

4-4-0T Built by Dubs & Co. Works nos 2778/9, 3077-9.
DW 5ft 3in, LW 3ft 0in, Cyls 16 x 22 O/S, Blr 3ft 10in (inside) x 10ft 6in,
THS 883 sq ft, WP 140lbs/sq in, WB 5ft 9in + 7ft 4in + 7ft 2in, Wt 42½tons
(101/2) 44tons (remainder). Frustrated order for FCU del E (Uraguay Eastern).
Stephenson gear. Valves above cylinders actuated by rocking levers.

Originally had covers over slide bars. Known as 'Yankee' tanks.

No	Name*	Date		LMS no	Withdrawn
101		9/1892		15013	7/1934
102		9/1892	Rebuilt 1906 with Drummond		
	Munlochy	1910	chimney	15014	12/1934
11		11/1893	Renumbered 51 1899		
			to duplicate list 51A 1919		
			renumbered 51B 1919	(15015)	1924
14		11/1893	Renumbered 50 1900		
	Portessie	1901	Renumbered 54 1901		
			to duplicate list 54B 1921	15017	1924
15		11/1893	Renumbered 52 1900		
	Fortrose	1901	to duplicate list 52A 1919		
			Renumbered 52B 1921		
			Reboilered 1906	15016	1927

*Names removed later

4-6-0 Built by Sharp Stewart & Co. Works nos 4022-36.
DW 5ft 3½in, LW 3ft 2½in, Cyls 20 x 26 O/S, Blr 4ft 7⅞in x 13ft 9in, THS
1672.5 sq ft, WP 170lbs/sq in, WB 6ft 6in + 5ft 3in + 5ft 6in + 7ft 9in,
Wt 56tons. Known at the time as Large Goods, nowadays more often referred
to as Jones Goods. First 4-6-Os to run in Britain. WP increased to
175lbs/sq in. Steel boilers, vacuum fitted. Nos 106 and 116 were dual
fitted with Westinghouse brakes. Nos 103/4/7/10-14/16/17 fitted with Drummond
chimneys 1930-7. Six wheel 3000 gallon tender. LMS class 4F.

No	Date		LMS no	Withdrawn
103	9/1894	Short Jones chimney c1922	17916	
		Drummond chimney c1930		7/1934
		Preserved at St Rollox in HR green		
	1959	Restored to running order St Rollox*		
	1965	Used in film Those Magnificent Men in		
		their Flying Machines.		
		Preserved in Glasgow Museum of		
		Transport.		
104	9/1894	Drummond chimney top c1920	17917	11/1939
105	9/1894	Drummond chimney top c1918	17918	1933
106	9/1894		17919	12/1934
107	9/1894	Drummond chimney c1935	17920	10/1937
108	10/1894		17921	1930
109	10/1894		17922	1929
110	10/1894	Drummond chimney by 1931	17923	11/1935
111	10/1894	Drummond chimney by 1932	17924	9/1934
112	10/1894	Drummond chimney by 1932	17925	2/1940
113	10/1894	Drummond chimney by 1934	17926	11/1939
114	10/1894	Drummond chimney by 1930	17927	9/1936
115	11/1894		17928	1933
116	11/1894	Drummond chimney 1936	17929	6/1936
117	11/1894	Drummond chimney by 1936	17930	11/1939

*1959 restoration of no 103 included repainting in Stroudly yellow but
unlikely that loco ever ran in traffic in this livery.

Drummond Classification System 1901

In 1901 Drummond introduced a classification scheme by letter as follows:

A	*Castle*	4-6-0	140 class
B	*Loch*	4-4-0	119 class
C	Small *Ben*	4-4-0	1 class
D	*Strath*	4-4-0	89 class
E	*Bruce*	4-4-0	76 class
F	*Duke*	4-4-0	60 class
G	*Glenbarry*	2-2-2	Nos 28, 35, 46, 47, 55
H	*Raugmore*	2-4-0	Nos 29/30
I	Large Goods	4-6-0	103 class
K	Drummond Goods	0-6-0	134 class
L	Skye Bogie	4-4-0	70 class
M	Medium Goods	2-4-0	36 class
N	Small Goods	2-4-0	18 class
O	Jones tank	2-4-0T	58 class
P	Yankee tank	4-4-0T	101 class
R	Stroudley tank	0-6-0T	56 class
S	*Strathpeffer*	0-4-4ST	No 13
T	Special tank	2-4-0T	No 118 (ex Duke of Sutherland)
U	*Needlefield*	0-4-0T	No 1A

Subsequent classes were given letters as detailed hereafter, the letter U being re-used in 1908 for the Large *Ben* class, *Needlefield* having been sold in 1902.

Drummond also produced somewhat of a revolution in Highland locomotive design by building 4-4-0s, 0-6-0s (the first of this otherwise ubiquitous wheel arrangement to run on the Highland) and 0-6-4Ts with inside cylinders.

The letter classification was not applied to Cunming locos.

Drummond Locomotives 1898-1913

4-4-0 Built by Dubs & Co. Works nos below.
                H R Lochgorm
                North British Locomotive Co. Works nos below

DW 6ft 0in, LW 3ft 6in, Cyls 18¼ x 26, Blr 4ft 6¼in x 10ft 6in, THS 1175 sq ft, WP 175lbs/sq in, WB 6ft 6in + 6ft 9in + 9ft 0in, Wt 46tons 4cwts. **Small Ben class C** similar but not identical to LSW 290 class. Inside cylinders. Stephenson link motion. Bogie pin 1in in front of centre, two injectors, double-slide type regulator (instead of double-beat type in Jones engines), safety valves on dome. Nos 2/3/14/15 had double bogie 3,200 gallon tenders from 0-6-0s (below). Remainder had six-wheel 3,000 gallon tenders of Drummond design Nos 2, 11-17 were dual brake fitted with Westinghouse and vacuum, the others vacuum only. Nos 2 and 7 had Smith feed-water heating. Being smaller than the *Loch* class these locos worked mostly north of Inverness and to Keith (and for a period when HR locos were working through over the GNSR, to Aberdeen). Only 8 & 15 still retained Drummond boilers in 1923. LMS class 2P (N34 (ex CR) boilers fitted by LMS as below).

The following were built by Dubs & Co. Works nos 3686-92.

No	Name	Date		LMS no	BR no	With-drawn
1	*Ben Nevis**	7/1898	N34 blr 1928	14397	(54397)	2/1949
	renamed *Ben-y-Gloe*	7/1898				
	renamed *Ben Y'Gloe*	1939				
2	*Ben Alder*	7/1898	Rebuilt by	14398	54398	2/1953**
			Hawthorn 1920-3			
			N34 blr 1929			

No	Name	Date		LMS no	BR no	Withdrawn
3	*Ben Wyvis*	7/1898	N34 blr 1927 Sto epipe chimney from 2 1951	14399	54399	5/1952
4	*Ben More*	2/1899	N34 blr 1927	14400		10/1946
5	*Ben Vrackie*	2/1899	N34 blr 1929	14401	(54401)	10/1948
6	*Ben Armin*	2/1899	N34 blr 1927 Carriage heating, Largs until 1942	14402		12/1939
7	*Ben Attow*	2/1899	N34 blr 1927	14403	(54403)	2/1949
8	*Ben Clebrig*	2/1899	N34 blr 1928	14404	54404	10/1950

*No 1 was renamed before entering traffic, appearing only for official photographs as *Ben Nevis*. The name was changed because the Board objected that Ben Nevis was not in Highland territory.

**54398 was set aside for preservation until 1964 but this was not effected.

The following were built by HR, Lochgorm.

No	Name	Date		LMS no	BR no	Withdrawn
9	*Ben Rinnes*	7/1899	N34 blr 1930	14405		9/1944
10	*Ben Slioch*	8/1899	N34 blr 1930	14406		7/1947
11	*Ben Macdhui*	11/1899		14407		12/1931
12	*Ben Hope*	4/1900	N34 blr 1927	14408		7/1947
13	*Ben Alisky*	6/1900	N34 blr 1928	14409	(54409)	4/1950
14	*Den Dearg*	8/1900	N34 blr 1928	14410	(54410)	12/1949
15	*Ben Loyal*	2/1900	Used for carriage heating. Scrapped	14411		10/1936 7/1937
16	*Ben Avon*	2/1901	N34 blr 1928	14412		4/1947
17	*Ben Alligan*	2/1901		14413		12/1933

The following were built by North British Locomotive Co (following amalgamation in 1903 under above title of Dubs & Co, Sharp Stewart & Co and Neilson & Co). Works nos 17398-400.

No	Name	Date		LMS no	BR No	Withdrawn
38	*Ben Udlaman*	4/1906		14414		12/1933
41	*Ben Bhach Ard*	7/1906	N34 blr 1928	14415	(54415)	5/1948
47	*Ben a'Bhuird*	7/1906	N34 blr 1927	14416	(54416)	9/1948

4-4-O Built by North British Locomotive Co. Works nos 18269-72, 18803-4. DW 6ft Oin, LW 3ft 6in, Cyls 18 x 26, Blr 5ft 3in x 10ft 6in, THS 1648.2 sq ft, WP 180lbs/sq in, Wt 52tons 6cwts. Other domensions as 'small *Ben*' class. **Large (or New) Ben class U** Increased boiler diameter. Drummond steam reverser. First four originally had six-wheel tenders, but 61 and 63 got double bogie tenders from the O-6-Os (below) 60 and 62 had new, larger 3,600 gallon double bogie tenders. Nos 60-3 dual brake fitted. Smith patent feed-water heating fitted 1914-15. Superheaters added to original boilers by LMS with extended smokebox (THS 1318.11 sq ft including 168.41 sq ft in 19-element superheater). WP reduced to 175lbs/sq in on dates below. LMS class 2P.

No	Name	Date	Rebuilt	LMS no	Withdrawn
61	*Ben na Caillich* renamed *Ben na Caillach*	5/1908 1926	1927	14417	5/1936
63	*Ben Mheadhoin*	5/1908	5/1924	14418	12/1932
66	*Ben Mholach* renumbered **64**	5/1908 1909	1925	14419	10/1935
68	*Ben a'Chait* renumbered **65**	5/1908 1909	6/1924	14420	4/1934
60	*Ben Bhreac Mhor* renamed *Ben Bhreac Mhor*	5/1909 1924	1924 Westinghouse brake removed	14421	10/1932

62	*Ben a'Chaoruinn*	5/1909	1926		14422	3/1937
	renamed *Ben*	1926	Carriage heating			
	Achaoruinn		scrapped			6/1938

0-4-4T Built by HR, Lochgorm.
DW 4ft 6in, TW 2ft 6in, Cyls 14 x 20 O/S, Blr 3ft 10½in x 8ft 2in, THS 719.5
sq ft, WP 150lbs/sq in, WB 6ft 0in + 7ft 3in + 5ft 0in, Wt 35¾tons.
Class W 55051/3 were last Highland locos in use (on the Dornoch branch).
Names removed 1920.

No	Name	Date		LMS no	BR no	Withdrawn
25	*Strathpeffer*	3/1905		15051	55051	6/1956
40	*Gordon Lennox*	9/1905		15052		12/1930
45		12/1905		15053	55053	1/1957
			Scrapped			2/1958
46		2/1906	N34 blr c1926	15054		10/1945

4-6-0 Built by Dubs & Co. Works nos 3848-53, 4244-47.
North British Locomotive Co. Works nos 19011/2, 20160-3.
DW 5ft 9in, LW 3ft 3in, Cyls 19½ x 26 O/S, Blr 4ft 9¾in x 14ft 4½in, THS
2050 sq ft, WP 175lbs/sq in, WB 6ft 6in + 5ft 6in + 6ft 0in + 8ft 3in, Wt
59tons 18¼cwts.
Castle class A Original design work had been done by Jones before his
retirement and was not greatly altered by Drummond except for Drummond type
cab, boiler mountings, marine big ends, Richardson type balanced slide
valves and Drummond steam reverser. Allan link motion and boiler were to
Jones practice. Bogie pivot two inches in front of centre. Double bogie.
3,350 gallon tenders. Nos 146-9 dual brake fitted. 1913 locos had extended
smokeboxes and deflector chimneys. LMS class 3P.

No	Name	Date		LMS no	Withdrawn
140	*Taymouth Castle*	6/1900		14675	8/1939
141	*Ballindalloch Castle*	6/1900	Phoenix superheater 1912-16 (and extended smokebox until 1914). Reboilered by R. Stephenson & Co 1917	14676	9/1937
142	*Dunrobin Castle*	6/1900		14677	2/1939
143	*Gordon Castle*	6/1900	Blr ex 14680 in 1930 with 1926 rebuild plate Reinstated 9/1940	14678	7/1939, 2/1946
144	*Blair Castle*	6/1900	Smith superheater 1912. Rebuilt 1926.	14679	2/1936
145	*Murthly Castle*	6/1900	Rebuilt 6/1926	14680	5/1930
146	*Skibo Castle*	7/1902	Ran trials on NB 1910 against NB 4-4-0 no 867	14681	10/1946
147	*Beaufort Castle*	7/1902	Rebuilt 1921	14682	11/1943
148	*Cawdor Castle*	7/1902	ex CR boiler and whistle 1930	14683	4/1937
149	*Duncraig Castle*	7/1902	ex CR blr and whistle 1930	14684	1/1940
30	*Dunvegan Castle*	3/1910	Rebuilt 1931	14685	1/1945
35	*Urquhart Castle*	2/1911	Rebuilt 1931	14686	7/1946
26	*Brahan Castle*	11/1913		14687	6/1935
27	*Thurso Castle*	7/1913		14688	2/1935
28	*Cluny Castle*	7/1913	Rebuilt 1921 (Hawthorn's) Reinstated 5/1941	14689	5/1939, 9/1944
43	*Dalcross Castle*	4/1913			
	Renumbered **29**	1913		14690	4/1947

O-6-O Built by Dubs & Co. Works nos 3842-7, 4240-3.
        North British Locomotive Co. Works nos 17896/7.
DW 5ft 0in, Cyls 18¼ x 26, WB 7ft 6in + 9ft 0in, Wt 43tons. Other domensions
as 'small *Ben*' class. Stephenson gear.   Known as 'Barney class'.
Boilers were interchangeable with 'small *Ben*' class. 1900 locos had 3,200
gallon double-bogie tenders, all being transferred to 4-4-0s as above.
Nos 18-21 (1902) had water-tube fireboxes. 1907 (NBL) locos had 3,185
gallon six-wheel tenders. N34 (ex CR) boilers fitted by LMS as below. LMS
class 3F.

No	Date			LMS no	BR no	With-drawn
134	2/1900	N34 blr 1926		17693	(57693)	6/1949
135	2/1900	N34 blr 1937		17694	(57694)	2/1950
136	2/1900	N34 blr 1931 HR blr refitted		17695		
		c1943 - 5/1948			57695	1/1952
137	2/1900	N34 blr 1944		17696		3/1946
138	2/1900	N34 blr 1936. Stove-pipe		17697		
		chimney 1946			57697	2/1951
139	2/1900	N34 blr 1945		17698	57698	12/1951
18	8/1902			17699	(57699)	2/1949
19	8/1902	N34 blr 1931		17700		12/1946
20	8/1902	Rebuilt 1923		17701		2/1936
21	8/1902	N34 blr 1936		17702	(57702)	11/1949
36	7/1907	N34 blr 1937. Stove-pipe		17703		
		chimney from 1946				7/1947
55	7/1907	Renumbered **37** 1921		17704		
		N34 blr 1936				12/1946

O-6-OT Built by HR, Lochgorm.
DW 5ft 2½in, Cyls 18 x 24 O/S, Blr 4ft 0in x 10ft 4in, THS 1186 sq ft, WP
160lbs/sq in, WB 14ft 2in total. Wt 47tons 18cwt. **Class V.** Wheels,
cylinders and some motion parts from 2-4-0 goods locos. Boilers from rebuilt
2-4-0 passenger locos; known as 'Scrap tanks'. LMS class 2F.

No	Date	LMS no	Withdrawn
22	10/1903	16380	1930
23	10/1903	16381	1932
24	5/1904	16382	1930

O-6-4T Built by North British Locomotive Co. Works nos 18805-8, 19013-16.
DW 5ft 0in, TW 3ft 3in, Cyls 18¼ x 26, Blr 4ft 6½in x 10ft 6in, THS 1268 sq
ft, WP 180lbs/sq in, WB 7ft 9in + 7ft 9in + 5ft 3in + 6ft 6in, Wt 69tons.
Class X Primarily intended for banking but also used on local passenger
and goods. WP later reduced to 175lbs/sq in. LMS class 4P. N55 blrs
(ex CR) fitted by LMS on dates below.

No	Date		LMS no	Withdrawn
39	1909	N55 blr 1931	15300	12/1936
64	1909	Renumbered **66** 1909	15301	10/1934
65	1909	Renumbered **68** 1909	15302	8/1933
69	1909		15303	10/1932
29	1911	Renumbered **43** 1913	15304	10/1932
31	1911		15305	11/1934
42	1911	N55 blr 1931	15306	11/1935
44	1911	N55 blr 1931	15307	11/1934

Smith Locomotives 1915

4-6-0 Built by Hawthorn Leslie & Co. Works nos 3095/6.
DW 6ft 0in, LW 3ft 3in, Cyls 21 x 28 O/S, Blr 5ft $1\frac{13}{16}$ x 14ft 4½in, THS
1949.6 sq ft (including superheater 350 sq ft), WP 160lbs/sq in, WB 6ft 6in
+ 5ft 7½in + 6ft 3in + 8ft 0in, Wt 71tons 16cwt.
River class Walschaerts valve gear, 24-element Robinson superheater, steam
reverse, Smith feed-water heating, dual brake fitted. Following trials of
no 70 the civil engineer ruled that these locos were too heavy for the
bridges (advance designs had not been submitted to him) and the whole order
of six locomotives were sold to the Caledonian (see page 102).
The first two below were painted in HR livery and it is generally stated
that they were both delivered, but there is some doubt whether no 71 was in
fact delivered to Inverness. The other four were still being built and
were diverted directly to St Rollox. Intended numbers and names in
brackets.

No	Name		Date	CR no
70	*River Ness*		1915	938
71	*River Spey*		1915	939
(72)	*(River Tay)*		1915	940
(73)	*(River Findhorn)*		1915	941
(74)	*(River Garry)*		1915	942
(75)	*(River Tummel)*		1915	943

Cumming Locomotives 1916-21

4-4-0 Built by North British Locomotive Co. Works nos 21456-8.
DW 6ft 3½in, LW 3ft 3in, Cyls 19 x 24 O/S.
As *Loch* class in all but minor details and dual brake fitted. LMS class 2P.

No	Name	Date		LMS no	With-drawn
70	*Loch Ashie*	1916		14394	9/1936
71	*Loch Garve*	1916	Drummond chimney	14395	
			by 1930		11/1935
72	*Loch Ruthven*	1916		14396	10/1934

4-4-0 Built by Hawthorn Leslie & Co. Works nos 3172/3.
DW 6ft 3in, LW 3ft 3in, Cyls 20 x 26 O/S, Blr 4ft $8\frac{9}{16}$in x 11ft 4⅝in, THS
1,320 sq ft (including 180sq ft superheater), WP 160lbs/sq in, Wt 54tons
19¾cwt. Walschaerts valve gear, Robinson superheater, Belpaire firebox.
Wakefield lubricator inside admission piston valves. Ross safety valves.
WP increased to 175lbs/sq in. LMS class 3P.

No	Name	Date		LMS no	With-drawn
73	*Snaigow*	1917	CR chimney c1934	14522	4/1936
74	*Durn*	1917		14523	4/1935

4-6-0 Built by North British Locomotive Co. Works nos 21459-61.
DW 6ft 0in, LW 3ft 3in, Cyls 19½ x 26 O/S, THS 2048 sq ft, WB 6ft 6in +
5ft 7½in + 6ft 3in + 8ft 3in, Wt 60tons 13cwts. Otherwise as Castle class
with larger DW and screw reverse instead of steam reverse. Six-wheel 4,000
gallon tender. LMS class 3P.

No	Name	Date	LMS no	Withdrawn
50	*Brodie Castle*	8/1917	14691	9/1938
58	*Darnaway Castle*	8/1917	14692	3/1946
59	*Foulis Castle*	8/1917	14693	4/1935

4-6-0 Built by Hawthorn Leslie & Co. Works nos 3286-9, 3371-4.
DW 5ft 3in, LW 3ft 0in, Cyls 20½in x 26 O/S, Blr 4ft $7\frac{3}{16}$ (1½in taper) x
13ft 9in, THS 1,440 sq ft (including superheater 241 sq ft), WP 175lbs/sq in,
WB 6ft 7in + 5ft 0in + 6ft 0in + 6ft 6in, Wt 56tons 9cwts.
Walschaerts valve gear. Robinson superheater, Belpaire firebox large cab
with roof projecting over tender front, straight splasher, screw reverse,
3,000 gallon tender. Built for heavy goods work they later became known as
Clan Goods due to similarity with larger *Clan* class below. Bogie pivot lin
in rear of centre. LMS class 5F.

No	Date		LMS no	BR no	Withdrawn
75	1918	CR chimney & snifting valves 1936	17950	57950	8/1950
76	1918	CR chimney c1940	17951	57951	5/1951
77	1918	CR snifting valves c1940	17952		
		CR chimney c1943			10/1946
78	1918		17953	(57953)	10/1948
79	1918	CR snifting valves c1944	17954	57954	10/1952
80	1919	CR chimney & snifting valves c1945	17955	57955	6/1952
81	1919		17956	57956	5/1952
82	1919		17957		3/1946

4-6-0 Built by Hawthorn Leslie & Co. Works nos 3329-32, 3443-6.
DW 6ft 0in, LW 3ft 0in, Cyls 21 x 26 O/S, Blr 4ft $9\frac{3}{16}$in (1½in taper) x 14ft
6in, THS 1723 sq ft (including superheater 256 sq ft), WP 175lbs/sq in, WB
6ft 7in + 5ft 2in + 6ft 9in + 7ft 3in, Wt 62tons 4¼cwts. **Clan class**
Walschaerts valve gear, Robinson superheater to the same design as goods
engines (above) but with larger DW and boiler. Nos 51/2/4/7 were dual-brake
fitted. LMS class 4P.

No	Name	Date		LMS no	BR no	Withdrawn
49	*Clan Campbell*	8/1919	CR chimney 1944	14762		6/1947
51	*Clan Fraser*	8/1919	Westinghouse removed 6/1936	14763		8/1944
52	*Clan Munro*	1919	Westinghouse removed 6/1936. CR chimney c1935.	14764		2/1948
53	*Clan Stewart*	8/1919	Fitted for oil fuel 1920. CR chimney by 1942	14765		2/1945
54	*Clan Chattan*	1921	Westinghouse removed 4/1936	14766		4/1944
55	*Clan Mackinnon*	1921		14767	54767	2/1950
56	*Clan MacKenzie*	1921		14768		4/1945
57	*Clan Cameron*	1921	Westinghouse removed 6/1936	14769		11/1943

Highland Number Index (originally Inverness and Aberdeen Junction)

1	1856	2-2-2 ex I&N		19	1863	2-4-O 18 class
	1874	Blank			1897	Blank
	1877	2-4-O 3 class			1902	O-6-O 134 class
	1898	4-4-O Small *Ben*		20	1863	2-4-O 18 class
2	1856	2-2-2 ex I&N		-21	1902	O-6-O 134 class
	1871	2-4-O No 2		22	1863	2-4-O 18 class
	1898	4-4-O Small *Ben*			1897	Blank
3	1856	2-2-2 3 class			1903	O-6-OT 22 class
	1870	Blank		23	1863	2-4-O 18 class
	1877	2-4-O 3 class			1903	O-6-OT 22 class
	1898	4-4-O Small *Ben*		24	1863	2-4-O 18 class
4	1857	2-2-2 3 class			1904	O-6-OT 22 class
	1873	Blank		25	1863	2-4-O 18 class
	1876	4-4-O *Duke* class			1905	O-4-4T 25 class
	1899	4-4-O Small *Ben*		26	1863	2-4-O 18 class
5	1858	2-4-O 5 class		-27	1913	4-6-O *Castle* class
	1897	4-4-O Skye bogie		28	1863	2-2-2/2-4-O 28 class
	1899	4-4-O Small *Ben*			1906	Blank
6	1858	2-4-O 5 class			1913	4-6-O *Castle* class
	1893	2-4-O ex 14		29	1863	2-2-2/2-4-O 28 class
	1897	4-4-O Skye bogie			1898	2-4-O ex 1
	1899	4-4-O Small *Ben*			1911	O-6-4T 39 class
7	1858	2-4-O/4-4-O 5 class		30	1863	2-2-2/2-4-O 30 class
	1898	4-4-O Skye bogie			1898	2-4-O ex 3
	1899	4-4-O Small *Ben*			1910	4-6-O *Castle* class
8	1858	2-4-O 5 class		31	1863	2-2-2/2-4-O 30 class
	1894	Blank			1899	4-4-O ex 4
	1899	4-4-O Small *Ben*			1911	O-6-4T 39 class
9	1858	2-4-O 5 class		32	1863	2-2-2 30 class
	1893	2-4-O ex 11			1897	2-4-O ex 6
	1898	Blank			1899	4-4-O ex 5
	1899	4-4-O Small *Ben*		33	1863	2-2-2/2-4-O 30 class
10	1858	2-4-O/4-4-O 5 class			1899	4-4-O ex 6
	1898	Blank		34	1863	2-2-2/2-4-O 30 class
	1899	4-4-O Small *Ben*			1898	Blank
11	1859	2-4-O 5 class			1899	4-4-O ex 7
	1893	4-4-OT 101 class		35	1863	2-2-2/2-4-O 30 class
	1899	4-4-O Small *Ben*			1911	4-6-O *Castle* class
12	1862	2-2-2 12 class		36	1864	2-4-O 36 class
	1899	Blank			1902	2-4-O ex 18
	1900	4-4-O Small *Ben*			1907	O-6-O 134 class
13	1862	2-2-O 12 class		37	1864	2-4-O 36 class
	1890	O-4-4ST *Strathpeffer*			1921	O-6-O 55
	1900	4-4-O Small *Ben*		38	1864	2-4-O 36 class
14	1862	2-4-O 14 class			1902	2-4-O ex 20
	1893	4-4-OT 101 class			1906	4-4-O Small *Ben*
	1900	4-4-O Small *Ben*		39	1864	2-4-O 36 class
15	1862	2-4-O 14 class			1902	2-4-O ex 21
	1893	4-4-OT 101 class			1909	O-6-4T 39 class
	1900	4-4-O Small *Ben*		40	1864	2-4-O 36 class
16	1862	O-4-OST ex Findhorn			1905	O-4-4T 25 class
	1873	Blank		41	1864	2-4-O 36 class
	1874	O-6-OT 56 class			1906	4-4-O Small *Ben*
	1901	4-4-O Small *Ben*		42	1864	2-4-O 36 class
17	1863	O-4-OT No 17			1911	O-6-4T 39 class
	1879	2-4-OT/4-4-OT 58 class		43	1864	2-4-O 36 class
	1901	4-4-O Small *Ben*			1913	4-6-O *Castle* class
18	1863	2-4-O 18 class			1913	O-6-4T ex 29
	1902	O-6-O 134 class		44	1864	2-4-O 36 class

Highland Name index (including I&AJ)

Aberfeldy	1886	2-4-OT 58 class no 17
Aldourie	1855	2-2-2 ex I&N
	1871	2-4-O No 2
		4-4-O *Duke* class no 69
Altyre	1858	2-4-O 5 class no 8
Ardross	1857	2-2-2 3 class no 4
	1876	4-4-O *Duke* class no 4
Ardvuela		4-4-O *Duke* class no 67
Atholl	1863	2-2-2 30 class no 33
	1886	4-4-O *Bruce* class no 79
Aviemore	1863	2-4-O 18 class no 22
	1864	2-4-O 36 class no 39
Auchtertyre	1901	4-4-O *Bruce* class no 4
Aultnaskiah	1858	2-2-2 5 class no 9
Aultwherrie	1903	4-4-O *Duke* class no 62
Badenoch		2-2-2 30 class no 50
Ballindalloch	1877	2-4-O 3 class no 3
Ballindalloch Castle	1900	4-6-O *Castle* class no 141
Balnain	1869	0-6-OT 56 class no 56
Beaufort	1885	4-4-O Duke class no 74
Beaufort Castle	1902	4-6-O Castle class no 147
Beauly	1863	2-4-O 18 class no 26
		2-4-O 5 class no 8
	1886	2-2-2 30 class no 47
Belladrum	1862	2-2-2 12 class no 12
	1864	2-2-2 30 class no 49
Ben a'Bhuird	1906	4-4-O small *Ben* no 47
Ben a'Chait	1908	large *Ben* no 68
Ben a'Chaoruinn	1909	large *Ben* no 62
Ben Achaoruinn	1926	correction of above
Ben Alder	1898	small *Ben* no 2
Ben Alisky	1900	small *Ben* no 13
Ben Alligan	1901	small *Ben* no 17
Ben Armin	1899	small *Ben* no 6
Ban Attow	1899	small *Ben* no 7
Ben Avon	1901	small *Ben* no 16
Ben Bhach Ard	1906	small *Ben* no 41
Ben Bhreac Mhor	1909	large *Ben* no 60
Ben Bhreac 'Mhor	1924	correction of above
Ben Clebrig	1899	small *Ben* no 8
Ben Dearg	1900	small *Ben* no 14
Ben Hope	1900	small *Ben* no 12
Ben Loyal	1900	small *Ben* no 15
Ben Macdhui	1899	small *Ben* no 11
Ben Mheadhoin	1908	large *Ben* no 63
Ben Mholach	1908	large *Ben* no 66
Ben More	1899	small *Ben* no 4
Ben na Caillach	1926	large Ben no 61 (correction)
Ben na Caillich	1908	original form of above
Ben Nevis	1898	small *Ben* no 1
Ben Rinnes	1899	small *Ben* no 9
Ben Slioch	1899	small *Ben* no 10
Ben Udlaman	1906	small *Ben* no 38
Ben Vrackie	1899	small *Ben* no 5
Ben Wyvis	1898	small *Ben* no 3
Ben-y-Gloe	1898	small Ben no 1
Ben Y'Gloe	1939	correction of above
Birnam	1863	2-4-O 18 class no 20
	1883	2-2-2 30 class no 33

Blair Atholl	1874	2-2-O 30 class no 51
Blair Castle	1900	4-6-O *Castle* class no 144
Brahan Castle	1913	*Castle* class no 26
Breadalbane	1871	2-2-2 12 class no 12
	1879	2-4-OT 58 class no 17
	1886	4-4-O *Duke* class no 75
Brodie	1864	2-4-O 36 class no 44
Brodie Castle	1917	4-6-O large Castle no 50
Bruce	1858	2-4-O 5 class no 6
	1864	2-2-2 30 class no 47
	1874	4-4-O *Duke* class no 60
	1884	*Duke* class no 72
	1886	*Bruce* class no 76
Burghead	1878	2-4-OT 58 class no 58
Cadboll	1864	2-2-2 30 class no 48
	1886	4-4-O *Bruce* class no 83
Caithness	1864	2-2-2 30 class no 51
	post 1874	4-4-O *Duke* class no 68
Caithness-shire	1874	*Duke* class no 68
Cawdor Castle	1902	4-6-O Castle class no 148
Clachnacuddin	1864	2-2-2 30 class no 46
	1883	4-4-O Duke class no 71
Clan Cameron	1921	4-6-O *Clan* class no 57
Clan Campbell	1919	*Clan* class no 49
Clan Chattan	1921	*Clan* class no 54
Clan Fraser	1919	*Clan* class no 51
Clan Mackenzie	1921	*Clan* class no 56
Clan Mackinnon	1921	*Clan* class no 55
Clan Munro	1919	*Clan* class no 52
Clan Stewart	1919	*Clan* class no 53
Cluny	1864	2-2-2 30 class no 55
	1874	30 class no 32
Cluny Castle	1913	4-6-O *Castle* class no 28
Colville	1886	4-4-O *Bruce* class no 81
Conon	1863	2-4-O 18 class
Cromartie	1877	4-4-O *Duke* class no 67
Dalcross	1864	2-4-O 36 class no 45
		2-4-O 18 class no 23
Dalcross Castle	1913	4-6-O *Castle* class no 43
Dalraddy		4-4-O *Duke* class no 65
Darnaway Castle	1917	4-6-O large *Castle* no 58
Dava	1864	2-4-O 36 class no 43
Dingwall	1863	2-4-O 18 class no 19
	post 1875	2-4-O 5 class no 7
	1886	2-2-2 30 class no 48
Dochfour	1888	4-4-O *Duke* class no 84
Dornoch	1902	0-6-OT 56 class no 56
Duke	1877	4-4-O *Duke* class no 61
Duncraig	1873	2-4-O 5 class no 10
Duncraig Castle	1902	4-6-O *Castle* class no 149
Dunkeld	post 1874	2-4-O 14 class no 15
Dunphail	1864	2-2-2 30 class no 52
Dunrobin	1870	2-4-OT Duke of Sutherland's
	1895	0-4-4T Duke of Sutherland's
Dunrobin Castle	1900	4-6-O *Castle* class no 142
Dunvegan Castle	1910	*Castle* class no 30
Durn	1908	4-4-O *Bruce* class no 82
	1917	4-4-O *Snaigow* class
Evanton		2-4-O 14 class no 14
Fife	1886	4-4-O *Bruce* class no 82
Findhorn	1860	0-4-OST Findhorn

Forres	1863	2-4-0 18 class no 21
		2-2-2 28 class no 29
Fort George	1899	0-6-0T 56 class no 16
Fortrose	1901	4-4-0T 101 class
Foulis		2-4-0 14 class no 15
Foulis Castle	1917	4-6-0 large *Castle* no 59
Glenbarry	1863	2-2-2 28 class no 28
Glenbruar	1892	4-4-0 *Strath* class no 100
Glenmore	1892	*Strath* class no 97
Glentilt	1892	*Strath* class no 96
Glentromie	1892	*Strath* class no 99
Glentruim	1892	*Strath* class no 98
Golspie		2-4-0 18 class no 19
		2-4-0 5 class no 9
	1886	2-2-2 30 class no 53
Gordon Castle	1895	2-4-0T ex Duke of Sutherland's
	1900	4-6-0 *Castle* class no 143
Gordon Lennox	1905	0-4-4T 25 class no 40
Grandtully	1897	4-4-0 *Strath* class no 90
Grange	c1886	4-4-0 Duke class no 72
Grantown		2-2-2 28 class no 28
Helmsdale		2-2-2 30 class no 49
	c1874	2-4-0 5 class no 6
Highlander	1863	2-2-2 28 class no 29
	1879	2-4-0T 58 class no 59
Hopeman	1863	0-4-0ST no 17
Huntingtower	1899	4-4-0 *Duke* class no 62
Invergordon	1863	2-4-0 18 class no 24
	1884	2-2-2 30 class no 55
Inverness	1863	2-4-0 18 class no 18
		4-4-0 *Duke* class no 63
Inverness-shure	1874	*Duke* class no 63
Isla Bank		2-2-2 30 class no 35
Keith	1864	2-4-0 36 class no 40
Kincraig	1864	36 class no 38
Kingsmills	1863	2-2-2 30 class no 35
Kingussie	1864	2-4-0 36 class no 41
	1883	2-2-2 30 class no 46
Lairg		2-4-0 18 class no 24
Lentran	1864	2-4-0 36 class no 42
Loch	1862	2-4-0 14 class no 14
Lochalsh	1886	4-4-0 *Bruce* class no 78
Loch an Dorb	1896	4-4-0 *Loch* class no 123
Loch Ashie	1916	*Loch* class no 70
Loch Ericht	1896	*Loch* class no 121
Loch Fannich	1896	*Loch* class no 130
Loch Garry	1896	*Loch* class no 127
Loch Garve	1916	*Loch* class no 71
Lochgorm	1872	0-6-0T 56 class no 57
Loch Insh	1896	4-4-0 *Loch* class no 119
Loch Laggan	1896	*Loch* class no 124
Loch Laschal		*Loch* class no 133 (correction)
Loch Laoghal	1896	Original form of above
Loch Luichart	1896	*Loch* class no 128
Loch Maree	1896	*Loch* class no 129
Loch Moy	1896	*Loch* class no 122
Loch Naver	1896	*Loch* class no 132
Loch Ness	1896	*Loch* class no 120
Loch Ruthven	1916	*Loch* class no 72
Loch Shin	1896	*Loch* class no 131
Loch Tay	1896	*Loch* class no 125

Loch Tummel	1896	*Loch* class no 126
Lovat	1862	2-2-2 12 class no 13
	c1874	2-2-2 30 class no 47
	1886	4-4-0 *Bruce* class no 77
Lybster	1903	0-4-4ST no 53 (ex 13)
Macduff	1864	2-2-2 30 class no 54
Monkland	1902	4-4-0 *Bruce* class no 83
Morayshire	1874	4-4-0 *Duke* class no 64
Muirtown		Duke class no 68
Munlochy	1910	4-4-0T 101 class no 102
Murthly	1863	2-4-0 18 class no 23
Murthly Castle	1900	4-6-0 *Castle* class no 145
Nairn	1864	2-4-0 36 class no 36
Nairnshire	1874	4-4-0 *Duke* class no 65
Needlefield	1880	0-4-0ST ex no 17
Novar	1863	2-4-0 18 class no 25
Perthshire	1874	4-4-0 *Duke* class no 62
	c1889	2-2-2 30 class no 34
Prince	1863	30 class no 30
Princess	1863	30 class no 31
Portessie	1901	4-4-0T 101 class no 14
Raigmore	1855	2-2-2 ex I&N
	1877	2-4-0 3 class no 1
River Ness	1915	4-6-0 *River* class no 70
River Spey	1915	*River* class no 71
Rosehaugh	1898	4-4-0 *Duke* class no 73
Ross-shire	1874	*Duke* class no 66
St Martins	1856	2-2-2 3 class no 3
	1874	0-6-0T 56 class no 16
Seafield	1858	2-4-0 5 class no 5
	1863	2-2-2 30 class no 34
	c1889	4-4-0 *Duke* class no 64
Sir George	1892	4-4-0 *Strath* class no 89
Sir James		4-4-0 Duke class no 69
Skibo		2-4-0 5 class no 11
Skibo Castle	1902	4-6-0 Castle class no 146
Snaigow	1917	4-4-0 Snaigow class no 73
Stafford	1859	2-4-0 5 class no 11
	1864	2-2-2 30 class no 53
	1886	4-4-0 *Bruce* class no 80
Stemster	1889	4-4-0 *Duke* class no 62
Strathcarron	1892	4-4-0 *Strath* class no 95
Strathdearn	1892	*Strath* class no 92
Strathnairn	1892	*Strath* class no 93
Strathpeffer	1885	2-2-2/2-2-2T 12 class no 12
	1890	0-4-4ST no 13
	1905	0-4-4T 25 class no 25
Strathspey	1892	4-4-0 *Strath* class no 91
Strathtay	1892	Strath class no 94
Sutherland	1862	2-4-0 14 class no 15
	1863	2-2-2 30 class no 32
	1874	30 class no 55
	1884	4-4-0 *Duke* class no 60
Sutherlandshire	1874	*Duke* class no 61
Tain		2-4-0 5 class no 5
Taymouth Castle	1900	4-6-0 *Castle* class no 140
The Duke	1874	4-4-0 *Duke* class no 67
The Lord Provost	1874	*Duke* class no 69
Thurlow	1885	*Duke* class no 73
Thurso	1874	2-2-2 12 class no 13
Thurso Castle	1913	4-6-0 *Castle* class no 27

Tweedale	1892	4-4-O	*Strath* class no 90
Urquhart Castle	1911	4-6-O	*Castle* class no 35
Westhall	1858	2-4-O	5 class no 10

FURNESS RAILWAY

INTRODUCTION

The Furness Railway was a small, locally based railway with 158 miles of route from the LNWR at Carnforth to Whitehaven with branches to Hincaster Junction north of Carnforth and south of Oxenholme on the LNW line. This gave access to the north (with running powers to Kendal and Tebay). There were branches to Lakeside (Windermere), Pierl and Coniston and a number of minor mineral lines. A second connection at Carnforth provided access to the Midland via the joint Carnforth - Wennington line. It also operated with the LNWR the joint lines of the Whitehaven, Cleator and Egremont Railway and had a joint interest with the LNWR in the Cleator and Workington Junction but this was not a controlling interest and this company was managed independently (see page no 257). The Furness, however, operated all the passenger trains and some of the goods trains on the C&W Jct.

It was centred on Barrow-in-Furness which town it largely created, building extensive docks. Barrow did not, however, develop as a major port despite the fact that the Midland used it from 1867 for their Irish traffic before building their own port at Heysham in 1904.

It maintained amicable relations with both the Midland and the LNWR and from an early date promoted itself as the principal railway providing access to the Lake District, building an hotel at Furness Abbey and operating passenger vessels on Lake Windermere and Lake Coniston.

The prime function of the railway, however, which was the reason for its incorporation in 1844, was to serve the mineral resources of the area, in particular iron ore deposits from which the original prospectus expected 60% of the revenue to come. This ultimately led to the creation of a large iron and steel making industry in Furness and in turn to Barrow becoming a major ship building centre, but the original function of the railway was to convey minerals to a causeway linking Roa Island to the mainland between Rampside and Piel which had been recently built by John Abel Smith.

The original 15 miles of railway was opened on 12 August 1846 from Kirkby-in-Furness to Dalton with a junction at Goldmire (facing Dalton) to Piel and a branch off this line to Barrow. Passengers were carried in four carriages from December of that year. An extension from Kirkby to Broughton was opened in February 1848 and one from Dalton to Ulverston was opened to Lindal in May or June 1851 and to Ulverston Road in May 1852, but not completed to Ulverston until 7 July 1854 due to delays caused by bad weather.

For the first six years just four locomotives were sufficient to operate the railway. In the meantime a connection with the Whitehaven and Furness Junction had been made at Broughton.

The remainder of the main line was built by the Ulverston and Lancaster Railway (registered under the spelling of Ulverstone) and opened on 10 August 1857 for goods traffic and for passengers in the following month, but worked by the Furness until absorbed in 1862.

Likewise the Coniston railway was a separate company but with common directors and was opened on 18 June 1859 from Broughton to Coniston. It also was worked by the Furness and was amalgamated in the same year, 1862.

A direct junction with the W&F Jct at Foxfield was opened in 1866 eliminating the need for reversal at Broughton.

In 1880 major changes were made at Barrow by the decision to build a 7½ mile line from Park South Junction south of Askam, making a loop line through Barrow to Roose, erecting a now central station and closing the old Barrow branch. This was opened on 1 June 1882, all regular passenger trains then being diverted to this line, only through goods trains and special passenger trains using the original line between Park South and Dalton.

Although increasing the mileage by five miles this had the effect of putting Barrow on the main line.

The fortunes of the railway tended to rise and fall with those of the iron and steel industry but on the whole it was a highly profitable company and had an individuality of its own which it retained for many years after it had ceased to

exist in a legal sense.
There was a close involvement between the company and the local, relatively isolated, community which it served and the chairman, the Duke of Devonshire, a local landowner, and the Ramsden family who ran the railway almost as a family business, for many years were local benefactors.

Locomotive Superintendents

James Ramsden	1846-50	Appointed General Manager
R. Mason	1850-96	Retired
William Frank Pettigrew	1896-1918	Retired
David L. Rutherford	1918-23	Formation of LMS

James Ramsden had served his apprenticeship with Bury, Curtis and Kennedy and had worked with Edward Bury at Wolverton on the London and Birmingham railway so it was natural that the early goods engines were of Bury type. He was appointed General Manager in 1850 and ultimately became Managing Director. In 1873 he was knighted for his services to trade and industry.
Throughout Mason's period all the locomotives continued to be of standard manufacturer's design, mostly by Sharp Stewart, the more numerous o-6-Os often being known as 'Sharpies'.
Pettigrew was undoubtedly the most talented of the FR loco superintendents. He had been with the Great Eastern and was works manager of Nine Elms, the LSWR loco works, when appointed to the FR. His title was later altered to CME and he designed locomotives especially suited to FR traffic.
Rutherford also, like Pettigrew, a Scot was a civil engineer and he came to the FR from the North British in that capacity in 1909 taking on the additional responsibility of Locomotive, Carriage and Wagon Superintendent on Pettigrew's retirement. His involvement in the Baltic tank design of 1920 was probably only supervisory.
Stephenson link motion was used on all locomotives.
The Furness was a vacuum braked railway and the driver's footplate position was on the left. The locos were painted Indian red and carriages ultramarine blue with white upper panels and subtly reflected the colours of haematite ore and the blue of the lakes on a sunny summer's day.

Dimensions are generally those stated by Rush but it should be noted that where comparison is possible with other sources there are some discrepancies and these have been amended where references in the contemporary technical press indicate otherwise.

FURNESS RAILWAY

CONSTITUENT COMPANIES

Whitehaven Junction
  Incorporated 1844. Opened Maryport to Workington 19 January 1846, to
  Harrington 18 May 1846, to Whitehaven 19 March 1847 (goods from 15 February
  1847).

Whitehaven and Furness Junction
  Incorporated 1847. Opened Whitehaven (Preston St) to Ravenglass 1 June 1849,
  to Bootle 19 July 1850, to Broughton 28 October 1850. Formed joint committee
  1854 with Whitehaven Junction which was taken over by the LNWR. W&F Jct
  taken over by FR and the joint locos were shared 1866.

  For complete list of these locomotives see Vol 2A pps 50-2. Variant versions
  of the allocations between LNW and FR have been published in *Loco Mag*, Vol 5,
  pps 58, 78 (1900) (repeated by Rush) and in McGowan Gradon. As noted in Vol
  2A a third version contained in unpublished notes by S.S. Scott made from
  Crewe records in the 1920s has been preferred as being more likely to be
  authentic.

  9 locomotives to FR stock 1866 as under:

  0-6-0 Built by R&W Hawthorn. Works no 1269.
    DW 4ft 6in, Cyls 16 x 24, Blr 4ft 2in x 9ft 0in, THS 918 sq ft, WP 120lbs/
    sq in, WB 6ft 0in + 6ft 8in, Wt 28tons 6cwts. Weatherboard only. Dome on
    raised firebox.

No	Name	Date		
19	*Lonsdale*	1864	To Furness **42**	Rebuilt 1886
		1866	Accident Ravenglass	
		1904	Withdrawn. Scrapped 1910	

  0-6-0 Built by R&W Hawthorn 4/1847. Works no 466.
    Purchased from L&Y (ex Blackburn, Darwen & Bolton) 1854 through a Mr Dees
    (see Vol 3B, p17).
    DW 4ft 8in, Cyls 16 x 24, Blr 3ft 11in x 10ft 0in, THS 605 sq ft, WB 7ft
    3in + 7ft 3in, Wt 23tons 11cwts.

No	Name	Date	
9	*King Lear*	1854	Rebuilt 1859. To Furness **43**
			Believed sold. Replaced 1871

  0-4-2 Built by R&W Hawthorn. Works no 975.
    DW 5ft 0in, Cyls 16 x 22. Dimensions possibly similar to no 3 below.

No	Name	Date	
1	*Excelsior*	10/1856	To Furness **44**
		1882	Sold to Wigan Colliery Co.

  0-4-2 Built by R&W Hawthorn. Works no 997
    DW 5ft 6in, Cyls 16 x 22 (Rush records DW 5ft 0in, LW 3ft 6in, Cyls 14 x 20,
    Blr 3ft 11in x 9ft 9in, THS 907 sq ft, WP 120lbs/sq in, WB 7ft 6in + 6ft 6in,
    Wt 27tons 11cwt, for this loco).

No	Name	Date	
3	*Mars*	7/1857	To Furness **45**. Scrapped 1882

  2-2-2WT Built by E B Wilson & Co.
    DW 5ft 3in, LW & TW 3ft 6in, Cyls 12 x 18, Blr 3ft 9in x 8ft 6in, THS 739
    sq ft, WP 120lbs/sq in, WB 6ft 6in + 6ft 8in, Wt 27tons. Inside frames.

No*	Name	Date	
4	*Oberon*	1851	In accident Broughton 1857.
		1863	Rebuilt
		8/1866	In accident Whitehaven tunnel
		1866	To Furness **46**
		1872	To duplicate list 46A

```
    5    Titania              1851  Rebuilt 1864.  To Furness 47.
                              1872  Sold
      *Order of numbering not certain
```

2-4-0 Built by R&W Hawthorn. Works no 601.
DW 5ft 6in, Cyls 15 x 21.

No	Name	Date
4	Maryport	9/1847

```
                              1854  Renumbered joint stock 7
                                    Renamed Petrel
                              1857  Rebuilt 2-2-2T
                              1866  To Furness 48. Sold 1872
```

0-4-0ST Built by Fletcher Jennings. Works no 29 *(Banshee)*
               Neilson & Co. Works no 571 *(Bob Ridley)*
   DW 4ft 0in, Cyls 10 x 16. Not identical apart from dimensions. Used for
   transfers between Preston St & Whitehaven Harbour.

No	Name	Date
16	Banshee	4/1863	To Furness 49. Sold 1883 to Cousins, Whitehaven. Resold 1898 to Ellenborough Colliery, Maryport.
15	Bob Ridley	1862	Purchased second hand, built 1860
		1866	To Furness 50. Sold 1883 to Cousins, Whitehaven.

Whitehaven, Cleator and Egremont

Incorporated 1854. Opened 11/1/1855 (goods), 1857 (passenger). Junction
with Whitehaven and Furness Junction at Mirehouse, one mile South of Corkickle
to Egremont with branch from Moor Row to Cleator and Frizington. Egremont
branch extended to join W&F Jct at Sellafield 1868. Northern extension to
Lamplugh opened early 1864 to Marron Junction on LNWR Cockermouth line 6 1864.
Taken over by LNWR 1877. After protests about previous agreements from the
FR it was agreed that the WC&E should be taken over jointly by the LNWR and
FR. Locos to FR 1878, names removed, (no LNWR numbers allotted).

17 locomotives as under:

0-6-0ST Built by Robert Stephenson & Co. Works nos below (RS)
               Fletcher Jennings & Co. Works no below (FJ)
   DW 4ft 6in, Cyls 17 x 24, Blr 4ft 0in x 10ft 9in, THS 995 sq ft, WP 150lbs/
   sq in. WB 6ft 6in + 7ft 9in, Wt 44tons. Nos 1,2 & 4 originally had cyls
   16 x 24. Generally flat-sided saddle tanks with round tops covering boiler
   only but with some covering firebox as well, all had O/S frames. Rebuilt
   with cabs, DW 4ft 7½in, bunkers with curved up side panels and straight
   back panels. (No 10 was not given a cab at first rebuilding but this was
   added later). Nos 5 and 10 had semi-circular tanks. Nos 1 & 2, 4 & 5 were
   originally domeless. No 6 was given a more elaborate cab.

No	Name	Date		Works no	FR no	Rebuilt	Duplicate no	year	With-drawn
1	Ennerdale	1855	RS	1008	98	*			1895
2	Carlisle	1855	RS	1009	99	*			1886
4	Keeble	1858	FJ	21	100	1882 1/1895	100A	1904	1918
5	Hercules	1860	RS	1310	101	*			1895
6	Parkside	1862	RS	1437	102	*			1900
7	Egremont	1863	RS	1487	103	*			1887
8	Cleator	1863	RS	1488	104	*			1900
9	Loweswater	1867-8	RS	1804**	105	*	105A	1904	1921
10	Crummock	1867-8	RS	1798**	106	*	106A	1904	1918
11	Newton Manor	1869	RS	1960	107	1880	107A	1904	1918
13	Springfield	1871	RS	1997	109	*	109A	1898	7/1924***
14	Derwentwater	1873	RS	2109	110	*	110A	1907	1920
15	Buttermere	1873	RS	2110	111	*	111A	1907	1920

*Date of rebuilding not known
**Rush records no 9 as RS1798 and no 10 as RS1804
***LMS 11547 allotted

0-6-OT Built by R&W Hawthorn. Works no 989.
DW 4ft 0in, Cyls 14 x 22, Blr 4ft 0in x 9ft 8in, THS 787 sq ft, WP 150lbs/
sq in, WB 5ft 8in + 5ft 10in, Wt 34tons. 'Stovepipe' chimney, Hawthorn type
dome, weatherboard only. Rebuilt early '80s with normal dome, Salter valves
and primitive cab with rounded top.

No	Name		
3	*Victoria*	To FR no **113**.	Sold 1898.

2-4-OT Built by Stothert & Slaughter 1854.
Purchased 1870 from North London (Vol 2A p55).
DW 5ft 3in, LW 3ft 6in, Cyls 15 x 22 O/S, Blr 4ft 0in x 10ft 3in, THS 911 sq
ft, WP 120lbs/sq in, WB 6ft 0in + 8ft 3in, Wt 36tons. Rebuilt DW 5ft 0in,
Cyls 15 x 20 with ugly design of cab by Fletcher Jennings.

No	Name		
12	*Marron*	To Furness **108**.	Scrapped 1898

0-6-OST Built by A. Barclay Sons & Co, Kilmarnock.
DW 4ft 6in, Cyls 17 x 24, Blr 4ft 0in x 10ft 8in, THS 992 sq ft, WP 150lbs/
sq in, Wt 43tons 19cwts. Inside frames.

No	Name	Date	
16	*Ullswater*	1875	Sold 1877 (purchaser in Wales*)
17	*Watswater*	1875	To Furness **112**. Rebuilt 1896
	(works no 154)	1898	Renumbered **108**
		1907	To duplicate list 108A
		1915	Rebuilt
		1923	Allotted LMS 11548. Scrapped 8/1924

Locomotive Magazine Vol 5 (1900) and the S.S. Scott list records the above
information but Rush (p83) records no 16 as being 0-4-OST and retained by
the L&NW for shunting at Crewe works before being sold and eventually coming
into possession of Whitehaven Iron & Steel Co in 1916, being scrapped about
1919.

All WC&E locos had second pair of buffers between main ones for shunting
chaldron wagons.

FURNESS LOCOMOTIVES 1844-96

All locomotives in this period were to manufacturer's designs.

O-4-O Built by Bury, Curtis and Kennedy.
   DW 4ft 9in, Cyls 13 x 24, Blr 3ft 9in x 10ft 0in, THS 740.4 sq ft, WP 90lbs/
   sq in, WB 7ft 5in, Wt 17¾tons. Normal Bury type. Four-wheel tenders.

No	Date	
1	1844	Sold 1870 to a contractor
2	1844	Sold 1870 to colliery in Northumberland

O-4-O Built by Bury, Curtis and Kennedy.
   DW 4ft 9in, Cyls 14 x 24, Blr 3ft 10in x 10ft 0in, THS 854 sq ft, WP 110lbs/
   sq in, WB 7ft 5in, Wt 19½tons. Larger version of 1 class.

No	Date	
3	1846	Withdrawn 12/1898. Nicknamed 'Old Copper Knob'. Placed in glass stand outside Barrow Central station 1907. Damaged in air raid 1941 and stored at Horwich. Subsequently exhibited at Clapham, now in NRM, York.
4	1846	Scrapped 1/1898

O-4-O Built by Fairbairn & Co.
   DW 4ft 6in, Cyls 15 x 24, Blr 4ft 2in x 10ft 8in, THS 940 sq ft, WP 120lbs/
   sq in, WB 7ft 9in, Wt 21tons 9cwt (7-10), 24tons 4cwts (13-16). Bury type
   closed splashers (13-16 of different design).

No	Date	
7	1854/5	Sold 1899*
8	1854/5	Sold 1899*
9	1854/5	To duplicate list 9A 1899. Sold 1899/1900*
10	1854/5	To duplicate list 10A 1899. Sold 1899/1900*
13	1858	Replaced 1899
14	1858	Replaced 1899
15	1861	Replaced 1899
16	1861	To duplicate list 16A 1899

*Sold to Barrow Haematite Steel Co and converted to saddle tank.

O-4-O Built by Sharp Stewart & Co. Works nos 1434/5, 1447/8, 1585/6, 1663/4.
   DW 4ft 9in, Cyls 15½ x 24, Blr 4ft 2in x 10ft 8in, THS 926 sq ft, WP 120lbs/
   sq in, WB 7ft 9in, Wt 24tons 18cwts. Plate frames, dome on first ring of
   boiler cover, Salter safety valves, normal round top firebox, raised
   footplating over wheels with deep valance. Four-wheel tenders. Springs
   above running plate.

No	Date	
17	1863	Sold 1870*
18	1863	Sold 1870*
19	1863	Sold 1870*
20	1863	Sold 1870*
25	1865	Sold 1873*
26	1865	Sold 1873*
27	1866	To duplicate list 27A 1914. Withdrawn 1918.
28	1866	To duplicate list 28A 1914. Withdrawn 1918.

*Sold to Barrow Haematite Steel Co. Ex no 18 was converted to saddle tank
and is preserved at the Hastwell Training Centre, Barrow. Ex no 25 was
converted to saddle tank and is preserved at Stone Cross Special School,
Ulverston.

2-2-2WT Built by Sharp Stewart & Co. Works nos 696/7.
   DW 5ft 6in, LW & TW 3ft 7in, Cyls 14 x 18, Blr 4ft 0in x 9ft 8in, THS 835 sq
   ft, WP 120lbs/sq in, WB 7ft 3in + 7ft 3in, Wt 30½tons. Outside sandwich
   frames (straight). No cab as built, but bent-over weatherboard later fitted.
   Raised firebox dome on first ring of boiler cover.

No	Date	
5	1852	Scrapped 1873
6	1852	Scrapped 1873

2-2-2WT Built by Sharp Stewart & Co. Works nos 1016, 1019.
DW 5ft 6¼in, LW & TW 3ft 7in, Cyls 14 x 20, Blr 4ft 2in x 9ft 7in, THS 840
sq ft, WP 120lbs/sq in, WB 7ft 3in + 7ft 0in, Wt 30tons 2cwts. As 5 class
with larger dimensions and curved O/S frames.

No	Date	
11	1857	Withdrawn 1873. Sold back to Sharp Stewart 1875.
12	1857	Accident Broughton 1857
		To duplicate list 9A 1872
		Sold to Weston Clevedon & Portishead 1898
		No 2 *'Clevedon'*

2-2-2WT Built by Sharp Stewart & Co. Works nos as below.
DW 5ft 6¼in, LW & TW 3ft 7in, Cyls 15 x 18, Blr 4ft 2in x 9ft 7in, THS 868
sq ft, WP 120lbs/sq in, WB 7ft 3in + 7ft 0in, Wt 30½tons. As 11 class,
larger domensions.

No	Date	Works no	Duplicate no	year	
21	1864	1500	21A	1896	Sold 1899
22	1864	1501			Sold 1899 to Whitburn Colliery Co
34	1866	1763	34A	1896	Withdrawn 1898
35	1866	1707	35A	1896	Sold 1899 to Weston Clevedon and
					Portishead. No 1 *Weston*.
36	1866	1708	36A	1896	Stationery work 1896-8.
37	1866	1762	37A	1896	Stationery work 1896-8.

2-4-0 Built by Sharp Stewart. Works nos as below.
DW 5ft 6in, LW 3ft 6in, Cyls 16 x 20, Blr 4ft 0in x 9ft 9in, THS 910.5 sq ft,
WP 120lbs/sq in, WB 6ft 6in + 8ft 6in, Wt 30½tons. Similar to Cambrian
Railway 28 class. Later fitted with automatic vacuum brake. 7 rebuilt
2-4-2T with TW 3ft 6in, WB 6ft 6in + 8ft 6in + 6ft 6in, Wt 44tons 11cwt.

No	Date	Works no	Duplicate no	year	
1	1870	2057	1A	1913	Rebuilt 1895. Scrapped 1916.
2	1870	2058	2A	1913	Rebuilt 1896. Withdrawn 1918.
57	1870	2093			Scrapped 1918
58	1870	2094			Withdrawn 1918
70	1872	2245	70A	1920	Rebuilt 2-4-2T 1891
					Allotted LMS 10619. Withdrawn 2/1924.
71	1872	2246	71A	1920	Rebuilt 2-4-2T 1891. Allotted LMS
					10620. Withdrawn 8/1924
72	1872	2247			Rebuilt 2-4-2T 1891. Scrapped 1919
73	1872	2248			Rebuilt 2-4-2T 1891. Scrapped 1919
74	1872	2249			Rebuilt 2-4-2T 1891. Replaced 1920
46	1872	2256			Scrapped 1920
75	1872	2257			Withdrawn 1914
47	1872	2258			Rebuilt 2-4-2T 1891. Scrapped 1919.
48	1872	2259			Rebuilt 2-4-2T 1891. Scrapped 1920
5	1873	2364	5A	1906	Withdrawn 1907
6	1873	2365	6A	1906	Withdrawn 1907
11	1873	2366			Renumbered **3** 1899
			3A	1906	Withdrawn 1916
12	1873	2367			Renumbered **4** 1899
			4A	1906	Scrapped 1920
44	1882	3086	44A	1920	Rebuilt 1898. Allotted LMS 10002.
					Withdrawn 1924. Scrapped 4/1925
45	1882	3087	45A	1920	Withdrawn 1921

4-4-0 Built by Sharp Stewart & Co. Works nos 3618-21.
DW 5ft 7½in, LW 3ft 1½in, Cyls 17 x 24, Blr 4ft 2in x 10ft 4½in, THS 1041 sq
ft, WP 140lbs/sq in, WB 5ft 9in + 6ft 6½in + 8ft 0in, Wt 36tons 2cwts.
Seperate coupled wheel splashers. Bogie version of 2-4-0s. Known as
'Seagulls'. Enlarged four-wheel tenders 2,500 galls. LMS class 1P, red
livery.

			LMS	
No	Date		no	Withdrawn
120	1890	Rebuilt 1908 superheater	10131	5/1927
121	1890		10132	12/1924
122	1890		10133	10/1927
123	1890		10134	9/1925

4-4-0 Built by Sharp Stewart & Co. Works nos 4174-9, 4651-2.
DW 6ft 0in, LW 3ft 6in, Cyls 18 x 24, Blr 4ft 2in x 10ft 4½in, THS 1208.5 sq
ft, WP 150lbs/sq in, WB 5ft 9in + 6ft 8in + 8ft 6in, Wt 41tons 6cwts.
Seperate coupled wheel splashers. Flush fireboxes. Similar to Manson
4-4-0s on Great North of Scotland. Six-wheel tenders 2,500 gallons. LMS
class 1P.

		Renumbered			LMS	
No	Date	no	year	Rebuilt	no	Withdrawn
21	1896	32	1910			
		44	1920		10137	12/1930
22	1896	33	1910			
		45	1920		10138	10/1929
34	1896	46	1920	1913 Phoenix superheater		
				(removed 1914) 1924	10139	8/1929
35	1896	47	1920	1909 superheater	10140	9/1929
36	1896				10135	10/1929
37	1896			1913 Phoenix superheater		
				(removed 1914)	10136	12/1931
124	1900				10141	1/1929
125	1900				10142	9/1929

0-4-0ST Built by Sharp Stewart & Co. Works nos 1543/4, 2448/50.
DW 4ft 0in, Cyls 14 x 20, Blr 3ft 5in x 10ft 6in, THS 669 sq ft, WP 120lbs/
sq in, WB 7ft 9in, Wt 24½tons. Domed boiler with safety valves over firebox.
Bentlover weatherboard. Nos 23/4 had saddle tank over smokebox but not over
firebox. Nos 94-7 had dome over first ring of boiler cover. Nos 95 and 97
latterly had Ross 'pop' safety valves.

		1898	Duplicate			
No	Date	no	no	year	Withdrawn	
23	1864	98			1904	
24	1864	99			1904	
94	1874		94A	1912	1914	
95	1874		95A	1912	1916	
96	1874		96A	1907	1916	
97	1874		97A	1907	8/1924	Allotted LMS 11258

0-6-0T Built by Sharp Stewart & Co. Works nos 1842/3, 2204/5, 2300/1.
DW 4ft 6in, Cyls 18 x 24, Blr 4ft 0in x 10ft 0in, THS 1111sq ft, WP 140lbs/
sq in, WB 7ft 0in + 8ft 6in, Wt 44tons 14cwts. Long side tanks almost to
front of smokebox possibly giving resemblence to horse's blinkers and
nickname of 'Neddies'. Oblong cut out at bottom of each tank between first
and second axles for attention to motion. Centre dome, safety valves in
brass casing over raised firebox. Bent over weatherboard supported by poles
at rear. Used for banking on Lindal bank and on joint lines in Cleator Moor
area. Moor Row locos had unofficial home made wooden side sheets. LMS
Class 2F.

No	Date	1915 no	Rebuilt	LMS no	Withdrawn
51	1867				1915
52	1867	84			1918
68	1872			(11549)	4/1925
69	1872			(11550)	5/1925
82	1873			(11551)	10/1925
83	1873		1906	(11552)	6/1926

O-6-O Built by Sharp Stewart & Co. Works nos as below.
DW 4ft 6½in, Cyls 16 x 24, Blr 3ft 11¼in x 10ft 4in, THS 959.27 sq ft, WP 120lbs/sq in, WB 6ft 9in + 8ft 0in, Wt 26tons. Raised firebox. Salter safety valve in brass casing over firebox. Centre dome. Locos built before 1873 had weatherboard only. Later locos had cab similar to Stirling GN design (Wt 30tons 19cwts). Originally fitted with four-wheel 1,500 gallon tenders. Fourteen further locos were ordered but cancelled by FR and subsequently sold as follows:

	SS 2339/47	Mid Wales 9 & 10 (Intended FR nos 88,91)
	2342/6	NSR 69 & 70 (88/90)
	2510	Denbigh, Ruthin & Corwen No 4 (94)
	2511/3	Cambrian 14 & 15 (95/97)
	2512	Sold abroad (96)

Locos rebuilt 1897-1901 were given flush boilers standard with 112 class O-6-2Ts with Ramsbottom safety valves. 1910-13 rebuilds were given boilers standard with 19 class O-6-OTs. 1916-18 rebuilds had similar boilers but with extended smokeboxes. All were vacuum brake fitted and given more modern cabs with large oblong rear splasher except 1916-18 rebuilds which had cabs without rear splasher.
The LMS numbering distinguished between the two types of rebuild boiler (12000-14: Wt 50½tons; 12065-76: Wt 53tons 7cwts class 1F).

No	Date	Works no	Renumbered no	year	Duplicate no	year	Rebuilt	LMS no*	Withdrawn	Scrapped
29	1866	1697	61	1918			1900	12001	7/1925	
30	1866	1698	62	1918			1899	12007	12/1925	
31	1866	1764	48	1920			1899	12000	5/1925	
32	1866	1765			32A	1896				1900
33	1866	1766			33A	1896				1900
38	1866	1760								1915
39	1866	1761								1915
40	1867	1784	80	1916			1900	12008	6/1927	
41	1867	1785								1916
17	1870	2064	23	1899			1899			
			42	1910						
			66	1916				12003	10/1925	
18	1870	2065	24	1899						1910
19	1870	2095								1910
20	1870	2096	25	1910	25A	1913	1900	12002	2/1924	1925
53	1871	2097								1916
54	1871	2098	78	1916			1898	12005	7/1925	
55	1871	2099					1898			1918
56	1871	2100					1899			1918
59	1871	2145								1913
60	1871	2146	64	1918			1900			1921
61	1871	2147					1899			1916
62	1871	2148					1900			1916
63	1871	2149					1899			1918
64	1871	2150								1918
65	1871	2151					1918	12065	3/1930	
66	1871	2152								1916
67	1871	2153								1914

43	1871	2154	**67**	1916		1901	12004	6/1925	
									1910
25	1873	2278							
26	1873	2279	**59**	1913	✓	1916			
			63	1918			12066	12/1929	
76	1873	2280				1901	12006	1925	12/1926
77	1873	2283							1914
78	1873	2284				1899			1915
79	1873	2285				1916	12067	6/1930	
80	1873	2316							1916
81	1873	2317				1900			1921
84	1873	2337							1915
85	1873	2338				1900	12009	7/1925	
86	1873	2340				1898	12010	10/1924	
87	1873	2341				1898	12011	2/1924	
92	1874	2422	**75**	1914		1897	12012	1924	2/1926
93	1874	2423	**77**	1914		1899	12013	9/1924	
88	1875	2506				1911	12068	1926	8/1927
89	1875	2507				1912	12069	1926	4/1927
90	1875	2508				1918	12070	6/1930	
91	1875	2509	To Dept no 1		1918	1900			1924
114	1881	2945	**115**	1898					
			70	1920		1910	12071	6/1925	1926
115	1881	2946							1892**
116	1881	2947	**71**	1920		1901	12014	11/1925	
117	1881	2948	**72**	1920		1913	12072	11/1927	
118	1881	2949	**73**	1920		1911	12073	8/1925	1927
119	1881	2950	**74**	1920		1910	12074	10/1925	1926
49	1884	3170				1916	12075	6/1928	
50	1884	3171				1912	12076	11/1927	1928
120	1884	3172 ⎫	Sold to Lancaster Southport & Preston Jct						
121	1884	3173 ⎭	nos 1 & 2 in 1887. See vol 3B, p26.						

*Locos withdrawn before about 1926 may not all have carried LMS numbers.

**No 115 fell into a cavern when old mine workings subsided under the track while the loco was shunting at Lindal on 22 September 1892 and had to be abandoned.

Some locos transferred to work the Joint lines were fitted with back weatherboards for tender-first running. Possibly (unconfirmed) nos 49, 63, 66, 74 (ex 119) & 75 (ex 92).

Pettigrew Locomotives 1898-1916

4-4-0 Built by Sharp Stewart & Co. Works nos 4716-9.
DW 6ft 6in, LW 3ft 6in, Cyls 18 x 26, Blr 4ft 4in x 10ft 8⅜in, THS 1263.25 sq
ft, WP 160lbs/sq in, WB 6ft 0in + 7ft 3½in + 8ft 6in, Wt 43tons. 3,000 gallon
tenders. Used on principal express passenger trains. LMS class 1P.

No	Date	Rebuilt	LMS no	Withdrawn
126	1901		10143	12/1931
127	1901		10144	5/1930
128	1901		10145	6/1930
129	1901	1924 at Horwich	10146	12/1930

4-4-0 Built by North British Locomotive Co. Works nos 20071-2, 20867-8.
DW 6ft 0in, LW 3ft 6in, Cyls 18 x 26, Blr 4ft 7in + 10ft 0in, THS 1193 sq ft,
WP 170lbs/sq in, WB as 126 class, Wt 46tons 12cwts, 3,300 gallon tenders.
Did not usually work north of Barrow. Used on through Euston trains. 1914
locos had boilers 6in longer. THS 1246 sq ft. Wt 47tons 12cwts. LMS class
2P.

No	Date	Rebuilt	LMS no	Withdrawn
130	1913		10185	8/1932
131	1913		10186	11/1932
132	1914		10187	9/1932
133	1914	1924 at Horwich	10188	4/1932

Railmotor 0-4-0T. Built by FR at Barrow.
DW 2ft 10in, Cyls 11 x 14 O/S, Blr 4ft 0in x 3ft 6in, THS 509.1 sq ft, WP
160lbs/sq in, WB 8ft 0in, Wt (including coach) 43½tons. Engine enclosed in
coach body with 8ft 0in carriage bogie. Walschaerts valve gear. Twelve
first and thirty-six third-class passengers. Guards compartment combined
with rear end driving controls. Two four-wheel trailers seating twenty-eight
third class passengers were provided. Both later had a small first class
compartment as well. These had control gear at one end. The loco units
were the only ones built at Barrow works. Used on Coniston branch. They
suffered the usual vibration problems.

Motor nos (engine & coach)	Trailer nos	Date	
1	128 (carriage stock)	1905	Scrapped about 1914
2	193 (carriage stock)	1905	Scrapped earlier after collision with buffer stop.

4-4-2T Built by Kitson & Co   (K). Works nos below
            Vulcan Foundry   (VF). Works nos below
DW 5ft 8in, LW 3ft 2in, TW 3ft 9in, Cyls 17½ x 24, Blr 4ft 3in x 10ft 0in,
THS 1070 sq ft (1915 locos); 1127 sq ft (1916 locos) WP 160lbs/sq in, WB
6ft 0in + 7ft 3½in + 8ft 0in + 7ft 9in, Wt 59tons 9cwts. Boilers standard
with 19 class 0-6-0T below. Primarily intended for use on branch lines.
LMS class 1P.

No	Date		Works no	LMS no	Withdrawn
38	1915	K	5119	11080	12/1930
39	1915	K	5120	11081	12/1932
40	1916	VF	3176	11082	12/1930
41	1916	VF	3177	11083	9/1932
42	1916	K	5172	11084	12/1930
43	1916	K	5173	11085	2/1931

0-6-0T Built by Vulcan Foundry (VF). Works nos below
            Kitson & Co   (K). Works nos below
DW 4ft 7½in, Cyls 17½ x 24, Blr 4ft 3in x 10ft 0in, THS 1070 sq ft,

WP 160lbs/sq in, WB 7ft 4in + 7ft 8in, Wt 48tons 17cwts. 1915/16 locos had
boiler pitched 2in higher at 7ft 8in, water capacity increased by 20 gallons
to 1,070 gallons, coal by 5cwts to 2¼tons. Wt 49½tons. LMS class 2F.

No	Date		Works no	1918 no	LMS no	Withdrawn
19	1910	VF	2523	55	11553	1943
20	1910	VF	2524	56	11554	6/1930
21	1910	VF	2525	57	11555	7/1930
22	1910	VF	2526	58	11556	12/1932
23	1910	VF	2527	59	11557	9/1932
24	1910	VF	2528	60	11558	5/1935
51	1915	K	5121		11559	11/1934
52	1915	K	5122		11560	6/1930
53	1916	VF	3174		11561	11/1936
54	1916	VF	3175		11562	7/1930

O-6-2T Built by Sharp Stewart & Co. Works nos 4364-6.
DW 4ft 8in, TW 3ft 8½in, Cyls 18 x 26, Blr 4ft 4in x 10ft 6in, THS 1134 sq ft,
WP 140lbs/sq in, WB 7ft 5in + 7ft 0in + 6ft 3in, Wt 54tons 11cwts. LMS class
3F.

No	Date	LMS no	Withdrawn
112	1898	11622	12/1927
113	1898	11623	3/1928
114	1898	11524	4/1928

O-6-2T Built by Nasmyth Wilson & Co (NW). Works nos below.
        North British Locomotive Co (NBL). Works nos below.
DW 5ft 1in, TW 3ft 8½in, Cyls 18 x 26, WB 7ft 9in + 8ft 6in + 7ft 9in,
WP 160lbs/sq in, Wt 55tons 3cwts. Other domensions as 112 class. 190T locos
had shorter side tanks and longer bunkers (coal capacity increased by 10cwts
to 2tons). Wt 56tons 17cwts. LMS class 3F.

No	Date		Works no	LMS no	Withdrawn
98	1904	NW	689	11625	10/1935
99	1904	NW	690	11626	2/1930
100	1904	NW	691	11627	4/1936
101	1904	NW	692	11628	1945
102	1904	NW	693	11629	10/1931
103	1904	NBL	16113	11630	5/1934
104	1904	NBL	16114	11631	8/1930
105	1904	NBL	16115	11632	5/1933
106	1904	NBL	16116	11633	3/1931
107	1904	NBL	16117	11634	12/1929
96	1907	NBL	17808	11635*	8/1938
97	1907	NBL	17809	11636	1941
108	1907	NBL	17810	11637	8/1935
109	1907	NBL	17811	11638	1/1933
110	1907	NBL	17812	11639	11/1931
111	1907	NBL	17813	11640	7/1933

*11635 was rebuilt in 1927 with L&Y Belpaire boiler. Possibly one other of
class as well.

O-6-2T Built by Kitson & Co. Works nos 4855/6, 5042/3.
DW 4ft 7½in, TW 3ft 8½in, Cyls 18 x 26, Blr 4ft 7in x 9ft 3in, THS 1016 sq ft,
WP 170lbs/sq in, WB 7ft 5in + 7ft 3in + 6ft 10in, Wt 56tons 18cwts. Improved
Cleator tanks. Nos 92/3 had Blr 4ft 7in x 10ft 6in standard with later 1
class O-6-Os. THS 1246 sq ft, Wt 58tons 12cwt.

		LMS	
No	Date	no	Withdrawn
94	1912	11641	11/1934
95	1912	11642	9/1929
92	1914	11643	8/1934
93	1914	11644	8/1932

0-6-0 Built by Nasmyth Wilson & Co. Works nos 552-7.
            Sharp Stewart & Co. Works nos 4563-8.
DW 4ft 8in, Cyls 18 x 26, Blr 4ft 5in x 10ft 6in, THS 1134 sq ft, WP 150lbs/
sq in, WB 7ft 9in + 7ft 9in, Wt 38½tons. Used for express goods and Tebay-
Barrow coke trains. Fitted with automatic vacuum brake and steam heating
apparatus. 2,500 gallon tenders. LMS class 2F.

			LMS	
No	Date	Rebuilt	No	Withdrawn
7	1899		12468	1/1928
8	1899	L&Y Belpair blr fitted by LMS	12469	7/1930
9	1899		12470	12/1932
10	1899		12471	5/1930
11	1899		12472	8/1930
12	1899		12473	10/1929
13	1899		12474	8/1930
14	1899	6/1910 Superheater, later removed	12475	11/1932
15	1899		12476	7/1930
16	1899		12477	4/1930
17	1899		12478	12/1929
18	1899	1/1910 Superheater, removed 1919		
		L&Y Belpair blr fitted by LMS	12479	8/1936

0-6-0 Built by North British Locomotive Co. Works nos 17840-3.
DW 5ft 1in, Cyls 18 x 26, WP 160lbs/sq in, Wt 40tons 8cwt. Other dimensions
as 7 class above. Six more were ordered from Nasmyth Wilson & Co, but sold
to North Staffordshire instead (NW 588-93, NSR 159-64). Intended for mixed
traffic work. Vacuum brake and steam heating apparatus, 2,500 gallon tender.
LMS class 2F.

			LMS	
No	Date	Rebuilt	no	Withdrawn
3	1906	1924 L&Y Belpair boiler (at Horwich) 12480		5/1930
4	1906		12481	7/1930
5	1906	1926 L&Y Belpair boiler	12482	12/1934
6	1906	1924 L&Y Belpair boiler (at Horwich) 12483		5/1930

0-6-0 Built by North British Locomotive Co (NBL). Works nos below.
            Kitson & Co. (K). Works nos below.
DW 4ft 7½in, Cyls 18 x 26, Blr 4ft 7in x 10ft 0in (1913 locos), 4ft 7in x
10ft 6in (remainder), THS 1246 sq ft, WP 170lbs/sq in, WB 7ft 9in + 7ft 9in,
Wt 42tons 13cwts (1913 locos), 44tons 17cwts (remainder). Extended smokebox.
1913 locos had Phoenix superheaters which were removed in 1914. Above wt
is after removal. Vacuum brake and steam heating apparatus 3,300 gallon tenders. LMS class 3F.

			Works		LMS	BR	
No	Date		no		no	no	Withdrawn
1	1913	NBL	20073	L&Y Belpair blr by LMS	12494	52494	4/1956
2	1913	NBL	20074		12495		12/1932
25	1913	NBL	20075		12496		7/1932
26	1913	NBL	20076		12497		8/1935
27	1914	NBL	20665		12498		8/1932
28	1914	NBL	20666	c1927 L&Y Belpair blr	12499	52499	2/1957
19	1918	K	5195		12500		9/1932
20	1918	K	5196	L&Y Belpaire blr later	12501	52501	6/1957
21	1918	K	5197		12502		5/1930

22	1918	K	5198		12503		12/1930
23	1918	NBL	21993		12504		11/1932
24	1918	NBL	21994		12505		4/1930
29	1918	NBL	21995		12506		11/1930
30	1918	NBL	21996		12507		6/1935
31	1920	NBL	22572		12508	52508	9/1950
32	1920	NBL	22573	L&Y Belpaire blr later	12509	52509	12/1956
33	1920	NBL	22574	L&Y Belpaire blr later	12510	52510	8/1957
34	1920	NBL	22575		12511		11/1932
35	1920	NBL	22576		12512		12/1932

Rutherford Locomotives 1920-1

4-6-4T Built by Kitson & Co. Works nos 5292-6.
DW 5ft 8in, LW & TW 3ft 2in, Cyls 19½ x 26, Blr 5ft 0in x 15ft 0in, THS
2003 sq ft, WP 170lbs/sq in, WB 7ft 0in + 6ft 9in + 6ft 7½in + 6ft 7½in +
6ft 9in + 7ft 0in, Wt 92tons 15cwts. Built to the limits of the loading
gauge with boiler pitched at 8ft 9in and height to top of chimney of 13ft
6in. Original plans for design possibly carried out by Pettigrew but much
of the design is credited to Barrow Chief Draughtsman, a man named Sharples.
They were the only inside cylinder Baltic tanks in the UK and the only
non superheated ones. Belpair fireboxes, running plate raised from front of
smokebox, additional well tanks under bunker. Nicknamed 'Jumbos', they were
forbidden to work north of Barrow. LMS class 3P.

No	Date	LMS no	Withdrawn
115	1920	11100	5/1935
116	1920	11101	7/1935
117	1920	11102	11/1934
118	1920	11103	1940
119	1921	11104	5/1935

1	1844	0-4-0 1 class
-2	1870	2-4-0 1 class
	1913	0-6-0 1 class
3	1846	0-4-0 3 class
-4	1899	2-4-0 ex 11/12
	1906	0-6-0 3 class
5	1852	2-2-2WT 5 class
-6	1873	2-4-0 1 class
	1906	0-6-0 3 class
7	1854/5	0-4-0 7 class
-10	1899	0-6-0 7 class
11	1857	2-2-2WT 11 class
-12	1873	2-4-0 1 class
	1899	0-6-0 7 class
13	1858	0-4-0 7 class
-14	1899	0-6-0 7 class
15	1861	0-4-0 7 class
-16	1899	0-6-0 7 class
17	1863	0-4-0 17 class
-18	1870	0-6-0 29 class
	1899	0-6-0 7 class
19	1863	0-4-0 17 class
-20	1870	0-6-0 29 class
	1910	0-6-OT 19 class
	1918	0-6-0 1 class
21	1864	2-2-2WT 21 class
-22	1896	4-4-0 21 class
	1910	0-6-OT 19 class
	1918	0-6-0 1 class
23	1864	0-4-OST 23 class
-24	1899	0-6-0 ex 17/18
	1910	0-6-OT 19 class
	1918	0-6-0 1 class
25	1865	0-4-0 17 class
	1873	0-6-0 29 class
	1910	0-6-0 ex 20
	1913	0-6-0 1 class
26	1865	0-4-0 17 class
	1873	0-6-0 29 class
	1913	0-6-0 1 class
27	1866	0-4-0 17 class
-28	1914	0-6-0 1 class
29	1866	0-6-0 29 class
-30	1918	0-6-0 1 class
31	1866	0-6-0 29 class
	1920	0-6-0 1 class
32	1866	0-6-0 29 class
-33	1896	Blank
	1910	4-4-0 ex 21/22
	1920	0-6-0 1 class
34	1866	2-2-2WT 21 class
-35	1896	4-4-0 21 class
	1920	0-6-0 1 class
36	1866	2-2-2WT 21 class
-37	1896	4-4-0 21 class
38	1866	0-6-0 29 class
-39	1915	4-4-2T 38 class
40	1867	0-6-0 29 class
-41	1916	4-4-2T 38 class

42	1866	ex W&F Jct
	1910	0-6-0 ex 23
	1916	4-4-2T 38 class
43	1866	ex W&F Jct
	1871	0-6-0 29 class
	1916	4-4-2T 38 class
44	1866	ex W&F Jct
-45	1882	2-4-0 1 class
	1920	4-4-0 ex 32/33
46	1866	ex W&F Jct
	1872	2-4-0 1 class
	1920	4-4-0 ex 34
47	1866	ex W&F Jct
	1872	2-4-0/2-4-2T 1 class
	1920	4-4-0 ex 35
48	1866	ex W&F Jct
	1872	2-4-0/2-4-2T 1 class
	1920	0-6-0 ex 31
49	1866	ex W&F Jct
-50	1884	0-6-0 29 class
51	1867	0-6-OT 51 class
-52	1915	0-6-OT 19 class
53	1871	0-6-0 29 class
-54	1916	0-6-OT 19 class
55	1871	0-6-0 29 class
-56	1918	0-6-OT ex 19/20
57	1870	2-4-0 1 class
-58	1918	0-6-OT ex 21/22
59	1871	0-6-0 29 class
	1913	0-6-0 ex 26
	1918	0-6-OT ex 23
60	1871	0-6-0 29 class
	1918	0-6-OT ex 24
61	1871	0-6-0 29 class
-62	1917	Blank
	1918	0-6-0 ex 29/30
63	1871	0-6-0 29 class
	1918	0-6-0 ex 59
64	1871	0-6-0 29 class
	1918	0-6-0 ex 60
	1922	Blank
65	1871	0-6-0 29 class
66	1871	0-6-0 29 class
-67	1916	0-6-0 ex 42/43
68	1872	0-6-OT 51 class
-69		
70	1872	2-4-0/2-4-2T 1 class
-74	1920	0-6-0 ex 115-9
75	1872	2-4-0 1 class
	1914	0-6-0 ex 92
76	1873	0-6-0 29 class
77	1873	0-6-0 29 class
	1914	0-6-0 ex 93
78	1873	0-6-0 29 class
	1916	0-6-0 ex 54
79	1873	0-6-0 29 class
80	1873	0-6-0 29 class
	1916	0-6-0 ex 40
81	1873	0-6-0 29 class
	1922	Blank

82	1873	0-6-0T 51 class
-83		
84	1873	0-6-0 29 class
	1915	0-6-0T ex 52
	1919	Blank
85	1873	0-6-0 29 class
-87		
88	1874	0-6-0 29 class
-90		
91	1875	0-6-0 29 class
	1919	Blank
92	1874	0-6-0 29 class
-93	1914	0-6-2T 94 class
94	1874	0-4-0ST 23 class
-95	1912	0-6-2T 94 class
96	1874	0-4-0ST 23 class
-97	1907	0-6-2T 98 class
98	1878	ex WC&E
	1896	Blank
	1898	0-4-0ST ex 23
	1904	0-6-2T 98 class
99	1878	ex WC&E
	1887	Blank
	1898	0-4-0ST ex 24
	1904	0-6-2T 98 class
100	1878	ex WC&E
	1904	0-6-2T 98 class
101	1878	ex WC&E
	1896	Blank
	1904	0-6-2T 98 class
102	1878	ex WC&E
	1901	Blank
	1904	0-6-2T 98 class
103	1878	ex WC&E
	1888	Blank
	1904	0-6-2T 98 class
104	1878	ex WC&E
	1901	Blank
	1904	0-6-2T 98 class
105	1878	ex WC&E
-107	1904	0-6-2T 98 class
108	1878	ex WC&E
	1898	0-6-0ST ex 112
	1907	0-6-2T 98 class
109	1878	ex WC&E
	1899	Blank
	1907	0-6-2T 98 class
110	1878	ex WC&E
-111	1907	0-6-2T 98 class
112	1878	ex WC&E
-113	1898	0-6-2T 112 class
114	1881	0-6-0 29 class
	1898	0-6-2T 112 class
115	1881	0-6-0 29 class
	1893	Blank
	1898	0-6-0 ex 114
	1920	4-6-4T 115 class
116	1881	0-6-0 29 class
-118	1920	4-6-4T 115 class
119	1881	0-6-0 29 class
	1921	4-6-4T 115 class

120	1884	0-6-0 29 class
-121	1888	Blank
	1890	4-4-0 120 class
122	1890	4-4-0 120 class
-123		
124	1900	4-4-0 21 class
-125		
126	1901	4-4-0 126 class
-129		
130	1913	4-4-0 130 class
-131		
132	1914	4-4-0 130 class
-133		

MARYPORT AND CARLISLE

INTRODUCTION

Incorporated 1837. Opened Maryport to Arkleby Pits 15 July 1840, to Aspatria 12 April 1841, Carlisle Crown St to Wigton 3 May 1843, throughout Carlisle Crown St (London Road from 3/1849) to Maryport 10 February 1845. Aspatria to Mealsgate 2 April 1866, Aikbank Jct to Blaithwaite (1¾ miles) 1 October 1877, Blaithwaite to Mealsgate 1 October 1877 (possible completed earlier but relaid and officially opened as above). Derwent branch Bullgill to Brigham (connection with Cockermouth and Workington Railway) 1 June 1867 (completed 15 February 1867). Connection at Maryport with Whitehaven Junction Railway and at Carlisle with North Eastern Railway at Rome St Jct and Bog Jct and with Citadel Station Joint Committee lines at M&C Joint Line Jct from 1 June 1851.

The M&C was a highly profitable railway and apart from a brief period from 1 October 1848 until 1 January 1850, when it was leased by George Hudson, was never involved in any amalgamations and retained its independence until 1923 when the LMS was formed.
Hugh Smellie was Locomotive, Carriage and Wagon Superintendent from 1870 to 1878 when he left to take up his appointment with the Glasgow and South Western. His predecessor George Tosh had started building locomotives at Maryport in 1859 and introduced coal firing and fitted the locos with steel tyres, the first steel boiler being fitted in 1862.
Loco building by the company was continued by Robert Campbell (1878-93), William Robertson (1893-8). William Coulthard (1898-1904) only ordered one loco to be built at Maryport in 1900, after which the practice was discontinued.
J B Adamson was Loco Superintendent during 1904-23.
Most of the locos built by Tosh had domeless boilers, but those of Smellie's period had domes and Stirling type rounded cabs. Domeless boilers were again introduced by Campbell both for new locos and for rebuilds.
There were never more than three locomotives exactly alike.
   Brake: automatic vacuum
   Drivers position on footplate: right-hand side
   Colours: engines - green
            carriages - cream with green bodies
            wagons - lead colour
   Route mileage: 42 miles 63 chains
   The LNWR had running powers over the railway.

Maryport and Carlisle Locomotives

2-2-2 Built by Tulk & Ley, Whitehaven. Works no 1.
  DW 5ft 0in, Cyls 12 x 18

No	Name	Date	
1	*Ellen*	1840	Laid up 1/1848 after boiler explosion
			Sold for scrap 1850

0-6-0 Built by Tulk & Ley, Whitehaven. Works no 2.
  DW 4ft 6in, Cyls 14 x 18

No	Name	Date	
2	*Brayton*	1840	Rebuilt 1854 as 0-4-2. **R**eplaced 1869

0-6-0 Built by R&W Hawthorn & Co
  DW 4ft 6in, Cyls 14 x 18

No	Name	Date	
3	*Ballantyne*	1842	Rebuilt 1858. Replaced 1873.
	Dykes		
5	*Sir Wilfrid*	1843	Replaced 1857

2-2-2 Built by Tulk & Ley, Whitehaven. Works no 3.
  DW 5ft 6in, Cyls 13 x 18

No	Name	Date	
4	*Harrison*	1843	Replaced 1864

0-4-2 Built by R&W Hawthorn
  DW 5ft 0in, Cyls 14 x 21

No	Name	Date	
6	*Senhouse*	1845	Rebuilt 1853. Replaced 1860.

0-4-2 Built by Tulk & Ley, Whitehaven. Works nos below.
  DW 4ft 9in, Cyls 14 x 21

No	Name	Date	Works no	Rebuilt	Replaced
7	*Lowca*	1845	4	1855	1865
8	*Harris*	1845	9	1852	1862
9	*Cocker**	1845	5		1859

*Name not confirmed. Simmons gives building date as 1847.

0-6-0 Built by R&W Hawthorn
  DW 4ft 6in, Cyls 15 x 24

No	Name	Date	
10	*Derwent*	1848	Rebuilt 1854. Replaced 1862

0-6-0 Built by Thomas Richardson & Sons, Hartlepool. Works no 168.
  DW 5ft 0in, Cyls 15 x 22

No	Date	
11	2/1850	Rebuilt 1856. Scrapped 1868.

0-4-2 Built by Tulk & Ley, Whitehaven.
  Dimensions not recorded. Wt 25tons.

No	Date	
1	1852	Replaced 1866

This locomotive is not recorded in the Simmons list and is only vaguely
alluded to by Lowe under the works no 20 without positive identification or
date and he adds the note that it might in fact refer to a rebuild,
presumably that of no 2 above in 1854. E. Craven, however, who carried out
extensive research into early locomotive history came to the conclusion
that this was a replacement for the original no 1 at the above date and that
the Tulk & Ley works no was 19. There is this no positive confirmation of

the existence of this locomotive but it seems highly probable that no 1
was replaced since it is unlikely that the number would otherwise have been
left blank for sixteen years.

4-2-0 Built by Tulk & Ley. Works no 17, 1850.
DW 7ft 0in, Cyls 16 x 20 O/S (Lowe states 18 x 20).
Tulk & Ley held a licence under T.R. Crampton's patent and this was the last
of eight locomotives built to his type by them. Purchased from stock 1854.
No   Date
12   1854 Rebuilt 2-2-2 1860. Scrapped 1870

0-6-0 Built by E.B. Wilson
DW 4ft 9in, Cyls 15 x 22
No   Date
13   1855 Withdrawn 1873. Scrapped 1874.

0-6-0 Built by Sharp Stewart & Co.
DW 5ft 0in, Cyls 15 x 28.
No   Date
14   1855 Rebuilt 1868. To Duplicate list R1 1877
              Scrapped 1879

2-2-2 Built by M&C at Maryport
DW 6ft 0in, Cyls 14 x 22
No   Date
5   1857 Scrapped 1872

0-6-0 Built by Sharp Stewart & Co.
DW 5ft 6in, Cyls 15 x 24. Simmons records this locomotive as an 0-4-2 but
Gordon Lowther points out in correspondence that Sharp Stewart records show
an 0-6-0 being supplied in 1859 to order E354, Works no 1131, although the
M&C running number is not identified.
No   Date
15   1859 Rebuilt 1869. To duplicate list R1 1880.
              Scrapped 1884.

0-4-0 Built by M&C at Maryport
DW not recorded, Cyls 15 x 22
No   Date
9   1859 Rebuilt 1869. Scrapped 1875.

0-4-2 Built by M&C at Maryport
DW 5ft 6in, Cyls 15 x 22
No   Date
6   1860 Withdrawn 1871. Scrapped 1872.

0-4-2 Built by M&C at Maryport
DW 6ft 0in, Cyls 15 x 22
No   Date
8   1862 Scrapped 1876.

0-4-2 Built by M&C at Maryport
DW 5ft 6in, Cyls 15 x 22
No   Date
10   1862 To duplicate list R2 1878.
              Rebuilt 1880. Scrapped 1897

0-4-2ST Built by M&C at Maryport
DW 4ft 9in, Cyls 15 x 22
No   Date
4   1864 Sold 1878

O-4-2ST Built by M&C at Maryport
  DW 4ft 6in, Cyls 14½ x 22

No	Date	
7	1865	Rebuilt 1879. To duplicate list R3 1882.
		Scrapped 1892

O-6-O Built by M&C at Maryport
  DW 4ft 6in, Cyls 16 x 22

No	Date	
16	1865	Rebuilt 1873. Scrapped 1895.

O-4-2T Built by M&C at Maryport
  DW 4ft 9in, Cyls 15 x 22. Stephenson valve gear.

No	Date	
17	1865	Rebuilt 1907 as O-6-OT, DW 4ft 9½in, WP 140lbs/sq in, Wt 35½ tons
	1923	To LMS 11563. Withdrawn 12/1927.

O-6-O Built by M&C at Maryport
  DW 5ft Oin, Cyls 15¾ x 24. Stephenson valve gear.

No	Date	
1	1866	Rebuilt 1888. To duplicate list R4 1900
		Rebuilt 1903. DW 5ft 1½in, Cyls 17 x 24, WP 140lbs/sq in, Wt 33¼tons approx (standard with no 6 as built 1871).
	1923	To LMS 12077. Withdrawn 8/1924

O-4-2T Built by M&C at Maryport
  DW 5ft 2in, Cyls 15 x 22

No	Date	
18	1867	To duplicate list R5 1908. Scrapped 1923.

2-4-O Built by M&C at Maryport
  DW 6ft Oin, Cyls 15 x 22

No	Date	
19	1867	To duplicate list R1 1884. Scrapped 1921.

O-6-O Built by M&C at Maryport
  DW 5ft Oin, Cyls 15¾ x 24.

No	Date	
11	1868	To duplicate list R3 1881. Scrapped 1882.
2	1869	Scrapped 1886

O-6-O Built by M&C at Maryport
  DW 5ft 1in, Cyls 17 x 24. Stephenson valve gear

No	Date	
12	1870	Rebuilt 1883
		Rebuilt 1901. DW 5ft 1½in, WP 140lbs/sq in, Wt 33¼tons approx (standard with no 6 1871).
	1923	To LMS 12078. Withdrawn 3/1925 (LMS no possibly not carried)

O-6-O Built by M&C at Maryport
  DW 5ft 1½in, Cyls 17 x 24. Stephenson valve gear

No	Date	Rebuilt		LMS no	Withdrawn
6	1871	1880	WP 140lbs/sq in		
		1895	Wt 33¼tons as		
		1907	finally rebuilt	12079	5/1928
20	1871	1881			
		1906	as 6 above	12080	9/1929
		1921			

0-6-0 Built by Beyer Peacock & Co
DW 4ft 8½in, Cyls 17 x 24. Stephenson valve gear

No	Date	Rebuilt		LMS no	Withdrawn
21	1871	1903	DW 4ft 9in, WP 140lbs/sq in,		
			Wt 33¼tons approx	12081	7/1924
22	1872	1897	as 21 above		1923
24	1873	1899	as 21 above	(12082)	11/1924

0-4-2 Built by Beyer Peacock & Co. Order no 2804. Works no 1144
DW 4ft 8½in, Cyls 16 x 24

No	Date	
23	1872	Rebuilt 1891. Sold 1923 to Marple & Gillott

0-4-2 Built by M&C at Maryport
DW 5ft 7½in, Cyls 16 x 22

No	Date	
3	1873	Rebuilt 1886, 1904. Scrapped 1923.

2-4-0 Built by M&C at Maryport
DW 6ft 1½in, Cyls 17 x 24. Smellie design with Stephenson valve gear.

No	Date	Rebuilt		LMS no	Withdrawn
13	1873	1887	WP 135lbs/sq in		
		1894	Wt 33tons 2cwts		
		1905	as finally rebuilt	(10005)	3/1925
8	1876	1895	as 13 above	(10006)	10/1924
10	1878	1898, 1910	as 13 above	(10007)	3/1925

0-4-2 Built by M&C at Maryport
DW 5ft 7½in, Cyls 16 x 22

No	Date	
5	1873	Rebuilt 1884, 1903. Scrapped 1921

0-6-0 Built by M&C at Maryport.
DW 5ft 1½in, Cyls 18 x 28. Stephenson valve gear

No	Date	Rebuilt		LMS no	Withdrawn
9	1875	1883	WP 140lbs/sq in		
		1898	Wt 36½tons		
		1922	as finally rebuilt	12484	7/1930
14	1877	1887	as 9 above	12485	9/1924
				(Scrapped 1925)	

0-6-0 Built by Beyer Peacock & Co. Order nos 3661, 7347, 8340. Works nos 1799,
DW 5ft 1½in, Cyls 18 x 26. Stephenson valve gear   3284, 4060.

No	Date	Rebuilt		LMS no	Withdrawn
25	6/1878	1879	WP 140lbs/sq in		
			Wt 39tons approx	12486	12/1930
27	1890	1900	as 25 above	12490	6/1928
28	1899	1922	as 25 above	12491	8/1930

0-6-0 Built by M&C at Maryport
DW 5ft 1½in, Cyls 18 x 26. Stephenson valve gear.
All had the same dimensions but were not all identical.

No	Date	Rebuilt	LMS no	Withdrawn
11	5/1881	1891, 1902 as 25 above	12487	12/1928
7	10/1882	1903, 1921 as 25 above	12488	8/1930
19	1884	1905, 1922 as 25 above	12489	6/1930
1	1900	1919 as 25 above	12492	5/1930

0-6-0 Built by North British Locomotive Co. Works no 18285
DW 5ft 1½in, Cyls 18 x 26, Blr 4ft 5in diam, THS 1208 sq ft, WP 140lbs/sq in,
WB 8ft 0in + 8ft 10in, Wt 39¾tons. Stephenson valve gear. Similar to
G&SW 361 class.

No	Date	
18	1908	Rebuilt 1919 as 25 above
	1923	To LMS 12493. Withdrawn 12/1925
		(LMS no possibly not carried).

O-4-OT Built by Neilson & Co. Works nos 2640, 2737.
DW 3ft 8in, Cyls 14 x 20

		Duplicate		LMS	
No	Date	no	year	no	Withdrawn
15	1880	R3	1892	(11259)	8/1924
26	1881	R2	1897	(11260)	4/1924

O-4-2 Built by M&C at Maryport
DW 5ft 7½in, Cyls 17 x 24. Stephenson valve gear

			LMS	
No	Date	Rebuilt	no	Withdrawn
4	1879	1889, 1904 WP 150lbs/sq in		
		Wt 33½tons	10010	11/1928*
			10012	6/1928
15	1892	1916 as 4 above		
16	1895	1920 Beyer Peacock & Co		
		as 4 above	10013	10/1928

*Boiler off 10010 fitted in 1920 was used in Derby works until 1953

O-4-2 Built by M&C at Maryport
DW 5ft 7½in, Cyls 17 x 26. Stephenson valve gear

No	Date	
2	4/1889	Rebuilt 1903 WP 140lbs/sq in, Wt 32tons.
	1923	To LMS 10011. Withdrawn 11/1928

O-4-4T Built by M&C at Maryport
DW 5ft 1½in, Cyls 16 x 22

No	Date	
26	1897	To LMS (10618). Withdrawn 3/1925

O-6-O Built by Yorkshire Engine Co.
DW 5ft 0in, Cyls 19 x 26, WP 170lbs/sq in, Wt 49tons 12cwts. Stephenson
valve gear.

No	Date	LMS no	Withdrawn
29	1921	12513	12/1933
30	1921	12514	3/1934

1	1840	2-2-2		26	1881	0-4-4T
	1851	Blank		27	1890	0-6-0
	1852	0-4-2		28	1899	0-6-0
	1866	0-6-0		29	1921	0-6-0
	1900	0-6-0		30	1921	0-6-0
2	1840	0-6-0				
	1869	0-6-0				
	1887	Blank				
	1889	0-4-2				
3	1842	0-6-0				
	1873	0-4-2				
4	1843	2-2-2				
	1864	0-4-2ST				
	1879	0-4-2				
5	1843	0-6-0				
	1857	2-2-2				
	1873	0-4-2				
	1922	Blank				
6	1845	0-4-2				
	1860	0-4-2				
	1871	0-6-0				
7	1845	0-4-2				
	1865	0-4-2ST				
	1882	0-6-0				
8	1845	0-4-2				
	1862	0-4-2				
	1876	2-4-0				
9	1845	0-4-2				
	1859	0-4-0				
	1875	0-6-0				
10	1848	0-6-0				
	1862	0-4-2				
	1878	2-4-0				
11	1850	0-6-0				
	1868	0-6-0				
	1881	0-6-0				
12	1854	4-2-0/2-2-2				
	1870	0-6-0				
13	1855	0-6-0				
	1873	2-4-0				
14	1855	0-6-0				
	1877	0-6-0				
15	1859	0-6-0				
	1880	0-4-0T				
	1892	0-4-2				
16	1865	0-6-0				
	1895	0-4-2				
17	1865	0-4-2T/0-6-0T				
18	1867	0-4-2T				
	1908	0-6-0				
19	1867	2-4-0				
	1884	0-6-0				
20	1871	0-6-0				
21	1871	0-6-0				
22	1872	0-6-0				
23	1872	0-4-2				
24	1873	0-6-0				
25	1878	0-6-0				

NORTH STAFFORDSHIRE RAILWAY

INTRODUCTION

The 'Knotty' as it was affectionately known was a small intensely operated network of lines centred on Stoke-on-Trent and serving the closely knit community of the Potteries and surrounding areas with some 216 route miles including the leased and worked lines of the Silverdale and Newcastle, the Talke o'the Hill branch and the Leek and Manifold Valley Light Railway.

The main line was officially considered to be from Willington Junction on the Midland to Crewe and North Staffordshire trains ran between Crewe (LNW) and Derby (Midland) over this line and the branch from Marston Junction to the Midland at Burton-on-Trent.

However the line from the LNW Macclesfield branch to the LNW main line at Colwich provided a shorter route for LNW Manchester to London trains than via Crewe (as it still does for their modern counterparts today) and consequently this line became a north-south main line also. It was customary for the NS Railway who had running powers into Manchester London Road to work the train between Manchester and Stoke and the LNW locomotive to work between Stoke and Euston. Originally hauled by 2-4-0s these heavy trains were later worked by 4-4-2Ts with occasionally a 4-4-0 or 0-6-0 and from 1916 by the Class F 0-6-4Ts. The trains were tightly timed over the 37½ miles to Stoke and banking assistance was usually provided between Macclesfield Hibel Road and Macclesfield Moss. Occasionally the LNW would provide a pilot to Congleton instead. The LNW routed three trains a day via Stoke latterly.

There were also branches from Stone to Norton Bridge on the LNW main line north of Stafford and from Stoke to Market Drayton on the Great Western, and a line from Silverdale to the Crewe line at Alsager through Audley. From the Crewe line there was also a branch to Sandbach on the LNW Manchester to Crewe line. There were numerous branch lines in the Stoke area connecting with many private mineral lines and an intensely operated 'loop line' (always referred to as such) between Kidsgrove and Etruria and serving the pottery towns of Hanley, Burslem and Tunstall.

East of Stoke there was the Biddulph valley line between Congleton and Stoke Junction just south of Stoke station where the Derby line also joins and the company's locomotive works were opposite this junction on the other side of the line.

The Churnet Valley line ran from North Rode on the Macclesfield line through Leek to the Derby line at Uttoxeter. From this line there was a branch connection with the Biddulph Valley line between Milton Junction and Leek Brook and a branch from Leek to Waterhouses to connect with the Leek and Manifold narrow gauge railway. There was also a 3ft 6in gauge railway serving the quarries at Caldon Low.

A further branch loop linked the Biddulph valley line at Botteslaw Junction near Bucknall with the Derby line at Millfield Junction near Normacot on the Derby line.

Ashbourne was served by a branch from Rocester on the Churnet Valley line. This met the LNW line from Buxton in a joint station at Ashbournw and there were also short branches to Cheadle (Staffs) and Trentham Park.

Colwich station was also jointly owned with the LNW, as was the goods station at Macclesfield, but two seperate passenger stations were maintained at Macclesfield: Central for the North Staffordshire and Hibel Road for the LNW. From the former the NS operated the line to Marple Wharf Junction jointly with the MS&L/Great Central and Central station was built (roughly on the site of the present station) by the 'Macclesfield Committee' which controlled this joint line, the LNW having declined to participate in a joint station controlled by all three companies.

Trains ran via Marple to Manchester London Road over the joint line, but the NS did not work into Manchester via this route and the main service was provided by the MS&L/GC, the NS being confined only to working morning and evening peak period short workings to Bollington and, from 1885, a Summer dated service between Macclesfield and Buxton via a connecting spur to the LNW line at Middlewood.

The company was incorporated in 1845 following failure to persuade the Manchester and Birmingham to build their line through the Potteries and leased the Trent and Mersey Canal on 15 Jan 1848, this being vested in the NSR on the following 26 June.

The first section of line to be opened was that from Stoke to Norton Bridge on 3 April 1848 (passenger from 17 April) but the junction with the LNW here was not made until 1850. The line to Uttoxeter was opened on 7 August 1848, Burton 11 September 1848, Crewe and Congleton 9 October 1848, Colwich 1 May 1849, Macclesfield 18 June 1849, Churnet Valley and Marston Junction to Willington Junction 13 July 1849.

This was the system until 1862 and most of the other lines were built between then and 1880. The Middlewood curve was opened in 1885, the Cheadle branch was completed on 1 January 1901, the Waterhouses branch on 1 July 1905 and the Trentham Park branch on 1 April 1910.

In addition to the running powers already mentioned to Manchester and Buxton the NS also had running powers over the LNW to Llandudno, Warrington, Liverpool, Wolverhampton, Birmingham and Rugby, over the GW to Wellington and the Midland and Great Northern routes to Derby and Nottingham. All of these companies enjoyed reciprocal running powers over the NS, the GN running passenger trains over the 12 miles from Eggington to Bromshall to reach their Stafford branch from Derby Friargate. NS goods trains ran as far as Wellingborough on the Midland.

The LNW originally expected that it would be able to take over the railway, but the directors adopted an independent line resenting some of the methods used by the larger company to coerce them and, playing off the LNW against the GW's desire for an independent line to Manchester and Merseyside, they also promoted a traffic regulation bill in 1850 in Parliament to outlaw some of these practices. Although this failed many of its principles were included in the Railway and Canal Traffic Act 1854. Two attempts by the LNW to promote an amalgamation bill had to be withdrawn and a third in 1875 resulted in proposals by the Midland and later the MS&L and GN for a joint take-over bid and opposition from the GW. The LNW withdrew its proposals for the last time and although the MS&L made a further independent approach in 1876 this came to nothing and the Knotty remained an independent railway, ultimately profitable and held in great affection by the local community and all who came into contact with it.

Locomotive Superintendents

Robert N. Angus	1874-5	Died
(Locomotive Foreman from 1847)		
C. Clare	1875-82	Died
Luke Longbottom	1882-1902	Died
John Henry Adams	1902-1915	Died
John Albert Hookham	1915-23	Formation of LMS

Until 1874 the post of locomotive superintendent was combined with that of engineer, the day-to-day running of the locomotives being in the charge of Angus as locomotive foreman. Four men filled the post of engineer and locomotive superintendent prior to the promotion of Angus himself in 1874. They were S.P. Bidder (1846-8), John Curphey Forsyth (1848-64), James Johnson (1865-70) and Thomas Weatherburn Dodds (1870-4). They were all primarily civil engineers and were responsible for the Trent and Mersey Canal as well as the railway and they relied in the early years on manufacturer's supplying suitable locomotives to general specifications.

Bidder was appointed general manager in 1848 in which position he continued to exert considerable influence on the choice of locomotives until he resigned in 1853, when Forsyth reluctantly succeeded him combining the posts of general manager and engineer until he resigned from both in 1864. At this period the company was hard pressed financially and no doubt this was a necessary economy. There is also little doubt that much of the practical work of rebuilding and maintaining the locomotives fell increasingly to Angus, especially after

Forsyth's resignation when a consultant's report criticised the suitability of the locomotives and recommended a widespread rebuilding programme.

In 1868 a significant step was taken when the first locomotive was built at Stoke works, but just how much of the credit for this should go to Johnson and how much to Angus is not known. It is possible, indeed known in some cases, that at first locomotives were only assembled there from parts supplied by manufacturers.

Dodss was in partnership from 1850 with his father Isaac Dodds in a small engineering works at Holmes near Rotheram which had, inter alia, built the rolling stock for the Santander and Alar railway in Spain and Isaac Dodds and another named Owen had taken out a patent for Dodds' wedge motion which dispensed with links and relied for reversing on sliding wedges which altered the position of the eccentric in relation to the appropriate crank.

After the failure of the engineering works in the depression of 1866 Dodds improved the design of the wedge motion and on taking up his appointment on the NS Rly fitted it to many of the locomotives.

Difficulty was encountered however because the wedges frequently jammed, often requiring the strengths of both driver and fireman on a crow-bar to free them. After an accident in 1873 involving some runaway wagons in which a locomotive was unable to avoid the runaways despite adequate warning because the wedge motion jammed, the attention of the board was drawn to the matter and they were so annoyed that Dodds was asked to resign in 1874.

At last Angus was given his just due and promoted to the position of locomotive superintendent but regrettably he died in 1875.

Under Clare a standardisation of the locomotives was started and from this period most locos were built by the company at Stoke works, outside suppliers only being resorted to at times of stress. This was a very creditable achievement for a small railway and a total of 197 locomotives (slightly less if some renewals shown here as such are regarded only as rebuilds) were built up to 1923, well over half the total number of locomotives owned at all periods. The works were closed by the LMS after a few years doing only repair work in July 1927.

Longbottom apprenticed with Fenton, Murray and Jackson in Leeds and following the failure of this firm completed his apprenticeship with E.B. Wilson. He then joined Kitson, Thompson & Hewitson in Leeds and after a period as works manager at Bray & Waddington, Leeds, he was appointed general engineer of the Kendal & Windermere railway becoming locomotive foreman for the Tebay and Preston area of the LNWR on the amalgamation of the K&W in 1860. He was appointed locomotive, carriage & wagon superintendent of the NSR in 12/1882.

During his twenty years of office at Stoke the standardisation policy started by Clare was carried through to completion with interchangeable parts and boilers between classes. It was Longbottom who laid down the locomotive policies of the company for the rest of its independent existence, there being a significant shift of emphasis in favour of tank engines as being more suitable for a railway with many short hauls.

Adams was the third son of Williams Adams, locomotive superintendent of the North London, GE and LSW railways. He apprenticed under his father at Stratford GE and transferred to Nine Elms when his father was appointed to the LSW. After completing his training he worked as a fireman and later a driver on the LSW for two years before going to Tannett, Walker & Co to gain experience with hydraulic engineering.

In 7/1887 he was appointed locomotive, carriage and wagon superintendent of the Donna Teresa Christina Railway in Brazil and in 1/1889 became assistant works manager of the SE&C at Ashford.

On joining the NS Rly he began the construction of bogie passenger carriages at Stoke in addition to locomotives after reorganising and re-equipping the works. He also introduced several new types of locomotives such as the 4-4-O (class G), O-4-4T (Class M), 4-4-2T (Class K) and O-6-4T (Class C). He modernised some of the Longbottom classes and in common with other contemporary companies introduced Belpaire fireboxes and superheating.

Hookham apprenticed under William Kirtley on the London, Chatham and Dover Railway remaining with the company as a draughtsman until 1887 when he worked in the drawing office of the Pulsometer Engineering Co, Nine Elms, Lambeth and later in the Glengall Ironworks, Millwall, on marine engines, dredgers and barges returning to the LC&D drawing office in 1891. In 1899, when the Joint Managing Committee with the SE was formed, he was transferred to Ashford under Adams. In 6/1900 he also went to the DTC Railway in Brazil as locomotive, carriage and wagon superintendent, possibly on Adams's recommendation and when Adams joined the NS he was appointed works manager at Stoke, succeeding Adams when he died.

His four-cylinder 0-6-0T was designed for working local trains on steeply graded lines. It had cranks set at 90° and 135° giving even torque and an eight-beat exhaust, but the LMS showed little interest in the experiment and the locomotive had steaming difficulties, being rebuilt as an 0-6-0 goods engine.

The North Staffordshire was a vacuum-braked railway and the driver's position was on the right (in contrast to the neighbouring LNW on the left). Its later carriages were comfortable with leather seating and it switched straight from oil lighting to electric lighting, never using the gas lighting that proved so disastrous in so many accidents.

Locomotive livery was originally gamboge green, but was changed by Longbottom to Victoria brown - a rich red-brown. He also introduced the famous Staffordshire Knot emblem on tender and tank sides from which the railway's nickname derived.

Under Adams the colour was changed to madder lake lined in yellow and the coat of arms replaced the Knot emblem.

Carriages were formerly crimson and white but in later days were crimson lake all over. Some issues of the *Railway Year Book* state that the upper panels of the early coaches were green but give no further details.

NORTH STAFFORDSHIRE RAILWAY ASSOCIATED COMPANY

Leek and Manifold Valley Light Railway (2ft 6in gauge)

Worked by NSR
Incorporated and authorised 6 March 1899 as the Leek, Caldon Low and Hartington
Light Railway by an order under the Light Railway Act 1896. Opened 27 June 1904,
Waterhouses (connection NSR) - Hulme End. Line closed 12 March 1934.

2 locomotives as under
  2-6-4T Built by Kitson & Co Ltd. Works nos 4258, 4257*.
    DW 3ft 6in, LW & TW 1ft 1in, Cyls 11½ x 16 O/S, Blr 3ft 0in diam, THS 405 sq
    ft, WP 150lbs/sq in, Total WB 20ft 6in, Wt 26tons 16cwts. Named after the
    engineer and resident engineer. The engineer E R Calthrop had been a
    locomotive inspector on the Great Indian Peninsular Railway from 1882 and
    from 1892 had been a consultant, building in 1895, the Barsi Light Railway, a
    2ft 6in gauge line in Maharashtra, India. The locos were scaled down versions
    of 4-8-4Ts built by Kitsons for the Barsi line. They had Walschaerts valve
    gear, outside frames, two injectors, a pump, vacuum brake and left-hand
    driving position. The wheel balance weights were carried outside the wheels
    on the axles rather than on the wheels. Ramsbottom safety valves were
    replaced by 'pop' safety valves. Bunker sides were later raised to increase
    coal capacity. The locos (and also the carriages) had a distinctly oriental
    appearance with large double-roof cabs and brass headlamps. Livery was
    originally light chocolate brown with double white lining, later changed to
    NSR madder lake with single cream line. Standard LMS crimson lake edged in
    black and yellow was at first applied, but from the late 1920s unlined black
    was applied. No LMS numbers were allotted.

    *Works nos are frequently transposed but the locos were numbered on the
    railway in reverse order to the Kitson nos.

No	Name	Date	
1	E R Calthrop	1904	Withdrawn 12/1936. Used in demolition train from 2/1937 and purchased by contractor, George Cohen, Sons & Co 5/1937. Scrapped at Waterhouses 10/1937.
2	J B Earle	1904	Withdrawn at Crewe 2/1935. Sold to Cohen's for scrap 5/1937 and broken up at Stanningley Leeds. One number plate survived and was recovered in 1954 and is now in the Narrow gauge Museum at Tywyn, Gwynedd.

North Staffordshire Railway

1848-62 Locomotives ordered by engineers S P Bidder and J C Forsyth.

2-2-2 Built by Sharp Brothers.   Works nos 484, 486, 549-51, 552, (Christianen/
                Miller give 554).
DW 5ft 6in, Cyls 15 x 20, Blr 3ft 6in diam, THS 748.2 sq ft.   Sharp standard
design (A W G Cope *Rly Mag* Volume 61 (1927) gives cylinders 15 x 22).

| | | | 1870 | | |
No	Name	Date	no	Rebuilt	Replaced
1	*Dragon**	1848	1	1866 2-2-2ST	1891
2		1848	26	c1867 2-4-0	1882
23		1848	27	c1867 2-4-0	1883
24		1848			
Renumbered 81		1868	28	c1867 2-4-0	1882
27		1848	2	1866 2-2-2ST	1890
29		1848	29	c1867 2-4-0	1883

*Hauled first train.   Name removed later.

2-2-2 Built by Kitson, Thompson & Hewitson.   Works nos 238-41.
DW 6ft 1in, LW & TW 4ft 0in, Cyls 15 x 22, Blr 3ft 6¾in diam, THS 806 sq ft.
Outside frames, centre domes, raised fireboxes, Salter safety valves bell
capped chimneys.   Original weather boards replaced by shallow rounded cabs,
some with side drop light.

No	Date	1870 no	Replaced
54	1851	22	1882
55	1851	23	1886
56	1851	24	1886
57	1851	25	1882

2-2-2WT See note below.   Purchased second hand 1860.
DW 4ft 6in, Cyls 14 x 18, THS 872 sq ft.   Tall chimney.   Cope, *Rly Mag* Vol 61
(1927) identified this locomotive as R Stephenson & Co no 754 built 1850 and
delivered 2/1850 to Shrewsbury and Birmingham no 3 as a 2-2-2 tender engine,
becoming GW 37 in 4/1852, but this is not confirmed.   It is stated to have
been rebuilt 2-2-2WT 1859 with front and rear weatherboards.

No	Date	1870 no	
65	1860	3	Scrapped 1883

2-4-0 Built by Jones & Potts
DW not known, Cyls 15 x 22 O/S.   Long boiler type.

| | | 1870 | |
No	Date	no	
3	1848	38	Replaced 1874
4	1848	39	Replaced 1874
12	1848		Renewed 1866 by Hudswell & Clarke
14	1848		Renewed 1865 by Hudswell & Clarke
22	1848	34	Rebuilt c1866*. Replaced 1884
25	1848		Renewed 1866 by Hudswell & Clarke
38	1848	40	Rebuilt c1872. Replaced 1881
39	1848		Renewed 1865 by Hudswell & Clarke
40	1848	36	Rebuilt 1867* at Stoke. Replaced 1883
42	1848	37	Rebuilt 1867* at Stoke. Replaced 1883

*normal boiler

2-4-0 Built by R Stephenson & Co.   Works no 671-7.
DW 5ft 6in, LW 3ft 6in, Cyls 15 x 22 O/S.   Long boiler type of similar diam to
Kitson singles.   Four rebuilt with normal boilers.

No	Date	1870 no	Rebuilt	Replaced
9	1848	31	1867	1879
10	1848	32	1867	1884
11	1848	41		1874
13	1848			1868
19	1848	33	1867	1883
20	1848	42		1874
28	1848	35	c1866	1881

2-4-0 Built by Hick Hargreaves & Co
DW 5ft 6in, Cyls 14 x 21 O/S. Long boiler type. Dome/safety valves over high raised fireboxes.

No	Date	1870 no	
5	1848		Possibly later had 15 x 22 cyls. Replaced 1868
6	1848	30	Rebuilt c1866 normal boiler. Replaced 1881
7	1848	4	Rebuilt 1851 2-2-2T. Replaced 1881
8	1848	5	Rebuilt 1851 2-2-2T. Replaced 1881

2-4-0 Built by Kitson, Thompson & Hewitson. Works nos 176-81.
DW 5ft 6in, LW 3ft 6in, Cyls 15 x 22, Blr 3ft 8in x 13ft 10in, THS 914 sq ft. Dome close behind smokebox, long boiler type, tall chimney. No cab or weatherboard as built. All rebuilt 2-4-OST with front and rear weatherboards.

No	Date	1870 no	Rebuilt 2-4-OST	Replaced
30	1848	6	c1865	1878
31	1848	7	c1865	1874
32	1848	8	c1865	1878
45	1849	9	c1865	1874
46	1849	10	c1865	1874
47	1849	11	c1865	1874

2-4-0 Built by Kitson, Thompson & Hewitson. Works nos 226-31.
DW 6ft 1in, LW 4ft 0in, Cyls 15 x 22, Blr 3ft 6½in x 10ft 6in, THS 806 sq ft. Oval boilers with centre dome. Outside leading bearings. No cab or weatherboard until rebuilt as singles. (TW 4ft 0in).

No	Date	1870 no	Rebuilt 2-2-2	Replaced
48	1850	16	1851	1884
49	1850	17	1851	1882
50	1850	18	1851	1882
51	1850	19	1851	1872
52	1850	20	1851	1883
53	1850	21	1851	1882

0-6-0 Built by Vulcan Foundry. Works nos 279-88, 383-6.
DW 4ft 9in, Cyls 16 x 24, THS 1061.796 sq ft, Total WB 11ft 6in. Double frames, long boiler type.

No	Date	1870 no	Rebuilt	Replaced
15	1848	64		1874
16	1848	65		1874
17	1848	66		1877
18	1848	67		1875
21	1848	68		1875
26	1848	69		1873
37	1848	70		1873
41	1848	71		1874
43	1848	72		1876

44	1848	73	1875		1888
60	1855	60	1870	O-6-OST	1884
61	1855	61	1870	O-6-OST	1887
62	1855	62	1870	O-6-OST	1885
63	1855	63	1870	O-6-OST	1884

O-6-O Built by R Stephenson & Co. Works nos 406, 422-4 in 1844. Purchased
     1848 from Grinell & Peto, contractors.
DW 4ft 9in, Cyls 15 x 24

No	Date	Replaced*	
33	1848	1866	*Christiansen/Miller record that one or two
34	1848	1866	of these locos were sold to Moss of
35	1848	1866	Stafford and that one was part exchanged
36	1848	1866	with another from the LNW who broke it up
			under 'cut up' no 1858.

O-6-O Built by R Stephenson & Co. Works nos 678-83.
DW 4ft 9in, Cyls 16 x 24. Long boiler.

No	Date	
58	1849	Nos 58-63 were sold in 1850 to
59	1849	Wright of Birmingham. Nos 58-62 were
60	1849	resold by him to the Midland Railway
61	1849	in 1/1851. For subsequent history see
62	1850	Vol 3A pps 79-80
63	1850	No 63 resold 1850 to Rhenish Railway

O-6-O Built by Kitson, Thompson & Hewitson. Works nos 316/7
DW 5ft Oin, Cyls 16 x 24, Blr 4ft Oin in diam, THS 994 sq ft. Double frames.
Tall copper topped chimney, tall brass domes and weatherboard. Later
standardised as class F - double framed O-6-O. Blr 4ft 2in x 10ft 4½in.

No	Date	1870 no	Replaced
58	1853	102	1897
59	1853	103	1898

O-6-O Built by R Stephenson & Co. Works nos 1330/1.
DW 5ft Oin, Cyls 16 x 24, THS 1010 sq ft. Double frames similar to 58 class
above. Later standardised Class F.

No	Date	1870 no	Replaced
64	1860	100	1896
66	1860	101	1897

O-6-OST Built by R Stephenson & Co. Works nos 1414/5.
DW 4ft Oin, Cyls 16 x 22, THS 1083, Wt 34tons. Double frames, long boilers
flat-sided saddle tanks.

No	Date	1970 no	
67	1862	56	Both sold 3/1888 to Kidsgrove Steel
68	1862	57	and Iron Co*

*Named Ada and Marion. One resold 1910 to Chatterley-Whitfield Collieries
 and renamed Sampson

2-2-2T Ballast engine
    Christiansen/Miller refer to the purchase in 1848 of a 2-2-2T from Price &
    Leishman but there are no known details of its origin or dimensions. It
    was not entered into stock, being what would in later days be referred to as
    a departmental locomotive, and was referred to as the 'ballast engine'.

1865-77 Locomotives in this period were ordered by engineers James Johnson until 1870 and by Thomas Weatherburn Dodds until 1874, when he was asked to resign following board disatisfaction with his experiments with his design of wedge motion. Some existing locomotives were renewed following a consultant's report and the details of these and locomotives built by the company at Stoke from 1868 came increasingly under the influence of Angus as locomotive foreman until his appointment as locomotive superintendent in 1874 gave him sole responsibility.

2-4-0 Built by Hudswell & Clarke. Works nos 57, 58 or 59, 60/1.
Dimensions not known. Renewals of Jones & potts locos of 1848 (3 class above). O/S cylinders retained.

		1870	
No	Date	no	Replaced
39	1865	**43**	1883
14	1865	**44**	1883
25	1866	**45**	1884
12	1866	**46**	1884

2-4-0 Built by NSR at Stoke
DW 6ft 6in, Cyls 16½ x 22, Blr 4ft 2½in diam, WP 140lbs/sq in, THS 804 sq ft. Originally fitted with wedge motion replaced by Stephenson valve gear. Neat, large rectangular cab with drop light similar to carriage doors. Original tender had outside springs.

No	Date	Rebuilt	
19	1872	1886	WP 150lbs, THS 914 sq ft
		1901	17 x 24 cyls. Renewed 1906

2-4-0 Built by NSR at Stoke
                Dubs & Co. Works nos 858-60.
DW 6ft 1½in, LW 4ft 0in, Cyls 16½ x 22, Blr 4ft 2½in diam, THS 821.5 sq ft, Wt 36½tons. Stephenson valve gear. Later standardised as Class C.

The following, built at Stoke had only bent over weatherboards originally, cabs being fitted later.

No	Date	Rebuilt	
38	1874	4/1893	17 x 24 cyls. Renewed 1897
39	1874	12/1892	17 x 24 cyls. Renewed 1897

The following were built by Dubs & Co with cabs.

No	Date	Rebuilt		Withdrawn
13	1875	17 x 24 cyls, later 18 x 24 dates not recorded		1912*
14	1875	1888, 9/1903 17 x 24 cyls		1919**
15	1875	2/1894 17 x 24 cyls		Renewed 1905

  *No 13 to duplicate list 13A in 1912
**No 14 to duplicate list 14A in 1912 and in accident Uttoxeter

2-4-0 Built by NSR at Stoke
DW 5ft 6in, LW 3ft 7in, Cyls 16 x 22 O/S, WB 6ft 6in + 7ft 9in. Angus design of goods locomotive with cabs. Standard Longbottom cabs substituted and new boilers. WP 150lbs/sq in, THS 914 sq ft later. Officially regarded as renewals.

No	Date	
7	1874	To duplicate list 7A 1895. Withdrawn 1897
10	1874	Replaced 1894
71	1874	Replaced 1894

2-4-OT Built by NSR at Stoke
                Sharp Stewart & Co. Works nos 2445-7.
DW 5ft 6in, Cyls 16 x 24. All had Sharp characteristics, SS&Co supplying

the parts for the Stoke built locos, (Nos 9 & 11). Front and rear weatherboards bent over to form round roof. Standard cabs and boilers 1894 (Blr
4ft 0in x 10ft 4¼in, Cyls 16½ x 24). The two Stoke built locos were
replaced in 1907 by class M O-4-4Ts, the others being rebuilt 2-4-2T in
1899 and likewise replaced in 1908.

		Rebuilt 2-4-2T*	
No	Date		Replaced
9	1874		1907
11	1874		1907
12	1874	1899	1908
41	1874	1899	1908
42	1874	1899	1908

*LW 3ft 9in, TW 4ft 0in, WB 6ft 6in + 7ft 9in + 6ft 0in.

O-6-O Built by Hudswell & Clarke. Works nos 35/6, 39/40, 43/4.
                    Neilson & Co. Works nos 1145-50.
DW 5ft 0in, Cyls 16 x 24. Double frames. Similar to MS&L and GN locos at
this period. Standardised 1888-97 as **class F**, blr 4ft 2in x 10ft 4¼in,
WP 140lbs/sq in, WB 8ft 0in + 7ft 6in, Cyls 17 x 24.

The following were built by Hudswell & Clarke.

No	Date	1870 no	
69	1864	78	Also rebuilt 1880. Replaced 1899
70	1864	79	Also rebuilt 1879. Replaced 1898
71	1865	80	Also rebuilt 1879. Replaced 1899
72	1865	81	Also rebuilt 1877. Replaced 1899
73	1865	82	Replaced 1907
74	1865	83	Replaced 1907

The following were built by Neilson & Co, and had long fireboxes originally.

No	Date	1870 no	Replaced
75	1865	84	1909
76	1865	85	1909
77	1865	86	1910
78	1865	87	1910
79	1865	88	1909
80	1865	89	1913

O-6-O Built by Hudswell & Clarke. Works nos 69/70
DW 5ft 0in, Cyls 16½ x 24. Double frames, long firebox. Renewals of
earlier Stephenson locos (33 class). Later standardised as class F.

		1870 no	
No	Date		Replaced
33	1866	76	1902
35	1866	77	1902

O-6-O Built by Worcester Engine Co. Works nos 7-16.
DW 5ft 0in, 16½ x 24 (later increased to 17 x 24). Double frames. Later
standardised as Class F.

		1870		Duplicate		With-
No	Date	no	Rebuilt	no	year	drawn
90	1867	90	7/1890, 10/1903			1910
91	1867	91	6/1892, 3/1904			1911
92	1867	92	5/1893, 10/1901			1911
93	1867	93	5/1890			1909
94	1867	94	10/1891	94A	1909	1911
95	1867	95	1882, 4/1898	95A	1909	1910
96	1867	96	10/1890			1913
97	1867	97	4/1891, 1907			1913
98	1867	98	6/1891	98A	1908	1910
99	1867	99	9/1892	99A	1908	1910

0-6-0 Built by NSR at Stoke
DW 5ft 0in, Cyls 17 x 24.   Inside frames.   Later standardised as **class E**
(below).   LMS class 1F.

No	Date	Rebuilt	Duplicate no	year	LMS numbers 1923*	1927	With-drawn
74	1871	1/1895, 1911	74A	1919	2320	8650	6/1934
75	1871	1885, 1901, 1912	75A	1919	2321		11/1926

0-6-0 Built by Vulcan Foundry.   Works nos below.
         Sharp Stewart & Co.   Works nos below
         Beyer Peacock & Co.   Works nos below
         NSR at Stoke
DW 5ft 0in, Cyls 16½ x 24, THS 921 sq ft (except Beyer Peacock), WP 140lbs/
sq in (unless stated 150lbs/sq in).   All except the Sharp Stewart locos
were standardised as **class E**, blr 4ft 2in x 10ft 4½in.   WB 7ft 3in + 7ft 9in,
Wt 33tons 7cwts.   LMS class 1F.

The following were built by Vulcan Foundry.   Works nos 642-51.

No	Date	Rebuilt	LMS numbers 1923*	1927	Withdrawn
104	1872	9/1887, 2/1903	2322	8651	12/1932
105	1872	12/1887, 9/1902	2323		11/1926
106	1872	3/1888, 8/1903	2324	8652	10/1932
107	1872	2/1887, 11/1903	2325		6/1927
108**	1872	8/1887, 5/1903	2326	8653	12/1930
109**	1872	6/1887, 1906	(2327)	8654***	12/1930
110**	1872	1885, 4/1895, 11/1909	2328	8655	12/1929
111**	1872	1909, 12/1914	2329	8656***	3/1930
112	1872	1902, 1914	2330	8657	12/1928
113**	1872	2/1896, 1/1909, 1913	2331	8658	12/1928

The following were built by Sharp Stewart & Co.   Works nos 2342/6/78/9/2424-7.
They were not rebuilt to class E and became a seperate class 69, blr 3ft 11in
diam, THS 870 sq ft, WB 6ft 9in + 8ft 0in.   Nos 69/70 were originally intended
for the Furness Railway and were built with cylinders 16 x 24.   Standard
blrs on rebuilding.

No	Date	Rebuilt	Duplicate no	year	LMS no	With-drawn
69	1873	16½in cyls date not known	69A	1913		1922
70	1873	1903 16½in cyls	70A	1914	2332	5/1927
64	1874	11/1888, 2/1905	64A	1913		1919
65	1874	6/1888	65A	1913		1919
114	1874	1913	114A	1916		1920
115	1874	1913	115A	1913		1920
116	1874	6/1889, 2/1901, 1911	116A	1916	2333	9/1926
117	1874	1913	117A	1916		1916

The following were built by Beyer Peacock & Co.   Works nos 1348-53 and had
THS 1,061 sq ft and a larger firebox.

No	Date	Rebuilt	Duplicate no	year	LMS numbers 1923*	1927	With-drawn
118**	1874	12/1892, 11/1904 6/1913	118A	1918	2334		8/1927
119**	1874	1/1892, 5/1904	119A	1918	2335		12/1926
120	1874	8/1885, 6/1901	120A	1918	2336	8659	3/1930
121**	1874	7/1891, 6/1904	121A	1919	2337		7/1927
122**	1874	11/1884, 1907			2338	8660	12/1933
123**	1874	1889, 4/1902, 1920			2339	8661	12/1933

The following were built by NSR at Stoke with standard boilers for class E
but had WB 7ft 6in + 7ft 9in.

No	Date	Rebuilt	LMS numbers		Withdrawn
			1923*	1927	
67	1875	1884, 6/1900	2340	8662	12/1928
68**	1875	1886, 5/1899, 1911	2341	8663	5/1928
72	1876	10/1889			1919
66	1877	9/1894, 1905	2342	8664	12/1930

*Not certain all 1923 LMS numbers were carried on above two classes
**WP 150lbs/sq in
***No 8654 applied 5/1928, no 8656 7/1928.

0-6-OST Built by Hudswell & Clarke. Works nos 67/8.
DW 5ft 0in, Cyls 16½ x 24. Believed to have been intended to replace 3
class 2-4-0 nos 40 & 42 and to have been delivered with these numbers but
to have been renumbered before entering traffic when it was decided to
rebuild the above locos which was done in 1867 (q.v.)

No	Date	1870 no	Renewed
34	1866	**58**	1880
36	1866	**59**	1881

0-6-OST Built by Hudswell & Clarke (no 82). Works no 77.
NSR at Stoke (first locos built at Stoke).
DW 3ft 0in, Cyls 13 x 18 (not confirmed).

No	Date	1870 no	Replaced
82	1866	**51**	1880
5	1868	**52**	1879
13	1868	**53**	1880
24	1868	**54**	1882

0-6-OST Built by Dodds & Son, Rotherham - 1856
Dimensions not known. Possibly rebuilt standard with 82 class above. May
have been on the NSR from 1866, but not added to stock until 1870.

No **55** 1870 Replaced 1882

0-6-OST Built by R Stephenson & Co. Works nos 2251-4.
DW 4ft 0in, Cyls 16 x 22. Half cabs, otherwise like 67 class of 1862

No	Date	
47	1875	Sold 5/1890 to Madeley Coal & Iron Co, named *Pioneer*. Destroyed by boiler explosion 11/1895.
48	1875	Replaced 1887
49	1875	Replaced 1885
50	1875	Replaced 1889

Clare locomotives 1878-95

2-4-0 Built by NSR at Stoke.
DW 6ft 0in, LW 4ft 0in, Cyls 16½ x 24, Blr 4ft 2½in x 10ft 4¼in, THS 822 sq
ft, WP 150lbs/sq in, WB 7ft 7in + 7ft 9in, Wt 45tons. **Class C.**

No	Name	Date	Rebuilt 17in cyls	Withdrawn
54	*John Bramley Moore*	1882	2/1900	1906*
55	*Colin Minton Campbell*	1882	5/1903	1906*
45		1884	1903	1911
46		1884	1901	1911

*Nos 54/5 were renewed in 1906

2-4-OT Built by NSR at Stoke
DW 4ft 6in, LW 4ft 0in, Cyls 16½ x 24, Blr 4ft 2in x 10ft 4¼in, THS 823 sq ft, WP 140lbs/sq in, WB 6ft 8in + 7ft 10in, Wt 43tons 2cwts. **Class A.**
Five were rebuilt 17 x 24 cyls, DW 5ft 1½in, Blr 4ft 2in x 10ft 7in.
Longbottom cabs substituted for Clare originals. Ramsbottom safety valves and flush boilers as built.
Three of rebuilt locos rebuilt again as 2-4-2Ts. LMS class 1P.

No	Date	Rebuilt	Duplicate no	year	LMS no	Withdrawn
6	1878	c1888 larger dimensions (above)				1910
8	1878		8A	1911		1914
31	1879		31A	1914		1921
52	1879	larger dimensions, date unknown 1898 2-4-2T Wt 56tons 8cwts			1454	8/1932
51	1880		51A	1913		1914
53	1880	larger dimensions, date unknown	53A	1914		1921
35	1881	larger dimensions, date unknown 1898 2-4-2T as 52			1455	10/1932
40	1881	larger dimensions, date unknown 1898 2-4-2T as 52			1456	7/1932

2-4-OT Built by NSR at Stoke
DW 5ft 6in, Cyls 16½ x 24, Wt 43tons 18cwts. Otherwise as Class A.
Class B. Boilers and cabs as class A, Longbottom cabs being substituted.
1894/5 locos had 17 x 24 cyls and ten were so rebuilt. Three were rebuilt as 2-4-2T. Wt 56tons 8cwts. LMS class 1P.

No	Date	Rebuilt	Duplicate no	year	LMS no	Withdrawn
4	1881		4A	1915		1921
5	1881		5A	1915		1922
30	1881	1906 17in cyls, 1913	30A	1914		1921
17	1882	1898 17in cyls	17A	1920	1440	6/1928
18	1882	1903 17in cyls, 1910	18A	1921	1441	6/1933
21	1882	1901 2-4-2T, 1912			1457	7/1932
22	1882		22A	1921	1442	12/1932
25	1882	1904 17in cyls	25A	1921		1921
26	1882					1921
28	1882					1922
27	1883	1901 17in cyls	27A	1922	1443	7/1925
29	1883	1898 17in cyls	29A	1921	1444	10/1932
23	11/1886	1903 17in cyls, 1913	23A	1922	1445	6/1928
24	1886	1901 2-4-2T			1458	1/1934
48	6/1887	1908 17in cyls	48A	1923	1446	6/1929
61	1887	1900 2-4-2T			1459	8/1934
2	12/1890	1903 17in cyls	2A	1923	1447	11/1930
1	4/1891	1904 17in cyls, 1913	1A	1923	1448	12/1930
71	6/1894	1903			1450	9/1933
10	12/1894	1903	10A	1923	1449	2/1928
7	6/1895	1904, 1912			1451	2/1928

O-6-OST Built by NSR at Stoke
DW 4ft 0in, Cyls 16½ x 22, Boiler as class A, WB 7ft 3in + 7ft 9in, Wt 39tons 3cwts. **Class ST.** LMS class 1F.
Renewals of Hudswell & Clarke locos, same numbers, of 1866.

No	Date	Rebuilt	Duplicate no	year	LMS no	Withdrawn
58	1880	1909	58A	1899	1600	6/1927
59	1881	1909	59A	1902	1601	12/1930

Longbottom locomotives 1883-1900

2-4-0 Built by NSR at Stoke
DW 6ft 6in, Cyls 18 x 24. Otherwise as class C. Renewals of nos 38/9 of
1874 (38 class).

No	Date	
38	1897	Replaced 1912
39	1897	Replaced 1912

0-6-OT Built by NSR at Stoke
DW 4ft 6in, Cyls 16½ x 24, Blr 4ft 2in + 10ft 4¼in, THS 818 sq ft, WP 150lbs/
sq in, WB 6ft 10in + 7ft 10in, Wt 44tons 7cwts. **Class D.** Last twelve from
no 142 (1894) were built with cylinders 17 x 24 and the others were all
subsequently rebuilt with 17in cylinders. LMS class 2F.

No	Date	Rebuilt 17in cyls	Rebuilt other	Duplicate no	Duplicate year	LMS no	With-drawn
3	1883	1902				1550	8/1930
20	1883	1903	1915			1551	12/1931
33	1883	1902				1552	10/1929
36	1883	1902				1553	8/1935
37	1883	1902				1554	10/1931
43	1883	1904				1555	10/1931
44	1883	1913				1556	12/1931
16	1884	1902				1557	8/1936
32	1884	1903				1558	1/1929
34	1884	1902				1559	12/1930
60	1884	1903				1560	4/1928
63	1884	1903				1561	9/1929
49	1885	1903				1562	2/1931
62	1885	1903				1563	9/1929
124	1885	1900		124A	1904	1564	5/1932
125	1885	1905		125A	1904	1565	1/1928
126	1886	1903				1566	12/1931
127	1886	1904				1567	11/1937
128	1887	1903				1568	4/1928
129	1887	1904				1569	12/1931
57	1888	1905				1570	12/1937
73	1888	1904				1571	8/1929
50	1889	1906				1572	1/1932
56	1889	1903				1573	5/1929
47	1890	1906				1574	6/1929
130	1891	1907				1575	8/1929
131	1891	1906				1576	12/1936
132	1892	1905				1577	6/1929
133	1892	1905				1578	1/1930
134	1892	1904				1579	5/1934
135	1892	1906				1580	10/1931
136	1892	1905				1581	10/1928
137	1892	1908				1582	1/1929
138	1893	1908				1583	8/1936
139	1893	1906				1584	5/1934
140	1893	1907				1585	12/1930
141	1894	1906				1586	10/1931
142	1894		1903			1587	1/1929
143	1895		1905			1588	11/1927
144	1895					1589	9/1935
145	1895		1909			1590	12/1930
146	1896		1908			1591	4/1932
147	1896		1904			1592	8/1931
148	1896		1912			1593	1/1932
149	1897					1594	3/1930

150	1897	1912	1595	4/1932
151	1897	1908	1596	3/1932
152	1897		1597	8/1936
153	1899		1598	11/1929

0-6-2T Built by NSR at Stoke
DW 4ft 6in, TW 3ft 6in, Cyls 18 x 24. Blr as Class D. THS 921 sq ft,
WB 7ft 5in + 8ft 5in + 7ft 6in, Wt 55tons 5cwts. **Class DX.** Enlarged version
of D class. Longer fireboxes and bunkers. Radial truck. LMS class 2F.

No	Second no 1902	Date	LMS no	Withdrawn
58		1899	2234	10/1929
154		1900	2235	3/1929
155		1900	2236	7/1929
156	76	5/1902	2238	9/1931
157	59	1902	2237	6/1929
(158)	77	1902	2239	11/1927

0-6-0 Built by NSR at Stoke.
DW 4ft 6in, Cyls 17 x 24, Blr 4ft 2in x 10ft 4½in, THS 910 sq ft, WP 150lbs/
sq in, WB 7ft 6in + 7ft 9in, Wt 37tons 9cwts.
100 class. Very similar to E class (1875-7 Stoke built locos of E class had
the same WB the others having WB 3in shorter q.v.). LMS class 2F.

No	Date	Rebuilt	LMS numbers 1923*	1927	Withdrawn
100	1896		2347	8669	9/1931
101	1897		2348	8670	12/1928
102	1897		2349	8671	4/1929
103	1898		2350	8672	12/1928
79	1898		2344	8666	10/1929
78	1899		2346	8668	4/1931
81	1899	1911	2343	8665	12/1928
80	1899		2345	8667	10/1929

* 1923 numbers possibly not applied.

0-6-0 Built by Nasmyth Wilson & Co. Works nos 588-93.
DW 5ft 0in, Cyls 18 x 26, Blr 4ft 4in x 10ft 6in, THS 1128 sq ft, WP 150lbs/
sq in, WB 7ft 9in + 7ft 9in, Wt 40tons 14cwts. Ordered by Furness Railway.
159 class. Last three had cyls 18½ x 26. LMS class 2F.

No	Date	Rebuilt	LMS numbers 1923*	1927	Withdrawn
159	1900	1912	2351	8673	10/1936
160	1900	1912	2352	8674	11/1933
161	1900		2353	8675	2/1936
162	1900		2354	8676	8/1929
163	1900	1913	2355	8677	9/1936
164	1900		2356	8678	3/1934

*1923 nos possibly not applied.

0-6-0 Built by LNW at Crewe. Crewe nos as below.
DW 5ft 2in, Cyls 17 x 24, THS 980 sq ft, WP 140lbs/sq in, WB 7ft 3in + 8ft
3in, Wt 31tons approx. Purchased from LNW 1900 (see Vol 2A pp126/9/31/50).
All had been rebuilt 'Special DX'. NSR chimneys fitted and locos placed
immediately on the duplicate list.

No	Date	Crewe no	Date built	Rebuilt SDX	Withdrawn
114A	4/1900	513	10/1861	8/1887	1913
115A	4/1900	1261	4/1869	10/1883	1915
116A	5/1900	431	3/1860	7/1885	1914
117A	5/1900	569	8/1862	8/1883	1916

O-4-OST (3ft 6in gauge). Builders below.
DW 3ft 3in, Cyls 7 x 12 O/S. For Caldon Low Quarry railway.

Name	Date	Built by
Toad	1877	Henry Hughes & Co, Loughborough
Frog	1877	Henry Hughes & Co, Loughborough
Bobs	1901	W.G. Bagnall & Co. Works no 1634

All were scrapped on site 5/1936 still in NS livery.

Adams locomotives 1903-15

2-4-O Built by NSR at Stoke
   DW 6ft 6in, Cyls 18 x 24, Blr 4ft 4in x 10ft 8in, THS 950.5 sq ft, WP 160lbs/
   sq in, WB 7ft 7in + 7ft 9in, Wt 41tons 1cwt. 2,650 gallon tenders. **Class C.**
   Renewals of earlier locos with same numbers. Some sources merely record
   rebuilds at this date for 54/5. They were the last 2-4-Os built in the UK.

		Duplicate		
No	Date	no	year	Withdrawn
15	1905	15A	1920	1923
19	1906	19A	1920	1920
54	1906	54A	1920	1920
55	1906			1911

4-4-O Built by NSR at Stoke
   DW 6ft 0in, LW 3ft 7in, Cyls 18½ x 26, Blr 4ft 9in x 10ft 10in, THS 1,226
   sq ft, WP 175lbs/sq in, WB 5ft 9in + 7ft 10½in + 9ft 6in, Wt 47tons 11cwts.
   Class G. Belpaire fireboxes, raised footplating, Adams chimney, round cab
   roof, drumhead smokebox 3,200 gallon tenders. LMS class 2P.

		LMS numbers		
No	Date	1923*	1927	Withdrawn
86	1910	595	5410	4/1929
87	1910	596	5411	6/1929
170	1910	597	5412	12/1928
171	1910	(598)	5413**	5/1933

*Not certain that all 1923 LMS numbers were carried.
**No 5413 applied 8/1928.

4-4-O Built by NSR at Stoke.
   DW 6ft 6in, LW 3ft 7in, Cyls 20 x 26, Blr as class G. THS 1,281 sq ft
   (including superheater 261 sq ft), WP 160lbs/sq in (later increased to 170lbs
   /sq in), WB as class G, Wt 50tons 14cwts.
   Class KT, Superheated with higher pitched boiler, Belpaire firebox, straight
   footplating. LMS class 2P.

		LMS numbers*		
No	Date	1923	1927	Withdrawn
38	1912	599	5414	9/1928

*LMS numbers may not have been applied.

O-2-2T Railmotor built by Beyer Peacock & Co. Works nos 4643-5.
   DW 3ft 8in, TW 3ft 8in, Cyls 8½ x 14 O/S, THS 368 sq ft, WP 180lbs/sq in,
   WB 9ft 7in. Total WB with carriage 40ft 2in to centre pivot of carriage
   bogie. Wt 32½tons. Walschaerts valve gear, Belpaire firebox, all to Beyer
   Peacock design. Cab enclosed the boiler to the rear of the smokebox and
   was to the same dimensions as the integral coach unit which was carried at
   the rear on an 8ft carriage bogie. A 450 gallon water tank was slung
   beneath the front of the carriage and a small bunker carried 15cwts of coal.
   The carriage had the usual driving compartment at the rear for reverse
   running and a third-class only saloon seating forty which was designated

non smoking. Behind the engine unit was a separate luggage space in which
six third-class smoking seats were also provided.
The three units all built in 1905 were sold by the LMS 5/1927.

O-4-4T Built by NSR at Stoke.
DW 5ft 6in, TW 3ft 7in, Blr 4ft 7in x 11ft 3in, THS 1,120 sq ft, WP 175lbs/
sq in, WB 8ft 0in + 9ft 9in + 5ft 6in, Wt 57tons.
Class M. Cab curved down to join cab sides similar to Midland style. Adams
bogie.

No	Date	Rebuilt	LMS no	Withdrawn
9	1907	1915	1431	1/1936
11	1907	1915	1432	10/1935
12	1908		1433	10/1935
41	1908		1434	3/1939
42	1908		1435	8/1930

4-4-2T Built by NSR at Stoke.
DW 6ft 0in, LW 3ft 7in, TW 4ft 0in, Cyls 20 x 26, Blr 4ft 9in x 10ft 10in
(as G), THS 1,281 sq ft (including superheater 261 sq ft), WP 160lbs/sq in,
WB 5ft 9in + 7ft 10½in + 9ft 6in + 8ft 0in, Wt 70½tons.
Class K. Tank version of 4-4-0s with Schmidt superheater, higher pitched
boiler and Belpaire firebox. LMS class 3P.

No	Date	LMS no	Withdrawn
8	1911	2180	11/1933
45	1911	2181	1/1934
46	1911	2182	1/1934
55	12/1911	2183	11/1933
13	1912	2184	5/1935
14	1912	2185	12/1933
39	1912	2186	11/1933

O-6-2T Built by Vulcan Foundry. Works nos 1891-6.
DW 5ft 0in, TW 4ft 0in, Blr 4ft 7in x 11ft 3in, THS 1165.6 sq ft, WP 175lbs/
sq in, WB 8ft 0in + 7ft 6in + 7ft 6in, Wt 59tons 12cwts, **Class L.** LMS
Class 3F.

No	Date	1904 no	LMS no	Withdrawn
165	1903		2242	8/1935
166	1903		2243	12/1933
167	1903		2244	5/1935
168	1903		2245	8/1934
170	1903	124	2240	8/1935
169	1903	125	2241	2/1936

O-6-2T Built by NSR at Stoke
DW 5ft 0in, TW 4ft 0in, Cyls 18½ x 26, Blr 4ft 9in x 10ft 9in, THS 1120sq ft,
WP 175lbs/sq in, WB 8ft 0in + 7ft 6in + 7ft 6in, Wt 59tons 15cwts. LMS class
3F.
Class New L. Larger diameter boiler and modified cab roof, higher bunker
sides. 1913 locos had Belpaire fireboxes and feed water heaters, hot water
injectors and pumps.

No	Date	LMS no	Withdrawn
98	1908	2246	5/1936
99	1908	2247	2/1928
156	1908	2248	6/1937
157	1908	2249	2/1936
93	1909	2250	7/1934
94	1909	2251	7/1936

95	1909	2252	4/1934	
158	1909	2253	4/1936	Sold to Longmoor Military Railway, Marlborough WD 70207
	1947			Sold for scrap
	1953			Broken up
51	1913	2254	4/1934	
64	1913	2255	5/1936	
65	1913	2256	5/1935	
69	1913	2257	5/1937	Sold to Manchester Collieries named *King George VI*
89	1913	2258	6/1934	
96	1913	2259	10/1936	
97	1913	2260	5/1934	
172	1913	2261	2/1937	

O-6-4T Built by NSR at Stoke.
DW 5ft 0in, TW 3ft 4in, Cyls 20 x 26, Blr 4ft 9in x 10ft 9in, THS 1274 sq ft, including superheater 258 sq ft, WP 160lbs/sq in, WB 8ft 0in + 8ft 0in 6ft 3in + 5ft 6in, Wt 74tons 15cwts.
Class C. Robinson superheater, feed water heating, hot water injectors and pumps, 'pop' safety valves, mechanical lubricators, Belpaire firebox. No vacuum ejector. LMS class 5F.

No	Date	LMS no	Withdrawn
30	1914	2040	4/1934
31	1914	2041	3/1935
53	1914	2042	4/1935
70	1914	2043	10/1935
173	1914	2044	3/1936
174	1914	2045	5/1924
4	1915	2046	12/1937
5	1915	2047	1939

O-6-O Built by NSR at Stoke.
DW 5ft 0in, Cyls 17 x 24, WP 160lbs/sq in. Otherwise as 100 class but amended cab and side panels with Adams chimney. **New 100 class.** LMS class 2F.

No	Date	LMS numbers 1923*	1927	Withdrawn
82	1907	2357	8679	8/1929
83	1907	2358	8680	11/1928

*1923 nos may not have been carried.

O-6-O Built by NSR at Stoke.
DW 5ft 0in, Cyls 18½ x 26, Blr 4ft 7in x 10ft 9in, THS 1,124 sq ft (round top), 1,197.5 sq ft (Belpaire), WP 175lbs/sq in, WB 8ft 0in + 8ft 6in, Wt 42tons 17cwts (round top), 43tons 12cwt (Belpaire).
Class H O-6-O version of L class. Older type arc roofs, larger tenders with solid fenders instead of coal rails. 1910/11 locos had Belpaire fireboxes. LMS class 3F.

No	Date	LMS numbers 1923*	1927	Withdrawn
84	1909	2359	8681	1/1930
85	1909	2360	8682	5/1929
88	1909	2361	8683	6/1928
169	1909	2362	8684	12/1928
6	1910	2363	8685	1/1929
90	1910	2364	8686	1/1930
91	1911	2365	8657	1/1930
92	1911	2366	8688	10/1930

*1923 and some 1927 nos may not have been carried.

Hookham locomotives 1916-23

0-4-0 Electric Battery Locomotive built by NSR at Stoke.
DW 3ft 1in, WB 8ft 0in, Length 19ft 8in over buffers, Wt 17tons. Built for
use at Oakamoor copper works of Thomas Bolton & Sons*. Central wooden cab
with sloping covers on battery compartments on either side of cab. BTH
motors, one on each axle series wound up to 250 volts.
*Sometimes recorded erroneously as the builders.

Built 1917, but not numbered in NS stock or LMS. Under BR became BEL no 2.
Withdrawn 1964. Preserved at NRM York.

0-4-4T Built by NSR at Stoke.
DW 5ft 6in, TW 3ft 7in, Cyls 18½ x 26.
As class M but with longer bunkers, 'pop' safety valves.
Class New M

No	Date	LMS no	Withdrawn
15	1920	1436	4/1939
17	1920	1437	6/1935
19	1920	1438	1/1936
54	1920	1439	12/1931

0-6-2T Built by NSR at Stoke.
DW 5ft 0in, Cyls 18½ x 26. As L class but without feedwater heaters. Wt
63tons 17cwts.
Class New L No 25 and all the 1923 locos were superheated. (Wt 64tons 19cwts,
THS 1,205 sq ft including superheater 261 sq ft). LMS class 3F.

No	Date	LMS no	Withdrawn	
72	1920	2262	2/1937	Sold to Manchester Collieries named *Sir Robert*.
18	1921	2263	10/1936	
22	1921	2264	5/1936	Sold to Manchester Collieries named *Kenneth*
25	1921	2265	6/1936	
26	1921	2266	12/1936	
29	1921	2267	4/1935	Superheated by LMS
27	1922	2268	2/1936	Superheated by LMS
28	1922	2269	12/1934	
1	1923	2270	11/1937	Sold to Manchester Collieries named *Queen Elizabeth*
2	1923	2271	11/1937	Sold to Manchester Collieries named *Princess*. Withdrawn by NCB 6/1960. Preserved at Chatterley Whitfield Mining Museum, Tnustall.
10	1923	2272	7/1935	
48	1923	2273	2/1937	

0-6-4T Built by NSR at Stoke.
DW 5ft 6in, Cyls 20 x 26. As Class C of 1914. Wt 77tons 7cwts.
Class F Two mechanical lubricators. Designed for express passenger work.
LMS class 4P.

No	Date	LMS no	Withdrawn
114	1916	2048	6/1934
115	1916	2049	6/1934
116	1916	2050	2/1935
117	1916	2051	11/1935
118	1918	2052	10/1936
119	1918	2053	6/1935

120	1918	2054	2/1936
121	1919	2055	8/1934

O-6-OT Built by Kerr Stuart & Co Ltd. Works nos 4079/80.
DW 3ft 9in, Cyls 15 x 20 O/S, Blr 3ft 8in x 8ft 11in, WP 160lbs/sq in,
WB 5ft 6in + 5ft 3in, Wt 34tons 3cwts.
Class KS To Kerr Stuart 'Argentina' design. LMS class 1F.

No	Date	LMS no	Withdrawn	
74	1919	1602	12/1932	
75	1919	1603	4/1933	Sold to Nunnery Collieries, Sheffield.

O-6-OT Built by NSR at Stoke.
DW 4ft 6in, Cyls (4) 14 x 24 (2 O/S). M class (round top) blr THS 1051.7 sq
ft, WP 160lbs/sq in, WB 8ft 0in + 8ft 6in, Wt 56tons 15cwts.
4 cylinder D class. Experimental engine intended for working local
passenger trains on heavily graded lines with two pairs of cranks set at 90°
and 135° in relation to each other giving eight exhaust beats per revolution
(as later on Southern *Lord Nelson* class). Superheated boiler (superheater
heating surface 195sq ft). Walschaerts valve gear. Rebuilt by LMS as O-6-0
tender due to steaming problems.

No	Date	Rebuilt O-6-0	LMS numbers 1923	1924	1927*	Withdrawn
23	1922	1/1924	(1599)	2367	8689	12/1928

*1927 no possibly not applied.

North Staffordshire Railway Number Index

1	1848	2-2-2/2-2-2ST 1 class
	1891	2-4-OT Class B
	1923	0-6-2T New L class
2	1848	2-2-2/2-4-O 1 class
	1870	2-2-2ST ex 27
	1890	2-4-OT Class B
	1923	0-6-2T New L class
3	1848	2-4-O 3 class
	1870	2-2-2WT ex 65
	1883	0-6-OT Class D
4	1848	2-4-O 3 class
	1870	2-2-2T ex 7
	1881	2-4-OT Class B
	1915	0-6-4T Class C
5	1848	2-4-O 5 class
	1868	0-6-OST 82 class
	1870	2-2-2T ex 8
	1881	2-4-OT Class B
	1915	0-6-4T Class C
6	1848	2-4-O 5 class
	1870	2-4-OST ex 30
	1878	2-4-OT Class A
	1910	0-6-O Class H
7	1848	2-4-O/2-2-2T 5 class
	1870	2-4-OST ex 31
	1874	2-4-O 7 class
	1895	2-4-OT Class B
8	1848	2-4-O/2-2-2T 5 class
	1870	2-4-OST ex 32
	1878	2-4-OT Class A
	1911	4-4-2T Class K
9	1848	2-4-O 9 class
	1870	2-4-OST ex 45
	1874	2-4-OT 9 class
	1907	0-4-4T Class M
10	1848	2-4-O 9 class
	1870	2-4-OST ex 46
	1874	2-4-O 7 class
	1894	2-4-OT Class B
	1923	0-6-2T New L class
11	1848	2-4-O 9 class
	1970	2-4-OST ex 47
	1874	2-4-OT 9 class
	1907	0-4-4T Class M
12	1848	2-4-O 3 class
	1866	2-4-O 39 class
	1870	Blank
	1874	2-4-OT/2-4-2T 9 class
	1908	0-4-4T Class M
13	1848	2-4-O 9 class
	1868	0-6-OST 82 class
	1870	Blank
	1875	2-4-O 38 class (C)
	1912	4-4-2T Class K
14	1848	2-4-O 3 class
	1865	2-4-O 39 class
	1870	Blank
	1875	2-4-O 38 class (C)
	1912	4-4-2T Class K
15	1848	0-6-O 15 class
	1870	Blank
	1875	2-4-O 38 class (C)
	1905	2-4-O Class C
	1920	0-4-4T New M class
16	1848	0-6-O 15 class
	1870	2-2-2 ex 48
	1884	0-6-OT Class D
17	1848	0-6-O 15 class
	1870	2-2-2 ex 49
	1882	2-4-OT Class B
	1920	0-4-4T New M class
18	1848	0-6-O 15 class
	1870	2-2-2 ex 50
	1882	2-4-OT Class B
	1921	0-6-2T New L class
19	1848	2-4-O 9 class
	1870	2-2-2 ex 51
	1872	2-4-O
	1906	2-4-O Class C
	1920	0-4-4T New M class
20	1848	2-4-O 9 class
	1870	2-2-2 ex 52
	1883	0-6-OT Class D
21	1848	0-6-O 15 class
	1870	2-2-2 ex 53
	1882	2-4-OT class B/2-4-2T
22	1848	2-4-O 3 class
	1870	2-2-2 ex 54
	1882	2-4-OT Class B
	1921	0-6-2T New L class
23	1848	2-2-2/2-4-O 1 class
	1870	2-2-2 ex 55
	1886	2-4-OT Class B
	1922	0-6-OT 4 cyl D
24	1848	2-2-2/2-4-O 1 class
	1868	0-6-OST 82 class
	1870	2-2-2 ex 56
	1886	2-4-OT Class B/2-4-2T
25	1848	2-4-O 3 class
	1866	2-4-O 39 class
	1870	2-2-2 ex 57
	1882	2-4-OT Class B
	1921	0-6-2T New L class
26	1848	0-6-O 15 class
	1870	2-4-O ex 2
	1882	2-4-OT Class B
	1921	0-6-2T New L class
27	1848	2-2-2/2-2-2ST 1 class
	1870	2-4-O ex 23
	1883	2-4-OT Class B
	1922	0-6-2T New L class
28	1848	2-4-O 9 class
	1870	2-4-O ex 81
	1882	2-4-OT Class B
	1922	0-6-2T New L class
29	1848	2-2-2/2-4-O 1 class
	1883	2-4-OT Class B
	1921	0-6-2T New L class
30	1848	2-4-O/2-4-OST 30 class

	Year	Description		Year	Description
	1851	Blank		1902	0-6-2T ex 156
	1855	0-6-0/0-6-0ST 15 class	77	1865	0-6-0 69 class (F)
	1884	0-6-0T Class D		1870	0-6-0 ex 35
61	1849	0-6-0 58 class		1902	0-6-2T Class DX
	1851	Blank	78	1865	0-6-0 69 class (F)
	1855	0-6-0/0-6-0ST 15 class		1870	0-6-0 ex 69
	1887	2-4-0T Class B/2-4-2T		1899	0-6-0 100 class
62	1850	0-6-0 58 class	79	1865	0-6-0 69 class (F)
	1851	Blank		1870	0-6-0 ex 70
	1855	0-6-0/0-6-0ST 15 class		1898	0-6-0 100 class
	1885	0-6-0T Class D	80	1865	0-6-0 69 class (F)
63	1850	0-6-0 58 class		1870	0-6-0 ex 71
	1851	Blank		1899	0-6-0 100 class
	1855	0-6-0/0-6-0ST 15 class	81	1868	2-4-0 ex 24
	1884	0-6-0T Class D		1870	0-6-0 ex 72
64	1860	0-6-0 64 class (F)		1899	0-6-0 100 class
	1870	0-6-0 ex 15	82	1866	0-6-0ST 82 class
	1874	0-6-0 69 class		1870	0-6-0 ex 73
	1913	0-6-2T New L class		1907	0-6-0 New 100 class
65	1860	2-2-2WT	83	1870	0-6-0 ex 74
	1870	0-6-0 ex 16		1907	0-6-0 New 100 class
	1874	0-6-0 69 class	84	1870	0-6-0 ex 75/6
	1913	0-6-2T New L class	-85	1909	0-6-0 Class H
66	1860	0-6-0 64 class (F)	86	1870	0-6-0 ex 77/8
	1870	0-6-0 ex 17	-87	1910	4-4-0 Class G
	1877	0-6-0 104 class (E)	88	1870	0-6-0 ex 79
67	1862	0-6-0ST 67 class		1909	0-6-0 Class H
	1870	0-6-0 ex 18	89	1870	0-6-0 ex 80
	1875	0-6-0 104 class (E)		1913	0-6-2T New L class
68	1862	0-6-0ST 67 class	90	1867	0-6-0 90 class (F)
	1870	0-6-0 ex 21		1910	0-6-0 Class H
	1875	0-6-0 104 class (E)	91	1867	0-6-0 90 class (F)
69	1864	0-6-0 69 class (F)	-92	1911	0-6-0 Class H
	1870	0-6-0 ex 26	93	1867	0-6-0 90 class (F)
	1873	0-6-0 69 class	-95	1909	0-6-2T New L class
	1913	0-6-2T New L class	96	1867	0-6-0 90 class (F)
70	1864	0-6-0 69 class (F)	-97	1913	0-6-2T New L class
	1870	0-6-0 ex 37	98	1867	0-6-0 90 class (f)
	1873	0-6-0 69 class	-99	1908	0-6-2T New L class
	1914	0-6-4T Class C	100	1870	0-6-0 ex 64
71	1865	0-6-0 69 class (F)		1896	0-6-0 100 class
	1870	0-6-0 ex 41	101	1870	0-6-0 ex 66
	1874	2-4-0 7 class		1897	0-6-0 100 class
	1894	2-4-0T Class B	102	1870	0-6-0 ex 58
72	1865	0-6-0 69 class (F)		1897	0-6-0 100 class
	1870	0-6-0 ex 43	103	1870	0-6-0 ex 59
	1876	0-6-0 104 class (E)		1898	0-6-0 100 class
	1920	0-6-2T New L class	104	1872	0-6-0 104 class (E)
73	1865	0-6-0 69 class (F)	-113		
	1870	0-6-0 ex 44	114	1874	0-6-0 69 class
	1888	0-6-0T Class D		1916	0-6-4T Class F
74	1865	0-6-0 69 class (F)	115	1874	0-6-0 69 class
	1870	Blank		1914	Blank
	1871	0-6-0 74 class (E)		1916	0-6-4T Class F
	1919	0-6-0T Class KS	116	1874	0-6-0 69 class
75	1865	0-6-0 69 class (F)	-117	1916	0-6-4T Class F
	1870	Blank	118	1874	0-6-0 104 class (E)
	1871	0-6-0 74 class (E)	-120	1918	0-6-4T Class F
	1919	0-6-0T Class KS	121	1874	0-6-0 104 class (E)
76	1865	0-6-0 69 class (F)		1919	0-6-4T Class F
	1870	0-6-0 ex 33	122	1874	0-6-0 104 class (E)

```
-123
 124    1885    O-6-OT Class D
-125    1904    O-6-2T ex 170/169
 126    1886    O-6-OT Class D
-127
 128    1887    O-6-OT Class D
-129
 130    1891    O-6-OT Class D
-131
 132    1892    O-6-OT Class D
-137
 138    1893    O-6-OT Class D
-140
 141    1894    O-6-OT Class D
-142
 143    1895    O-6-OT Class D
-145
 146    1896    O-6-OT Class D
-148
 149    1897    O-6-OT Class D
-152
 153    1899    O-6-OT Class D
 154    1900    O-6-2T Class DX
-155
 156    1902    O-6-2T Class DX
-157    1903    Blank
        1908    O-6-2T New L class
 158    1902    O-6-2T DX allotted
        1903    Blank
        1909    O-6-2T New L class
 159    1900    O-6-O 159 class
-164
 165    1903    O-6-2T Class L
-168
 169    1903    O-6-2T Class L
        1905    Blank
        1909    O-6-O Class H
 170    1903    O-6-2T Class L
        1905    Blank
        1910    4-4-O Class G
 171    1910    4-4-O Class G
 172    1913    O-6-2T New L class
 173    1914    O-6-4T Class C
-174
```

CLEATOR AND WORKINGTON JUNCTION

Incorporated 1876. Opened Cleator Moor to Workington October 1879. A branch to Rowrah connecting with the Whitehaven, Cleator and Egremont Railway and the Rowrah and Kelton Fell mineral railway was opened shortly after the Cleator Moor to Workington section. To Siddick Junction (LNW) October 1880, Moss Bay and Derwent branches 1885. Extended Rowrah to Linefoot Junction (Maryport and Carlisle Rly, Brigham branch) by 1886 and Lonsdale Dock branch opened by same year. Also worked Lowca light railway. Passenger trains and some goods trains were hauled by Furness locos. The railway tapped the output of forty blast furnaces, six coal mines, two iron ore mines and two quarries with nine junctions in sixteen route miles and goods traffic was heavy and complicated. Both the FR and the LNW had a joint interest in the line but this was not a controlling interest and the company was managed independently.

Vacuum brake was used and the loco names were carried on brass plates on the tank sides with numbers on circular brass plates on the cab sides. Domes were of polished brass and the locos were painted black lined out in red with vermilion connecting rods. Second pairs of buffers were fitted to permit working with chaldron wagons.

10 locomotives as under:

0-4-0ST Built by A Barclay Sons & Co.
Dimensions not certain. Possibly second hand.

No	Name	Date	
1	Ennerdale	1879	Withdrawn by 1923. Disposal unknown.

0-4-0ST Built by Fletcher Jennings & Co. Works no 187.
DW not known, Cyls 14 x 20 O/S, WP 130lbs/sq in. Provided with cab with spectacles fore and aft.

No	Name	Date	
2	Brigham Hall	10/1882	
	Renamed		
	Rothersyke	1894	Sold, date not confirmed

0-6-0ST Built by Robert Stephenson & Co. Works no 2553
DW 4ft 0in, Cyls 17 x 24

No	Name	Date	
3	South Lodge	1884	Sold 1907

0-6-0ST Built by Fletcher Jennings & Co. Works no 196 (4)
            Robert Stephenson & Co. Works no 2692 (5)
DW not certain, Cyls 17 x 24 (not confirmed for no 5). Similar to no 3

No	Name	Date	
4	Harecroft	8/1887	Sold 1913 to Moss Bay Iron & Steel Co (later United Steel) no 46
5	Moresby Hall	1890	Scrapped 5/1924 at Barrow (not allotted LMS no).

0-6-0ST Built by Robert Stephenson & Co. Works nos 2813/46.
DW 4ft 7in, Cyls 17 x 24, WP 160lbs/sq in, Wt 50¼tons.

No	Name	Date	LMS no	Withdrawn
6	Brigham Hill	1894	11564	12/1926
7	Ponsonby Hall	1896	11565	12/1927

0-6-0ST Built by Peckett & Sons. Works nos 1134, 1340
DW 4ft 6in, Cyls 18 x 24, Blr 4ft 5in x 16ft 5in, WP 180lbs/sq in, THS 1229 sq ft, WB 14ft, total Wt 48tons. Built to the design of H. Murray, locomotive engineer to the railway. 1,400 gallons water and 40 cwt coal

capacity. Ramsbottom safety valves. Wt recorded by LMS as 53tons 3cwts.
WP reduced to 140lbs/sq in (11566) and 135lbs/sq in (11567).

No	Name	Date	LMS no	Withdrawn
8	*Hutton Hall*	1907	11566	12/1927
9	*Millgrove*	1913	11567	5/1928

0-6-0ST Built by Hudswell Clarke & Co. Works mo 1400
DW 4ft 6in, Cyls 18 x 24, WP 180lbs/sq in, Wt 54½tons.

No	Name	Date	LMS no	
10	*Skiddaw Lodge*	1920	11568	Sold 6/1932 to R Fraser & Co, Hartley Main Colliery No 10.

GARSTANG AND KNOT-END

Incorporated 1864. Opened Garstang and Catterall Junction (LNW) to Pilling 5 December 1870 (official ceremony 14 December) Closed 27 March (Good Friday) 1872, except for occasional use for horse haulage and company passed into receivership. Reopened on behalf of the debenture holders 23 February 1875 (goods), 17 April 1875 (passengers). New company incorporated 1898 with title **Knott End Railway** extended line from Pilling to Knott End, opened 30 July 1908 and G&KE transferred to new company, releasing the railway from receivership.

The original company failed through over optimistic reliance on one locomotive only which became unserviceable. The company title used an archaic spelling of Knott End with only one 't'. Locomotives were not numbered and *Farmers Friend* and *Hope* were hired from a company formed by the debenture holders with the title of Garstang & Knot-End Railway Engine Co and were never the property of the railway company. The railway ultimately derived a reasonable revenue from the carriage of coal and salt but ultimately became a victim of road competition after take over by the LMS.
The local nickname 'Pilling Pig' originally referred to the whistle of *Farmers Friend* which was said to sound like a dying pig, but latterly became the nickname of the daily goods train.

8 locomotives as under:

0-4-2ST Built by Black Hawthorn & Co. Works no 118.
   DW 3ft 6in, TW 2ft 6in, Cyls 13 x 18 O/S, Blr 3ft 10in x 8ft 5½in, THS 321 sq ft, WP 140lbs/sq in, WB 5ft 6in + 5ft 0in. Purchase financed through the British Wagon Co by agreement dated 5/1871.

Name	Date	
Hebe	1870	Out of use 3/1872. Subsequent history not known.

0-4-0ST Built by Manning Wardle & Co. Works no 226 (class E) in 1868 for
         A Pilling, Fleetwood Salt Co.
         Not certain whether purchased or hired by G&KE.
   DW 2ft 9in, Cyls 9½ x 14 O/S, Blr 2ft 11in x 7ft 0in, THS 319 sq ft, WP 120lbs/sq in, WB 5ft 0in.

Name	Date	
Union	1874	To traffic 2/1875. Believed sold to Henry Lovatt and ultimately to Wilson, Sons & Rea Ltd and renamed *Mermaid*, but dates not known and confirmation not established.

0-6-0ST Built by Hudswell, Clarke & Rodgers. Works no 176 or 173.
   DW 3ft 3in, Cyls 11 x 16 O/S or 13 x 20, Blr 3ft 0in x 8ft 4in, WP 120lbs/sq in, WB 5ft 3in + 5ft 3in.

Name	Date	
Farmers Friend	1875	Sold 1900. Replaced by *New Century*

0-6-0ST Built by Hudswell, Clarke & Co. Works no 263 1883.
   DW 3ft 6in, Cyls 13 x 20 (probably O/S), Blr 3ft 0in x 9ft 6in, THS 464lbs/sq in, WP 120lbs/sq in, WB 6ft 0in + 6ft 0in. Hired from 1/1885.

Name	Date	
Hope	1/1885	Replaced by *Jubilee Queen* 1897

0-6-0ST Built by Hudswell, Clarke & Co. Works nos 484, 559.
   DW 3ft 6in, Cyls 15 x 20 O/S, Blr 3ft 5in x 9ft 3in, THS 660.49 sq ft, WP 140lbs/sq in, WB 6ft 0in + 6ft 0in, Wt 30tons.

Name	Date	
Jubilee Queen	8/1897	To LMS (11300) Scrapped at Crewe 4/1926
New Century	1900	To LMS (11301). Scrapped 10/1925 at Crewe

0-6-0ST Built by Manning Wardle & Co. Works no 1732.
   DW 3ft 9in, Cyls 14 x 20 O/S, Blr 3ft 11in x 8ft 0in, THS 660sq ft, WP
   160lbs/sq in, WB 5ft 3in + 5ft 3in, Wt 31½tons. Side tanks, Isaacson valve
   gear. Painted dark green 'East & West Yorkshire Union style'.
   Name   Date
   Knott End   5/1908   To LMS (11302). Scrapped 2/1924.

2-6-0T Built by Manning Wardle & Co. Works no 1747.
   DW 4ft 6in, LW 3ft 0in, Cyls 16 x 22, Blr 4ft 5in x 10ft 0in, THS 902 sq ft,
   WP 160lbs/sq in, WB 8ft 3in + 6ft 0in + 6ft 6in, Wt 40½tons. Isaacson's
   link motion. Delivered to Knott End Rly.
   Name   Date
   Blackpool   4/1909   To LMS 11680. Withdrawn 10/1927.

STRATFORD-UPON-AVON AND MIDLAND JUNCTION

Introduction

Two of the constituent companies of the SMJ were reputed to earn the lowest revenue per mile of any of the British railways. These were the Northampton and Banbury Junction Railway and the East and West Junction Railway. The other two constituents were the Evesham, Redditch and Stratford-upon-Avon Railway and the Stratford-upon-Avon, Towcester and Midland Junction Railway and were both worked by the E&WJ.

All these three companies had been in the hands of the receiver from an early date, being managed by a joint committee.

Completion of the joint line of these companies in 1891 from Ravenstone Wood Junction on the Midland Railway to Broom provided, in theory, a shorter route for MR Bristol freight traffic and the MR duly began operating goods trains by this route. The short lived Olney to Towcester passenger service was also provided by MR trains on hiring terms but was a dismal failure and was withdrawn after only four months, never to be reinstated.

Difficulties were encountered with the goods trains as MR locomotives were too heavy for the lightly laid flat bottomed track and three ex-LNW 'DX' goods engines had to be purchased to work MR trains. When the STMJ passed into receivership on 27 May 1898 the affairs of the E&WJ, who were working the whole line, were so complicated that it was no longer clear who the legal owners were and further legislation was considered the only solution.

The Midland Counties Junction Railways (Sales) Act of 1901 authorised the Joint Committee to sell the joint line to any one, or several jointly of the MR, GW, LNW or GC but no offers were received. Meanwhile with the completion of the GC London extension to Marylebone, which crossed the E&WJ between Byfield and Morton Pinkney, north and south facing connections were built to the new GC main line.

By 1907 the joint railway was £100,000 in debt, not counting accumulated interest, and from 1 August 1908 the Stratford-upon-Avon and Midland Junction Railway Act incorporated the new company to take over the ESJR, E&W Jct and STMJ from 1 January 1909. The Act gave running powers to the MR and GC over the whole of the line, the LNW between Roade and Stratford and the GW between Fenny Compton and Stratford.

The new company instigated improvements, strengthening bridges, relaying track extending and building sidings and extending and improving the platform and loop at Stratford-upon-Avon.

On 1 July 1910 the Northampton and Banbury Junction, the oldest of the companies, was taken over (by Act 29 April 1910). This had however been built to higher standards with bull-head rail. The Green's Norton junction was eliminated, two seperate single lines being laid between there and Towcester which was resignalled, and telegraph was installed between Towcester and Cockley Brake Junction. By 1914 the company was paying a dividend of £1.7s.6d per cent.

Excursions ran intermittently from 1891 from the LNW to Stratford via Blisworth with LNW stock. These were originally hauled by LNW 'Jumbos' as the E&WJ was a Westinghouse brake fitted line, but eventually some locos were dual brake fitted and the SMJ adopted the vacuum brake as standard, retaining some Westinghouse fitted locos for working ex-E&WJ stock. These excursions continued under the LMS and some were also run from the Midland Division.

Through carriages between Stratford and Marylebone were introduced by the GC from 16 June 1902, reaching a peak of four daily services and a single daily service survived until 31 January 1936.

The SMJ promoted itself as 'The Shakespeare Route'. The locomotives centre was at Stratford and the engineer and locomotive superintendent was Russell Willmott. Locomotives were painted black and lake lined in yellow, coaches were lake lined in gold and all were lettered 'SMJ'.

Route mileage owned was 67 miles 46 chains.

STRATFORD -UPON-AVON AND MIDLAND JUNCTION

Constituent Companies

Northampton and Banbury Junction

Incorporated 1863. Opened Blisworth (LNW) to Towcester 1 May 1866, to Cockley
Brake Junction (LNW) with running powers to Banbury over former Buckinghamshire
Railway 1 June 1872. Name changed to Midland Counties and South Wales 1866.
Original N&BJ title readopted 1870. Merged with Stratford-upon-Avon and
Midland Junction 1 July 1910. Locomotive(s) hired at first until working
agreement concluded with LNW from 1 October 1866. From December 1872 until
1 November 1876 the company worked its own traffic with second-hand
locomotives purchased from the LNW, after which time a further working agreement was negotiated with the LNW who continued to operate the line until the
SMJ took over.

Locomotive hired from I&W Boulton 1 May-30 September 1866
2-2-2ST (ex Manchester & Birmingham 2-2-2 no 19). For details see Volume 2A,
p23.

Locomotives ordered but not taken up due to lack of funds.
0-4-2WT Built by Neilson & Co. Works nos 1217/8
  Became Caledonian 540/1 ex Solway. See page no 38.
0-4-2 Built by Neilson & Co. Works nos 1219/20
  Became Caledonian 452/3 ex Solway. See page no 38.

Locomotives purchased from LNW 1872/3
0-6-0 Built by Vulcan Foundry. Purchased 6/1872
  ex South Staffordshire No 21 *Ajax* (ordered by Shrewsbury & Hereford), see
  Volume 2A, p30.
0-6-0 Built by R&W Hawthorn & Co. Works no 708. Purchased 2/1873
  ex LNW (S. Div) no 239. Resold to Seven & Wye 11/1875. See Vol 2A, p83 and
  Vol 3A, p37.
2-4-0T Built by Sharp Brothers. Purchased 4/1873.
  ex South Staffordshire no 15 *Safety*. See Vol 2A, p33 (often quoted as SS no
  14 *Sylph*).

East and West Junction

Incorporated 1864. Opened Fenny Compton (GW) to Kineton 1 June 1871, to
Stratford-upon-Avon (GW) and Kineton to Greens Norton Junction, Towcester
(connection Northampton and Banbury Junction) 1 July 1873 with running powers to
Blisworth over N&BJ. Receiver appointed 29 January 1875. Passenger service
suspended 31 July 1877. Worked Evesham, Redditch and Stratford-upon-Avon
Junction Railway (incorporated 1873, opened Stratford-upon-Avon to Broom Junction
on Evesham and Redditch Railway, MR 2 June 1879) including passenger service.
Formed joint committee with Stratford-upon-Avon, Towcester and Midland Junction
Railway (incorporated 1879 as Easton, Neston Mineral and Towcester, Roade and
Olney Junction Railway, name changed to above 1882) in 1883. Passenger services
restored between Stratford-upon-Avon and Blisworth 22 March 1885. STMJ opened
Towcester to Ravenstone Wood Junction (MR) and running powers to Olney over MR
and spur connection at Roade with LNW 13 April 1891 (goods) 1 December 1892
(passenger, permanently withdrawn 30 March 1893).

26 locomotives as under (plus four hired and one probably hired):

Locomotives hired (possibly others not positively identified).
In addition to the Manning Wardle 0-6-0ST hired for the opening of the Stratford
to Kineton section in 1871 from the contractor for the line T R Crampton and
subsequently at intermittent periods until eventually purchased (page no 264)
the following were hired from I&W Boulton:
  Two 0-6-0STs named *Wellington* and *Nelson* previously owned by Brassey & Co
  (rebuilt from 0-6-0s).
  Ex Somerset & Dorset 2-4-0s nos 3 & 4 (built by G England & Co 1861, see
  page no 274) which had been sent in part exchange to Fox Walker & Co in 1874.

The following Farlie double-engine type was probably hired rather than
purchased. It had been built in 1873 for a Mexican railway. Although there is
no indication that it was purchased a photograph in *Rly Mag* Vol 26 (1910) p268
shows that it carried a plate on one of the tank sides 'E&WJR' but no number.
   0-6-6-OT built by Yorkshire Engine Co in 1873.
   DW 3ft 4in, Cyls 17 x 24 (4), THS 1939 sq ft, WP 150lbs/sq in, WB of each
   engine bogie 8ft 6in, total WB 31st 11in. Dimensions as given by Dunn.
   Walschaerts valve gear, the first British loco so fitted.
   Acquired 1876, withdrawn 1877.

Locomotives returned to makers due to lack of funds
   0-6-0 Built by by Beyer Peacock & Co. Order no 2931. Works nos 1235-7.
   DW 4ft 6½in, Cyls 16 x 24, may have been 15 x 20 (given by Dunn as 11 x 17),
   Blr 4ft 0in x 9ft 11in, THS 1,003 sq ft, WP 120lbs/sq in approx, WB 7ft 2in
   + 7ft 6in, Wt 26tons 16cwts. Beyer Peacock design for Swedish Government
   Railways with double frames, copper topped chimneys and brass domes.
   Resold 1875 to L&Y (see Vol 3B, p47).

		L&Y no
		1875
No	Date	
1	2/1873	520
2	2/1873	521
3	2/1873	522

   2-4-OT Built by Beyer Peacock & Co. Order no 2933. Works nos 1238-40.
   DW 5ft 0½in, LW 3ft 6¾in, Cyls 15 x 20, Blr 3ft 11¼in x 9ft 6in, THS
   926.6 sq ft, WP 120lbs/sq in approx, WB 6ft 9in + 7ft 0in, Wt 31tons 11¼cwts.
   Also to a design originally for Swedish Railways. Resold 1875 to L&Y. See
   Volume 3B, pp46-7 (note amended measurements which have been checked
   against original BP order book).

		L&Y no
		1875
No	Date	
4	2/1873	517
5	2/1873	518
6	2/1873	519

Note A second Fairlie single engine 0-4-4T was run on the railway for
   demonstration purposes in 1876. It was named *Robert Fairlie*. Dunn
   states that this was built by R&W Hawthorn, works no 1699 and may have
   become Swindon, Marlborough and Andover no 4 which was of the same
   type although traditionally recorded as Avonside, works no 1244 of
   1878. It did not however enter E&W stock.

Locomotives purchased

   2-4-0 Builders unknown. Purchased from a French railway through W B Buddicom.
   DW 5ft 6in, O/S cyls dimensions not known.

No	Name	Date	
4A	*Ceres*	1874	Sold 1880 for scrap

   0-6-0 Builders unknown. Purchased from a French railway through W B Buddicom.
         Possibly ex Chemin de Fer de Rhone et Loire.
   DW 4ft 9in, Cyls 18 x 24 O/S

No	Name	Date	
5A	*La Savoie*	1874	
		1880	Rebuilt 0-6-OST
		1885	Sold to Bute Trustees no 25
			(later Bute Docks Co/Cardiff Railway. See
			Vol 7)

   0-6-OST Built by Beyer Peacock & Co. Order no 3721. Works no 1830.
   DW 4ft 0½in, Cyls 16 x 22, THS 961 sq ft, WP 120lbs/sq in, WB 6ft 9in +

7 ft 0in, Wt 31tons 2cwt.

No	Date	
1	8/1879	Sold 4/1890* to Rothervale Colliery no 1. Renumbered 1929 'O'. Scrapped by NCB 10/1959. *Replaced 8/1888.

0-6-0 Built by Beyer Peacock & Co. Order no 3872. Works no 1919.
DW 4ft 6½in, Cyls 17 x 24, THS 1208 sq ft, WP 120lbs/sq in, WB 8ft 0in +
8ft 3in, Wt 31tons 6cwts. Allan straight link motion, double frames, cab
with large square window until rebuilt in 1904. Copper top on chimney,
brass dome.

No	Date	SMJ no	
2	11/1880	2	Possibly later to duplicate list 02
	1904		Rebuilt new boiler and vacuum brake
	1923		To LMS 2300. Withdrawn 4/1926
			Scrapped 1927.

0-6-0 Built by Beyer Peacock & Co. Order nos 6021/6568. Works nos 2049/
2626.
DW 5ft 0½in, Cyls 17 x 24, THS 1087 sq ft, WP 120lbs/sq in, WB 8ft 0in +
7ft 0in, Wt 32tons 2cwts.
Double frames, copper topped chimneys and brass domes until rebuilt, but
no 3 retained the brass dome.

No	Date	SMJ no	Duplicate no	year	Rebuilt	LMS no	
3	3/1881	3	03	1913	1898 Belpaire boiler		Withdrawn 9/1924
						2301	
					1904 Vacuum brake fitted		Scrapped 1925
4	1/1885*	4			1898 reboilered	2302	
					renumbered		Withdrawn
					1926	2397	11/1929

*No 4 was fitted with Westinghouse brake as built.

2-4-0T Built by Beyer Peacock & Co. Order no 6423. Works nos 2466/7.
DW 5ft 6in, LW 4ft 0in, THS 1145 sq ft, WP 140lbs/sq in, WB 8ft 3in + 7ft
9in, Wt 40tons 4cwts. Outside bearings on LW. Copper topped chimneys
Westinghouse brake. Built in 1884 to the order of Swindon, Marlborough and
Andover Railway.

No	Date	SMJ no	Rebuilt	Withdrawn	Sold to War Dept
5*	2/1885	5	1907 New blr (from BP)		5/1916
6	2/1885	6	1907 New blr (from BP)	1913	5/1916

*No 5 carried a plate lettered 'E&W' for a period.

2-4-0T Built by Yorkshire Engine Co 1872
      ex Potteries, Shrewsbury and North Wales *Hope* , purchased 1888.
DW 5ft 0in, Cyls 15 x 22, THS 871 sq ft, Wt 29¼tons.

No	Date	
1	8/1888	Sold c1895 to B P Blockley, Bloxwich. Sold 1905 to Cannock & Rugeley Collieries, No 8 *Harrison*. Rebuilt 0-6-0T 1916. Scrapped by NCB 1955.

0-6-0ST Built by Manning Wardle & Co. Works no 178.
        Built 2/1866 for T R Crampton. Purchased 1895 or 1896.
DW 3ft 2in, Cyls 11 x 18. This was the loco hired for the opening of the
first section of the line in 1871 as shown in photograph of the first train
in *Rly Mag* Vol 26 (1910) p265 and at other periods intermittently. It was

employed by Crampton in Woodford gravel pits.

No	Date	
1	1895/6	Rebuilt 1896 new boiler and cylinders and better cab.
	1908	Withdrawn
	1910	Rebuilt and sold to Shropshire and Montgomeryshire Light Railway No 4 *Morous*.
	1924	To Hundred of Manhood and Selsey Tramway retaining number and name.
	1936	Scrapped.

0-6-0 Built by L&NWR at Crewe. Purchased 1891.
DW 5ft 2½in, Cyls 17 x 24, Blr 4ft 2in x 10ft 6in, THS 1074.5 sq ft, WP 150lbs/sq in, Wt 31tons. Obtained from LNW for working MR goods trains when MR locos found to be too heavy for the track.

No	Date	Crewe no	Rebuilt Webb	See Vol 2A page	SMJ no	
7	12/1891	652	12/1878	133	7	To duplicate stock 07 then restored to Capital List with second-hand LNW wheels. Scrapped 1920.
8	12/1891	894	11/1880	133		Withdrawn 1908
9	12/1891	894	2/1886	139		Scrapped 1903 (wheels to no 8).

0-6-0 Built by Beyer Peacock & Co. Order nos 7825/8037/8487. Works nos 3613/3812/4126.
DW 5ft 1½in, Cyls 17 x 24, THS 918 sq ft, WP 140lbs/sq in, WB 8ft 0in + 7ft 0in, Wt 35tons. Double frames. Dual brake fitted.

No	Built	Date Delivered	SMJ no		LMS no	With-drawn
10	1/1895	4/1895	10	Withdrawn 1914. Rebuilt 1917 new BP blr, new cyls and wheels and re-instated	(2304)	4/1924
11	5/1896	8/1896	11		2305	
				renumbered 1926	2398	6/1930
12	3/1900	3/1900	12		2306	
				renumbered 1926	2399	8/1930

2-4-0 Built by Beyer Peacock & Co. Order no 8999. Works no 4495.
DW 6ft 1in, LW 3ft 9in, Cyls 17 x 24, THS 1096 sq ft, WP 160lbs/sq in, WB 7ft 9in + 8ft 3in, Wt 39¼tons. For working GC through-coaches from Marylebone. Design as for Hull & Barnsley 33 class of 1885. Belpaire firebox. Stephenson link motion.

No	Date	SMJ no	LMS no	
13	7/1903	13	(290)	Withdrawn 4/1924 but tender retained as a water carrier.

0-6-0 Built by Beyer Peacock & Co. Order nos 9011/9245/9405. Works nos 4496/4633/4735.
DW 4ft 9in, Cyls 17 x 24, THS 1121½ sq ft, WP 160lbs/sq in, WB 7ft 6in + 7ft 6in, Wt 38tons 11cwts. Double frames. Stephenson link motion. Vacuum brakes.

No	Date	SMJ no	Rebuilt	LMS no	With-drawn	Scrapped
14	9/1903	14		2307	6/1926	1927
15	11/1904	15		2308*	9/1924	1925
16	3/1906	16	1910. Isaacson valve gear. Link motion restored 1919	2309	8/1927	11/1927

*LMS 2308 possibly not applied.

STRATFORD-UPON-AVON AND MIDLAND JUNCTION

0-6-0 Built by Beyer Peacock & Co. Order no 9258. Works nos 5102/3.
  DW 4ft 9in, Cyls 18 x 24, THS 1164 sq ft, WP 175lbs/sq in, WB 7ft 6in + 7ft
  6in, Wt 40tons 9cwts. Inside frames, Isaacson valve gear. Link motion
  substituted 1919.

		LMS	
No	Date	no	Withdrawn
17	12/1908	2310	3/1925
18	12/1908	2311	5/1927

0-6-0 Built by LB&SC Rly at Brighton 6/1884.
      Purchased 11/1920 ex LBSC 428. See Vol 8.
  DW 5ft 0in, Cyls 18¼ x 26, THS 1413 sq ft, WP 150lbs/sq in, WB 7ft 9in + 7ft
  6in, Wt 40tons 7cwts. Converted from Westinghouse to vacuum brakes. Had
  only feed water pumps when bought. Injector fitted soon after entering
  traffic.

		LMS
No	Date	no
7	11/1920	(2303) Acquired MR chimney. Withdrawn 11/1924.

WIRRAL RAILWAY

Constituent Companies

Hoylake

Incorporated 1863. Opened 2 July 1866 Birkenhead (Bridge Street) to Hoylake.
Following the failure of the company's bank, Overend & Gurney Ltd, the company
became bankrupt and the line was closed in 1869.

The company is thought to have possessed two locoomtives, but there are no
details known. Highet refers to a 2-2-2T with outside frames and bearings
sold to Haydock Colliery in 1880 and a locomotive built by Fox Walker in 1867
named Magnet subsequently also sold to colliery in the Burnley area and later
described as an 0-6-0. These details must, however, be regarded as very
speculative. Livery was chocolate, lined red, black and white.

Hoylake and Birkenhead Rail and Tramway Co

Incorporated 1872 as a subsidiary of the Hoylake and Birkenhead Tramway
Company to take over the railway and operate it as part of a street tramway
system with street extension to Woodside Ferry from the Docks station. Opened
1 August 1872. Extended to West Kirby 1 April 1878. Company transferred to
Birkenhead Tramways Co (owned by Birkenhead Corporation) in 1879.

4 locomotives (2 second-hand) as under:

2-2-2WT Built by L&SWR, Nine Elms 1852, ex LSW 36 *Comet*
DW 5ft 6in, LW & TW 3ft 6in, Cyls 14 x 20, THS 750sq ft, WP 120lbs/sq in,
Wt 27tons 2cwts.
LSW name and number and green livery retained on H&BR&T.

Purchased 12/1872. Scrapped 7/1883.

2-4-0T Built by Yorkshire Engine Co. Works nos 356/7.
DW 5ft 0in, LW 3ft 4in, Cyls 14 x 20 O/S, Blr 3ft 4¾in x 10ft 8¾in, THS
601 sq ft, WP 145lbs/sq in, WB 5ft 6in + 7ft 3in, Wt 24tons 4cwts.

No	Name	Date	SH&D no	
1	*West Kirby*	1877	1	Sold 1892 ro Josiah Hardman Mitton
2	*Birkenhead*	1877	2	To Wirral no 2 1892
				Sold 1894 to Talke o'th'Hill Colliery
				Staffs. Withdrawn 1904

2-4-0WT Built by Stothert and Slaughter 1850 (as 0-4-0) ex Monmouthshire
Railway and Canal no 14 (latterly 14A) sold 1873 to Neath & Brecon
and resold to H&BR&T 1879 (see Vol 7).
DW 4ft 0in (approx), Cyls 13 x 20 (assumed).

No	Date	
3	3/1879	Converted to stationery engine at Birkenhead

Seacombe, Hoylake & Deeside

H&BR&T reorganised seperating it from Tramway Company and name changed to
above 1881. New Brighton branch opened 2 January 1888 to Wallasey and 30
March 1888 to New Brighton. Extension from Birkenhead Docks to Birkenhead
Park linking railway with Mersey Railway opened 2 January 1888 by Wirral
Railway Ltd. (The latter was incorporated in 1883 by Board of Trade
certificate with the object of building a line to Hawarden connecting with
the Wrexham, Mold and Connah's Quay Railway and the MS&L). Livery: black,

lined white, yellow and vermilion. Buffer beams vermilion with black edge.
Buffer casings black.
7 locomotives as under:

2-4-OT Built by Beyer Peacock & Co. Order nos 6385/6657. Works nos 2408, 2676.
DW 5ft O½in, LW 3dt 6½in, Cyls 15 x 20, Blr 4ft Oin x 9ft 6in, THS 918 sq ft,
WP 140lbs/sq in, WB 6ft 9in + 7ft Oin, Wt 33tons 18¼cwts.

		Wirral		
No	Date	no	Rebuilt	Withdrawn
3	5/1884	3	12/1887 larger bunker	
			(2 tons) vacuum brake	2/1914
4	8/1885	4	12/1887 vacuum brake	1/1913

O-4-4T Built by Beyer Peacock & Co. Order no 6889. Works nos 2826/7, 2863/4,
2975
DW 5ft 2in, TW 3ft Oin, Cyls 16⅜ x 24, Blr 4ft 2in x 10ft Oin, THS 1017 sq
ft, WP 140lbs/sq in, WB 7ft 6in + 8ft 3in + 5ft Oin, Wt 40tons 18cwts.

		Wirral	1894	1921	LMS	
No	Date	no	no	no	no	Withdrawn
5	4/1887	5	2		(6770)	11/1923
6	4/1887	6		6B		1/1922
7	8/1887	7	5		(6771)	11/1923
8	8/1887	8			(6772)	10/1923
9	7/1888	9			(6773)	4/1924

WIRRAL

Incorporated 1891 taking over the 1883 Wirral Railway Company (powers to construct the Hawarden line having been transferred to the MS&L and WM&CQ companies jointly, opened 16 March 1896, goods; 28 March, Official Ceremony: 18 May 1896, passengers), and amalgamating with SH&D. Seacombe branch opened 1 June 1895.

9 locomotives as under (plus 4 from LNW & 1 from L&Y):

4-4-2T Built by Beyer Peacock & Co. Order no 7532. Works nos 3465.
DW 5ft 2in, LW 3ft 0in, TW 3ft 9in, Cyls 16 x 24, Blr 4ft 2in x 10ft 0in, THS 981.7 sq ft, WP 140lbs/sq in, Wt 48tons 2½cwts.

No	Date		LMS no	Withdrawn
1	1892	New BP blr fitted 2/1914	(6830)	2/1924

0-4-4T Built by Beyer Peacock & Co. Order no 7798. Works nos 3605/6.
DW 5ft 2in, TW 3ft 0in, Cyls 17 x 24, Blr 4ft 0in x 10ft 0in, THS 1025.6 sq ft, WP 160lbs/sq in, WB 7ft 6in + 8ft 3in + 5ft 0in, Wt 47tons 17¾cwts. Designed by Beyer Peacock to specifications supplied by Wirral Locomotive Superintendent Eric G. Barker.

No	Date	LMS no	Withdrawn
7	4/1894	(6774)	1/1924
10	4/1894	(6775)	4/1924

4-4-4T Built by Beyer Peacock & Co. Order no 8033. Works no 3808.
DW 5ft 2in, LW & TW 3ft 0in, Cyls 17 x 24, Blr 4ft 0in x 10ft 0in, THS 1021.6sq ft, WP 160lbs/sq in, WB 5ft 9in + 7ft 1½in + 7ft 6in + 5ft 6in + 5ft 9in, Wt 59tons 16¼cwts. A bold and highly successful decision by Barker, this being the first ever 4-4-4T to run in the British Isles. It proved highly economical on the many sharp curves, reducing tyre and flange wear. Screw reverse link motion, Gresham & Craven combination injector.

No	Date	1919 no	
11	3/1896		Withdrawn 6/1919. In service stock until 12/1919. Scrapped 2/1920.

0-6-4T Built by Beyer Peacock & Co. Order no 8480. Works nos 4120/1.
DW 5ft 3in, TW 3ft 1in, Cyls 18 x 26, Blr 4ft 2in x 10ft 6in, THS 1174.9 sq ft, WP 170lbs/sq in, Wt 62tons 1¼cwts. Primarily intended for goods traffic.

No	Date	LMS no	Withdrawn
12	4/1900	(6948)	2/1924
13	4/1900	(6949)	10/1923

4-4-4T Built by Beyer Peacock & Co. Order no 8950. Works nos 4493/4.
DW 5ft 3in, Cyls 18 x 26, THS 1050.2 sq ft, Wt 60¼tons. Other dimensions as no 11. Following the success of no 11 these were introduced in 1903 by Barker's successor, T B Hunter, with the addition of steam sanding apparatus.

No	Date	LMS no	Withdrawn
14	6/1903	(6850)	7/1924
15	6/1903	(6851)	5/1924

0-4-4T Built by Beyer Peacock & Co. Order no 0647. Works no 5742.
DW 5ft 6in, TW 3ft 1in, Cyls 18 x 26, Blr 4ft 2in x 10ft 6in, THS 1174.9 sq ft, WP 160lbs/sq in, WB 8ft 0in + 9ft 9in + 5ft 6in, Wt 54½tons.

No	Date	LMS no	Withdrawn
3	2/1914	6776 (applied 11/1926)	7/1928

2-4-2T Built by LNW, Crewe
DW 4ft 6in (+2½in tyres), LW & TW 3ft 3in, Cyls 17 x 20, Blr 4ft 0in x 9ft
10in, THS 971.6 sq ft, WP 150lbs/sq in, WB 6ft 9in + 7ft 9in + 6ft 9in. LNW
Webb **4ft 6in tanks** purchased as below. Joy valve gear.

No	Date purchased	Crewe no	Date built	LNW no	LMS no	With-drawn	See Vol 2B page no
4	2/1913	3608	8/1896	2282	(6758)	11/1927	209
11	6/1919	2523	4/1882	659	(6759)	1924*	206
16	11/1919	2725	3/1884	889**	(6760)	4/1924	207
17	1/1921	2637	5/1883	284	6761***	7/1928	206

    *Scrapped 4/1927
    **LNW no misprinted as 880 in Vol 2B
    ***LMS no applied 5/1928

2-4-2T Built by L&Y Rly at Horwich 7/1890. Ex L&Y 1041 (Horwich Lot 4 no 39).
     Aspinall 1008 class.
DW 5ft 8in, LW & TW 3ft 7¼in (radial); Cyls 18 x 26, Blr 4ft 2in x 10ft 7⅜in,
THS 1216.4 sq ft, WP 180lbs/sq in, WB 7ft 10½in + 8ft 7in + 7ft 10½in, Wt
55tons 19cwts. Joy valve gear. See Vol 3B, p63.

No	Date purchased	LMS no	BR no	Withdrawn
6	6/1921	6762	46762	9/1952

SOMERSET AND DORSET JOINT

Introduction

The Somerset and Dorset was probably more appreciated by railway lovers than by the general public. It was either the 'Slow and Dirty' or the 'Swift and Delightful' according to your point of view. Of these epithets only one had a direct relationship with the truth.

Travel on the S&D was comparatively slow, the 74 mile journey between Bath and Bournemouth taking around two hours. This was due partly to the heavy gradients over the Mendips including the 1 in 50 climb up from Bath Junction to the unpleasant single line Combe Down tunnel and equally severe gradients from Radstock to the summit at Masbury. From the south trains faced a steady 1 in 50 five mile climb from Shepton Mallet.

Secondly there were several single line sections and when traffic was heavy as on summer Saturdays when through trains would be running to and from the north, delays could multiply during the day, sometimes becoming quite excessive by the evening.

The railway remained a basically rural one, but carrying main line traffic, wherein lay its interest for the railway minded. These factors certainly produced very interesting locomotive working.

The Somerset Central, originally laid to the broad gauge and operated by the Bristol and Exeter Railway, with which it connected at Highbridge, amalgamated with the Dorset Central as the S&D with a through line from Burnham on Sea to the L&SW at Wimborne. As the railway passed through no major centres of population, the small town of Glastonbury being the largest place on the route and Blandford, about half the size, being the only other town served, its future prosperity lay in developing the railway as a through route.

Failing to attract traffic from Bristol and South Wales the company turned its attention to tapping the coal traffic from the North Somerset coalfield in the Radstock area, but schemes for a northern extension were overcome in 1866 by the financial failure of the company and appointment of a receiver.

Eventually, after two unsuccessful attempts the company was allowed to raise £160,000 in debenture stock and the receiver was discharged.

Nothing daunted they immediately turned their attention again to a northern extension. The Midland Railway had reached a temporary station at Bath in 1869 and a connection with this line now seemed an obvious choice. The route incorporated the old Somerset Coal Canal tramway from Radstock to the canal basin at Midford.

An Act was obtained in 1871 for the line from Evercreech Junction, south of Glastonbury, to Bath with running powers into the new MR station at Bath, opened the previous year. Bath Extension shares were issued taking the total consolidated capital to close on £1.75 million, nearly half of it in debentures. The new line, completed in July 1874, brought additional traffic but the revenue could not pay the interest charges on the huge debenture stock and the company approached the GW with a view to a takeover. In turn the GW consulted the Bristol and Exeter and L&SW, unwisely offering the latter the southern section of the line south of Templecombe where it crossed the L&SW Exeter line.

Archibald Scott, the L&SW General Manager saw this as an opportunity to reach the Midlands independently of the GW and immediately conferred with Allport of the MR at a hastily arranged meeting in Birmingham.

The result was a joint offer by the two companies on terms unlikely to be bettered by the GW and the S&DJ was born, its future determined as a north-south link slicing through GW territory with a branch to Burnham-on-Sea. GW lines were crossed in five places, at Bath, Midford, Radstock, Shipton Mallet and Cole, but only at Radstock was there a connection with the GW North Somerset line. A second connection had been planned, at the insistence of the Bristol and Exeter, at Cole but never completed.

The new owners immediately began channelling through freight and passenger traffic over the line.

The asset they had leased however was far from ideal and this was brought home to them when a serious head on collision occurred at Radstock on 7 August 1876. The line had been built as cheaply as possible by an impoverished company and abounded in steep gradients and sharp curves. However they set about improving the line for its new use as far as possible.

A new line was opened from Corfe Mullen to Broadstone on 14 December 1885 eliminating the previous necessity for Poole and Bournemouth trains to reverse at Wimborne.

Sections of the line were doubled where possible, Wincanton to Templecombe in 1887, Midford to Wincanton in stages up to 1894 and Corfe Mullen to Blandford in 1901. Meanwhile a new branch was opened to Bridgewater from Edington Junction in 1890.

Apart from the through freight traffic between the MR at Bath and the L&SW at Templecombe, Wimborne or Bournemouth there was indigenous traffic in the coal from Radstock and stone from quarries at Binegar or Winsor Hill. From five daily goods trains from Burnham to Templecombe or Wimborne and six through trains from Bath in 1877 in addition to the mineral traffic the number of trains from Bath had grown by 1906 to no less than twenty-one daily scheduled services, many during the night and additional special trains were often required. After the 1914-18 war the mineral traffic increased but other services began to decline and the line was reported to be losing money by 1922.

It remained, however, a valuable link between the Midland/LMS and LSW/Southern, passenger services reaching a peak in 1914 with seven through down trains and ten up trains all through the year. A train from Manchester introduced in 1910 was named 'The Pines Express' in 1927.

On summer Saturdays, apart from wartime periods, there would be a steady procession of through trains moving north and south requiring intricate timing, and no chance of recovery in the event of delay.

The S&DJ was unaffected by the Railways Act 1921 the managing companies becoming the LMS and Southern in 1923. From 1 January 1930 however, in order to effect economies, the locomotives were absorbed into LMS stock and the passenger carriages into Southern stock and the S&DJ, although still legally in existence, lost its individuality. The distinctive blue livery gave way to LMS black on the engines and Southern green on the carriages. Highbridge works was closed. British Railways kept the line open for the coal traffic until all but one of the collieries closed in 1966. The through passenger services, after enjoying somewhat of a revival in the 1950s were diverted via Reading and Basignstoke in 1962. The company was nationalised under the Transport Act 1947.

The Locomotive Superintendent of the Somerset Central was Robert Andrews who remained with the S&D until April 1868 when the post was (rather rashly) abolished by the receiver then in control of the railway. Andrews established the works at Highbridge. B S Fisher from the Taff Vale Railway was appointed on 27 August 1873 and was retained by the Joint Committee until he met with a fatal accident in Highbridge yard being crushed between the buffers of two loaded coal wagons on 10 May 1883. As the MR were responsible for the locomotives all the succeeding locomotive superintendents came from that company, naturally.

W H French was appointed 17 May 1883. Following his resignation from the railway in 1889 he was succeeded by A W Whitaker on 1 November 1889. Whitaker was undoutedly the most influential locomotive superintendent of the S&DJ introducing Midland Railway methods and ordering locos from Derby works rather than from outside firms. He reorganised the works, modernising the machinery and sending workers to Derby for short periods to widen their experience and enable them to meet and discuss with other men on similar work the problems involved. He was an inovative man and introduced token exchange apparatus amongst other things.

He retired on 24 July 1911 and was replaced by M F Ryan who in turn resigned on 13 September 1913 to become assistant to Urie on the L&SW.

R C Archbutt took office 1 October 1913 and remained until the absorption of the locomotive stock in 1930 when he returned to the Midland Division of the LMS. From February 1915 to January 1919 while Archbutt was serving in the army with the ROD Whitaker returned from retirement as acting locomotive superintendent.

The Somerset and Dorset livery before 1876 was dark green, but the MR introduced their standard pale green until 1883 when the new Johnson standard livery was introduced. The change was made to Prussian blue in 1886 at the instigation of the Joint Committee and was popular with the public. Coaches were painted in the same colour.

Total route mileage was 105 miles 54 chains.

SOMERSET AND DORSET JOINT

Constituent Companies

Somerset Central 7ft 0in gauge
  Incorporated 1852. Opened 28 August 1854 Highbridge to Glastonbury.
Connection at Highbridge with Bristol and Exeter. Extended to Burnham-on-Sea
3 May 1858. Opened Glastonbury to Wells 15 March 1859, Glastonbury to Cole
3 February 1862 joining Dorset Central. Mixed gauge laid throughout to
Burnham. Worked by Bristol and Exeter with broad gauge stock to Glastonbury.
The southern section was worked by the company's own locomotives from
3 February 1862 until amalgamation with Dorset Central effective from
1 September 1862. During this period they also took over the working of the
Dorset Central from Cole to Templecombe from the LSW. Hardly any trains
used the broad gauge rails from Glastonbury to Cole which had been laid at
the instigation of the Bristol and Exeter.

8 locomotives as under, all to Somerset and Dorset 1 September 1862 retaining
the same numbers:

2-4-0 Built by G England & Co.
  DW 5ft 0in, LW 3ft 6in, Cyls 15 x 18, Blr 3ft 10in x 9ft 0in, THS 860 sq ft,
WP 115lbs/sq in, WB 6ft 10in + 6ft 10in, Wt 25tons 4cwts. Domeless with
manhole cover on flush topped blr. Spring safety valves over firebox, O/S
LW bearings & frames. Four-wheel tender with weatherboards. Nos 1, 3, 4 &
5 were sold to Fox Walker & Co in part exchange for 1 class 0-6-0STs in 1874.

No	Date	
1	10/1861	
	11/1874	To Fox Walker & Co
	5/1875	Sold to Bishops Castle Rly. *Progress* Scrapped 1905
2	11/1861	
	1874	To duplicate list 'old no 2'
	6/1876	Renumbered S&DJ **25**
	8/1881	Renumbered 25A
	2/1882	Withdrawn and used as stationary boiler at Highbridge. Broken up 5/1885
3	11/1861	
	11/1874	To Fox Walker & Co. Hired to E&W Junction Rly.
4	11/1861	
	11/1874	To Fox Walker & Co. Hired to E&W Junction Rly.
5	11/1861	
	11/1874	To Fox Walker & Co
	1/1877	Sold to Bishops Castle Rly. *Bishops Castle*
	1893/4	Repaired by Wrexham, Mold & Connah's Quay Rly, at Wrexham. Scrapped 1904.
6	11/1861	Accident at Cole 7/10/1875
	6/1876	Renumbered S&DJ **26**
	8/1881	To duplicate list 26A
	10/1883	Withdrawn
	5/1884	Rebuilt 2-4-0T, LW 3ft 10in and reinstated
	1/1889	Broken up
7	11/1861	
	6/1876	Renumbered S&DJ **27**
	8/1881	To Duplicate list 27A
	5/1888	Rebuilt 2-4-0T, LW 3ft 6in, Cyls 16 x 18, Blr 3ft 11in x 8ft 9in, THS 830 sq ft, WP 140lbs/sq in, WB 6ft 10in + 7ft 4in, Wt 35tons 9cwts.
	7/1902	Reboilered, Midland type dome and safety valve cover over firebox THS 836 sq ft, Wt 36tons 4cwts.
	7/1925	Withdrawn

2-4-OWT Built by G England & Co.
DW 5ft 0in, LW 3ft 6in, Cyls 15 x 18. Other dimensions as 1 class 2-4-0
above, but Wt not known. Ordered as 2-4-0 with nos 1-7, but modified
during construction to a tank engine.

No   Date
8   11/1861   Possibly converted to a 2-4-0 tender engine 4/1872 until
                   1874.
       7/1876   Renumbered S&DJ **28**
       8/1881   To duplicate list 28A
       1/1883   Rebuilt 2-4-OST, Cyls 16 x 18, Blr 3ft 11in x 8ft 9in,
                   THS 830sq ft, WP 140lbs/sq in, Wt 37tons 4cwts.
       10/1904   Rebuilt 2-4-OT, Blr 4ft 0in x 8ft 10in, THS 836 sq ft, Wt
                   36tons 3cwts. Copper-capped chimney and brass dome cover
                   retained. Withdrawn 4/1928.

Dorset Central

Incorporated 1856. Opened Wimborne Junction (L&SW) to Blandford 1 November 1860 and worked by L&SW. Opened Templecombe to Cole November 1861, also worked by L&SW until 3 February 1862 and from that date worked by SC. Amalgamated with SC to form Somerset and Dorset 7 August 1862, effective from 1 September 1862.

During the period of working by L&SW the following locomotives are recorded as being operated:

Wimborne Jct to Blandford section 1 November 1860 - 31 August 1862.
2-2-2WT	No 15	*Mars*
2-4-0	No 41	*Ajax*

Templecombe to Cole section November 1861 - 2nd February 1862
2-2-2	No 53	*Mazeppa*
	No 58	*Sultan*
	No 61	*Snake*
2-4-0WT	No 145	*Hood*
0-6-0	No 49	*Bison*

Somerset and Dorset
Incorporated as above. Completed remaining section of line, Templecombe to Blandford 31 August 1863 with running powers over LSW to Poole (after reversal at Wimborne). Receiver appointed 30 June 1866. Discharge granted by Court of Chancery May 1870 after capital restructure. Obtained Act for extension from Evercreech Junction to the Midland Railway at Bath in 1871, opened 20 July 1874. Broad gauge rails removed about 1870. Leased to Midland and L&SW Railways jointly 1 November 1875, the Midland taking over responsibility for the locomotives and rolling stock and the LSW accepting responsibility for the permanent way, civil engineering and signalling. Lease confirmed by Act of 13 July 1876 as the Somerset and Dorset Joint.

23 locomotives as under (plus 4 similar ordered by S&DJ):

2-4-O Built by G England & Co.
DW 5ft Oin, LW 3ft 6in, Cyls 16 x 18, THS 849 sq ft, WP 115lbs/sq in, WB 6ft 7in + 7ft 5in. Similar to 1 class above but with larger raised firebox, modified framing and large cab with side windows. Tender sand boxes provided for tender-first running, but no tender weather-boards. Sold to Midland Rly by S&DJ to offset cost of new locos.

No	Date	S&DJ no	Date	Duplicate no	date	MR no	Date	
9*	8/1863	29	8/1876	29A	11/1877	1399	8/1878	See Vol 3A
10	8/1863	10	8/1876	10A	1877	1397	8/1878	page 124**

*No 9 in accident Wimborne 11/1/1866.
**Amends information in Vol 3A. MR numbers as above.

2-4-O Built by G England & Co.
DW 5ft Oin, LW 3ft 6in, Cyls 16 x 18. As nos 9 & 10 but with longer coupled wheelbase, sandbox on boiler barrel. Clarke patent smoke consuming apparatus fitted without S&D knowledge. Centre dome with safety valve attached.

No	Date	1870 no	S&DJ no	Duplicate no	year	locos Sold 8/1878 to offset costs of new/
12	9/1864	no	no	12A	1877	To LSW 148 *Colne*. See Vol 7
13	9/1864		13	13A	1877	To Midland 1398. See Vol 3A, p124*
14	9/1864		14	14A	1877	To LSW 7 *Fowler*. See Vol 7
15	9/1864	11	11	11A	1877	To LSW 147 *Isis*. See Vol 7

*Amends information in Vol 3A. MR no as above.

2-4-O Built by G England & Co.
DW 6ft Oin, LW 4ft 6in, Cyls 16 x 24, Blr 3ft 11in x 9ft 9in, THS 979 sq ft, WP 120lbs/sq in, WB 7ft 5in + 7ft 5in, Wt 30½tons. Part of South Eastern Railway order (Cudworth class 118) for twenty locos rejected when delivery date not kept. Long coal-burning fireboxes divided by longitudinal mid-feather. Double frames, the otuer one being of a composite nature and had to be strengthened at Highbridge.

No	Date	S&DJ no	Duplicate no	date	
17	11/1865	17	17A	5/1891	Restored to Capital list **45** 11/1895
					Reboilered and cab fitted 8/1879
					Blr 4ft 2in x 10ft Oin, THS 1115 sq ft.
					Withdrawn 1/1897
18	11/1865	18	18A	5/1891	Reboilered and cab fitted 3/1879 as 17
					Withdrawn 1/1897

*No 18 was in accident 5/10/1874 falling from Pecking Mill viaduct.

2-4-O Built by Vulcan Foundry. Works nos 562/3.
DW 5ft Oin, LW 3ft 6in, Cyls 17 x 22, Blr 4ft 3in x 9ft 8½in, THS 1097 sq ft, WP 120lbs/sq in, WB 7ft 3in + 6ft 9in, Wt 33½tons. Domed (centrally

placed) boilers, otherwise similar to England 2-4-Os, including large
cab with drop lights as in carriages. Six-wheel tenders (1,575 gallons).
Six locos were ordered but only two could be paid for, the others eventually
being sold (at some loss to Vulcan's) to Alsace-Lorraine Railway (nos 26-29).

No	Date	Renumbered 2/1871	S&DJ no	Duplicate no	date	Rebuilt as below	Withdrawn
19	9/1866	15	15	15A	5/1891	12/1880*	2/1901 but reinstated
						10/1902**	1/1914 (blr to no 44)
20	7/1866	15	16***	16A	5/1891	6/1881*	11/1899 but
						7/1903**	reinstated 1/1914 (blr to 37)

*Reboilered and new cylinders fitted. WB 7ft 3in + 7ft 9in, MR-type cab,
steam brakes, Wt 32tons 11cwts. Kirltey tenders (1,720 gallons). At these
dates (1880/1) no 15 had Allan motion, no 16, Stephenson.
**Reboilered THS 1119 sq ft, Wt 33tons 6cwts.
***No 16 in accident Wimborne 11/1890

2-4-OT Built by G England & Co, 1862
DW 4ft 0in, Cyls 11 x 17, Blr 3ft 8in, THS 645 sq ft. Built for
International Exhibition, 1862. Purchased 10/1863. Flush top firebox,
domed boiler, two spring-balance safety valves, tall copper-topped chimney
mounted on a square base. The footplate was partly covered by a bent plate.
Only the front part of the tanks held water (520 gallons) which helped to
increase fore-end adhesion weight.
On purchase the locomotive continued to be painted in the deep-blue colour
in which it had been exhibited, getting the nickname 'blue bottle' and
possibly giving rise to the blue livery adopted by the S&DJ in 1886. although
no 11 was later repainted in the then standard green.

No	Date	
11	10/1863	Sold to Admiralty, Sheerness 9/1870.

2-4-OT Built by E Bury & Co (as 2-2-0) 1842 ex SE, later LBSC 4 rebuilt
2-4-OT 3/1857 (see Vol 8) purchased from George Reed, a S&D Director
10/1865.
DW 5ft 6in, Cyls 14 x 18. Spare six-wheel tender also purchased.

No	Date	
16	10/1865	Renumbered 19 2/1871 exchanging numbers with Vulcan 2-4-0 above. Latterly* used as stationary boiler at Highbridge. Assumed sold for scrap 5/1876.
		*Presumably by 3/1874 as no re-used then as below.

0-6-0 Built by John Fowler & Co. Works nos 2125-30.
DW 4ft 6in, Cyls 17½ x 24, Blr 3ft 10½in x 10ft 0in, THS 1067 sq ft,
WP 140lbs/sq in, WB 7ft 3in + 8ft 3in, Wt 32tons 13cwts. Inside frames.
Similar to GN 474 class. First four had domeless boilers, rounded Stirling
type cabs and conical safety valve covers. Nos 23/4 had domes on boiler
centre at Fisher's instigation because he feared priming when the engine was
worked hard. All had steam brakes with large wooden shoes acting on all
wheels, wooden 'sandwich' buffer beams and these were the only locos fitted
with large elliptical number plates in brass on the cab side. Very solidly
built and intended for working the heavily graded Bath extension, later class
1P 2G LMS class 4F.

No	Date	S&DJ no	Rebuilt	With- drawn
19	3/1874	19*	Domed blr, 17in diam cyls 5/1888.	
			Blr 4ft 1in diam, THS 1162sq ft, WP 150lbs/sq in Wt 34tons 2cwts. Reboilered 3/1908 THS 1176 sq ft, WP 160lbs/sq in, Wt 35tons 11½cwts	6/1927

20	4/1874	20	Domed blr as 19 2/1893	
			Reboilered 12/1910, THS 1048 sq ft, WP 160lbs/	
			sq in, Wt 35tons 14cwts.	8/1928
21	5/1874	21	Domed blr as 19 9/1893 (17in cyls)	
			Reboilered as 20 2/1911	7/1928
22	6/1874	22*	Domed blr as 19 11/1892 (17in cyls)	
			Reboilered as 19 11/1911	8/1928
23	7/1874	23	Reboilered as 19 8/1892 (17in cyls)	
			Reboilered as 19 6/1910	8/1928
24	8/1874	24	Reboilered as 19 11/1893 (17in cyls)	
			Reboilered as 19 10/1910	8/1928

*No 19 was in accident at Blandford 15/6/1896 and at Highbridge 27/3/1898.
**No 22 was in an accident at Shapwick on 3/5/1877, at Binegar 3/2/1886 and
5/2/1895 and at Highbridge 27/3/1898.

0-6-0ST Built by Fox Walker & Co. Works nos 254-8, 320-3.
DW 4ft 0in, Cyls 17½ x 24, Blr 4ft 3in x 10ft 6in, THS 1141 sq ft, WP
140lbs/sq in, WB 7ft 3in + 7ft 9in, Wt 45tons 6cwts. Banking tanks for Bath
extension. 2-4-0s nos 1, 3, 4 & 5 sent to Fox Walker in part-exchange for
nos 1-3. Heavy construction and 'sandwich' buffer beams as on 0-6-0s with
bunker over-hanging rear buffer beam. Saddle tank extended from rear of
smoke box to rear of firebox, originally 8in inside cab, though this was
altered by shortening the cab at the first rebuild. Steam brakes (vacuum
brakes never fitted), sloping smoke box front originally, dished wheels
permitting larger bearing surfaces, gravity sanding. Brass domes and
chimney caps, the latter latterly replaced by cast chimneys. Nos 6-9 were
ordered by the Joint Committee with 17 x 24 cyls and minor differences
including curved bunker tops and plain bushed coupling rods. To pay for nos
6/7 it was necessary to sell the Fowler 0-6-0s and nos 1 & 2 below to
C Christian, Bristol and lease them back with a similar arrangement for
2-4-0s, 6/7 and 'old no 2' with the Railway Rolling Stock Co of Wolverhampton.
All are recorded as being 17 x 24 cyls by 1896. Later class 2G LMS class 2F.

| S&DJ | | | LMS | |
no	Date	Rebuilt	no	Withdrawn
1	7/1874	0-6-0 1/1888. Wt 33tons 16cwts		
		0-6-0ST 12/1908. DW 4ft 3in		
		WP 160lbs/sq in, THS 1050 sq ft,		
		Wt 43tons 17cwts	1500	11/1930
2	7/1874	Reboilered 8/1885. Blr 4ft 2in x		
		10ft 3½in, THS 1121 sq ft, Wt		
		41tons 1cwt. Reboilered 9/1906,		
		DW 4ft 0½in, Wt 43tons 15cwts,		
		other dimensions as 1908, details		
		for no 1.	(1501)	2/1930
3	9/1874	Rebuilt as 2 4/1893, DW 4ft 2in.		
		Rebuilt as 2 7/1911, DW 4ft 3in.		
		Painted black 1915	1502	9/1930
4	2/1875	Rebuilt as 2 10/1890		
		Rebuilt as 2 4/1909	(1503)	2/1930
5	2/1875	Rebuilt as 2 3/1890		
		Rebuilt as 2 2/1910	1504	10/1934
6	6/1876	Rebuilt as 2 12/1894		
		Rebuilt as 2 4/1911	1505	11/1934
7*	6/1876	Rebuilt as 3 5/1890		
		Rebuilt as 3 10/1909 DW 4ft 2in.	1506	10/1934
8**	8/1876	Rebuilt 0-6-0T 11/1889, vacuum		
		brake control, DW 4ft 6in, Wt 44tons		
		13cwts. Rebuilt 0-6-0 10/1908,		
		Wt 35tons 12cwts		5/1928
9	8/1876	Rebuilt as 2 7/1899. Rebuilt as		
		2 4/1910. Painted black 1915	1507	12/1930

*No 7 was in accident at Radstock 7/8/1876
**No 8 was in accident at Midsomer Norton 2/3/1882

SOMERSET AND DORSET JOINT

O-4-4T Built by Avonside Engine Co. Works nos 1184/5, 1187-9 1186, 1190-2.
Vulcan Foundry. Works nos 1071-4.
DW 5ft 3in, TW 3ft 0in, Cyls 17 x 24, Blr 4ft 2in x 10ft 6in, THS 1195 sq
ft, WP 140lbs/sq in, WB 8ft 0in + 8ft 6in + 5ft 6in, Wt 43tons 11cwts.
Similar to Johnson 6 class O-4-4Ts of 1875 on Midland with longer bogie
wheelbase. Johnson chimney and boiler fittings. No cabs but weatherboards
later roofed over. Deeley cab fitted at second rebuilding. Steam brakes on
all wheels but bogie brakes removed when vacuum brake fitted. Vulcan locos
delivered in MR red and had full MR cabs with doors, higher bunkers and
tanks which extended further forward. Screw reverse. Cylinders enlarged to
18in diam. Later class 1P 1G LMS 1P.

No	Date	Reboilered etc	LMS no	Withdrawn
10	11/1877	1/1891 THS 1251 sq ft. 3/1907 WP 160lbs/ sq in, THS 1074. Elongated Johnson chimney.	(1200)	2/1930
11	11/1877	2/1892 as 10. 10/1909 as 10	1201	9/1930
12	11/1877	3/1890 as 10. 1/1907 as 10	1202	10/1931
13	12/1877	10/1894 as 10. 10/1906 as 10	1203	11/1930
14*	12/1877	7/1891 as 10. 12/1907 as 10 To Duplicate list 14A 2/1897	(1204)	4/1930
29	11/1877	11/1889 as 10. 4/1907 as 10 To Duplicate list 29A 4/1926	1205	12/1930
30	12/1877	8/1893 as 10. 9/1906 as 10 To Duplicate list 30A 4/1926 Motor fitted 5/1928	1206	5/1932
31	12/1877	4/1891 as 10. 10/1910 as 10 To Duplicate list 31A 4/1926 Motor fitted 5/1928	1207	12/1932
32*	12/1877	12/1893 as 10. 2/1907 as 10 3/1925 G5½ Belpaire boiler, THS 1073½ sq ft, Wt 49tons 11cwts. Motor fitted 5/1928 Renumbered **52** 8/1928	1230**	6/1946 5/1928
52*	12/1884	9/1902 as 10 (1891)		
53*	1/1885	9/1902 as 10 (1891) 3/1925 G5½ blr as 32	1321	3/1930 11/1920
54*	1/1885	6/1907 as 10 (1891)		
55	1/1885	8/1906 as 10 (1891) 6/1925 G5½ blr as 32. Motor fitted 8/1927	1232	12/1932

*The following locos were in accidents as below:
    No 14 Wimborne 12/12/1881
        32 Midsomer Norton 2/3/1882
        52 Burnham on Sea 13/4/1914 (Easter Monday)
        53 Shepton Mallet 27/2/1885
            Binegar 31/7/1885
            Binegar 3/2/1886
        54 Broadstone Jct 23/12/1890
**LMS 1230 was painted in black livery.

O-4-4T Built by MR Derby. Order no 460 1884, ex-MR/LMS 1305 (previously 1651).
See Vol 3A, p138.
DW 5ft 3½in, TW 3ft 0½in, Cyls 18 x 24, Blr 4ft 1in x 10ft 6in, THS 1254 sq
ft, WP 150lbs/sq in, WB 8ft 0in + 9ft 9in + 5ft 0in, Wt 50tons 9cwts.
Replacement for no 54 above.

```
            Date
No       purchased
54          1/1921    Painted red but lettered 'SDJR'.
                      Motor fitted 5/1928
                      To LMS 1930 resuming old no 1305
                      Withdrawn 8/1931
```

The following four-coupled tank locomotives were acquired to shunt the coal
traffic at Radstock. They were all painted in the full SDJR livery of Prussian
blue and so smartly kept by their crews that they became known locally as 'The
dazzlers'.

O-4-OST Built by Slaughter Gruning & Co in 1852.
     Purchased 10/1882 and rebuilt 4/1883
     DW 3ft 0in, Cyls 10 x 14 O/S, THS 582 sq ft, WP 110lbs/sq in, WB 6ft 0in, Wt
     13¾tons. Weatherboards only. Worked in chalk quarry at Grays until 1866
     then hired out by I&W Boulton and latterly purchased by Widnes Alkali Co,
     becore being offered for sale by C P Philips in 1880.

```
No       Name        Date
5        Bristol      4/1883   To Duplicate list 45A 11/1891
                               Withdrawn 11/1895
```

O-4-2ST Built by S&DJ at Highbridge.
     DW 3ft 6in, TW 2ft 3in, Cyls 10 x 14 O/S, Blr 2ft 7in x 7ft 2in, THS 221½ sq
     ft, WP 140lbs/sq in, WB 5ft 1in + 4ft 9in, Wt 17tons 3cwts. Flush boiler
     dome and spring-balance safety valve over firebox, copper-capped chimney.
     Saddle tank extended from rear of smokebox to front of firebox. DW springs
     above running plate. Steam brakes. Original cab replaced by single sheet
     one at reboilering in 1896 and saddle tank enlarged to front of smokebox with
     taller chimney. (Blr 2ft 7in x 7ft 5in, THS 287 sq ft, WP 150lbs/sq in, Wt
     20tons 13cwts, 11 x 14 O/S cyls fitted 1906). Experimentally motor fitted
     with vacuum brake 10/1906 removed after trials on Burnham-on-Sea branch.

```
No       Date
25A      12/1885   Rebuilt 10/1896, 10/1906 as above.
                   Withdrawn 2/1929
```

O-4-OST Built by S&DJ at Highbridge
     DW 3ft 0in, Cyls 10 x 14 O/S, Blr 2ft 7in x 8ft 2in, THS 310 sq ft, WP 150lbs/
     sq in, WB 6ft 0in, Wt 19tons 8cwts. Saddle tank from front of smokebox.
     Springs above axleboxes, inclined cylinders, flush-topped boiler with tall
     dome and spring balance safety valves. Steam braking, gravity sanding. No 45A
     originally had an open footplate, but 26A had a single-sheet cab when built
     and 45A was later so fitted.

```
No       Date
45A      4/1895    Withdrawn 8/1929
26A      10/1895   To LMS (1509) 1930.  Withdrawn 12/1930.
```

O-4-OT Sentinel. Built by Sentinel Wagon Co Ltd. Works nos 7587/8
     DW 3ft 2in, Cyls (4) 6¾ x 9, THS 159 sq ft + 43 sq ft, superheater WP 275lbs/
     sq in, WB 5ft 6in, Wt 27tons 15cwts.
     Painted black. Standard Sentinel twin engines 100hp each with vertical
     boilers and chain drive.

No	Date	LMS no	BR no	Withdrawn
101	2/1929	7190	47190	3/1961
102	5/1929	7191	47191	8/1959

4-4-0 Built by MR Derby. Order nos 872 (15-18), 1431 (67/8), 1482 (14, 45).
     DW 5ft 9in, LW 3ft 0in, Cyls 18 x 24, Blr 4ft 1in x 10ft 0in, THS 1202 sq ft,
     WP 150lbs/sq in, WB 6ft 0in + 6ft 6in + 8ft 3in, Wt 39tons. Standard

Johnson A class boiler with C class firebox. Screw reverse, Stephenson
valve gear, Salter safety valves on central dome and half cabs. Steam
braking on engine controlled by vacuum train brake ejector. 2,200 gallon
tenders were built at Highbridge and followed Kirtley practice with springs
above the platform plate on the outside. Loco design generally followed
current MR practice although wheelbase was non standard. 1907-11 rebuilds
had MR H class boilers shortened by 6in and tenders enlarged to 2,600
gallons. Nos 17 & 45 had shortened Belpaire G7 boilers in 1926/7 (THS
1,326½ sq ft, Wt 47tons 2cwts). Cylinders later 18 x 26. Nos 14 & 45 had
steel boilers. Later class 2P 2G LMS class 2P.

No	Date	Reboilered	LMS no	Withdrawn
15	5/1891	4/1905 WP 160lbs/sq in, THS 1176 sq ft		
		9/1910 H blr, THS 1,353 sq ft (blr to 24)		8/1928
16	5/1891	4/1906 as 15 (1905)		
		4/1910 H blr as 15 (blr to 23)		8/1928
17	5/1891	8/1904 as 15 (1905)		
		1/1908 H blr THS 1282 sq ft (blr to 19)		
		11/1927 G7 blr as above	302	6/1931
18	5/1891	12/1904 as 15 (1905)		
		6/1911 H blr as 15 (blr to 22)		
		8/1928 blr ex 45 & renumbered 15	301	9/1931
67	1/1896	12/1907 H blr THS 1344 sq ft		8/1920*
68	1/1896	5/1908 H blr THS 1282 sq ft		11/1921*
14	2/1897	12/1910 H blr THS 1353 sq ft	(300)	1/1930
45	2/1897	8/1909 H blr THS 1282 sq ft		
		9/1926 G7 blr as above (blr to 18)	303	2/1932
		Renumbered 18 8/1928		

*Renewed

4-4-0 Built by MR Derby. Order nos 2588 (69-71), 3310 (77/8).
DW 6ft 0in, LW 3ft 1in, Cyls 18 x 26, Blr 4ft 8in x 10ft 6in, THS 1420 sq
ft (Order 2588), 1347 sq ft (Order 3310), WP 175lbs/sq in, WB 6ft 0in + 7ft
0½in + 8ft 6in, Wt 46tons 4cwts (Order 2588), 47tons 8cwts (Order 3310).
MR H class boiler on order 2588. H1 class on order 3310. Two Ramsbottom
safety valves and one 'lock up' type over firebox all in large brass casing.
Nos 77/8 (order 3310) had Deeley cabs. All had 2,950 gallon tenders with
large slots in frames and coal rails. Tenders of 77/8 to 0-6-0s 73 &76 in
exchange for 2,600 gallon tenders from 4-4-Os 67/8 above in 1921.

No	Date	Reboilered	LMS no	Withdrawn
69	11/1903			4/1921*
70	11/1903			4/1914*
71	11/1903			5/1914*
77	3/1908	5/1926 THS 1384 sq ft, Wt 48tons 9cwts**	320	9/1931
78	3/1908	9/1931 G7 blr as 17**	321	3/1938

*Renewed **As class 3P 2G (2P 2G after 1923) LMS class 2P.

4-4-0 Built by MR Derby. Order nos 4337 (70/1), 4476 (67-9).
DW 7ft 0½in. LW 3ft 6½in, Cyls 20½ x 26, THS 1170 sq ft + superheater 313 sq
ft, WP 160lbs/sq in, WB 6ft 0in + 7ft 2½in + 9ft 6in, Wt 53tons 7cwts.
Renewals of previous locos with the same numbers.
MR 483 class with Belpaire G7S boiler and Schmidt superheater. 3,250 gallon
tenders.

No	Date	Renumbered 8/1928	LMS no	BR no	Withdrawn
70	5/1914	39	322	40322	3/1953
71	4/1914	40	323	41323	9/1956
67	4/1921	41	324	40324	1/1953
68	4/1921	42	325	40325	10/1951
69	4/1921	43	326	40326	5/1956

4-4-0 Built by LMS Derby. Order no 6901
DW 6ft 9in, LW 3ft 6½in, Cyls 19 x 26, Blr 4ft 8in x 10ft 5$\frac{5}{16}$in, THS 1158
sq ft + superheater 253 sq ft, WP 180lbs/sq in, WB 6ft 0in + 7ft 2½in +
9ft 6in, Wt 54tons 1cwt. Standard LMS Class 2 (563 class) with modified
G75 boiler and 3,500 gallon tender. The locos were built as LMS 575, 576
and 580 but transferred from Derby direct when completed. Class 3P 2G LMS
                                                                class 2P

		LMS	BR	
No	Date	no	no	Withdrawn
44	6/1928	633	40633	11/1959
45	6/1928	634	40634	5/1962
46	7/1928	635	40635	2/1961

0-6-0 Built by Neilson & Co. Works nos 2269-74 (1878).
            Vulcan Foundry. Works nos 840-5, 896-9, 1055-60, 1264-9.
DW 4ft 6in, Cyls 17 x 24, Blr 4ft 2in x 10ft 0in, THS 1124 sq ft, WP 140lbs/
sq in, WB 7ft 4in + 7ft 8in, Wt 33tons 19cwt (Neilson) 34½tons (Vulcan).
Johnson design with boiler and other features similar to 1102 class MR
0-6-0Ts with smaller Johnson dome, half cabs and outside springs on 2,200
gallon tender. Steam brakes with cast iron shoes. As the first batch came
from Scotland the whole class became known as 'Scotties'. Nos 56-61 were
built with vacuum ejector and remainder so equipped from 8/1890. Steam
brake retained, controlled by vacuum handle. 1906-9 reboilerings had later
pattern Johnson boiler with closed dome and Ramsbottom safety valves THS
1023 sq ft, WP 160lbs/sq in. Class 1P 1G LMS class 1F.

		Renumbered			LMS	With-
No	Date	no	date	Reboiled	no	drawn
33	6/1878			12/1890		10/1914
34	7/1878			3/1891		10/1914
35	7/1878			5/1889, 6/1903		4/1922
36*	7/1878			10/1889, 11/1898		4/1922
37	7/1878			4/1893, 6/1903, 1/1914		4/1922
38	7/1878			3/1897		4/1922
39	12/1879			1/1896		4/1925
40	12/1879	67	8/1928	1/1890, 4/1898, 9/1908	2886	12/1930
41	12/1879			2/1896		7/1925
42	1/1880	68	8/1928	6/1890, 10/1898	2887	11/1932
43	1/1880			7/1891, 10/1901		10/1914
44	1/1880	69	8/1928	8/1890, 12/1908, 1/1914		
				5/1929 (2nd hand Derby blr)	2888	12/1930
25	7/1881			9/1903		12/1928
26	8/1881			1/1897, 11/1908		12/1928
27	8/1881			5/1892, 7/1899		10/1914
28**	8/1881			11/1891, 1/1900, 7/1908		12/1928
46*	8/1884			2/1903		9/1925
47	8/1884	70	8/1928	11/1900	2889	11/1932
48*	8/1884			5/1903		4/1925
49	8/1884	71	8/1928	11/1903, 11/1928 (2nd hand		
				Deeley Blr)	2890	10/1932
50	9/1884	51	8/1928	4/1901	2885	2/1931
51	10/1884			1/1903		11/1925
56	6/1890	33	4/1922	10/1906		10/1928
57*	6/1890	34	4/1922	11/1906, 12/1928 Belpaire G5		
				blr, THS 1,008 sq ft,		
				Wt 36tons 7cwts	2880	12/1932
58	6/1890	35	4/1922	1/1909, 3/1929 G5 blr as		
				34 above	2881	12/1932
59	6/1890	36	4/1922	7/1907, 5/1928 G5 blr as		
				34 above	2882	12/1932
60	7/1890	37	4/1922	5/1908, 1/1927 G5 blr as		
				34 above	2883	12/1932
61	7/1890	38	4/1922	9/1908, 3/1928 G5 blr as		
				34 above	2884	12/1932

*The following locos were in accidents as below.
    No 36 Binegar 3/2/1886
       46 Binegar 3/2/1895
       48 Binegar 31/7/1885
       57 Templecombe 10/7/1894
**No 28 was fitted with tender weatherboard in 1890s with spectacles made
  from original cab of 26A O-4-OST.

O-6-O Built by MR Derby. Order no 1449 (1896)
              Neilson & Co. Works nos 6030-34
DW 5ft 2½in, Cyls 18 x 26, Blr 4ft 2in x 10ft 6in, THS 1,251 sq ft, WP 150lbs/
sq in, WB 8ft 0in + 8ft 6in, Wt 38tons 11cwts. As MR Johnson 1873 class.
2,950 gallon tender with outside springs and coal rails. Neilson locos had
3,250 gallon tenders and were originally painted in Midland red but ltttered
'SDJR' having been diverted from current MR order with Neilson's for
standard goods. Nicknamed 'Bulldogs'. Class 3P 3G LMS class 3F.

No	Date	Reboilered	LMS no	BR no	Withdrawn
62	1/1896	5/1923 Belpaire G7 blr THS 1,380 sq ft, WP 175lbs/sq in, Wt 45tons 8cwts	3194	43194	12/1960
63	1/1896	10/1914 H blr, THS 1,332 sq ft, WP 175lbs/sq in, Wt 44tons 11cwts (ex 4-4-O no 70). 5/1920 G7 blr as 62.	3198		10/1947
64	2/1896	3/1921 G7 blr as 62	3201	43201	4/1957
65	2/1896	12/1921 G7 blr as 62	3204	43204	9/1956
66	3/1896	4/1914 H blr THS 1,347 sq ft WP & Wt as 63 (ex 4-4-O no 71) 5/1920 G7 blr as 62	3211	43211	/1961
72	9/1902	10/1925 G7 blr as 62	3216	43216	8/1962
73	9/1902	7/1924 G7 blr as 62	3218	43218	4/1960
74	9/1902	4/1924 G7 blr as 62	3228	43228	10/1952
75	9/1902	11/1924 G7 blr as 62	3248	43248	8/1959
76	9/1902	11/1923 G7 blr as 62	3260	43260	9/1949*

*No 43260 withdrawn after accident at Ashcott 19/8/1949.

O-6-O Built by Armstrong Whitworth & Co Ltd. Works nos 468-72.
DW 5ft 3in, Cyls 20 x 26, Blr 4ft 8in x 10ft 5⁵⁄₁₆in, THS 1170 sq ft + super-
heater 313 sq ft, WP 175lbs/sq in WB 8ft 0in + 8ft 6in, Wt 48tons 15cwts. As
MR class 4 goods with G7S boiler and piston valves.

No	Date	LMS no	BR no	Withdrawn
57	4/1922	4557	44557	9/1962
58	4/1922	4558	44558	12/1964
59	4/1922	4559	44559	1/1963
60	4/1922	4560	44560	9/1965
61	4/1922	4561	44561	3/1962

O-6-OT Built by W G Bagnall & Co. Works nos 2358-64.
DW 4ft 7in, Cyls 18 x 26, Blr 4ft 1in x 10ft 6in, THS 1064½ sq ft, WP 160lbs/
sq in, WB 8ft 0in + 8ft 6in, Wt 49½tons. As standard LMS Class 3F with G5½
boiler, screw reverse, vacuum brake and steam heating apparatus. Class 3P 3G.

No	Date	LMS nos 1930	1936	BR no	Withdrawn
19	12/1928	7150	7310	47310	4/1962
20	1/1929	7151	7311	47311	12/1960
21	1/1929	7152	7312	47312	3/1961
22	1/1929	7153	7313	47313	6/1967
23	1/1929	7154	7314	47314	11/1966
24	2/1929	7155	7315	47315	9/1959
25	2/1929	7156	7316	47316	11/1962

2-8-0 Built by MR Derby. Order no 4209 (1914)   (MR)
          R Stephenson & Co. Works nos 3892-6   (RS)
DW 4ft 7¾in, LW 3ft 3½in, Cyls 21 x 28 O/S
MR - Blr 4ft 8in x 11ft 11in, THS 1327.25 sq ft + superheater 290.75 sq ft,
    WP 160lbs/sq in, Wt 64tons 15cwts.
RS - Blr 5ft 3in x 11ft 11in, THS 1,471 sq ft + superheater 374 sq ft,
    WP 160lbs/sq in, Wt 68tons 11cwts.
WB 8ft 3in + 6ft 0in + 5ft 6in + 6ft 0in.
New design by James Clayton who had originally been employed by Paget to
design the MR experimental 2-6-2T Walschaerts valve gear, outside admission
piston valves. G9AS boiler on Derby-built locos as then being fitted to
Deeley 999 class 4-4-0s and later fitted to 1000 class compounds but with
smaller superheater. G9BS boiler on RS locos, both boilers with Belpaire
fireboxes. MR locos had Ramsbottom safety valves, RS locos had Ross 'pop'
type. Standard MR fittings were provided including Class 4 goods axle boxes
which were undersized and gave trouble with overheating until fitted with
mechanical lubricators. Steam brakes on all wheels and vacuum ejector
provided for occasional use on passenger trains. 3,500 gallon tenders, the
Derby batch originally having tender cabs as the locos were too long for the
existing turntables and had to run tender first on the north-bound journey.
These were found to be inefficient and, after consultation with the
enginemen, were removed in 1919/20.
RS locos had left-hand instead of right-hand drive and Lambert sanding
apparatus, a French design delivering wet sand. Original steam reversing
gear on MR locos was later changed for hand-operated screw reverse as
provided on RS locos, but MR locos continued to have right-hand drive. This
S&DJ design was used by the LMS for the basis of the 2-6-0 + 0-6-2 Garratt
locomotive built by Beyer Peacock & Co in 1927 and 1930 for the Toton-Brent
coal trains. RS locos were all fitted with G9AS boilers at dates below and
became standard with the original MR locos. These boilers were from MR and
LMS compounds. Class 5P 5G LMS class 7F.

		LMS nos		G9AS	BR	
No	Date	1930	1932	blr	no	Withdrawn
80	2/1914	9670	13800		53800	7/1959
81	3/1914	9671	13801		53801	7/1961
82	3/1914	9672	13802		53802	3/1960
83	4/1914	9673	13803		53803	2/1962
84	4/1914	9674	13804		53804	2/1962
85	8/1914	9675	13805		53805	3/1961
86*	7/1925	9676	13806	8/1955	53806	1/1964
87	7/1925	9677	13807	6/1954	53807	10/1964
88**	7/1925	9678	13808	12/1953	53808	3/1964
89***	7/1925	9679	13809	2/1930	53809	6/1964
90	8/1925	9680	13810	2/1930	53810	12/1963

  *No 86 was exhibited at Stockton and Darlington Centenery Celebrations in
   1925.
 **No 88 is preserved at Somerset and Dorset Museum Trust, Washford, W. Somerset.
***No 89 was in an accident at Bath on 20/11/1929 and is preserved at Midland
   Railway Centre, Butterley.

Somerset and Dorset Joint. Number Index

No.	Year	Description
1	1876	O-6-OST ex S&D
-9		
10	1876	2-4-O ex S&D
-13	1877	O-4-4T 10 class
14	1876	2-4-O ex S&D
	1877	O-4-4T 10 class
	1897	4-4-O 15 class
15	1876	2-4-O ex S&D
	1891	4-4-O 15 class
	1928	4-4-O ex 18
16	1876	2-4-O ex S&D
	1891	4-4-O 15 class
	1929	Blank
17	1876	2-4-O ex S&D
	1891	4-4-O 15 class
18	1876	2-4-O ex S&D
	1891	4-4-O 15 class
	1928	4-4-O ex 45
19	1876	O-6-O ex S&D
	1928	O-6-OT 19 class
20	1876	O-6-O ex S&D
-24	1929	O-6-OT 19 class
25	1876	2-4-O ex S&D 2
	1881	O-6-O 33 class
	1929	O-6-OT 19 class
26	1876	2-4-O ex S&D 6
	1881	O-6-O 33 class
	1929	Blank
27	1876	2-4-O ex S&D 7
	1881	O-6-O 33 class
	1915	Blank
28	1876	2-4-OT ex S&D 8
	1881	O-6-O 33 class
	1929	Blank
29	1876	2-4-O ex S&D
	1877	O-4-4T 10 class
	1927	Blank (29A to LMS)
30	1877	O-4-4T 10 class
-31	1927	Blank (30A/31A to LMS)
32	1877	O-4-4T 10 class
	1929	Blank
33	1878	O-6-O 33 class
	1915	Blank
	1922	O-6-O ex 56
	1929	Blank
34	1878	O-6-O 33 class
	1915	Blank
	1922	O-6-O ex 57
35	1878	O-6-O 33 class
-38	1922	O-6-O ex 58-61
39	1879	O-6-O 33 class
	1926	Blank
	1928	4-4-O ex 70
40	1879	O-6-O 33 class
	1928	4-4-O ex 71
41	1879	O-6-O 33 class
	1926	Blank
	1928	4-4-O ex 67
42	1880	O-6-O 33 class
43	1880	O-6-O 33 class
	1915	Blank
	1928	4-4-O ex 69
44	1880	O-6-O 33 class
	1928	4-4-O 44 class
45	1883	O-4-OST
	1892	Blank
	1897	4-4-O 15 class
	1928	4-4-O 44 class
46	1884	O-6-O 33 class
	1926	Blank
	1928	4-4-O 44 class
47	1884	O-6-O 33 class
	1929	Blank
48	1884	O-6-O 33 class
	1926	Blank
49	1884	O-6-O 33 class
-50	192	Blank
51	1884	O-6-O 33 class
	1927	Blank
	1928	O-6-O ex 50
52	1884	O-4-4T 10 class
	1928	O-4-4T ex 32
53	1885	O-4-4T 10 class
54	1885	O-4-4T 10 class
	1921	O-4-4T No 54 (ex MR)
55	1885	O-4-4T 10 class
56	1890	O-6-O 33 class
	1923	Blank
57	1890	O-6-O 33 class
-61	1922	O-6-O 57 class
62	1896	O-6-O 62 class
-66		
67	1896	4-4-O 15 class
	1921	4-4-O 70 class
	1928	O-6-O ex 40
68	1896	4-4-O 15 class
	1921	4-4-O 70 class
	1928	O-6-O ex 42
69	1903	4-4-O 69 class
	1921	4-4-O 70 class
	1928	O-6-O ex 44
70	1903	4-4-O 69 class
	1914	4-4-O 70 class
	1928	O-6-O ex 47
71	1903	4-4-O 69 class
	1914	4-4-O 70 class
	1928	O-6-O ex 49
72	1902	O-6-O 62 class
-76		
77	1908	4-4-O 69 class
-78		
79		Blank
80	1914	2-8-O 80 class
-85		
86	1925	2-8-O 80 class
-90		
91		Blank
-100		
101	1929	Sentinel
-102		

Dates of renumbering by British Railways

Somerset and Dorset Joint	
4-4-0	
40322	6/1948
40323	7/1948
40324	8/1948
40325	8/1949
40326	2/1951
40633	6/1948
40634	1/1950
40635	11/1949

0-6-0 Class 2G	
43194	12/1949
43201	10/1949
43204	12/1949
43211	6/1948
43216	7/1948
43218	1/1949
43228	1/1950
43248	8/1949

0-6-0 Class 4G	
44557	2/1950
44558	7/1948
44559	5/1948
44560	4/1949
44561	10/1949

Wirral 2-4-2T	
46762	9/1949

Somerset and Dorset Joint	
Sentinel	
47190	4/1949
47191	3/1952

0-6-0T	
47310	5/1948
47311	3/1949
47312	8/1949
47313	12/1948
47314	4/1950
47315	5/1949
47316	12/1950

Furness 0-6-0	
52494	3/1950
52499	2/1949
52501	8/1950
52508	12/1948
52509	8/1948
52510	9/1948

Somerset and Dorset Joint	
2-8-0	
53800	5/1948
53801	7/1949
53802	6/1948

53803	4/1949
53804	8/1948
53805	11/1949
53806	1/1950
53807	4/1950
53808	8/1949
53809	9/1949
53810	4/1949

Caledonian	
4-4-0 140 Class	
54363	3/1948

Highland	
4-4-0 *Ben*	
54398	10/1950
54399	1/1951
54404	10/1948

Caledonian	
4-4-0 140 class s'heat	
54438	4/1948
54439	

4-4-0 139 class	
54440	8/1948
54441	3/1950
54443	4/1950
54444	4/1948
54445	5/1948
54446	9/1948
54447	7/1950
54448	8/1948
54449	6/1950
54450	12/1949
54451	9/1949
54452	6/1949
54453	9/1948
54454	11/1951
54455	5/1948
54456	6/1948
54457	11/1948
54458	12/1948
54459	4/1949
54460	6/1948

Caledonian	
4-4-0 113 class	
54461	9/1950
54462	11/1948
54463	6/1948
54464	8/1948
54465	9/1948
54466	7/1948
54467	2/1951
54468	1/1950
54469	1/1949
54470	9/1948

54471	5/1948		55129	4/1948
54472	11/1949		55132	6/1949
54473	8/1948		55134	4/1949
54474	11/1948		55135	8/1949
54475	4/1949		55136	12/1949
54476	10/1950		55138	4/1948
			55139	10/1949
4-4-0 72 class			55140	11/1949
54477	4/1949		55141	8/1949
54478	2/1949		55142	5/1949
54479	4/1948		55143	9/1949
54480	9/1948		55145	11/1948
54481	2/1949		55146	4/1949
54482	6/1950			
54483	10/1949		**0-4-4T 439 class**	
54484	9/1948		55159	9/1948
54485	4/1948		55160	12/1949
54486	7/1950		55161	11/1948
54487	2/1951		55162	4/1949
54488	7/1948		55164	
54489	4/1950		55165	12/1948
54490	6/1949		55166	9/1948
54491	6/1948		55167	8/1949
54492	4/1949		55168	5/1950
54493	2/1950		55169	
54494	9/1950		55170	8/1950
54495	12/1949		55173	6/1948
54496	10/1948		55174	11/1951
54497	10/1948		55175	10/1950
54498	6/1949		55176	
54499	5/1948		55177	5/1949
54500	12/1949		55178	6/1948
54501	12/1949		55179	5/1949
54502	4/1949		55181	12/1948
54503	10/1949		55182	7/1951
54504	4/1948		55183	11/1948
54505	10/1948		55185	1/1949
54506	7/1948		55186	6/1949
54507	1/1950		55187	1/1949
54508	1/1949		55189	7/1949
			55191	6/1948
Highland			55193	6/1949
4-6-0 *Clan*			55194	9/1949
54767	8/1948		55195	
			55196	7/1948
0-4-4T			55197	7/1948
55051	4/1949		55198	5/1950
55053	1/1949		55199	
			55200	9/1949
Caledonian			55201	9/1948
0-4-4T 19 class			55202	11/1948
55119	1/1949		55203	12/1949
55121	10/1948		55204	11/1948
55122	3/1951		55205	
55123	1/1949		55206	1/1949
55124	10/1948		55207	12/1948
			55208	2/1949
0-4-4T 92 class			55209	1/1949
55125	10/1948		55210	5/1948
55126	6/1949		55211	7/1949

55212	9/1948		56157	
55213	11/1949		56158	5/1949
55214			56159	3/1949
55215	12/1949		56160	6/1948
55216			56161	2/1949
55217	3/1949		56162	8/1949
55218			56163	10/1949
55219	8/1948		56164	2/1952
55220	7/1948		56165	11/1949
55221	8/1948		56166	
55222			56167	5/1949
55223	10/1948		56168	3/1949
55224	12/1961		56169	10/1948
55225	5/1949		56170	5/1948
55226	2/1949		56171	9/1950
55227	12/1949		56172	2/1951
55228	7/1948		56173	10/1949
55229	12/1949			
55230	4/1951		**0-6-0T 29 & 782 classes**	
55231	12/1948		56230	
55232	6/1948		56231	2/1949
55233	10/1948		56232	10/1948
55234	10/1951		56233	
55235	7/1950		56234	2/1951
55236	12/1951		56235	
			56236	6/1950
0-4-4T 431 class			56237	10/1948
55237	8/1949		56238	4/1948
55238	4/1949		56239	3/1949
55239	5/1949		56240	1/1949
55240	7/1948		56241	4/1950
			56242	1/1951
4-6-2T 944 class			56243	11/1949
55350	4/1950		56244	11/1948
55352	5/1950		56245	6/1948
55353	7/1949		56246	11/1950
55356	4/1948		56247	7/1949
55359	6/1948		56248	6/1949
55360	6/1948		56249	6/1948
			56250	5/1950
0-4-0ST 264 class			56251	5/1950
56011	1/1952		56252	3/1949
56025	8/1948		56253	5/1949
56027	2/1950		56254	6/1948
56028	1/1949		56255	2/1951
56029	2/1952		56256	10/1948
56030	2/1951		56257	9/1950
56031	10/1951		56258	9/1950
56032	7/1949		56259	12/1949
56035	7/1951		56260	4/1949
56038	4/1948		56261	5/1948
56039	11/1952		56262	10/1948
			56263	
0-6-0T 498 class			56264	
56151	5/1949		56265	5/1950
56152	12/1949		56266	
56153	5/1948		56267	6/1950
56154	5/1950		56268	3/1949
56155	9/1948		56269	6/1948
56156	6/1949		56270	

56271	3/1949	56331	8/1950
56272	4/1948	56332	7/1949
56273		56333	
56274	8/1950	56334	12/1949
56275	8/1949	56335	5/1948
56276	9/1948	56336	6/1948
56277	3/1948	56337	9/1950
56278		56338	11/1949
56279	6/1948	56339	1/1949
56280	5/1950	56340	9/1948
56281	4/1948	56341	6/1948
56282	12/1948	56342	9/1949
56283	4/1948	56343	
56284	4/1948	56344	1/1949
56285	12/1949	56345	1/1949
56286	11/1948	56346	6/1948
56287	4/1949	56347	
56288		56348	3/1949
56289	12/1948	56349	5/1949
56290	9/1950	56350	11/1948
56291	6/1950	56352	11/1949
56292		56353	11/1949
56293	5/1951	56354	2/1951
56294	9/1949	56355	11/1949
56295	7/1949	56356	9/1949
56296	10/1951	56357	
56297	11/1948	56358	
56298	12/1948	56359	4/1948
56299	12/1948	56360	8/1949
56300	11/1950	56361	4/1948
56301		56362	11/1950
56302	1/1949	56363	3/1951
56303	11/1950	56364	
56304	9/1948	56365	1/1949
56305	5/1948	56366	8/1949
56306	11/1949	56367	12/1948
56307	5/1950	56368	9/1948
56308	2/1949	56369	9/1948
56309		56370	9/1949
56310	4/1948	56371	
56311	4/1949	56372	10/1950
56312	4/1949	56373	9/1949
56313		56374	5/1949
56314	12/1948	56375	2/1949
56315	6/1948	56376	3/1951
56316			
56317	4/1949	**0-6-0 294 class**	
56318	12/1949	57230	10/1949
56319	11/1950	57232	12/1948
56320		57233	9/1950
56321	6/1950	57234	6/1949
56322		57235	
56323	6/1949	57236	9/1948
56324		57237	5/1948
56325	4/1950	57238	10/1948
56326	9/1949	57239	6/1950
56327	8/1948	57240	10/1949
56328	12/1949	57241	5/1950
56329	7/1950	57242	
56330	4/1950	57243	4/1948

57244	5/1950	57317	4/1948
57245	7/1948	57318	5/1949
57246	11/1949	57319	9/1948
57247	9/1948	57320	10/1948
57249	2/1949	57321	11/1948
57250	8/1949	57322	6/1950
57251	12/1949	57323	7/1948
57252	5/1949	57324	
57253	5/1950	57325	11/1948
57254	9/1948	57326	7/1950
57256	11/1948	57328	9/1949
57257	8/1949	57329	9/1948
57258	6/1948	57331	12/1948
57259	6/1949	57332	6/1948
57260	6/1948	57334	4/1949
57261	5/1948	57335	9/1948
57262	4/1949	57336	5/1949
57263	9/1949	57337	8/1948
57264	6/1948	57338	8/1948
57265	4/1950	57339	11/1949
57266	9/1948	57340	3/1949
57267	8/1949	57341	1/1949
57268	5/1948	57344	10/1948
57269	10/1950	57345	10/1949
57270	12/1949	57346	3/1949
57271	8/1948	57347	
57272	11/1948	57348	5/1949
57273	12/1948	57349	8/1949
57274	10/1950	57350	9/1949
57275	12/1948	57351	5/1948
57276		57352	12/1948
57277	4/1949	57353	3/1949
57278	6/1950	57354	
57279	7/1948	57355	6/1949
57282	7/1949	57356	9/1949
57283	4/1949	57357	
57284	12/1948	57358	6/1948
57285	10/1949	57359	12/1949
57287	12/1948	57360	9/1948
57288	10/1949	57361	6/1948
57289	4/1948	57362	12/1949
57291	5/1948	57363	6/1949
57292	5/1948	57364	7/1950
57294	5/1948	57365	6/1949
57295	6/1949	57366	
57296	6/1950	57367	6/1950
57298	5/1948	57368	9/1948
57299	12/1948	57369	10/1949
57300	5/1949	57370	8/1948
57302	8/1949	57372	3/1949
57303		57373	4/1949
57304	4/1949	57375	1/1949
57306	4/1949	57377	8/1948
57307	5/1948	57378	4/1949
57309	9/1948	57379	6/1949
57310	5/1948	57383	7/1949
57311	10/1949	57384	
57312	9/1948	57385	5/1948
57314		57386	
57315	9/1948	57387	3/1948
57316	7/1948	57388	1/1949

57389	5/1948	57468	9/1948
57390	5/1948	57470	
57391	6/1948	57472	12/1948
57392		57473	4/1949

0-6-0 711 class		0-6-0 812 class	
57394	3/1949	57550	
57395	9/1950	57552	9/1949
57396	5/1950	57553	9/1949
57397	7/1948	57554	7/1949
57398	6/1948	57555	6/1949
57404	2/1949	57556	5/1948
57405		57557	11/1948
57407	9/1949	57558	
57409	4/1948	57559	2/1949
57410	4/1950	57560	
57411	7/1949	57562	4/1948
57412	3/1949	57563	10/1949
57413	9/1950	57564	2/1949
57414	9/1950	57565	12/1949
57416	9/1949	57566	7/1948
57417	12/1948	57568	12/1949
57418		57569	7/1949
57419	4/1949	57570	6/1948
57423	12/1948	57571	9/1950
57424	9/1950	57572	6/1949
57425	4/1948	57573	4/1948
57426		57575	10/1948
57429	3/1949	57576	9/1948
57430	6/1948	57577	1/1949
57431	1/1949	57579	
57432	3/1948	57580	4/1949
57433	4/1950	57581	10/1948
57434	11/1948	57582	7/1948
57435	9/1948	57583	6/1948
57436	10/1948	57585	9/1949
57437	12/1949	57586	6/1950
57439	6/1948	57587	
57441	1/1949	57588	5/1948
57443		57589	2/1949
57444		57590	6/1950
57445	9/1948	57591	11/1949
57446	4/1950	57592	6/1949
57447	11/1948	57593	12/1949
57448	6/1950	57594	5/1948
57450	11/1949	57595	1/1949
57451	11/1949	57596	5/1949
57453	8/1948	57597	8/1949
57455	6/1949	57599	8/1948
57456		57600	6/1949
57457	10/1949	57601	6/1949
57458	10/1950	57602	12/1949
57459		57603	5/1950
57460		57604	6/1948
57461	9/1948	57605	6/1949
57462		57607	6/1949
57463	9/1948	57608	5/1948
57464	5/1948	57609	
57465	3/1949	57611	
57467	8/1948	57612	

57613	1/1949
57614	6/1948
57615	3/1949
57617	3/1949
57618	2/1949
57619	7/1948
57620	2/1949
57621	8/1949
57622	10/1948
57623	6/1949
57625	8/1949
57626	11/1949
57627	
57628	

O-6-O 652 class

57630	6/1949
57631	6/1948
57632	7/1948
57633	
57634	
57635	6/1948
57637	6/1949
57638	11/1948
57640	11/1949
57642	12/1949
57643	5/1948
57644	2/1949
57645	4/1949

O-6-O 300 class

57650	12/1948
57651	9/1948
57652	9/1948
57653	11/1948
57654	7/1949
57655	
57658	5/1949
57659	6/1948
57661	6/1948
57663	5/1950
57665	4/1948
57666	
57667	7/1949
57668	11/1949
57669	7/1948
57670	5/1949
57671	10/1949
57672	
57673	9/1950
57674	3/1949
57679	1/1949
57681	4/1948
57682	
57684	2/1949
57686	7/1948
57688	8/1951
57689	12/1948
57690	6/1948
57691	

Highland

O-6-O 134 class

57695	5/1948
57697	10/1948
57698	11/1948

4-6-O *Clan goods*

57950	6/1949
57951	11/1948
57954	5/1949
57955	11/1948
57956	11/1948

BIBLIOGRAPHY

Abbreviations

Eng	*Engineer*
Engnrg	*Engineering*
HMRS	*Journal of the Historical Model Railway Society*
L&R	*Locomotives and Railways*
Loco Mag	*Locomotive, Railway Carriage and Wagon Review*
Mod Eng	*Model Engineer*
Mod Rlys	*Model Railways* (formerly *Model Railway News*)
MRC	*Model Railway Constructor*
MRN	*Model Railway News* (now *Model Railways*)
NPM	*Newnes Practical Mechanics*
Rly Eng	*Railway Engineer*
Rly Mag	*Railway Magazine*
Rly Mod	*Railway Modeller*
Rly Wld	*Railway World* (formerly *Railways*)
Rlys	*Railways* (now *Railway World*)
RO	*Railway Observer* (Railway Correspondence and Travel Society)
SLS	*Journal of the Stephenson Locomotive Society*
TI	*Trains Illustrated*

Caledonian Railway - Constituent Companies

Dundee and Arbroath
Dundee and Newtyle
Dundee and Perth
Aberdeen
  Dundee's Iron Horses: The Story of a lost industry
  George MacLennan Steel (Lindsay & Co Ltd 1974)

Dundee and Newtyle

Eng	Vol 55 (1883) 0-2-4
Rlys	Vol 1, p53 (1940) 0-2-4
MRC	Vol 1, p9 (1934) 2-2-0

Glasgow Paisley and Greenock

SLS	Vol 26, p180 (1950)

Scottish Central

SLS	Vol 24, p199 (1948)

Solway

MRN	Vol 41, p387 (1965); Vol 42, p44 (1966)
	Neilson 0-6-0 1868

See also General Surveys Loco Mag for references to all constituent companies

Caledonian Railway: General Surveys

Locomotive and Train Working in the Latter Part of the Nineteenth Century
Volume 3, E.L. Ahrons (Edited L.L. Asher) (Heffer, Cambridge 1952). Also
printed in Rly Mag in complete form Vol 42, pp151, 230, 291, 363 (1918).
The Caledonian Railway O.S. Nock (Ian Allan 1962, 1973)
Caledonian Railway Centenary 1847-1947 (SLS 1947)
Centenary of the Caledonian Railway 1847-1947 (LMS 1947)
The McIntosh Locomotives of the Caledonian Railway MacLeod A.B. (Ian Allan 1944, 1948)

Drummond Locomotives Brian Haresnape & Peter Rowledge (Ian Allen 1982)
Forty Years of Caledonian Locomotives 1882-1922 Cornwell, H.J. Campbell
(David & Charles 1974)
A Livery Register: The Caledonian Railway Locomotives (Historical Model
Railway Society) 1883-1923)

Loco Mag *Locomotives of the Caledonian Railway**
          Jas F. McEwan Vol 46, pp150, 204, 256, 293 (1940); Vol 47, pp12,
          37, 61, 77, 107, 122, 154, 171, 200, 208, 231, 250 (1941);
          Vol 48, pp33, 73, 107, 139, 173, 207 (1942); Vol 49, pp39, 68,
          106, 140, 170 (1943); Vol 50, pp4, 35, 71, 101, 142 (1944);
          Vol 51, pp7, 38, 74, 117, 135 (1945); Vol 52, pp13, 41, 61, 101,
          135, 183 (1946); Vol 53, pp24, 55, 90, 144, 177, 193 (1947);
          Vol 54, pp41, 73, 94 (1948)
          *to 1895 including constituent companies.

SLS   The 'Genesis of the Caledonian Locomotive List' Alan G. Dunbar
          Vol 33 (1957) pp120, 140, 262

MRN   *The Lambie Locomotives of the CR.* A.B. MacLeod
          Vol 20, pp135, 136, 166 (1944)

Rly Mag   *Notes on Scottish Locomotives and Railway Working*
          'No 1 Caledonian', S.R. Yates
          Vol 70, pp1, 105, 189 (1932)

Rly Mag   *The McIntosh Locomotives of the CR.* Alex K. Bowman
          Vol 34, p201 (1914)

TI   *Latter-day Caledonian Locomotive Design.* A.G. Dunbar
          Vol 9, p540-5 (1956); Vol 10, p49 (1957)

Rly Wld   *Dugald Drummond at St Rollox* 1882-85. Alan J.S. Paterson
          Vol 22, pp21, 88 (1961)

Caledonian Railway: Locomotive Types

Singles
SLS   Vol 14, pp159, 168, 223, 263, 264, 296, 359 (1938)

2-2-2
4 class
Loco Mag Vol 16 (1910)
Eng   Vol 56 (1883)
76 class
Eng   Vol 13 (1862), Vol 16 (1863), Vol 91 (1901), Vol 115 (1913)

4-2-2 No 123
Eng   Vol 62 (1886, working drawing)
Engnrg   Vol 42 (1886, working drawing)
Rly Eng   Vol 12 (1891, working drawing)
Rly Mag   Vol 73, p1 (1933) with colour plate
MRN   Vol 6, p306 (1930); Vol 9, p6 (1933)
Mod Eng   *Library of Locomotives.* Robin Orchard
          Vol 122, p572 (1960). Also Vol 115, p62 (1956)
Rly Wld   *Exhibition Engines of 1886.* A.J.S. Paterson
          Vol 21, p15 (1960)
Locomotives I Have Known, p132, Maskelyne J.N.
(Percival Marshall, 1959)
Locomotives Worth Modelling, p73, Hambleton E.C.
(Percival Marshall 1949, Allied Publications 1977)

0-4-2
216 class
Eng   Vol 134 (1922)

670 class
  HMRS   Vol 1, p168

2-4-0
197 class
  L&R   Vol 4, p36 (1904)
98 class
  Eng   Vol 33 (1872)
130 class
  MRN   Vol 39, p16 (1963)

4-4-0
179 class
  L&R   Vol 1, p125 (1900)
  Rly Mod Vol 25, p73 (1974)
Drummond 4-4-0s
  SLS   Vol 12, p270 (1936)
No 124
  Rly Wld Vol 21, p15 (1960). As above under 4-2-2
66 class
  Eng   Vol 134 (1922)
  Engnrg   Vol 42 (1886, working drawing)
  Rly Eng Vol 14 (1893)
80 class
  Eng   Vol 65 (1888, working drawing)
  Rly Mod Vol 21, p316 (1970)
13 class
  Eng   Vol 79 (1895)
  MRN   Vol 20, pp135, 166 (1944)
  Rly Mod Vol 17, p55 (1966)
721 class
  Eng   Vol 81 (1896)
  Engnrg   Vol 69 (1900)
  Rly Eng Vol 17 (1896, part working drawing)
             Vol 18 (1897)
  NPM   1938
  Mod Eng Vol 102, p791 (1950)
  TI   *Dunalastair I 4-4-0s of the CR*. A.G. Dunbar
             Vol 12, p85 (1959). Also Vol 2 (1949)
  No 724 fitted for oil fuel
  Engnrg   Vol 93 (1912)
  Rly Eng Vol 33 (1912)
766 class
  Eng   Vol 85 (1898)
  Engnrg   Vol 67 (1899, working drawing) Vol 69 (1900)
  Loco Mag Vol 3 (1898, colour plate)
  SLS   Vol 13, p137 (1937)
  MRN   Vol 28, p216 (1952)
  Mod Eng Vol 115, p770 (1956)
  Further Locomotives I Have Known, p70, J.N. Maskelyne
  (Percival Marshall, 1952)
900 class
  Eng   Vol 100 (1905)
  Engnrg   Vol 69 (1900, working drawing)
  L&R   Vol 1, p43 (1900)
  Rly Mod Vol 21, p83 (1970)
  SLS   Vol 13, p137 (1937)
140 class
  Rly Eng Vol 26 (1905, working drawing)
  MRC   Vol 45, p154 (1978)

139 class
  Rly Eng   Vol 35 (1914, working drawing)
43 class
  TI   *The Caledonian 40 class 4-4-0s.* A.G. Dunbar
              Vol 7, p11 (1954)
113 class
  Rly Mag   Vol 40 (Jan 1917, colour plate)
  Eng   Vol 132 (1921)
  Engnrg   Vol 102 (1916, working drawing)
  SLS   Vol 43, p238 (1967)
General
  Mod Eng   *The Famous 'Dunalastair' Family*
              Vol 113, pp270, 314 (1955)
  T *The Caledonian 'Dunalastairs' and Associated Classes*
  O.S. Nock (David & Charles, 1968)

0-4-0ST
  Mod Eng   *Dugald Drummond's Waddling Pugs.* Robin Orchard
              Vol 124, pp392, 454 (1961)

0-4-2ST
  MRN   Vol 14, p181 (1938)
  SLS   *The Killin Branch Tanks.* L. Ward
              Vol 19, p40 (1943)
  MRN   Vol 14, pp181, 189 (1938)
  Rly Mod   Vol 17, pp310, 380 (1966)

4-4-0T (condensing)
  Engnrg   Vol 62 (1896)
  MRN   Vol 20, pp135, 166 (1944)
  Rly Wld   Vol 24, p378 (1963) A.G. Dunbar

0-4-4T
19 class
  Engnrg   Vol 62 (1896)
  L&R   Vol 3, p37 (1901)
  Rly Mod   Vol 23, p86 (1972)
439 class
  0-4-4 Tanks of the Caledonian Railway Scottish Railway
  Preservation Society (1963)
  Loco Mag   Vol 32, p45 (1926)
  Rly Mod   Vol 6, p264 (1955)
  SLS   *Last Years of the CR 0-4-4Ts*
              Vol 40, p18 (1964)

2-4-2T
  Rly Wld   *Misfortunes of the Caley Radials*
              Vol 33, p404 (1972); Vol 34, p25 (1973)
  SLS   Vol 14, pp160, 209, 221, 259 (1938)

4-6-0
55 class
  Engnrg   Vol 74 (1902, working drawing)
  Rly Eng   Vol 23 (1902)
  Loco Mag   Vol 12, p145 (1906)
  MRN   Vol 19, p176 (1943)
  Rly Mod   Vol 17, pp18, 59, 158 (1966)
49 class
  Eng   Vol 95 (1903)
  Engnrg   Vol 76 (1903)
  Rly Eng   Vol 24 (1903)

Rly Wld	*CR no 50 'Sir James Thompson'*. John A. Lines Vol 34, p211 (1973)

903 class

Engnrg	Vol 81 (1906), Vol 83 (1907, working drawing)
Rly Eng	Vol 30 (1909)
Rly Mag	Vol 21 (Sept, 1907, colour plate)
Loco Mag	Vol 12, p201 (1906)
HMRS	Vol 7, p4 (1970)
TI	*'Cardeans' of the CR*. A.G. Dunbar Vol 12, pp309, 456 (1959)
SLS	*Some Notes on the McIntosh 6ft 6in 4-6-0s of the Caledonian Railway* (49 & 903 class) A.J.S. Paterson Vol 41, p246 (1965); Vol 42, p36 (1966); Vol 45, p185 (1969)
HMRS	Vol 1, p168

908 class

Eng	Vol 102 (1906); Vol 103 (1907)
Engnrg	Vol 82 (1906)
Rly Eng	Vol 27 (1906)
Rly Mag	*New Six coupled bogie locomotives* Vol 19, p559 (1906)

918 class

Eng	Vol 102 (1906)
Engnrg	Vol 82 (1906)
Rly Eng	Vol 27 (1906)
Rly Mag	Vol 20 (Mar 1907, colour plate)
Rly Wld	Vol 25, p191 (1964) A.G. Dunbar

179 class

Rly Eng	Vol 35 (1914, working drawing)

938 class

Rly Wld	*The 'Hillman' at work*. A.G. Dunbar Vol 42, p481 (1981)

60 class

Eng	Vol 132 (1921, working drawing)
Rly Mod	Vol 20, p78 (1969)
SLS	*The Caley '60' class*. D. Newlands Vol 22, p138 (1946). Also Vol 30, p160 (1954)

956 class

Eng	Vol 133 (1922)
Rly Eng	Vol 42 (1921, working drawing)
Rly Mag	Vol 48, p168 (1921); Vol 111, p290 (1965)
Loco Mag	Vol 27 (1921)
MRC	Vol 2, p144 (1935)
SLS	*Y125 - And All That* A.G. Dunbar Vol 24, p192 (1948)

191 class

Eng	Vol 137 (1924)
Loco Mag	Vol 29 (frontispiece 1923), p305
SLS	Vol 12, p68 (1936)

General Surveys

TI	*Pickersgill 4-6-0s of the CR*. W.J. Probert Vol 6, pp273, 339, 476 (1953)

The Scottish 4-6-0 Classes. Atkins C.P. (Ian Allan, 1976)

0-6-0 and 2-6-0

631 class

L&R	Vol 2, p7 (1901)

294 class

Rly Eng	Vol 5 (1884, working drawing)
MRN	Vol 20, pp135, 156, 166 (1944)
Rly Mod	Vol 4, p156 (1953)

812 class
    The Story of 828. The working life, threatened extinction and
    restoration of the McIntosh 812 class. John Thomas
    (David & Charles, 1967)
    Rly Eng   Vol 20 (1899)
    L&R   Vol 1, p136 (1900)
652 class
    Engnrg   Vol 86 (1908, part working drawing)
    Rly Eng   Vol 29 (1908)
300 class
    Eng   Vol 132 (1921)
34 class (2-6-0)
    SLS   Vol 15, p174 (1939)
    Rly Wld   Vol 24, p18 (1963)
General
    SLS   The McIntosh 0-6-0s and 2-6-0s of the Caledonian Railway
               A.J.S. Paterson, Vol 38, p325 (1962)

0-6-0ST
    SLS   Jubilee Pugs
               Vol 12, p246 (1936); Vol 14, pp173, 221, 224 (1938)
    MRN   Vol 20, pp156, 166 (1944), 211 class
    Mod Rlys   Vol 4, p388 (1975), 323 & 486 classes

0-6-0T
    Engnrg   Vol 62 (1896), 29 class (condensing)
    SLS   Vol 27, p181 (1950), 782 class
    Rly Mod   Vol 14, p167 (1963)

4-6-2T
    Eng   Vol 125 (1918, working drawing) Vol 132 (1921)
    SLS   Vol 13, p8 (1937); Vol 30, p19 (1954)

0-8-0
    Engnrg   Vol 72 (1901)
    Rly Eng   Vol 22 (1901)
    L&R   Vol 2, p112 (1901)
    HMRS   Vol 8, pp74, 143 (1974)

0-8-0T
    Rly Eng   Vol 25 (1904)
    HMRS   Vol 8, p74 (1974)
    Rly Mod   Vol 28, p84 (1977)

Eight coupled
    Rly Wld   Vol 24, p16 (1963) A.G. Dunbar

Bogie tender
    Rly Eng   Vol 23 (1902, working drawing)

Chimneys
    HMRS   Vol 4, p45 Pickersgill 4-4-0s & 4-6-2T

Proposed designs not built
    Rly Mag   Proposed De Glehn Compound Atlantic
               Vol 88, p22 (1942)
               Proposed 2-6-0 Vol 92, p145 (1946)
    TI   A McIntosh Pacific Design Vol 11, p491 (1958)

Cab details
    MRN   Vol 34, p145 (1958), Vol 40, p173 (1964)

MRC   Vol 31, p289 (1964)

Connel Bus
SLS   Vol 25, p177 (1949)

Glasgow and South Western Railway – Constituent Companies
The Little Railways of South West Scotland. D.L. Smith
(David & Charles, 1968)

Wigtownshire
Loco Mag Vol 49, pp27, 53, 85, 119, 149 (1943)

Girvan and Portpatrick Junction
Loco Mag Vol 52, pp29, 39, 73, 93, 120, 156 (1946)
Rly Mag   Vol 29, p136 (1911)
SLS   Vol 7, p53 (1931); Vol 32, p334 (1956)

Glasgow, Paisley, Kilmarnock and Ayr
Loco Mag Vol 28, pp117, 141, 275 (1922)
          Vol 38, p275 (1932)
Eng   Vol 135 (1923), 2-2-2

Glasgow and South Western Railway: General Surveys
The Locomotives of the Glasgow and South Western Railway
D.L. Smith (David & Charles, 1976)
The Glasgow and South Western Railway. Campbell Highet
(Oakwood, 1965)
The Glasgow and South Western Railway (SLS, 1950)
Loco Mag Vol 28, pp202, 203, 239, 272, 292, 366, 368 (1922);
          Vol 29, pp46, 83, 136, 205, 262, 337 (1923); Vol 30, pp23,
          30, 89, 160, 212 (1924)
SLS   *Glasgow and South Western Railway Notes*
          Vol 11, pp145, 181, 205, 298 (1935); Vol 15, p172 (1939)
          Vol 17, pp78, 108, 130, 137 (1941); Vol 27, pp257, 267, 283 (1951)
          Kilmarnock Works List 1906-15, Vol 4, p56 (1928)
Loco Mag *Famous Locomotive Engineers: James Manson.* C.H. Ellis
          Vol 47, p126 (1941)
Rlys   *Manson Locomotives*, Vol 7, p50 (1946)
Rly Mag   *James Manson.* Campbell Highet, Vol 110, pp182, 249 (1964)
Rly Wld   *Manson Bogies.* David L. Smith, Vol 40, p618 (1979)
Rlys   *Locos on NCB*, Vol 9, p190 (1948)
Locomotive and Train Working in the Latter Part of the Nineteenth Century
Vol 3, E.L. Ahrons (edited L.L. Asher) (Heffer, 1952). Also in complete
form Rly Mag Vol 39, pp22, 105 (1916)

Glasgow and South Western Railway: Locomotive Types

0-4-0 (jackshaft type)
Eng   Vol 134 (1922)

0-4-2 *221 class*
MRN   Vol 37, p218 (1961)
SLS   Vol 21, p122 (1945) as rebuilt

2-4-0
75 class
L&R   Vol 4, p60 (1903)
157 class
Engnrg   Vol 30 (1880, working drawing)

4-4-0
  6 class
    Engnrg   Vol 20 (1875, working drawing)
  119 class
    Engnrg   Vol 36 (1883, working drawing)
  153 class
    Eng   Vol 67 (1889, working drawing)
  8 class
    Eng   Vol 79 (1895)
    Rly Eng   Vol 16 (1895)
  No 11 4 cylinder
    Eng   Vol 85 (1898)
    Engnrg   Vol 70 (1900, working drawing)
    SLS   Vol 11, p290 (1935); Vol 14, p166 (1938)
    TI   Vol 9 (1956)
  as rebuilt 1923
    Rly Mag   Vol 52, p224 (1923)
    Loco Mag Vol 29, p52 (1923)

Tank Engines
    SLS   Vol 11, p290 (1935)

0-4-0T *272 class*
    Rly Mod   Vol 15, p137 (1964)

0-4-2T
    Rly Mod   Vol 4, p237 (1953)

0-4-4T *326 class*
    MRN   Vol 30, p159 (1954)
    SLS   Vol 18, p155 (1942)
    Engnrg   Vol 60 (1895, working drawing)

Railcars
    Rly Mag   *Scottish Steam Railcars.* Campbell Highet
              Vol 15, p672 (1969)
    MRN   Vol 40, p498 (1964)
    Eng   Vol 99 (1905); Vol 102 (1906)
    Rly Eng   Vol 25 (1904)
    Engnrg   Vol 82 (1906)

4-6-0
  The Scottish 4-6-0 classes. C.P. Atkins (Ian Allan, 1976)
  381 class
    Eng   Vol 96 (1903); Vol 100 (1905, working drawing); Vol 101
              (1906, working drawing)
    Engnrg   Vol 76 (1903, working drawing)
    Rly Eng   Vol 24 (1903)
    MRC   Vol 15, pp104, 120 (1948)
  128 class
    Rly Mod   Vol 22, p91 (1971)

0-6-0 *361 class*
    L&R   Vol 1, p160 (1900)

0-6-0T *5 class*
    Eng   Vol 125 (1918)

0-6-2T
    Rly Mod   *Drummond and Whitelegg 0-6-2Ts,* Vol 28, p54 (1977)
    SLS   Vol 13, p8 (1937)

4-6-4T
Eng   Vol 133 (1922); Vol 134 (1922, working drawing); Vol 135 (1923)
Rly Eng   Vol 43 (1922, working drawing)
SLS   Vol 17, p34 (1941)
Rly Mag   Vol 119, p174 (1973) C.P. Atkins

Highland Railway - Constituent Companies

Inverness and Nairn
Loco Mag Vol 21, p229 (1915)

Inverness and Aberdeen Junction
Loco Mag Vol 21, pp231, 272 (1915); Vol 22, p46 (1916)

Duke of Sutherland's
Rly Mag   *Dunrobin Emigrates*, Vol 111, p290 (1965)

Highland Railway: General Surveys
A History of Highland Locomotives. M.C.V. Allchin (Railway Hobbies, 1947)
Highland Engines and their work. C.H. Ellis (London, 1930)
The Highland Railway Company and its Constituents and Successors 1855 to 1955 (SLS 1955)
The Highland Railway. O.S. Nock (Ian Allan, 1965)
The History of the Highland Railway. H.A. Vallance (London, 1938, David & Charles, 1963)
Locomotives and Train Working in the latter part of the Nineteenth Century E.L. Ahrons (edited L.L. Asher) Vol 3 (Heiffer, 1952). Also in complete form in Rly Mag Vol 49, pp233, 310 (1921)
Highland Railway Album (2 vols) A.J. Lambert (Ian Allan, 1974 & 1978)
Highland Locomotives. Peter Tatlow (Oxford Publications, 1979)
Loco Mag Vol 22, pp46, 111, 177, 243 (1916); Vol 23, pp47, 102, 139,
           197 (1917); Vol 24, pp31, 104 (1918); Vol 25, pp27, 37, 159,
           185 (1919)
L&R   Vol 1, p107 (1900)

Highland Railway: Locomotive Types

Tank Engines
SLS   Vol 9, p147 (1933); Vol 11, p145 (1935)

2-2-2T *No 12 Strathpeffer*
MRN   Vol 36, p85 (1960)

2-4-0 *Raigmore (1877)*
MRN   Vol 28, p10 (1952)

4-4-0
Jones
Eng   Vol 49 (1880) rebuilt from 2-4-0 with four-wheel tender
Engnrg   Vol 20 (1875, working drawing) *Duke class*
Rly Eng   Vol 7 (1886) *Duke class*
HMRS   Vol 1, p184 *Nairnshire Duke class*
SLS   Vol 15, p244 (1939)
         Vol 22, p150 (1946) *Duke and Bruce classes*
Engnrg   Vol 52 (1891, working drawing) *Bruce class*
Eng   Vol 79 (1895) *Strath class*
SLS   Vol 24, p15 (1948) *Strath class*
Rly Mod   Vol 4, p91 (1953) *Strath class*
MRN   Vol 7, p283 (1931) *Loch class*

Drummond Bens
    SLS   Vol 15, p292 (1939)
    MRC   Vol 46, pp158, 224, 371 (1980)
    Eng   Vol 119 (1915, working drawing) *Detail of smokebox and
               chimney for small Ben*
          as rebuilt
    Loco Mag   Vol 30, p135 (1924)
    Rly Mag   Vol 74, p106 (1934)
  Cumming 73 class
    Rly Eng   Vol 38 (1917)
    MRC   Vol 43, p18 (1976)

4-4-0T
    SLS   Vol 16, p124 (1940)
    MRC   Vol 27, p282 (1960) *58 class*
    Rly Wld   Vol 33, p76 (1972)

0-4-4T
    SLS   Vol 16, p54 (1940); Vol 17, p112 (1941); Vol 38, p44 (1962)
    Mod Rlys   Vol 1, p25 (1971)
    Rly Mod   Vol 24, p158 (1973)

4-6-0
    The Scottish 4-6-0 classes. C.P. Atkins (Ian Allan, 1976)
    Rly Mag   Six-coupled locomotives and their work. B. Purves
               Vol 32, p238 (1913)
  Large Goods
    Eng   Vol 78 (1894, working drawing)
    Loco Profile no 17 (Windsor)
    Locomotives in profile (Profile Publications, 1971/2)
    SLS   Vol 11, p138 (1935); Vol 36, p194 (1960)
    MRC   Vol 41, p366 (1974)
    MRN   Vol 13, p249 (1937); Vol 37, p58 (1961)
    Mod Rlys   Vol 1, p912 (1972)
  Castle
    Rly Eng   Vol 21 (1900, part working drawing)
    SLS   Vol 15, p280 (1939)
    Rly Wld   Vol 37, p406 (1976)
  River
    Rly Mag   Vol 113, pp505, 657 (1967); Vol 114, p48 (1968)
               Highland Locomotive Controversy. E. McKenna
               Vol 120, pp9, 245, 357 (1974)
    Rly Wld   Vol 39, p75 (1978)
  Clan
    Eng   Vol 134 (1922)
    SLS   Vol 14, p369 (1938)
    MRN   Vol 7, p283 (1931); Vol 13, pp182, 277 (1937)
    MRC   Vol 45, p428 (1978)
    Fitted for oil fuel
    Rly Eng   Vol 42 (1921, part working drawing)

0-6-0
    L&R   Vol 1, p34 (1900)
    SLS   Vol 15, p316 (1939)

0-6-0T
    SLS   Vol 16, pp31, 69 (1940)
    MRN   Vol 28, p254 (1952) *Lochgorm*

0-6-4T
    MRC   Vol 44, pp58, 278 (1977)
    Loco Mag   Vol 21 (1915)

         MRN   Vol 7, p283 (1931)

Details
    Rly Eng   Vol 18 (1896, working drawing) *motion*
    MRN   Vol 7, pp310, 347, 374 (1931); Vol 9, p80 (1933)

Locomotive Names
    SLS   *Origin and Meaning*, Vol 34, p216 (1958)

Furness Railway - Constituent Companies

Whitehaven, Cleator and Egremont
    Loco Mag Vol 5, pp106, 123, 138 (1900)
    SLS   Vol 27, p306 (1951)

Furness Railway: General Surveys
    The Furness Railway (with Locomotive and Rolling Stock Supplement)
    R. W. Rush (Oakwood, 1973)
    Locomotive and Train Working in the latter part of the Nineteenth Century
    E.L. Ahrons (edited L.L. Asher) Vol 2 (Heiffer, 1952). Also in complete
    form in Rly Mag Vol 49, p157 (1921)
    Loco Mag Vol 5, pp4, 22, 44, 58, 78, 86, 161, 197 (1900)
    TI   Vol 7, pp422, 462 (1954); Vol 8, pp9 78 (1955)

Furness Railway: Locomotive Types

2-2-2WT
    Eng   Vol 79 (1895)
    SLS   Vol 31, p86 (1955); Vol 32, pp25, 137 (1956)
    Rly Mod   Vol 16, p304 (1965); Vol 19, p343 (1968); Vol 23, p48 (1972)

0-4-0
    L&R   Vol 1, p6 (1900) *3 class*
    Eng   Vol 82 (1896); Vol 135 (1923) *3 class*
    Rly Mod   Vol 14, p64 (1963) *3 & 17 classes*

0-4-0ST
    Rly Mod   Vol 17, p342 (1966); Vol 18, p342 (1967)

2-4-0
    Rly Mod   Vol 17, p246 (1966)
    MRN   Vol 40, p608 (1964); Vol 41, p116 (1965)

4-4-0
    120 class
    Eng   Vol 79 (1895)
    Rly Mod   Vol 15, pp74, 166 (1974)
    MRN   Vol 38, pp264, 365 (1962)
    21 class
    Rly Mod   Vol 17, p243 (1966)
    126 & 130 classes
    Eng   Vol 93 (1902)
    SLS   Vol 32, p297 (1956)
    Rly Mod   Vol 17, p148 (1966)

2-4-2T
    MRN   Vol 7, p173 (1931)
    Rly Mod   Vol 16, p304 (1965)

4-4-2T
Rly Mag	Vol 38, p197 (1915). Also TI Vol 6 (1953)
MRN	Vol 37, p356 (1961)
Rly Mod	Vol 16, p324 (1965)
MRC	Vol 30, p70 (1963)

Railcars
Rly Mod	Vol 9, p287 (1958); Vol 10, pp46, 92, 112, 168 (1959)

0-6-0
29 class
Rly Mod	Vol 19, p20 (1968)

Pettigrew
SLS	Vol 28, p41 (1952); Vol 34, p247 (1958)
Eng	Vol 88 (1899, working drawing)
Engnrg	Vol 76 (1903)
Rly Mod	Vol 16, pp162, 220 (1965) *3 class*
Mod Rlys	Vol 4, p289 (1975) *1 class*

0-6-0T
51 class
Rly Mod	Vol 17, p342 (1966)

19 class
HMRS	Vol 2, p26
Rly Mod	Vol 17, p181 (1966)

0-6-2T
98 class
Rly Eng	Vol 79 (1905, working drawing)
Rly Mod	Vol 13, p268 (1962); Vol 16, pp162, 220 (1965); Vol 17
	Vol 17, p214 (1966)
MRN	Vol 10, p185 (1934); Vol 37, pp136, 235, 311, (1961)

94 class
Rly Mod	Vol 17, pp118, 188 (1966)

4-6-4T
Eng	Vol 111 (1921, working drawing)
Rly Eng	Vol 42 (1921)
MRC	Vol 6, p98 (1939)
Rly Mod	Vol 17, p116 (1966); Vol 28, p21 (1977) C.P. Atkins

Maryport and Carlisle Railway: General Surveys

Maryport and Carlisle Railway. Jack Simmons (Oakwood, 1947)
Locomotive and Train Working in the latter part of the Nineteenth Century
E.L. Ahrons (edited L.L. Asher) Vol 2 (Heiffer, 1952). Also in complete
form in Rly Mag Vol 51, p420 (1922)

Maryport and Carlisle Railway: Locomotive Types

4-2-0 Crampton
MRN	Vol 42, pp238, 465 (1966)

0-4-2 & 0-4-2ST *nos 4 & 7*
Rly Mod	Vol 16, pp47, 135 (1965)

0-4-4T *no 26*
MRC	Vol 27, p86 (1960)

0-6-0 *nos 29 & 30*
Rly Mod	Vol 22, p126 (1971)

Leek and Manifold Valley Light Railway

The Leek and Manifold Valley Light Railway 'Manifold' (the authors, 1955)
The Manifold Valley and its Light Railway. R. Keys and L. Porter
(Moorland, 1972)
The Leek and Manifold Valley Light Railway. Keith Turner
(David & Charles, 1980)

Locomotives 2-6-4T

MRC   Vol 23, p242 (1956); Vol 24, pp57, 87 (1957)

North Staffordshire Railway: General Surveys

*Locomotives of the North Staffordshire and London, Tilbury and Southend
Railways.* M.C.V. Allchin (the author, 1943)
The North Staffordshire Railway 'Manifold' (the authors, 1952)
The North Staffordshire Railway. Rex Christiansen and R.W. Miller
(David & Charles, 1971)
The North Staffordshire Railway Locomotives and Rolling Stock. R.W. Rush
(Oakwood, 1981)
Locomotive and Train Working in the latter part of the Nineteenth Century
E.L. Ahrons (edited L.L. Asher) Vol 2 (Heiffer, 1952). Also in complete
form in Rly Mag Vol 48, pp317, 377 (1921)

SLS   *Later locomotives 1906-15,* Vol 3, pp3, 27, 44, 71, 74, 88 (1927);
             Vol 4, p69 (1928)
             Notes on North Staffordshire Locomotives
             Vol 24, pp107, 139, 146, 253, 317 (1948); Vol 25, pp32, 34 (1949);
             Vol 27, pp41, 85, 104, 114, 131, 141, 154 (1951); Vol 28, p77,
             (1952); Vol 29, pp107, 116 (1953)
Rly Mag   *Locomotives of the late North Staffordshire Railway.* A.W.G. Cope,
             Vol 61, pp98, 196, 303 (1927); Vol 62, p236 (1928)
RO   *The North Staffordshire Railway - A Retrospect.* E. Haigh
             Vol 11, pp178, 241, 253, 318, 367, 372 (1939);
             Vol 12, p102 (1940)
Rlys   *Locomotives of the North Staffordshire Railway 1897-1923*
             Vol 12, p188 (1951)
             Locomotive Activity on the NSR, Vol 12, pp216, 245, 266 (1951);
             Vol 13, p18 (1952)
TI   *The Staffy, impressions of the NSR and its locomotives*
             H.C. Casserley, Vol 4, p81 (1951)

North Staffordshire Railway: Locomotive Types

2-4-0 *Nos 15 & 54*
Rly Mod   Vol 17, pp182, 252 (1966)

4-4-0 *Class G*
Eng   Vol 110 (1910, working drawing)

0-4-4T *Class M*
Eng   Vol 106 (1908, working drawing)

4-4-2T *Class K*
Eng   Vol 113 (1912, working drawing)
MRC   Vol 11, pp71, 125, 165 (1944); Vol 12, pp 43, 104 (1945)

Railcar
Eng   Vol 102 (1906)
Engnrg   Vol 82 (1906)

0-6-0 *58 class*
    L&R   Vol 2, p17 (1901)

0-6-2T
  Class L
    Eng   Vol 100 (1905, working drawing)
  Class New L
    Rly Mag   *The Knotty Steams again.* W.S. Darby
                 Vol 109, pp153, 358 (1963)
    Fitted for oil fuel
    Rly Eng   Vol 42 (1921)

0-6-4T *Classes C & F*
    Eng   Vol 123 (1917) *Class F*
    Rly Eng   Vol 36 (1915) *Class C*
    MRC   Vol 29, p172 (1962)

0-6-0T 4 cylinder
    Eng   Vol 135 (1923)
    Loco Mag   Vol 29, p1 (1923); Vol 30, p109 (1924)
    Rly Mag   Vol 52, p122 (1923); Vol 55, p264 (1924)

Battery locomotive
    Eng   Vol 125 (1918)
    Rly Mod   Vol 17, p286 (1966)

Details
  Boiler mountings classes C, K & KT
    MRC   Vol 11, p164 (1944)
  Standard buffer
    MRC   Vol 12, p105 (1945)
  6 coupled motion
    Rly Eng   Vol 20 (1899, working drawing)
  Drewry petrol inspection car
    Mod Rlys   Vol 4, p170 (1975)

Cleator and Workington Junction Railway
        *The Tracks of the Ironmasters: The History of the Cleator and Workington
        Junction Railway.* W. McGowan Gradon (the author, 1952)
        SLS   Vol 16, pp156, 222 (1940); Vol 17, p29 (1941)
        Rly Mag   Vol 127, p84 (1981)

0-6-0ST
        Eng   Vol 105 (1908)

Garstang and Knott End Railway
        The Garstang and Knott End Railway. R.W. Rush and M. Price (Oakwood, 1964)
        The Garstang and Knott End Railway. Margaret Edwards
        (Lancaster Museum, 1975)
        Loco Mag   Vol 21 (1915); Vol 6 (1901)
        Rly Mag   Vol 55, p444 (1924) G.A. Sekon
        Rly Wld   Vol 19, p207 (1958) J.I.C. Boyd

Northampton and Banbury Junction Railway
        Loco Mag   Vol 52, p171 (1946)

East and West Junction Railway
    Loco Mag Vol 39, pp98, 129 (1933); Vol 7 (1902)

  0-6-0ST
    SLS   Vol 5, p4 (1929)

Stratford-upon-Avon and Midland Junction Railway
    The Stratford-upon-Avon and Midland Junction Railway. J.M. Dunn
    (Oakwood, 1952, 1979)
    The Stratford-upon-Avon and Midland Junction Railway. Arthur Jordon
    (Oxford Publications, 1982, mainly general descriptive matter but
    including some useful photographs of locomotives)
    Rly Mag   Vol 26, p265 (1910)

Wirral Railway
    The Wirral Railway. Campbell Highet (Oakwood, 1961)
    Loco Mag Vol 30, pp122, 149 (1924) W.E.S. Brown
    RO   Vol 10, p156 (1938) E. Haigh
    SLS   Vol 23, pp150, 178 (1947)
    Rly Mag   *Recollections of the Wirral Railway,* Vol 100, p167 (1954)

  Hoylake tank
    SLS   Vol 27, p153 (1951)

  4-4-4T
    Eng   Vol 82 (1896) *No 11*
    MRN   Vol 43, p610 (1967) *No 11*
    MRC   Vol 28, p36 (1961) *No 14*

Somerset and Dorset Joint Railway – Constituent Companies

  Somerset Central
    Loco Mag Vol 44, pp18, 81, 157, 188 (1938)

  Somerset and Dorset
    Loco Mag Vol 14, p118 (1908); Vol 39, p270 (1933); Vol 44, pp189, 255,
            322, 349 (1938); Vol 45, pp18, 74 (1939)

Somerset and Dorset Joint Railway: General Surveys
    Locomotives of the Somerset and Dorset Joint Railway and the Irish
    Narrow Gauge. M.C.V. Allchin (the author, 1944)
    The Somerset and Dorset Railway. D.S. Barrie and C.R. Clinker
    (Oakwood, 1959, 1978)
    The Somerset and Dorset Railway. Robin Athill (David & Charles, 1967)
    Somerset and Dorset Locomotive History. D.L. Bradley and D. Milton
    (David & Charles, 1973)
    Highbridge in its Heyday. Colin G. Maggs (Oakwood, 1973)
    Locomotive and Train Working in the latter part of the Nineteenth Century
    E.L. Ahrons (edited L.L. Asher) Vol 5 (Heiffer, 1952). Also in complete
    form Rly Mag Vol 54, pp98, 173 (1924)
    Loco Mag *LMSR Locomotives. A History of the Somerset and Dorset Joint*
              Railway. P.C. Dewhurst, Vol 45, pp70, 133, 193, 249,
              339 (1939); Vol 46, pp43, 122, 177, 231, 282, 311 (1940);
              Vol 47, pp8, 42, 59, 89, (1941); Vol 48, p196 (1942)
    RO   Vol 2, p58 (1930); Vol 9, pp195, 223, 264, 316, 346, 379 (1937)
    Rly Mag   *Modern Locomotives of the Somerset and Dorset Joint Railway*
              1900-30. Vol 69, p235 (1931)

L&R   Vol 1, pp48, 62, 96, 114, 125, 155, 173 (1900);
           Vol 2, pp28, 83, 96, 114, 133 (1901)

Somerset and Dorset Joint Railway: Locomotive Types

4-4-0
  15 class (Class A)
    Rly Mod   Vol 19, p178 (1968) *as built*
    MRN   Vol 25, p222 (1949) *as rebuilt*
  69 class
    MRC   Vol 13, p89 (1946) *No 67*
    MRN   Vol 16, p1 (1940) *No 78*

2-4-0T *No 11*
    Rly Mod   Vol 14, p217 (1963)

0-4-4T
    MRN   Vol 42, p557 (1966); Vol 43, pp28, 33 (1967)
              Vol 43, p74 (1967) *rebuilt*

0-4-2ST and 0-4-0ST
    MRN   Vol 30, p166 (1954)
    Rly Mag   *A Peculiar Locomotive History.* J.B. Radford
              Vol 117, p592 (1971) *0-4-0ST Bristol*

Sentinel
    Loco Mag Vol 35, p142 (1929)
    Mod Rlys Vol 4, pp144, 282 (1975)

0-6-0 *MR class 4 (S&DJ class 4G)*
    MRN   Vol 41, pp53, 100 (1965) *Details*

2-8-0
    Somerset and Dorset 2-8-0s. D. Milton (Somerset & Dorset Museum
    Trust, 1971, 1980)
    Mod Eng   *Library of Locomotives.* Robin Orchard
              Vol 123, pp522, 586, 722 (1960)
    Loco Mag Vol 31, p337 (1925)
    Rly Mag   Vol 57, p454 (1925)
    Eng   Vol 117 (1914 working drawing), Vol 119 (1915)
    Rly Eng   Vol 35 (1914 working drawing), Vol 47, p350 (1925)

The following general works contain relevant material *inter-alia*
    The Railways of Great Britain and Ireland. F. Whishaw
    (London, 1841, 1842. Reprinted David & Charles, 1970)
    The British Steam Locomotive 1825-1925. E.L. Ahrons
    (London, 1927. Reprinted Locomotive Publishing Co, Ian Allan, 1961)
    Locomotives at the Grouping Vol 3: LMS. H.C. Casserley and
    S.W. Johnstone (Ian Allan, 1966)
    British Steam Locomotive Builders. James W. Lowe (Goose & Son, 1975)
    Scottish Locomotive History 1831-1923. Campbell Highet
    (George Allen & Unwin, 1970)
    The British 4-6-0. John F. Clay (New English Library, 1977)
    The Springburn Story. John Thomas (David & Charles, 1964, 1974)
    The Callander and Oban Railway. John Thomas (David & Charles, 1966)